Praise for
Beginning Excel® S

"A must read for anyone wanting to learn how Excel Services revolutionizes the world of spreadsheets!"

Richard McAniff
Corporate Vice President,
Microsoft Office

"This book will guide you through everything you need to know about the great new functionality in Excel Services. Microsoft Office SharePoint Server 2007 is Microsoft's platform for business applications. Excel Services provides great new business intelligence functionality and helps users control and manage their spreadsheets. We're already seeing these tools and services unleashing tremendous creativity in the developer community."

Kurt DelBene
Corporate Vice President,
Office Business Platform Group

"Microsoft Excel's sophisticated calculation and analysis capabilities, combined with ease of use and programmability, have led to wide deployment in Capital Markets for critical applications such as pricing and risk management. To date, management and auditing, of what can be highly complex linked workbooks, have posed challenges.

"Excel Services, part of Microsoft Office SharePoint Server 2007, now provides a powerful solution for management of mission-critical spreadsheet applications by centralizing workbook content and calculations and providing controlled web browser access to Excel applications and data on a client/server basis.

"We at HCL technologies see huge take-up of Excel Services in Capital Markets and are making significant investments in developing deployment capabilities. If you want to learn more about Excel Services, you must get this book."

Peter Bennett
Principal, Capital Markets,
HCL Former CIO of London Stock Exchange

"Excel Services is a critical enhancement to the analysis tool that the world knows and loves. This is the definitive book on Excel Services, from the team that dreamed it up and built it."

Bill Baker
Distinguished Engineer,
General Manager Business Intelligence,
Microsoft Corporation

"A crucial introduction to the most important addition to Office in years."

Avi Bryant
Co-CEO,
Dabble DB

"Microsoft Excel is a critical business tool in most organizations. As our customers use Excel in ever more demanding ways, they have asked the Excel team for a server to enable sharing of spreadsheets, to simplify controlling critical business information, and to provide web-based access to their spreadsheet models. In Office 2007, the Excel team introduced Excel Services — a server-based version of Excel — to meet precisely those needs.

"Eran, Liviu, and Craig — the authors of this book — led the development of Excel Services 2007, so they are uniquely qualified to explain what Excel Services is, how to deploy and run it, and how to get the most business benefit from the technology."

David Gainer
Group Program Manager,
Microsoft Excel

"Now, the analysis and models in your spreadsheets can instantly be part of a scalable enterprise-class application. I spent eight years working at Wells Fargo and Ernst & Young, and I have seen hundreds of examples of spreadsheets being used as part of a reccurring business process. *Beginning Excel Services* clearly and concisely shows you how to use Excel Services to start to automate those spreadsheet-based business processes and thus save substantial amounts of time, effort, and money."

Rod Boothby
Senior Director, Solution Marketing,
Teqlo Inc.

Beginning
Excel® Services

Liviu Asnash
Eran Megiddo
Craig Thomas

Wiley Publishing, Inc.

Beginning Excel® Services

Published by
Wiley Publishing, Inc.
10475 Crosspoint Boulevard
Indianapolis, IN 46256
www.wiley.com

Copyright © 2007 by Wiley Publishing, Inc., Indianapolis, Indiana

Published simultaneously in Canada

ISBN: 978-0-470-10489-7

Manufactured in the United States of America

10 9 8 7 6 5 4 3 2 1

Library of Congress Cataloging-in-Publication Data is available from the publisher.

For general information on our other products and services please contact our Customer Care Department within the United States at (800) 762-2974, outside the United States at (317) 572-3993 or fax (317) 572-4002.

Wiley also publishes its books in a variety of electronic formats. Some content that appears in print may not be available in electronic books.

To my amazing wife, Nurit, who inspires me in everything I do. You mean everything to me. And to my son, Edan, who reminds me that everything is possible.

—*Liviu Asnash*

To my wife, Inbal, for making me laugh when I need it most, and our two beautiful daughters, Yael and Adi, for making me smile every step of the way. You make life fun and wonderful. And to the Maximal team who "make things happen."

—*Eran Megiddo*

To my wife, Mele, and daughters, Emma and Cecelia, for inspiring me each and every day. I'm truly blessed. I love you all very much.

—*Craig Thomas*

About the Authors

Liviu Asnash is a Principal Development Lead at Microsoft, and currently manages the development of Excel Services (which is part of Microsoft Office SharePoint Server 2007). Asnash has more than 15 years of experience in enterprise-level software development. In the past five years, he has worked on Microsoft Office in areas related to Business Intelligence, Excel, and Excel Services. Prior to joining Microsoft, he was the director of Research and Development at Maximal Innovative Intelligence, a software company that developed data visualization tools for Business Intelligence. Before that, he worked for six years on mission-critical server systems based on UNIX and Oracle technologies. Asnash holds a B.S. degree in Computer Science and an M.B.A. degree. He lives in Bellevue, Washington, with his wife and son.

Eran Megiddo is an entrepreneur at heart and is the Principal Group Program Manager at Microsoft, responsible for the team that defines the functionality and product road map for Excel Services. Megiddo has been designing and developing data analysis software for more than 14 years. Prior to joining Microsoft, he co-founded Maximal Innovative Intelligence, back home in Israel. Maximal developed data visualization and exploration tools that were eventually acquired by Microsoft. The tools were initially released as Microsoft Data Analyzer and are now part of Microsoft Office Excel 2007. The inspiration for Maximal was in student-assessment software developed at Memad Educational Systems, where Megiddo led the software development and product marketing efforts. He began his professional career as an officer in an elite Israeli Military Intelligence unit. Megiddo enjoys spending his free time traveling and hiking with his wife and two daughters. He is an avid theatergoer, but on most nights, you will find him in the kitchen, where he enjoys cooking for family and friends.

Craig Thomas is a Senior Test Lead who works for Microsoft in Redmond, Washington. For the Office SharePoint Server 2007 release, he is the Release Test Lead for Excel Services. He also leads a team of testers who focus primarily on server performance and reliability. Prior to joining the Office team, he was contributing to shipping Exchange Server 2003 with a focus on leading a test team responsible for the Outlook Web Access component of Exchange. Thomas discovered his technology passions later in life, after an 11-year career as a submariner in the United States Navy. He programmed with C and C++ early on, but now prefers C#, and keeps his coding skills fresh by staying involved with tools development, authoring test automation scripts, and, of course, writing custom solutions for Excel Services.

Credits

Acquisitions Editor
Katie Mohr

Development Editor
Kevin Shafer

Technical Editor
Dan Battagin

Copy Editor
Kathryn Duggan

Editorial Manager
Mary Beth Wakefield

Production Manager
Tim Tate

Vice President and Executive Group Publisher
Richard Swadley

Vice President and Executive Publisher
Joseph B. Wikert

Compositor
Laurie Stewart, Happenstance Type-O-Rama

Proofreader
Jen Larsen, Word One

Indexer
Melanie Belkin

Anniversary Logo Design
Richard Pacifico

Acknowledgments

This book is the culmination of an effort we've all been involved with for more than three years as Excel Services progressed from thoughts and ideas to code running in production. Along the way, a lot of people crossed our paths and helped us get to where we are today. The words here cannot adequately express our gratitude to the Excel Services Testing, Development, and Program Management teams at Microsoft, who put together this amazing product and gave us something to write about. Thank you all.

Also, thanks to Wiley Publishing, especially Katie Mohr, for the support and for giving us this opportunity to complete our first book.

Contents

Contents

Part II: Working with Excel Services 73

Contents

Contents

Contents

Introduction

Excel is, by far, the most popular spreadsheet tool available. It is used by millions of end users each day to solve a wide range of problems. It provides solutions that span the gamut from simple list-keeping to mission-critical trading solutions that drive multimillion dollar trades on Wall Street. Everyone with an M.B.A. knows how to use it (and probably was already introduced to it somewhere back in middle school). Every financial department relies on it. Managers in business in every industry and at every level of the organization make decisions based on the numbers presented by and calculated in Excel.

Given how critical Excel is for business and users, it is not surprising that the need for better management, distribution, and incorporation of spreadsheets in larger applications is ever-increasing. Excel Services is an exciting new technology being delivered as part of Microsoft Office SharePoint Server 2007 to address this need. Excel Services enables the execution and sharing of workbooks on the server, thereby providing one version of the truth. It enables managed and secure distribution of Excel reports, incorporating spreadsheets in business intelligence (BI) dashboards and portals, protecting the proprietary information in spreadsheets, and building custom applications with Excel-based logic.

The authors of this book led the development of Excel Services at Microsoft. By sharing their insights into the benefits and usage of Excel Services here, they hope to help you solve your business problems.

Whom This Book Is For

This book is an introduction to Excel Services for all those who want to understand what it is, what it does, what the benefits are, and how to get started with Excel Services. If you share a need to provide a solution for your customers or organization, then this book is for you. This book is also targeted at anyone who is tasked with evaluating and later deploying Office 2007, and, specifically, Office SharePoint Server 2007. The book is technical and walks you through setting up and using the server, and discusses the architecture behind the scenes. This book is great if you are an IT developer or technical decision maker who is considering whether to use Excel Services within your organization. This book is also great for all Microsoft partners, including system integrators, consulting companies, hosting companies, value-added resellers, and independent software vendors who want to build and deploy solutions for their customers based on the new Office technologies. Anyone currently managing or developing solutions with Excel, Windows SharePoint Services, SharePoint Portal Server, or BI solutions should read this book to understand the basics of Excel Services.

This book assumes an understanding of Excel and basic knowledge of Excel 2007. It also assumes that you are familiar to some extent with Windows SharePoint Services. Knowledge of SharePoint Portal Server would also be a benefit. The last chapter of this book is a coding chapter, and to best understand it, you need basic coding skills, including knowledge of C# and JavaScript.

What This Book Covers

This book covers the Excel Services functionality that ships as part of Microsoft Office SharePoint Server 2007. Although it mentions other products (such as Excel 2007 and other features of Microsoft Office Share-Point Server 2007), explaining those products and features is outside the scope of this book.

Because this is the first version of the Excel Services technology, the book begins with the basics, explaining what Excel Services is for and how to use it. The book takes you from deploying an evaluation copy of the server, to administrating it, and provides step-by-step procedures for how to use the server in each of the scenarios it was designed for. It also covers the underpinnings of the server, delving into the server's architecture.

How This Book Is Structured

The first part of this book, "Overview of Excel Services," includes the following chapters:

❑   Chapter 1, "Introduction to Excel Services," explains the problems that Excel Services addresses. It then discusses what Excel Services is at a high level and what key scenarios are targeted.

❑   Chapter 2, "Getting Started with Excel Services," walks you through setting up an evaluation version of the product on your server.

❑   Chapter 3, "Architecture," explains the main components and how they work.

The second part of this book, "Working with Excel Services," goes into more detail about various aspects of the technology, and includes the following chapters:

❑   Chapter 4, "Workbook Support," discusses what types of workbooks and which Excel features are supported by Excel Services.

❑   Chapter 5, "External Data," discusses querying data from external databases into Excel Services, and the relevant security and performance implications.

❑   Chapter 6, "Capacity and Deployment Planning," starts by explaining the supported topologies and then discusses capacity planning.

❑   Chapter 7, "Administration of Excel Services," drills down into the various administrative settings and other features intended for system administrators.

❑   Chapter 8, "Security," discusses the most important security threats, and then explains the features and recommended configurations to mitigate them.

The third part of this book, "How-To Scenarios," provides several step-by-step procedures to implementing important Excel Services scenarios, and includes the following chapters:

❑   Chapter 9, "Sharing Workbooks with the Browser," describes the steps needed to publish a workbook to the server and view it in the browser.

❑   Chapter 10, "Interacting with Workbooks in the Browser," describes the functionality available to interact with the workbook in the browser.

❏ Chapter 11, "Controlling Workbook Distribution," explains how to use Excel Services to control the workbook distribution and maintain one central version with appropriate permissions.

❏ Chapter 12, "Business Intelligence Solutions," discusses how to use Excel Services in Business Intelligence (BI) scenarios. It discusses reporting, interacting with data, dashboards, and key performance indicators (KPIs).

❏ Chapter 13, "Offloading Workbook Calculation to the Server," examines the ability to use Excel Services to offload calculation-intensive workbooks to a server farm.

❏ Chapter 14, "Building Custom Solutions," provides an introduction to developing solutions on top of Excel Services.

The appendix of this book can help you troubleshoot common errors you might encounter when using Excel Services.

What You Need to Use This Book

Read the first two parts of this book to get a good understanding of Excel Services. To practice this understanding and to go through the step-by-step instructions in Part III, you need a deployment of Excel 2007 and of Microsoft Office SharePoint Server 2007. Chapter 2 helps you get started with Excel Services by walking you through deploying an evaluation copy of the server. To do this, you need access to an updated Windows 2003 Server machine.

For the client, you can use any machine that has Microsoft Internet Explorer 6 or 7. The experience is the same, and both were used to create the screenshots in this book. In addition, some screenshots show Microsoft Windows XP and others show Microsoft Windows Vista. You can use either operating system to run the browser and Excel 2007.

Chapters 9 through 13 use a sample workbook. You can download this workbook from www.wrox.com.

Conventions

To help you get the most from the text and keep track of what's happening, a number of conventions have been used throughout the book.

Try It Out

The Try It Out sections are exercises that you should work through, following the text in the book.

1. They usually consist of a set of steps.
2. Each step has a number.
3. Follow the steps through with your installation of the product.

How It Works

Following the Try It Out sections, the results of your actions are explained in detail.

Text that appears like this provides important, not-to-be forgotten information that is directly relevant to the surrounding text.

As for styles in the text:

- ❏ Important words are *italicized* when they are introduced.
- ❏ Keyboard strokes are shown like this: Ctrl+A.
- ❏ Code and URLs within the text is shown like this: `persistence.properties`.
- ❏ Code examples are presented in the following way:

```
Code examples are highlighted with a gray background.
```

```
The gray highlighting is not used for code that's less important in the
present context, or has been shown before.
```

Source Code

As you work through the examples in this book, you may choose to either type in all the code manually, or use the source code files that accompany the book. All of the source code used in this book is available for download at `www.wrox.com`. On this site, simply locate the book's title (either by using the Search box or by using one of the title lists), and click the Download Code link on the book's detail page to obtain all the source code for the book.

Because many books have similar titles, you may find it easiest to search by ISBN. This book's ISBN is 978-0-470-10489-7.

After you download the code, decompress it with your favorite compression tool. Alternately, you can go to the main Wrox code download page at `www.wrox.com/dynamic/books/download.aspx` to see the code available for this book and all other Wrox books.

Errata

We make every effort to ensure that there are no errors in the text or in the code. However, no one is perfect, and mistakes do occur. If you find an error in one of our books (such as a spelling mistake or faulty piece of code), we would be very grateful for your feedback. By sending in errata, you may save another reader hours of frustration and, at the same time, you will be helping us provide even higher quality information.

To find the errata page for this book, go to `www.wrox.com` and locate the title using the Search box or one of the title lists. Then, on the book details page, click the Book Errata link. On this page, you can view all errata that has been submitted for this book and posted by Wrox editors. A complete book list, including links to each book's errata, is also available at `www.wrox.com/misc-pages/booklist.shtml`.

If you don't spot "your" error on the Book Errata page, go to www.wrox.com/contact/techsupport .shtml and complete the form there to send us the error you have found. We'll check the information and, if appropriate, post a message to the book's errata page and fix the problem in subsequent editions of the book.

p2p.wrox.com

For author and peer discussion, join the P2P forums at p2p.wrox.com. The forums are a Web-based system for you to post messages relating to Wrox books and related technologies, and to interact with other readers and technology users. The forums offer a subscription feature to email you topics of interest of your choosing when new posts are made to the forums. Wrox authors, editors, other industry experts, and your fellow readers are present on these forums.

At http://p2p.wrox.com, you will find a number of different forums that will help you not only as you read this book, but also as you develop your own applications. To join the forums, just follow these steps:

1.   Go to p2p.wrox.com and click the Register link.

2.   Read the terms of use and click Agree.

3.   Complete the required information to join, as well as any optional information you wish to provide, and click Submit.

4.   You will receive an e-mail with information describing how to verify your account and complete the joining process.

You can read messages in the forums without joining P2P, but to post your own messages, you must join.

After you join, you can post new messages and respond to messages other users post. You can read messages at any time on the Web. If you would like to have new messages from a particular forum e-mailed to you, click the Subscribe to this Forum icon by the forum name in the forum listing.

For more information about how to use the Wrox P2P, be sure to read the P2P FAQs for answers to questions about how the forum software works, as well as many common questions specific to P2P and Wrox books. To read the FAQs, click the FAQ link on any P2P page.

Part I

Overview of
Excel Services

Introduction to Excel Services

Microsoft Office Excel has existed on the desktop for more than 20 years. It is by far the most broadly used spreadsheet tool available. And in Microsoft Office 2007, Excel is significantly enhanced. In Figure 1-1, you can see that quite a bit has changed in the last 20 years.

Today, spreadsheets are used more broadly than ever. Spreadsheets are often business- and mission-critical, and calculations range from trivial to those that require hours of compute time. There is a whole new set of needs for sharing spreadsheets broadly, incorporating them in web-based applications, and meeting compliance and regulation demands. In Office 2007, Microsoft has introduced a new product to address these and other needs: Microsoft Office SharePoint Server. Excel Services is a part of Office SharePoint Server that extends Excel to the server, enabling server-based workbook calculations, browser-based access to workbooks, and a web services interface to workbooks.

As with any new technology, there is a lot to learn, and many questions to answer. This book will help you get acquainted with Excel Services. The book is intended for people learning about, deploying, and using Excel Services. After reading the book, and going through the exercises, you will have a firm understanding of the benefits that Excel Services offers end users, how administrators can set up and manage Excel Services, and how developers can leverage Excel Services programmatically.

This chapter introduces Excel Services. It first explains what problems Excel Services was designed to address. It then discusses what Excel Services is at a high level, and the key scenarios that are targeted with the initial release. Finally, it attempts to preempt any misconceptions by discussing what Excel Services is not.

The remaining chapters of this book guide you through installing, setting up, and using Excel Services.

> *This book does not cover what is new in Excel 2007, nor does it cover Microsoft Office SharePoint Server broadly. The focus is on Excel Services functionality.*

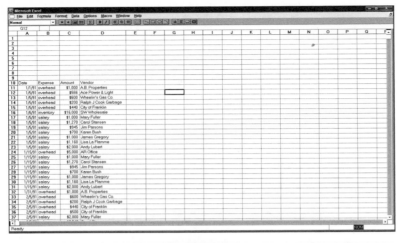

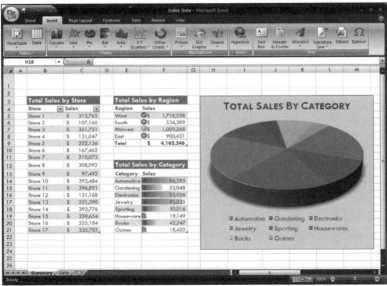

Figure 1-1

Who Hasn't Heard of Excel?

Excel is by far the most popular spreadsheet tool available. It is used by millions of end users each day. It is used to solve a very wide range of problems — solutions that span the gamut from simple list-keeping to mission-critical trading solutions driving multimillion dollar trades on Wall Street. Everyone who has an M.B.A. knows how to use it (and probably was already introduced to it somewhere back in middle-school). Every financial department relies on it. Managers in business in every industry and at every level of the organization make decisions based on the numbers presented by and calculated in Excel.

Whether it is being used for forecasting sales, analyzing a return on investment, developing a budget, tracking an investment portfolio, or calculating commission models, it is safe to say that Excel is at the heart of the business world. Excel formulas are the lingua franca, and much of the logic that drives businesses worldwide is captured in Excel models.

Given how critical Excel is for business, it is not surprising that there are ever-increasing needs for better management, distribution, and incorporation of spreadsheets in larger applications. The next section takes a look at these needs in more detail.

Why Excel on the Server?

Spreadsheets are used everywhere, and as they become more important to an organization, one or more of the following needs arise:

- ❑ There is a need to distribute the spreadsheet broadly.

- ❑ There is a need to control and manage the distribution and life cycle of the spreadsheet. (This is especially true in this age of compliance and regulations.)

- ❑ The spreadsheet needs to be viewed in the context of additional data as part of web applications and business intelligence (BI) dashboards.

- ❑ The results of the spreadsheet calculation need to be incorporated in other applications.

- ❑ The spreadsheet calculation takes a long time, preventing users from doing other things on their computers while it is processing.

This list is not all-encompassing. There many other needs that exist for users and organizations working with spreadsheets. This book focuses on the needs addressed by this first version of Excel Services. The "What Excel Services Is Not" section later in this chapter covers some of the things Excel Services does not do in this release.

The Problems with Distributing Spreadsheets

Today, when a spreadsheet author is working on an Excel workbook and wants to share it broadly (either for review or to distribute the final results), the most common way to do it is through e-mail. Sending an e-mail with an attached spreadsheet is simple and straightforward, but it also poses a problem. Every recipient of the e-mail with the attached spreadsheet receives his or her own copy of the spreadsheet. Now, instead of having one copy of the spreadsheet that everyone is looking at, there are as many copies as there were recipients on the To line of the e-mail. If the spreadsheet author makes a change to the workbook, he or she must send out an updated copy. But even then, the author has no way of verifying that everyone is looking at the latest copy sent. And, because each recipient has his or her own copy, they can each make changes to the workbook, making it out of sync with the version that is controlled by the spreadsheet author. Figure 1-2 shows this process.

The same problem holds true if the spreadsheet is placed on a file-share or document-management system. Each user opens a local copy of the spreadsheet, which he or she can then modify, making it out of sync with the sanctioned version.

Another problem that is exists when sharing spreadsheets this way is security. The spreadsheet may contain certain areas that its author does not want to share broadly (for example, the author may be interested in sharing the aggregated summary and not the detailed data on a different sheet in the workbook). In fact, in many cases, the actual model represented in the workbook and the formulas that comprise it are considered proprietary or a trade-secret that the spreadsheet author would like to protect. When all the recipients receive a copy of the entire spreadsheet file, it is practically impossible to guarantee that these elements will remain secured.

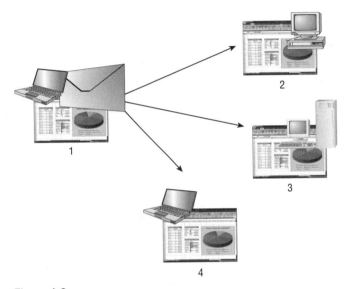

Figure 1-2

Controlling Spreadsheet Distribution

Distributing a workbook broadly may require additional control and management. The author may need to have the workbook reviewed and approved prior to it being made available broadly. Notifications may need to be sent out to all those tracking updates to the workbook. And after the spreadsheet has been distributed, there may be a need for an audit log to track who saw the spreadsheet, which version they saw, and who changed it. These types of requirements may be part of internal procedures, or mandated by external industry and government regulations. In addition, the workbook life cycle is not over when it is distributed. There may be records-management or document-retention policies that need to be enforced. For example, automatic backups and snapshots may need to be retained for archival purposes.

These needs usually span more than just workbooks. Documents (such as legal documents, human resource records, and product specifications), presentations, and e-mails all need to be controlled and managed. But there is no doubt that these requirements are especially relevant for workbooks that may include official financial reports, organizational budgets, trade records, and so forth.

Workbooks stored on local machines, copied from file share systems, and distributed as e-mail attachments are hard to track, control, and manage. This creates the potential for inefficiency and costly mistakes when people are basing their work and decisions on the wrong workbook. In this age of compliance and regulations, the concerns are even more acute.

The needs discussed thus far focused on distributing workbooks. The next two sections focus on incorporating workbooks, the models they represent, and the results of those models in web-based applications, dashboards, and custom solutions.

Incorporating Spreadsheets in Dashboards

The Excel client is perhaps the most used tool for data analysis and reporting. Whether the data originates in Excel or in some back-end system, users find a way to get it into Excel so that they can manipulate it, analyze it, and format the data and their findings for printing and sharing more broadly.

But when you look at what are considered the BI solutions within companies, Excel is usually not formally part of them. In fact, it is often explicitly called out as not being part of the sanctioned data analysis and reporting solution. Why? Here are two primary reasons.

BI solutions are essentially used for decision support, and it is critical that the numbers viewed in them are 100 percent trusted and secure. As mentioned previously, distributing workbooks as e-mail attachments may result in errors due to people looking at the wrong version or changing data they are not supposed to. When you look at typical BI solutions, they usually include a portal element that enables web-based report and analysis distribution. Distributing reports and analysis this way provides easy broad access, as well as the security and control necessary to ensure that the consumers of a report are looking at the correct report, can only access the data they are privileged to access, and cannot change (by accident or on purpose) the sanctioned data and results.

In addition, BI solutions often include dashboards, which enable the visual display of critical data in summary form. For example, a management dashboard may provide a complete view on the operations of a project, department, or company A customer dashboard may provide a sales representative with all the information and data available about a customer. The key to dashboards is the ability to combine different views on data, different data, and different content types all on the same page to give you a complete view for tracking information and making decisions. Although you can embed different data and objects in Excel workbooks, and build dashboards directly in the workbook, most BI dashboards are web-based. This allows for the greatest flexibility in incorporating different content types.

Leveraging Spreadsheet Models in Custom Solutions

The business logic that drives many applications is first defined in Excel workbooks. Excel workbooks are used to model such things as sales commissions, pricing and discounts models, and stock trades. Excel affords rapid development of these models in the hands of users who understand the business logic. The workbooks then serve as a specification for the developers who recode the logic in a formal programming language, and incorporate it in the target applications. This process is error-prone and costly. The developer needs to mimic the Excel model exactly and guarantee the same results. The cost of recoding and maintaining the code with every change to the workbook are high.

Excel can be called programmatically, but this solution is often not robust enough. This is especially true when the application calling the model must scale to support many such calculations with high availability. Excel is designed as a client application and, as such, there are limitations that affect these scenarios. There is, therefore, a need to support leveraging the business logic defined in Excel workbooks programmatically as part of scalable applications.

Offloading Spreadsheet Calculations to Servers

Some workbooks take a long time to calculate. Although many workbooks calculate instantaneously, there are also workbooks that take minutes and even hours to calculate. In some cases, calculating a single instance of the workbook may be very quick, but you have to repeat the calculation many times with different inputs. A great example for this is calculating risk using a Monte Carlo simulation. Though each calculation of the workbook may be short, it could require thousands of iterations with different input to return the needed results.

There is no doubt that the need to distribute workbooks is applicable to a broader set of users than dealing with workbooks that take a significant amount of time to calculate. But the cost this issue creates is significant. When these long-running calculations are taking place, you're blocked from using your computer for any additional work. When the calculation takes minutes or even hours, the ramifications are obvious.

The following section introduces you to Excel Services and how it can help address these needs.

What Is Excel Services?

Excel Services is a new server-side technology that is shipping in Microsoft Office 2007. It is not a product onto itself, but rather an integrated set of features that is part of the new Microsoft Office SharePoint Server 2007 (more on this product in the next section).

At its core, Excel Services enables you to calculate workbooks authored in the Excel client on a server, and distribute the updated results through either a browser-based interface or a programmatic interface in the form of web services. Excel Services extends the Excel client to the server, and, together with the rest of Office SharePoint Server functionality, provides an answer to the problems and needs described earlier.

With Excel Services, you can broadly distribute workbooks in a secure, controlled, and managed way. You can guarantee that only the correct version of the workbooks you author are accessed; that the details and formulas in the workbook are hidden and secure; and that the workbook has gone through the appropriate approval processes and is managed by the records-management policies of the organization. You can orkbooks as integral parts of BI dashboards and portals, and offload workbook calculations to free up desktop machines. And you can use workbook models and their results directly inside applications. All of this is fully integrated with the Excel client, leveraging all the capabilities and knowledge already out there.

Excel Services is designed to be a server product that supports many concurrent users, workbooks, and requests. It leverages server hardware and advanced configurations, from single-box deployments to multiple-tier and multiple-box scaled-out farms. It can work inside of the firewall as part of a point solution for a department, or as an enterprise-wide solution. It can also be deployed as part of an extranet topology to support scenarios that extend beyond the organization to external partners and customers through the Internet.

Next, you will take a step back and take a quick look at the rest of the functionality in Office SharePoint Server.

Microsoft Office SharePoint Server

Before going any deeper into Excel Services, you need to first zoom out and take a look at the broader product of which it is part: Microsoft Office SharePoint Server 2007. This, too, is a new product from Microsoft. In a nutshell, Office SharePoint Server is Microsoft's portal, document management, and business and collaboration application server all in one. The primary interface is through the web browser, as shown in Figure 1-3, but Office SharePoint Server functionality can also be accessed directly from the client.

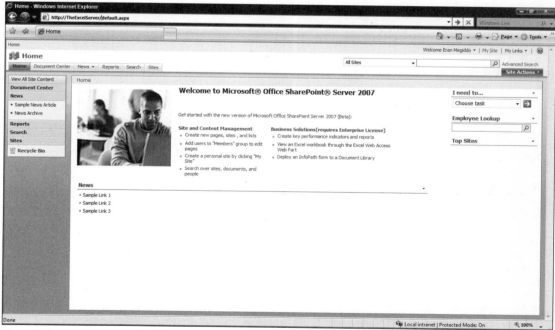

Figure 1-3

9

Office SharePoint Server provides the core storage, security, and administration framework. Beyond these, it includes a core set of six integrated capabilities:

❑   *Collaboration* — Document, task, and calendar sharing, and support for blogs and wikis

❑   *Portal* — Enterprise portal templates, personalization, news and content aggregation, and social networking.

❑   *Content Management* — Core document management (for example, check-in, check-out, and versioning), records management, and web content management

❑   *Search* — Enterprise-level search, including contextual relevance and rich people and data searching

❑   *Business process and forms* — Web-based forms and line-of-business application integration

❑   *Business Intelligence* — Dashboards, key performance indicator lists, report libraries, and web-based spreadsheets through Excel Services

As you can see, Office SharePoint Server is an extremely rich product. Each one of the six areas could be the subject of an entire book unto itself. This book does not attempt to cover all the functionality provided by Office SharePoint Server, neither in breadth nor in depth. The focus is Excel Services.

With that said, Excel Services is an integral part of Office SharePoint Server, and, as such, the solutions to the needs described earlier rely on many of the other capabilities of the product. This book will freely cross the line between features that are specific to Excel Services and features that are part of the Office SharePoint Server as a whole. The distinction is of no significance, because one set of features does not exist without the other.

As the name suggests, the heart of Office SharePoint Server is what used to be known as Microsoft SharePoint Portal Server. This is Microsoft's portal offering. Like SharePoint Portal, Office SharePoint Server is based on and requires Windows SharePoint Services. Windows SharePoint Services provide the base storage repository, document (and workbook) management functionality, as well as the end-user and administrator web user interface. Windows SharePoint Services also provides the base pro-grammability and extensibility model for developing custom web-based applications, which in turn is based on ASP.NET 2.0.

In Office 2007, both Windows SharePoint Services and the technology for SharePoint Portal Services are new versions with new functionality. In addition to these core technologies, Office SharePoint Server integrates what used to be the Content Management Server for web content management, the new Forms Server functionality for web-based forms and forms management, and Excel Services. Together, these provide the platform and capabilities described. The following sections cover a few of the core capabilities and key Office SharePoint Server concepts in more detail.

Security

Office SharePoint Server provides two fundamental building blocks for security: authentication and authorization. A user or application looking to calculate and view a workbook with Excel Services is first authenticated through Office SharePoint Server. The authentication is based on ASP.NET 2.0 authenti-cation, and a number of methods are supported. These include Windows-based authentication, forms-based authentication, and anonymous access. The authentication model is pluggable, and third-party authentication solutions such as Lightweight Directory Access Protocol (LDAP) directories can be used.

After a user or the calling application is authenticated, authorization is done against the resource being requested. This can be any resource in the SharePoint store. The scenarios and examples in this book cover libraries of workbooks, specific workbooks, and dashboards. Office SharePoint supports specific rights, and users or groups of users can be granted these rights. For example, a user may have the rights to open, view, and edit a workbook in the browser and the client, or the user may have only the right to view the workbook in the browser.

Office SharePoint Server also includes a single sign-on (SSO) store. This provides an additional mechanism by which users are authenticated, and is especially relevant for scenarios that include workbooks connected to external data sources. The SSO store infrastructure is pluggable, and third-party solutions can replace the built-in solution.

Chapter 8 describes the security model, the various authentication mechanisms, and the specific user rights in more detail. Later in this book, you will see how Excel Services uses this infrastructure to load workbooks, query external data sources, and provide results.

Web Part Pages

A key underlying concept for Office SharePoint Server is *Web Part Pages*. Practically all the web pages served by Office SharePoint Server are Web Part Pages. This is an ASP.NET 2.0 technology that enables you to place numerous web parts (equivalent to web controls) on a single web page, and defines how these web parts are laid out, as well as how they can interact with one another. Office SharePoint Server ships with a large selection of out-of-the-box web parts, and developers can create their own and deploy them to the server. Out-of-the-box web parts enable you to display documents in a specific document library, views on a task list, RSS content aggregation, a list of links, and simple Hypertext Markup Language (HTML) or rich text content, among other things. Excel Services has a web part component as well, through which spreadsheets are rendered in the browser.

Web parts can have numerous properties that control and customize them. Many of these settings can be personalized so that different users will receive different behaviors when they view the same page. Using this functionality, it is possible to set up a page that includes a list of tasks, and users logging in will see the tasks assigned to them.

Web parts on the same page can also interact, passing data between them. For example, the author of a Web Part Page can connect a web part that lists workbooks in a document library to an Excel Services web part. A user viewing the page can select from the list of workbooks, and the selected workbook is displayed. Behind the scenes, the workbook URL is passed between the two web parts.

Web parts are the foundation for building composite applications as well as BI dashboards.

Content Storage and Management

Office SharePoint Server provides the default content store for Excel Services scenarios. The core storage container is a *document library*, which, in turn, is associated with a site. Document libraries are conceptually equivalent to file system folders. As shown in Figure 1-4, they can contain virtually any file, including images, Word documents, PowerPoint presentations, Excel workbooks, and web pages. Document libraries can also contain additional document libraries or subfolders.

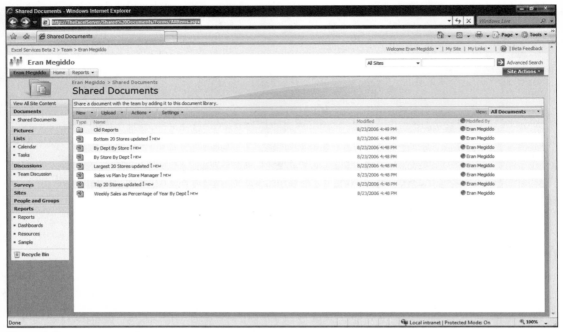

Figure 1-4

The content security and management functionality that is part of Office SharePoint Server accrues to any content stored in document libraries. As described previously in the "Security" section, users can be granted specific rights to a specific document library or a specific spreadsheet (or any other file) in a document library. Files in a document library can be controlled through enforced check-out and check-in procedures. Versions can be automatically kept for each file. These can be major versions and/or minor versions. Document approval settings can govern whether a file is made available broadly prior to being approved by the moderator of the document library. Notifications can be set to alert (through e-mail or RSS feeds) users when a new file is added to a document library, or when an existing file is updated or deleted.

More advanced document management capabilities include the following:

❑ Workflow

❑ Records management policy

❑ Auditing support

Office SharePoint Server's workflow support is built on Windows Workflow services. Workflows can be associated with a document library such that any time a file is added, updated, or deleted, a workflow is triggered. Workflows can also be triggered manually by users or programmatically. Office SharePoint Server includes a number of out-of-the-box workflows, and you can develop additional custom workflows using SharePoint Designer or Visual Studio. Following are the included workflows:

❑ Collect Feedback

❑ Approval

❑ Disposition Approval (to support retention policies)

❑ Collect Signatures

❑ Translation (for managing human document translation)

❑ A three-state workflow that assigns items in SharePoint lists between people based on changes to a specific column

In East Asia, there is also a more complex approval workflow to support specific routing options relevant in those markets. Figure 1-5 shows the web-based user interface for setting up workflows.

To further support records management, compliance, and regulation needs, Office SharePoint Server enables you to define policies for such things as document retention. For example, you can define which documents in a certain document library will be automatically archived for a given period of time without the possibility of anyone deleting them. You can specify the date when these documents are to be removed from the archive and deleted. As with workflows, there is a web-based user interface (as shown in Figure 1-6). Users can choose to customize the out-of-the-box policies, or they can be extended programmatically.

The document management functionality is completed by an auditing capability. Practically any event associated with a document can be audited, including documents being created, edited, viewed, and deleted. You can extend this capability programmatically so that custom events can be audited.

Office SharePoint Server also extends content management to include web content management by integrating the functionality of the Content Management Server.

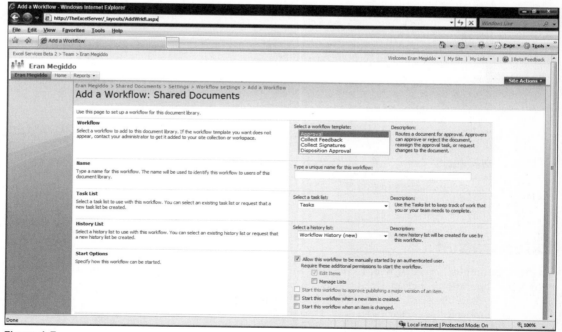

Figure 1-5

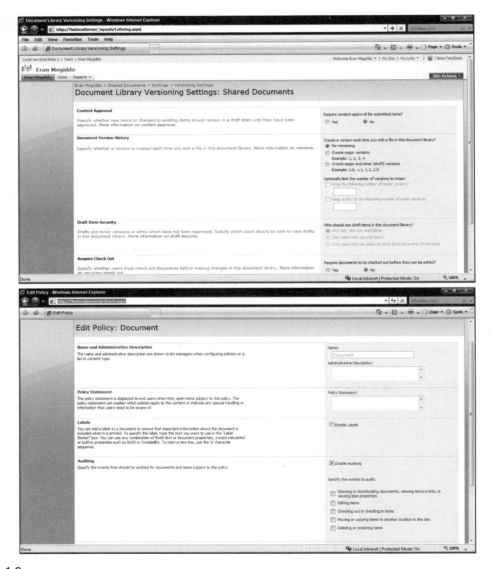

Figure 1-6

Collaboration

Office SharePoint Server provides a hub for storing and managing content, as well as for collaborating on it. Collaboration functionality includes support for discussion groups, shared task and calendar management, wikis, blogs, integration with e-mail systems, and (together with the Live Communications Server) support for presence awareness. The latter enables users to directly interact with one another from within the context of their dashboard, collaboration site, or application, as shown in Figure 1-7.

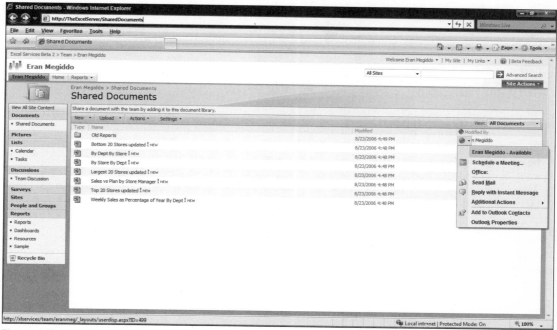

Figure 1-7

Users can collaborate on a document or set of documents. They can collaborate on tasks and entire projects. Entire sites and applications can be hubs for collaboration, as is the case with a blog or wiki. For example, you can set up a fully featured wiki by simply selecting that template when creating a new site. Using the My Site feature, you can also create personal sites to share data and documents. Audience-targeting features enable you to personalize content and target it to specific sets of users.

Search

The document and content stored in Office SharePoint Server can be indexed and subsequently searched. Searching is available from within any site. It can also be incorporated into custom pages and applications. In addition to searching within the content stored in the server, you can connect to external data stored in line-of-business applications and databases. The data is indexed, and you search and view it directly from within Office SharePoint Server. For example, you can search for people, colleagues, and experts in a specific field. The search indexer can also connect to third-party content repositories.

Forms Services

Yet another component of the server is Forms Services, which enables server-side forms authoring and management. Forms Services is the server-side extension of Microsoft Office's InfoPath tool. You can author electronic forms in InfoPath client and publish these forms to the server. The forms can then be filled out through either the InfoPath client or, using Forms Services, in the browser.

Forms can contain different controls (such as data pickers and combo boxes). The forms can be backed by simple input validation or custom code. Forms can display data that comes from external data sources because they push the data entered in the form back to an external data source.

Office SharePoint Server provides a complete forms-management solution, as well, that leverages all the document-management functionality provided.

Business Intelligence

BI functionality is also built into Office SharePoint Server. It supports the creation of BI portals and dashboards in Excel Services by providing browser-based spreadsheets that users can interact with to explore data. In addition, Office SharePoint Server includes Report Center site templates, report libraries, key performance indicator (KPI) lists and parts, Data Connection Libraries (DCLs), and support for building and using dashboards.

Report Centers

Office SharePoint Server includes a template for Report Centers, which are sites focused on disseminating BI information through the portal. As shown in Figure 1-8, the site includes a Report Library (which is a customized document library that is tailored to support reports), a DCL, a report calendar, and a set of default views and pages onto these collections.

Figure 1-8

Report Libraries

Report Libraries are document libraries tailored to contain reports and dashboards. The primary addition to regular document libraries is the support for retaining report histories for each report in the library. A good example is a monthly inventory report. If you want to keep a copy of your monthly inventory reports (so you can return to any given month and view inventory, for example), you'll need a copy of the report as it was at the end of every month. However, a simple document library would quickly become cluttered if you tried to store all of these reports in it.

Report Libraries enable you to save the history for the report and collapse it behind a single entry point for the inventory report. In the basic views of the Report Library, you see only the latest copy of the inventory report listed. Through the Report Library menu, you can expand and see all the historical copies of this report.

Report Libraries also include a number of default fields and views that are common in reporting scenarios.

Data Connection Libraries

Data Connection Libraries (DCLs) are document libraries extended and tailored to contain data connection definitions. In general, DCLs are geared to hold files that contain connection information for applications such as Excel to connect to external data sources.

Because data sources are stored in a central location on an Office SharePoint Server, end users and administrators can locate and maintain them more easily. For example, if you are in Excel and want to connect to an external data source, you can browse through the list of data connections that have already been defined and saved in a DCL. These connections are represented by descriptive names and text, making them easy to identify. Based on these, you can select the data source that you're interested in and Excel will connect to it. You don't need to know the various technical details of the data connection definition (such as the server name, the database name, and query).

Storing data connection definitions in central DCLs also makes it easier to manage data connections. Because the data definition is stored in one location, you only need to update it in that location.

As an example, consider a data connection file that defines the connection information for a sales database. Many Excel users have authored workbooks that connect to that sales database, all using the data connection information stored in that file. If the administrator of that database needs to move the data to a different machine, he or she only has to update the data connection definition in the one central location stored in the DCL. The next time the Excel workbooks that use this connection are opened, they will automatically update to the new connection information and the new machine name, and the data is refreshed. This saves the administrator from needing to maintain and update every single workbook manually.

Chapter 5 covers data connections and DCLs as they pertain to Excel Services in depth.

Key Performance Indicator Lists and Parts

Key performance indicators (KPIs) provide the basis for tracking key measurements in an organization. In addition to the actual values being tracked, KPIs include goals and trends. Many BI systems enable tracking KPIs on dashboards, as part of lists, in reports, or as part of more complex score carding applications. Office SharePoint Server provides basic functionality for displaying KPIs in dashboards using the KPI web part, or as part of KPI lists, as shown in Figure 1-9.

Figure 1-9

KPI lists contain KPIs and can present them visually. The KPIs can be contained in a flat list and be grouped hierarchically. The status, goals, and trends for the KPI can be sourced from values in a SQL Server Analysis Services 2005 cube, in an Excel workbook, or in a SharePoint list, and simply entered into the KPI.

These different KPI types can all exist in the same list, providing a great aggregation and view across multiple data sources.

The KPI web part displays the value and additional information for a single KPI. Users can get to these parts either by clicking on a KPI in the list, or by placing the KPI part directly on a dashboard.

Dashboards

A dashboard is an aggregation of related data and content in the form of reports, tables, and charts. These are presented on the same page, and provide an aggregate, contextualized view. For example, a regional sales manager can have a dashboard page that displays the latest sales numbers, current customer support escalations, the target sales for the period, and a list of current leads.

Office SharePoint Server supports building such BI dashboards based on the core Web Part Pages capabilities described earlier. In addition, it provides features that target common BI dashboard needs and makes it easy to create such dashboards.

To create a BI dashboard, you use the dashboard page template, which guides you through a wizard-like setup process. For example, you can choose the default parts to include in the dashboard and additional customization options. When you are finished with the setup, you are presented with the dashboard page, and can then continue to assemble it by configuring the content to display in the dashboard.

Another core feature of BI dashboards in Office SharePoint Server is a set of filters that enable you to connect all the content on the dashboard. This is done by filtering the different elements of the dashboard together. For example, the sales dashboard described earlier can include filters for the product line and for the sales region. The sales manager viewing the dashboard can select a region and all the various parts of the dashboard (such as the latest sales numbers or support escalations) will show the data for only that region.

Office SharePoint Server includes several filters out-of-the-box, and more can be added programmatically. The out-of-the-box filters include those that support filtering based on an authored list of values, values that come from a database query, data based filtering, and others. Figure 1-10 shows an example of such a dashboard.

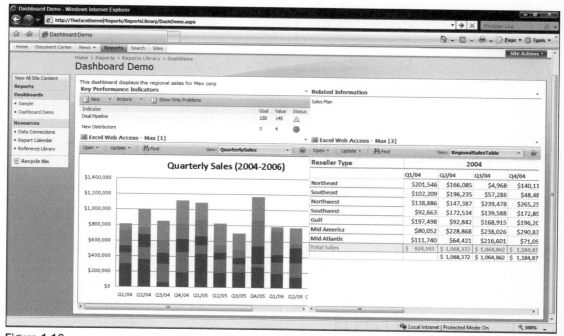

Figure 1-10

Chapter 12 describes how you can build a dashboard with Office SharePoint Server using Excel Services to include workbooks in the dashboard.

Administration

Tying together all the functionality described is a unified setup, deployment, administration, and monitoring system. It starts with one setup that delivers all the functionality described. Managing topologies, administrating server settings, and monitoring server status and health is all unified as well. Chapters 2 and 7 go into far more detail on all these topics as they pertain to Excel Services functionality. For now, it is important to understand that Excel Services administration is an integral part of Office SharePoint Server integration, and not a separate solution. With that said, there are numerous settings that are specific to managing Excel Services functionality, which this book covers in depth as well.

The key to Office SharePoint Server is that all the capabilities are completely integrated into a single product. Though you can use it as a document management system or as a portal, the real strength is building solutions and applications that leverage all this functionality in an integrated way. The same is true for the functionality provided by Excel Services. The needs described previously are best addressed when you leverage Excel Services capabilities with the broad functionality of Office SharePoint Server.

There are many more capabilities and features of Office SharePoint Server that are definitely worth learning about. This book can only provide a brief overview. As the book continues and expands on Excel Services and walks you through setting-up, administrating, and using it, additional Office SharePoint Server concepts are described. Excel Services is the Office SharePoint functionality that supports loading, calculating, and rendering an Excel workbook on the server. The solutions that are detailed in the following section, and described in further detail in Chapters 9 through 13, all focus on Excel Services functionality, but also apply to additional Office SharePoint server features from the sets described.

Now that you have a basic understanding of the core set of needs users have for Excel, what Excel Services is, and how it fits in the bigger Office SharePoint Server product, the next section describes the five key ways that you can use Excel Services.

Five Key Ways to Use Excel Services

This section examines five key uses for Excel Services. These use cases line up with the needs described. They also serve as examples in Chapters 9 through 13, which provide step-by-step guides to using Excel Services for each one of these scenarios.

Distributing Workbooks Through the Browser

With Excel Services, you can calculate a workbook on the server and view the results in the browser. This is the foundation for broad and secure distribution of workbooks. You use the Excel client to author a workbook, or you can create or update the workbook programmatically. Then the consumers of the workbook only need a browser to access, view, and explore it.

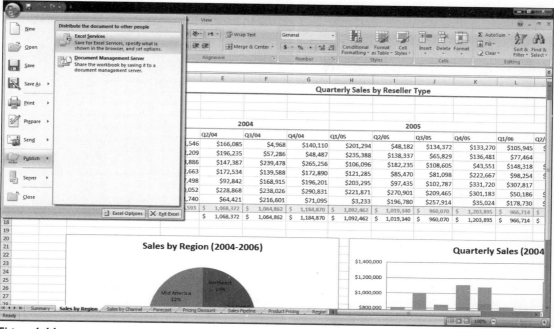

Figure 1-11

The scenario is straightforward. After you author a workbook, you save it to a document library or file share, and provide a link to that location. Figure 1-11 shows a workbook being authored in Excel client.

You can send the link to your workbook to others in an e-mail message, through a notification, or otherwise. Then the recipients just follow the link, and the workbook is calculated by Excel Services and the results are displayed in the browser.

In the browser, users can manipulate the workbook to explore the data in it. For example, they can sort and filter data, drill down or up on a PivotTable, or change input parameters that affect calculation. However, they cannot change the original workbook or values in it. The browser-based rendering looks true to the original, as shown in Figure 1-12.

This sounds simple, at first, but consider how this is different and better than simply sharing the workbook through e-mail or by placing it on a file share and having people load a copy of the workbook in Excel.

When a user opens a workbook in the Excel client from an e-mail attachment or from a file share, a copy of that workbook is downloaded locally. Even if users do not have permission to save over the original workbook, they can save a complete local copy. The next time the user wants to access the workbook, he or she may go back to the copy in the e-mail, or to the copy that was saved locally and, by that time the user is potentially not looking at the correct, updated version of the workbook. The workbook author may have updated it or made changes in the meantime.

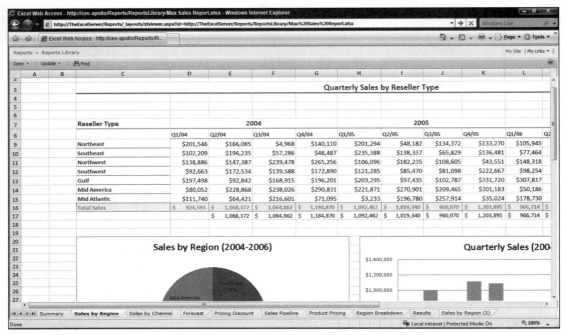

Figure 1-12

When the workbook is shared using Excel Services, only one copy of the workbook exists (where the workbook author saved it). Every time the consumers of the workbook want to view it, they navigate to the link that they were provided. In this way, they are guaranteed to always see the latest version available. In theory, you could also do this by sending an updated attachment or using a simple file share; however, in both those cases the consumers of the workbook have a local copy (either in the e-mail or ones that are saved), so there are no guarantees. Furthermore, for workbooks stored in Office SharePoint Server document libraries and viewed using Excel Services, you can ensure that users do not have permission to download and save a local copy of the workbook. Rather, they will only be allowed to view the workbook through the browser. In this way, it is guaranteed that they are looking at the sanctioned copy.

Accessing workbooks through Excel Services provides additional security. Users viewing workbooks in the browser cannot change the values or formulas in those workbooks. In fact, they cannot see the formulas at all. So, the workbook author is guaranteed that the model developed is protected, and the values in the author's analysis are not changed (either by mistake or on purpose). Authors know that the workbook they distributed for others to view is the one they are seeing. Finally, as you will see in greater detail in Chapter 9, the workbook author can also control which parts of a workbook are made visible to users viewing the workbook through the browser. This provides an additional level of security.

Distributing workbooks through Excel Services and viewing them in the browser meets the need to broadly share workbooks. It ensures that the sanctioned workbooks are being viewed, and that the proprietary data and models in them are secure. There are a couple of additional benefits that are worth calling out.

First, people viewing workbooks in the browser do not need to have Excel installed on their machines. A second benefit is a performance benefit. There are many workbooks that are large. It is not uncommon to see workbooks that are several megabytes in size. When users access these workbooks through e-mail or file shares, they need to download these large files locally. This can be especially slow if the user is working remotely. When you're viewing the workbook in the browser, Excel Services loads the large file, but only the result ranges designated by the workbook author are presented to the user in the browser. Even if the entire workbook is accessible, Excel Services lets the user page through sheets sections at a time. In this way, only a few hundred kilobytes of data need to be transferred across to the local machine, potentially saving significant time.

This is different from simply saving the workbook as HTML and providing a link to generated web page (a feature that exists in Excel today). When a workbook is saved as HTML, it is transformed into what can be considered a snapshot or frozen picture of the workbook. The HTML page shows the values as they were when the workbook author saved it as HTML. Users viewing the HTML page do not see any updated values from external data sources, or volatile functions (such as time-based functions). They also cannot interact with the workbook in any way to change parameters, drill down, or filter values.

On the other hand, when you access a workbook through Excel Services and view it in the browser, it is *live*. When you request to see the workbook through the browser, Excel Services loads and calculates the workbook, which means that any volatile data or functions are updated. The browser-based interface provided by Excel Services also allows users to interact with the workbook and changes are calculated by Excel Services with the results updating in the browser.

The following section describes how you can combine this capability with additional Office SharePoint Server functionality to provide control and management for workbook distribution.

Controlling and Managing Workbook Distribution

Controlling and managing the distribution of workbooks is critical, especially when the workbooks have key business impact. As discussed, this need is even more important given the various regulations and compliance requirements being set. Managing and controlling workbooks with Office SharePoint Server takes advantage of the core capability to calculate a workbook on the server, and display the results in the browser.

Consider a simple example. A workbook author must distribute monthly sales results broadly and must ensure that the results people are viewing are always the latest quarter results so that no confusion occurs. The author also must verify that the people viewing the report only see the results once they have been approved by the division's financial analyst. Finally, each quarterly report must be backed up and retained for future reference.

Office SharePoint Server and Excel Services can provide a solution to this scenario. To begin with, a Report Library is created that will contain all the quarterly reports. The library is configured for content approval and an approval workflow that is triggered every time a major version is checked in. In addition, a retention policy is set up that creates a backup copy of each major version of the workbook in an official file repository.

Only the workbook author and the analyst that reviews it are set up to have permission to view and edit the workbook in the Excel client. Everyone else has only the permission to view the workbook in the browser.

With this setup, the workbook author can manage and control the distribution of the workbook and verify that the intended recipients are always viewing the correct version of the report. Figure 1-13 shows how you can access these features directly from within Excel 2007.

After the workbook author saves and checks in a major version of the workbook, the approval workflow is activated. The financial analyst receives a link to the workbook by e-mail and is asked to review it for accuracy.

At this point, the workbook is not accessible to anyone but the workbook author and the analyst. After the analyst reviews the workbook and approves it, everyone else is authorized to view the workbook. But they can do so only in the browser. This ensures that the workbook they are looking at is the approved distribution copy, and that they cannot download and create copies of this workbook. It also protects any proprietary information represented by the model or sections of data in the workbook.

In addition, after the workbook has been approved, a second workflow is triggered. This one creates a copy of the workbook in the official records-management repository. That document library includes various retention settings to ensure that the document is archived according to corporate regulations.

The site administrator can view an audit log that shows who exactly has seen the workbook, which version, and when.

As you can see, integrating Excel Services capabilities with the rest of the Office SharePoint Server features provides a great solution for managing and controlling workbook distribution.

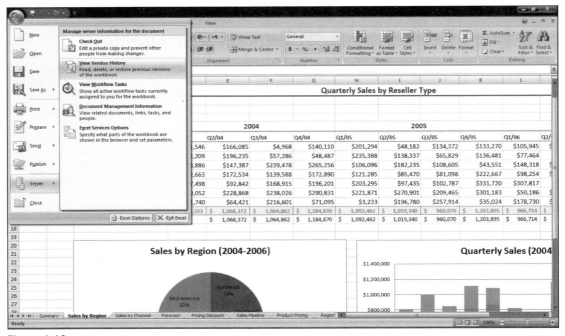

Figure 1-13

Building Business Intelligence Portals and Dashboards

In order for Excel to be considered a complete BI solution, there must be a way to incorporate workbooks that contain data analysis inside of portals and dashboards.

Excel Services and the BI features of Office SharePoint Server provide an answer to this need. With these features, you can use Excel to analyze your business data, and then distribute your analysis through Office SharePoint Server. You can use the BI functionality to build Report Centers and Report Libraries that become the hub for BI and reporting needs.

The Report Libraries can contain Excel workbooks that have been published by the various analysts. Users can then view these workbooks in the browser, ensuring that they remain managed and controlled. They can also incorporate the workbooks (or parts of the workbooks) as part of dashboards built using Office SharePoint Server. The dashboards can contain live workbooks, as well as KPI lists created from Excel.

Leveraging Workbook Calculation in Custom Solutions

As mentioned, Excel Services includes a web services interface. The interface is basic and focused on a couple of core scenarios.

One of these scenarios is building applications that directly leverage Excel workbooks as their business logic. The key capabilities of the Application Programming Interface (API) are loading a workbook, calculating it, setting values into cells, and retrieving values from individual cells or the entire updated workbook.

With these core interfaces, you could conceivably use Excel workbooks as functions in custom-developed applications. The workbooks become an integral part of the application, and are called programmatically to calculate results for specific inputs.

The Excel workbook is calculated by Excel Services, which provides a robust and scalable platform for calculating workbooks. This is very different from calling a client productivity tool, and can be leveraged as part of large enterprise applications.

To better understand how Excel Services can help solve your needs, consider this use case. Assume a pricing analyst in the Marketing Department is responsible for developing pricing and discounts for a specific range of products. The analysts must develop the discount schedule based on various factors (such as the amount being purchased and the type of reseller). The discount model is first developed in the Excel client.

The same discount model must be called by the company's web-based order quotation system. Without Excel Services, a developer would be tasked with recoding the logic represented in the Excel workbook in code so that it can be leveraged as part of the application.

With Excel Services, the workbook author can continue to maintain the workbook, and the developer can leverage the business logic stored in it programmatically. After the details for a new order are entered in the online quotation tool, the program calls on Excel Services to load the pricing workbook, plug the values from the input form, calculate the workbook, and retrieve the resulting values to present the user with the discount that is offered. Using this method, the developer does not need to track every change in the workbook and update the code. On the flip side, the analyst can update the discount model in Excel with immediate effect on the running application.

As discussed, Excel Services is designed to be a server from the ground up. Thus, the calling application can rely on the server being up and workbooks being calculated, even if many requests are entered simultaneously by different sales representatives asking for quotes.

Offloading Workbook Calculation to Excel Services

A core capability of Excel Services is loading and calculating a workbook on a server. In this first release, Excel Services does not do much to improve the performance of calculating a single workbook when compared with the client. But, because the workbook is calculated on the server, solutions can be built that free up the client computers and by doing that, allow users to continue to work in parallel with the workbook being calculated.

There is no direct out-of-the-box solution for this use case. It relies on the web services interface and a custom solution, such as offloading the workbook calculation through a job-submitting process. You, as a developer, could build a custom interface that enables users to submit a workbook to be calculated by the server directly from within Excel client. Or, you could build a solution that schedules batch calculation of workbooks. Chapter 13 of this book covers the latter example in more detail.

All of these solutions rely on using the web services interface to load and calculate the workbook on the server. The key to these solutions is that the client machines remain free for other activities. Although in general calculation, a workbook on the server does not improve the performance of that specific calculation, there are a number of cases in which it may, such as when all or parts of the workbook are already in the server cache or external data is retrieved. Chapter 3 examines the architecture and discusses the various levels of caching and how they affect performance.

The five use cases described are by no means the complete list of potential uses for Excel Services, although they do represent the key scenarios that Excel Services was designed for in this first version. There are many other ways to leverage server-side spreadsheet calculation and rendering. When these capabilities are incorporated with the rest of Office SharePoint Server's functionality, the uses and solutions that can be built increase even more.

Who Is Excel Services For?

Excel Services functionality and the Office SharePoint Server are server products. Server products require some level of IT-supported setup and administration, and they assume multiple users, so this is probably not a product you will find consumers installing at home. The benefits and scenarios of Excel Services are geared at primarily medium and large businesses. This can be as part of a point solution for a department or branch in a larger organization, or a broader solution for an entire enterprise. Excel Services does not target any specific industry or company type. It also does not target specific workbook applications (such as sales and marketing analysis, or budgeting). The use cases are many and varied.

So who is Excel Services for? Anyone who uses Excel and is looking to solve the needs described can benefit from Excel Services. Whether you are looking for an easy way to share workbooks over the web, or a complete solution for controlling and managing workbook distributions, Excel Services can provide an answer. If you are building a BI portal and dashboards, you can use Excel Services and the rest of the Office SharePoint Server BI capabilities to do just that. If you are a developer who wants to incorporate the business logic defined in workbooks directly, Excel Services and the web services API it provides could be your solution. Whether you are looking to offload calculations to the server or leverage server-side workbook calculations in any other way, Excel Services can provide the solution.

In addition, if you're trying to solve server-side Excel problems, Excel Services is for you. For example, if you are using Office Web Components to try to build BI dashboards authored in Excel, automating saving workbooks as web pages to broadly distribute them, or automating the client application (Excel.exe) on a server or set of servers to schedule or batch-calculate and distribute workbooks, then you will probably find that Excel Services provides a better solution to your needs.

Also, companies that already have or are looking at deploying Microsoft Office SharePoint Server for other uses (for example, as their corporate portal or document management solution) can gain from the leveraging of the capabilities of Excel Services that they are already deploying.

The next section looks at some of the key things Excel Services is not, and does not do in this first version.

What Excel Services Is Not

This chapter introduced Excel Services and the core needs that are addressed by this new functionality. As outlined, the needs for server-side workbook calculations are real and many. In this first release of Excel Services, a number of these needs are met. But there are many more needs and scenarios for server-side workbook calculation and management that are not solved by this version of Excel Services. A few of these are worth calling out to further define what Excel Services is by describing what it is not.

Although the version of Excel Services shipped with Office 2007 does not support functionality listed here, this may change in future versions.

Following are the top five things Excel Services is not:

- ❏ Although Excel Services provides full calculation fidelity with the client Excel.exe through shared calculation code, Excel Services is not the Excel client (Excel.EXE) adapted to run on the server. It is a new set of services designed from the ground up to run on servers and support many users, workbooks, and requests.

- ❏ Excel Services is not a product, nor is it a standalone server. Excel Services functionality is packaged as part of Microsoft Office SharePoint Server 2007. It cannot be purchased as a standalone product from Microsoft.

- ❏ Excel Services is not a solution for web-based spreadsheet authoring. Excel Services can calculate and render an existing workbook. It is assumed that the workbooks are authored in the Excel client, or programmatically.

- ❏ Excel Services does not support simultaneous, multiuser workbook authoring (such as budgeting applications). It is primarily designed for read-only access to workbooks in the context of workbook distribution.

- ❏ Excel Services does not support every Excel workbook. Certain Excel features are not supported by Excel Services (as detailed in Chapter 4).

This is not a complete list of what Excel Services is not. And this chapter did not address all the potential uses that Excel Services does address. This is a new technology that is part of a new product. As you discover and use Excel Services, you will find many more uses for this new technology than this book can cover, as well as scenarios and needs that are yet unmet.

Summary

Excel client has been around for more than 20 years and is probably the most commonly used business software. In Microsoft Office 2007, Excel is extended to the server. Microsoft Office SharePoint Server and Excel Services solve problems that exist today, and enable a broad new range of scenarios. Whether it is managing workbook distribution, or building BI dashboards that incorporate Excel workbooks, server-side Excel capabilities are new and exciting.

The rest of this book covers setting up and deploying the server, managing it, and using Excel Services for the key scenarios discussed in this chapter. Chapter 2 walks you through setting up and configuring Office SharePoint Server with Excel Services. You will set up an evaluation copy on a single-box deployment, which will provide you with a server to use in the remainder of the examples in the book.

Getting Started with Excel Services

Chapter 1 provided you with information outlining the many capabilities of Excel Services. Future chapters focus more on the Excel Services features and provide hands-on experience to facilitate your Excel Services learning experience. This chapter focuses on the steps necessary to get Excel Services up and running, and then, as you progress through the remainder of this book, you will have a deployment on which to try out Excel Services scenarios and administrative tasks.

In this chapter, you learn the following:

❑ The prerequisites for a single box installation of Microsoft Office SharePoint Server 2007 (MOSS)

❑ How to install an evaluation version of MOSS

❑ The state of Excel Services upon completion of an evaluation version setup

Installation Types

Microsoft offers four Office Servers as part of the 2007 release: Forms, Groove, Project, and Share-Point. Excel Services runs on Microsoft Office SharePoint Server 2007 (MOSS). It is only installed and available with MOSS. Installing the Forms, Groove, or Project server will not install Excel Services.

MOSS can be deployed through three types of installations.

❑ *Web Front-End* — The only components that will be installed on the server are those required to render content to users. You can add servers to your SharePoint farm when you choose this type of installation, and it will install the necessary Excel Services components on the web front end (WFE). A separate application server is also necessary to use Excel Services. No database engine will be installed.

❑   *Complete* — All components will be installed on the server. You can add servers to your Share-Point farm when you choose this type of installation. The application server where you are going to run the Excel Calculation Server (ECS) requires a Complete installation. You can also use this installation type on a server that is going to be the WFE. No database engine will be installed.

❑   *Stand-alone* — All components will be installed on the server. You cannot add servers to create a SharePoint farm with this type of installation. This server will represent both the application server and the WFE. Microsoft SQL Server 2005 Express Edition (SQL Server Express) will be installed as part of the installation.

The Stand-alone installation type is also referred to as an *evaluation installation*. That is not to say that you cannot use a Stand-alone installation in a production environment, because you can. There are many very good reasons why you might choose to deploy a standalone server. For example, you can use this config-uration to evaluate the product's features and capabilities, without spending too much time installing and configuring MOSS. If you expect your deployment to consist of only a few sites, then the Stand-alone installation may be all that you need.The remainder of this chapter focuses solely on a MOSS Stand-alone installation. The Complete and Web Front-End setups are not covered in this book.

Platform Requirements

Before you proceed with installing MOSS, ensure that your system meets both the hardware and soft-ware requirements. The requirements described here are for a single-server deployment, such as an evaluation server.

Hardware

Like most other software products, Microsoft Office SharePoint Server 2007 has requirements for the platform. The following table outlines the requirements you will need to meet when choosing the hardware for your evaluation server.

Component	Requirement
Processor	Dual-processor with a clock speed of at least 2.5 GHz
RAM	Minimum 1GB (2GB recommended for evaluation); minimum 2GB (4GB recom-mended) for a farm
Disk space	Up to 2GB for installation; at least 5GB of free disk space after installation

In keeping with the evaluation theme, if you adhere to the processor and RAM requirements and rec-ommendations, then you can expect to have a good experience while you're learning about and test driving Excel Services. Chapter 6 provides additional information that will be relevant to your hard-ware procurement decisions.

The 1GB minimum for RAM is a starting point for Excel Services. For performance reasons, Excel Services was designed and built with the understanding that it could be a memory-intensive application. Of course, the amount of memory available to Excel Services is configurable and the amount of system memory you will need is dependent on the scenarios you plan to support.

Software

You must also ensure that you meet the software requirements, including the correct operating system and some specific Windows components and applications. The installation and configuration order for these items is as follows:

1. *NTFS file system* — The partition where MOSS will be installed must be the New Technology File System (NTFS).

2. *Microsoft Windows Server 2003 with Service Pack 1 (SP1)* — You can use the Standard, Enterprise, or Datacenter installation for this. Web Edition is not supported for a single server.

3. *Microsoft Internet Information Services (IIS) 6.0* — You configure this as a Web Server running IIS 6.0 in worker process isolation mode. IIS 6.0 configuration instructions are provided next in this chapter.

4. *Microsoft .NET Framework 2.0* — You can download this from `http://msdn.microsoft.com/netframework/`. ASP.NET 2.0 must be enabled after installing the Framework, and instructions are provided later in this chapter.

5. *Microsoft Windows Workflow Foundation* — This is a technology included in the Microsoft .NET Framework 3.0 release (formerly known as WinFX). Download and install the Framework from `http://msdn.microsoft.com/winfx/default.aspx`.

Installing IIS 6.0

Complete the following steps to configure your server as a Web Server with IIS 6.0 running in worker process isolation mode:

1. Choose Start ⇨ All Programs ⇨ Administrative Tools ⇨ Configure Your Server Wizard.

2. Click Next on the Welcome to the Configure Your Server Wizard page, and then click Next on the Preliminary Steps page.

3. Select Application server (IIS, ASP.NET) on the Server Role page, and then click Next.

4. Click Next on the Application Server Options page and then click Next on the Summary of Selections page.

5. When the configuration is completed, the message "This Server is Now an Application server" is displayed. Click Finish.

    If this is a new installation of Windows Server 2003 (and not an upgrade from Windows 2000), you will not need to perform steps 6 through 9 because IIS 6.0 will already be configured to use IIS 6.0 worker process isolation mode.

6. Choose Start ⇨ All Programs ⇨ Administrative Tools ⇨ Internet Information Services (IIS) Manager.

7. Locate the IIS Manager tree and click the plus sign (+) next to the server name, right-click the Web Sites folder, and then click Properties.

8. Click the Service tab in the Web Sites Properties dialog box.

9. Deselect the Run WWW Service In IIS 5.0 Isolation Mode option and click OK.

Enabling ASP.NET 2.0

After you have successfully installed and configured IIS 6.0, you must install Windows .NET Framework 2.0. After you do this, enable ASP.NET 2.0 as follows:

1. Choose Start ➪ All Programs ➪ Administrative Tools ➪ Internet Information Services (IIS) Manager.

2. Locate the IIS Manager tree and click the plus sign (+) next to the server name. Select the Web Service Extensions folder.

3. Select ASP.NET v2.0.50727 in the details page, and then click the Allow button. The status for ASP.NET v2.0.50727 changes to Allowed.

You now have the software and components required for an evaluation installation of Microsoft Office SharePoint Server 2007. To proceed with MOSS setup, you must be a member of the Administrators group or a member of a group that is a member of the Administrators group for the server.

Excel 2007 Client

Eventually, you'll need a Microsoft Office Excel 2007 client to fully explore the capabilities of Excel Services and to try out the scenarios outlined throughout this book. However, you do not need the Excel 2007 client to install the evaluation server.

A compatible Excel 2007 workbook is made available in a SharePoint document library as part of the evaluation server installation. The "After Setup Completes" section, later in this chapter, describes how you can leverage that workbook on the server for evaluating Excel Services. Chapter 9 provides more detailed information on using the Excel client with Excel Services.

The evaluation server will only load workbooks saved in either the xlsx (Excel Workbook) or the xlsb (Excel Binary Workbook) file format. The Excel Workbook file format is the Excel 2007 default, and is an XML-based file format. The Excel Binary Workbook file format is a binary format that is also referred to as BIFF12. Workbooks saved by previous releases of the Excel client will not be loaded by Excel Services.

Installing an Evaluation Copy

The evaluation server installation is very straightforward. There is an option to customize a couple of folder paths, but that step isn't required because you can use the defaults. You can even set up MOSS from the command line using a configuration file, but that setup approach won't be discussed in this book. However, you will want to consider it if you want to set up a farm with MOSS installed on multiple servers.

Setup Wizard

Now that you have met both the hardware and software requirements for installing MOSS, you can launch Setup and install your evaluation server. Every page of the Setup wizard is not shown here because many of them are simply status pages.

A page may appear briefly to let you know that the necessary files are being processed, and then the Product Key page appears (see Figure 2-1). Enter your 25-character product key. When the key is recognized as valid, the Continue button is enabled. Click it to proceed with the setup.

When the Microsoft Software License Terms page appears (see Figure 2-2), click the check box to agree to the terms. Then click the Continue button to proceed.

On the next page that appears, you specify a Basic or Advanced installation (see Figure 2-3). If you select Basic, the setup will proceed with no further actions from you. If you select Advanced, you can change the default settings during setup.

If you click the Advanced button, the Server Type page is displayed next (see Figure 2-4). The Stand-alone option will install the evaluation server and, if you make no changes on any of the tabs, the installation will be the same as if you had selected Basic (no further action from you is required).

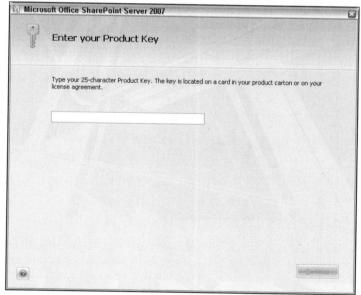

Figure 2-1

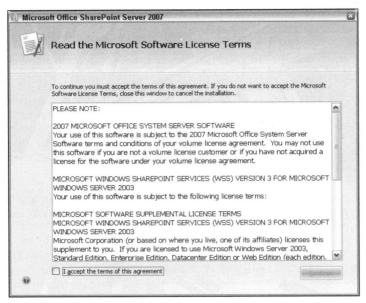

Figure 2-2

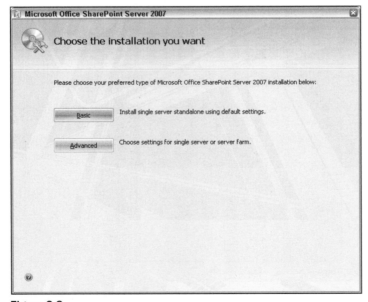

Figure 2-3

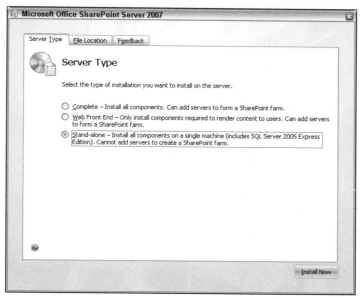

Figure 2-4

You can use the Feedback tab on the Server Type page to indicate your preference for sending anonymous product-improvement suggestions to Microsoft. The default setting is I'll Choose Later.

The File Location tab is shown in Figure 2-5. The two file locations specified on this page are the only evaluation server configuration settings that will be presented to you through the Setup wizard. After you are satisfied with the file location settings, click Install Now.

The Advanced and the Basic installation paths converge at this point. Setup proceeds with the installation, and you can track its progress by watching the Installation Progress page. When setup completes, a final Setup wizard page is displayed (see Figure 2-6). The check box on this page specifies that the SharePoint Products and Technologies Configuration Wizard will automatically start. Leave the check box selected and click the Close button.

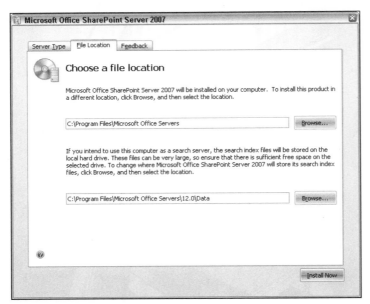

Figure 2-5

Figure 2-6

Configuration Wizard

The SharePoint Products and Technologies Configuration Wizard is required to set up an evaluation server. As the name implies, it configures your server. As described at the end of the previous section, you can launch the configuration wizard from the final page of setup, or you can run it independently by choosing Start ⇨ All Programs ⇨ Microsoft Office Server ⇨ SharePoint Products and Technologies Wizard. If the configuration wizard (see Figure 2-7) is not already running, go ahead and start it.

Click Next on the first page of the configuration wizard (Figure 2-7) to get started with the configuration. A dialog box appears, asking if it is OK to cycle the specified services (see Figure 2-8). Click the Yes button to continue with the configuration of your evaluation server.

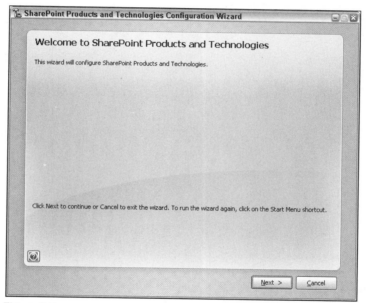

Figure 2-7

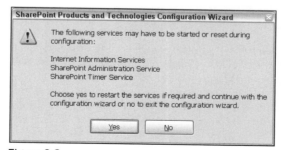

Figure 2-8

The configuration proceeds and you can track its progress by watching the configuration wizard progress page. When the configuration completes, a Configuration Successful page appears (see Figure 2-9). Click Finish to exit the SharePoint Products and Technologies Configuration Wizard. This action also automatically starts an instance of your browser and loads your portal's default page using the corresponding URL (such as `http://TheExcelServer/Pages/Default.aspx`).

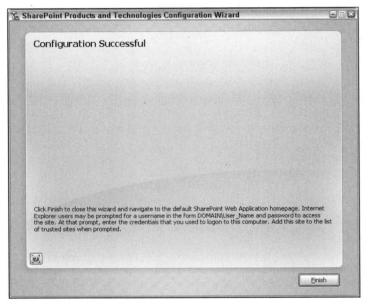

Figure 2-9

After Setup Completes

After both the setup wizard and the configuration wizard are completed, Excel Services is ready to load a workbook. The evaluation server setup is unique in that Excel Services will load and render a workbook without any further configuration. This section describes what is available to you on the evaluation server immediately after you run these two wizards.

Keep in mind that additional configuration may be necessary as the complexity of the scenario increases. The other two setup types, WFE and Complete, require additional manual configuration steps to get Excel Services properly configured to load and render workbooks.

A single trusted file location has been defined. An evaluation installation configures a trusted location automatically, so, by default, all content contained in the portal is trusted by Excel Services. For example, the address of the trusted location could be `http://TheExcelServer`. Take a look at the "Trusted Location Properties" section in Chapter 7 to better understand the settings for this trusted location.

Excel Web Access

The wizards create a Report Center dashboard and save a single Excel 2007 workbook to the Report Center's reports library. For example, if the sample dashboard is loaded to `http://TheExcelServer/Reports/ReportsLibrary/Sample%20Dashboard.aspx`, the workbook loaded by the sample dashboard is at `http://TheExcelServer/Reports/ReportsLibrary/SampleWorkbook.xlsx`.

You can use the sample dashboard to verify that Excel Services is working properly after the evaluation server setup finishes. Just open the sample dashboard and confirm that the Excel Web Access (EWA) Web Parts have successfully loaded the content. Figure 2-10 shows the sample dashboard.

The sample dashboard includes three instances of the EWA Web Part, each configured to load a different view of the data from the sample workbook. Two of the EWA Web Parts are connected to a single text filter Web Part, which is used to send text to the EWA Web Parts where it is used to filter the data displayed by the EWA Web Part.

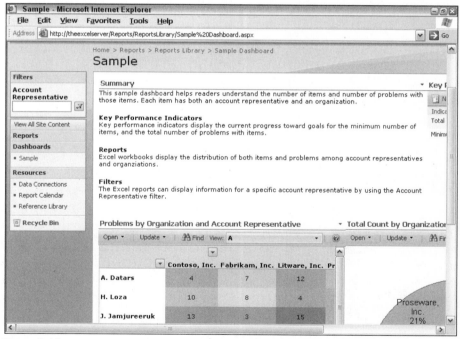

Figure 2-10

To better understand the details behind the dashboard's configuration, put the sample dashboard page in edit mode. This mode reveals the properties of each EWA Web Part and the filter Web Part. You can also see the established relationships between the Web Parts more clearly in this mode. Complete the following steps to edit the dashboard page:

1. Load the dashboard by navigating the browser to the URL `http://TheExcelServer/Reports/ReportsLibrary/Sample%20Dashboard.aspx`, for example.

2. Click the Site Actions link located in the upper-right corner of the page, and then click Edit Page. The layout of the dashboard changes to look something like Figure 2-11.

While you're in edit mode, you can add, remove, or modify Web Parts. To access the properties associated with a Web Part, select its Edit link and then select Modify Shared Web Part. This action opens the property pane, and the properties associated with the Web Part are displayed as shown in Figure 2-12. You can add more Web Parts to the dashboard by clicking the Add a Web Part link and then choosing the desired Web Part from the provided list. Chapter 12 provides more detailed information about building and working with dashboards.

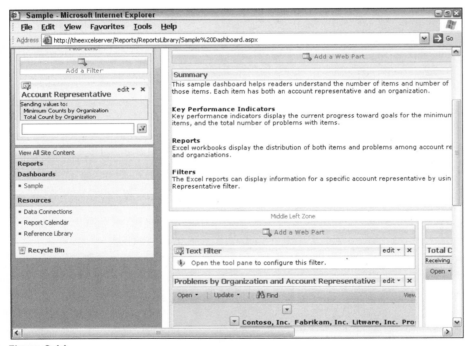

Figure 2-11

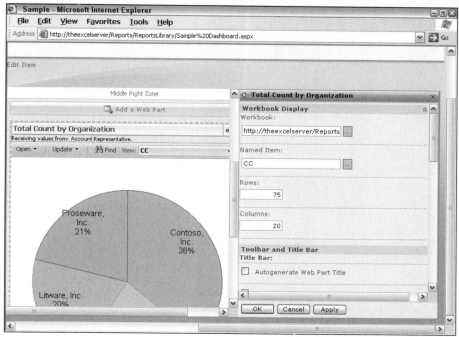

Figure 2-12

You can also use the sample workbook independently of the sample dashboard to further explore Excel Service's features, such as loading a workbook with the EWA outside of a SharePoint page or site. Follow these steps to load the workbook using xlviewer.aspx:

1. Load the Report Center reports library by navigating the browser to the URL `http://TheExcelServer/Reports/ReportsLibrary`, for example.

2. Use the View control to select Current Reports if it is not already selected. (The Report Center refers to Excel workbooks as *reports*.) The SampleWorkbook.xlsx workbook is now visible in the reports library.

3. Move the mouse over the SampleWorkbook.xlsx text, click the ECB menu edit button, and then click View In Web Browser. The workbook will now render using the EWA as shown in Figure 2-13.

The browser URL for rendering the workbook using xlviewer.aspx will now be something like `http://TheExcelServer/Reports/_layouts/xlviewer.aspx?listguid={guid}&itemid={id}&DefaultItem Open=1`. You can add parameters to make the URL friendlier and extend the xlviewer.aspx feature.

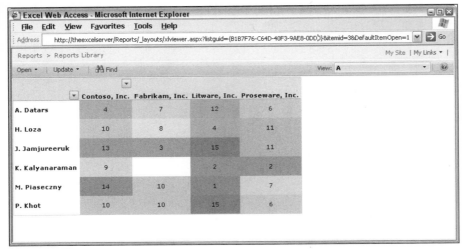

Figure 2-13

You can replace the `listguid={guid}&itemid={id}` URL parameters with `id=<path>`, where `path` is the complete path to a workbook in a trusted location. Windows SharePoint Services (WSS) and a Universal Naming Convention (UNC) trusted location examples are shown here:

```
http://TheExcelServer/Reports/_layouts/xlviewer.aspx?id=http://TheExcelServer/
Reports/ReportsLibrary/SampleWorkbook.xlsx&DefaultItemOpen=1

http://TheExcelServer/Reports/_layouts/xlviewer.aspx?id=\\TheServer\TheShare\
TheWorkbooks\SampleWorkbook.xlsx&DefaultItemOpen=1
```

Excel Web Services

After you have performed an evaluation server installation, the Excel Server public web service API is available and fully functional. Chapter 14 provides more detailed information for using the API.

Summary

In this chapter, you learned what the hardware and software requirements are for successfully installing an evaluation version of the MOSS. The three available types of server installation were described, and then the steps necessary to install an evaluation server were discussed. The setup and the configuration wizards were included in the walkthrough.

You were introduced to the Report Center's sample dashboard, and you were shown how to work with it in edit mode. You saw how to use the `xlviewer.aspx` to render a workbook by leveraging the sample workbook in the Report Center.

To summarize, you should now have a grasp on the following:

❑   How to install an evaluation version of MOSS

❑   The state of Excel Services following setup

❑   How to use the sample dashboard and sample workbook to explore Excel Web Access features

The architecture of Excel Services is explored in Chapter 3, where the main components are broken down and explained in detail.

Architecture

This chapter goes behind the scenes and explains how the scenarios discussed in Chapter 1 work. After reading this chapter, you should have a better understanding of what Excel Services does, and how it does it.

The first part of this chapter begins with a discussion of the Microsoft Office SharePoint Server architecture. It then examines the main components of Excel Services — the Excel Calculation Server (ECS), the Excel Web Access (EWA) Web Part, and the Excel Web Services API — and the flow of information between them.

The second part of this chapter examines the basic operational concepts of Excel Services: sessions, workbook operations, querying from external databases, caching, scaling the system, thread management, and charting.

The last section of this chapter revisits many of these topics and a few more from the point of view of performance. It recaps the architecture of the server and describes how you can make the most out of the hardware. Here you will explore the use of load balancing, networking, memory resources, CPU resources, I/O, and charting, as well as the interaction between the client machine and the browser.

Getting to Know Excel Services

To get started, take a look at a simple scenario and the main server components that are involved. Say you are a user who authors an Excel workbook and saves it to a SharePoint document library. You create a new SharePoint web page and add an EWA Web Part to it. You modify the EWA properties to point it to the workbook. Then you browse to the web page to see the workbook displayed as HTML in the browser inside the EWA. Figure 3-1 shows an example of what this web page might look like.

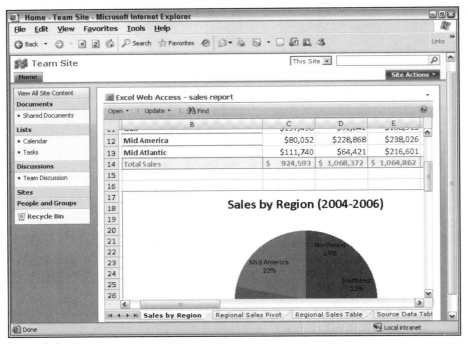

Figure 3-1

This book assumes that you have at least basic knowledge about SharePoint, and does not go into the details about how to create an Excel workbook or a SharePoint web page.

When the web page is opened in the browser, SharePoint builds the HTML for the page and asks each Web Part to generate its HTML snippet. The EWA and Excel Services open the file from the document library, calculate it, and generate its HTML representation. The main Excel Services components are the EWA Web Part and the ECS. Figure 3-2 shows these components and their relationship to the browser and the SharePoint document library.

The ECS is the engine behind Excel Services. It contains the logic to open workbooks, calculate them, query workbook data, and perform operations. The EWA is a layer on top of the ECS that transforms the ECS information to the HTML rendering.

In this example, the EWA sends a request to the ECS to open a workbook and display a range of data from it. The ECS downloads the workbook from the document library, opens it, calculates it, and returns the information from the requested range. The EWA receives the range information, transforms it to its HTML representation, and returns it to SharePoint, which sends it back to the browser as part of the whole web page. The EWA also generates a number of JavaScripts that are sent to the browser as part of the page. These scripts are used primarily for interactivity.

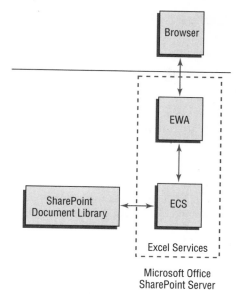

Figure 3-2

When the user switches to the second sheet in the browser, the EWA asks the ECS for the range on that sheet, and the ECS returns it from the already opened workbook. When the workbook was originally opened, a session was created and is maintained on the ECS. Any further operation that the user does (for example, refreshing data from a pivot table in the workbook) is performed in a similar fashion. The EWA sends the request to the ECS. The ECS performs the operation (in this case, it queries an external database for the pivot data), recalculates the workbook as needed, and returns the range information. The EWA then generates the HTML.

The following section takes a closer look at each of the main components of Excel Services to help you better understand this example scenario.

Understanding the Architecture

There are four key components of Excel Services:

- ❏ Microsoft Office SharePoint Server
- ❏ Excel Calculation Server (ECS)
- ❏ Excel Web Access (EWA) Web Part
- ❏ Excel Web Services API

Office SharePoint Server Architecture

This section explains at a high level the Microsoft Office SharePoint Server architecture. The main components in the SharePoint Server architecture are the web front end (WFE), the application server, and the database server (see Figure 3-3).

The WFEs are responsible for rendering the pages for the user requests. They might query data directly from the database server, or communicate with the appropriate application server to perform the operation. All the WFEs are mirrors of each other, and are usually load-balanced using network load balancing (NLB). (Load balancing is discussed in more detail later in this chapter.)

The application servers perform the more resource-intensive operations. This applicative logic is separated from the WFE to allow the WFE to be lightweight and scale independently. (Scaling is discussed in more detail later in this chapter.) Each application server has one or more roles, which define the features that are enabled on that machine. For example, one application server might be assigned the role of ECS, and a second application server might be assigned the roles of search querying and indexing. When a WFE needs to use a specific application from an application server, it uses a machine that contains the relevant role.

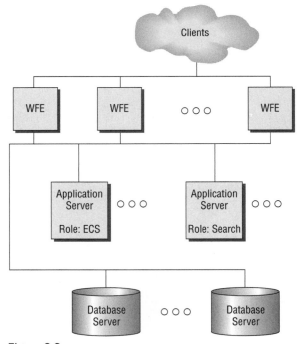

Figure 3-3

The database servers store the user, application, and configuration data. The user data contains information such as documents that are saved in document libraries. The application data is specific to each feature running in the SharePoint farm, which is described shortly. For example, it may contain some of the search indexing information. The configuration data contains the administrative settings at the farm and application level.

These components can be deployed on the same machine, or scaled out to multiple machines. Chapter 6 discusses the various topologies that are supported.

The SharePoint Hierarchy

A *SharePoint farm* is a collection of one or more machines that have the roles of WFE, application server, and database server, and are managed by the same central administrator.

A SharePoint farm is composed of one or more *web applications*. Each web application, also known as Windows SharePoint Services (WSS) Virtual Server (vServer), is a separate Internet Information Server (IIS) application pool and has a different IIS port. Most farms will have one web application, but in large enterprises, the central Information Technology (IT) manages several web applications in the same farm. Each web application has a separate content database for storing its user data.

A web application has one or more WSS site collections. The *site collection* is the top-level container for *sites* and *subsites*.

Each of the WFE machines supports all the web applications and all their site collections and sites. Figure 3-4 shows the SharePoint hierarchy.

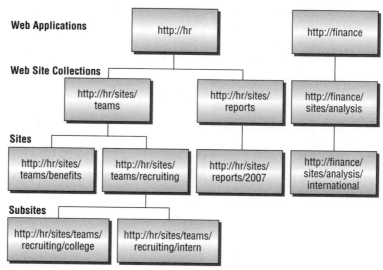

Figure 3-4

In the figure, the following are web applications:

- ❑ http://finance
- ❑ http://operations
- ❑ http://hr

The following are web site collections:

- ❑ http://hr/sites/reports
- ❑ http://hr/sites/teams

And the following are sites and subsites:

- ❑ http://hr/sites/teams/benefits
- ❑ http://hr/sites/teams/recruiting
- ❑ http://hr/sites/teams/recruiting/college

Shared Services Provider

A *Shared Services Provider* (SSP) is a group of services on the application servers (such as ECS and Search) that support the WFE. By default, there is one SSP in each SharePoint farm, and it supports all its web applications and site collections.

The administrator can create additional SSPs and map each web application to an SSP. Each SSP runs its services on the application servers in a separate process. This means each group of web applications on the WFE can have a separate ECS process, and each process can be managed separately.

Figure 3-5 shows an example of three web applications, each mapped to one of two SSPs that exist in the farm.

All SSPs run on all the application server machines. Each application server that contains the ECS role has a separate ECS process for each SSP. Figure 3-6 shows an example of two application server machines, with different roles enabled on them. Each of these machines has two SSPs running on them, each with the roles that are enabled on that machine.

The Excel Calculation Server (ECS)

The ECS is a web service and runs as part of the IIS on each application server machine. As mentioned, there is a separate process (application pool) for each SSP.

The WFE components (that is, the EWA and the API) communicate with the ECS via Web services. This Web service is not supported and not documented by Microsoft. The recommended way to interact with Excel Services is via the WFE API (described shortly). Following is the URL for the ECS Web service:

```
http://ECSMachineURL/TheSSPName/ExcelCalculationServer/ExcelService.asmx
```

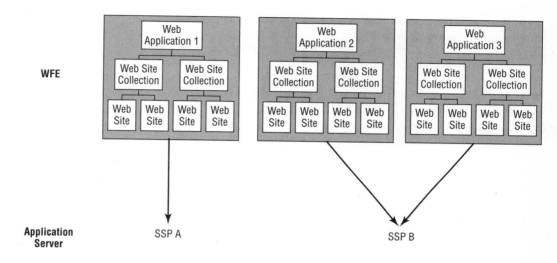

Figure 3-5

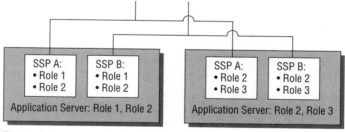

Figure 3-6

The Excel Web Access (EWA) Web Part

The EWA is a SharePoint Web Part. It can be used inside a SharePoint Web page by itself, or together with other Web Parts to form a dashboard.

The Excel Viewer is a predefined Web page that has one instance of the EWA on it. It can be used to view one workbook specified as a parameter on the URL.

The flow described in the basic example at the beginning of this chapter is an oversimplification. In practice, when the web page is rendered on the WFE, the EWA has a small HTML file that is generated quickly, without a call to the ECS. This small HTML file contains an `iframe` element and a progress message. The `iframe` message is sourced back to the WFE, and it will do the more expensive operation of actually opening the workbook through the ECS. The progress message is displayed until the `iframe` comes back with the HTML for displaying the spreadsheet.

When a user performs an operation in the workbook, only the `iframe` is refreshed, without requiring a postback of the entire page (which might have additional Web Parts and controls).

The Excel Web Services API

Excel Services exposes an API to allow programmatic access to its functionality. The API is exposed as a web service on the WFE, and also enables applications running on the WFE to link with it locally, as shown in Figure 3-7.

Whether you access Excel Services through the EWA or the API, the basic concepts of sessions, requests, state management, publishing workbooks, loading workbooks on the server, accessing external data, performing operations, and memory management are the same. With very few exceptions, the same administrator settings apply for both the EWA and the API.

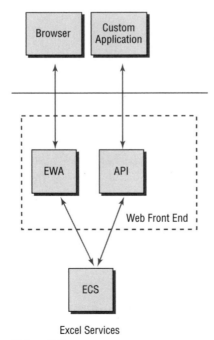

Figure 3-7

Each SharePoint web application and site has an instance of the web service. You must access the API from the correct site to ensure that the site context is used for authentication and authorization. For example, the URL of the API for the web application at `http://vServer` is the following:

```
http://vServer/_vti_bin/ExcelService.asmx
```

And the URL of the API for the site at `http://vServer/site` is the following:

```
http://vServer/site/_vti_bin/ExcelService.asmx
```

Chapter 14 provides more details about using the API.

Understanding Operational Concepts

This section drills down into various aspects of these components and their interactions. It starts with a discussion about *sessions*, which are the isolation unit for the user and provide the context in which all the operations run. Sessions start when users open a workbook, and end when they close the workbook or when the session times out. The state of a session is private to the user of the session, and it is not seen by other sessions.

The discussion then examines the concepts related to performing requests (or operations) on the server. Examples of such requests are opening a workbook, paging down, filtering a table, and drilling in a pivot table.

Next, you will look into the process of publishing workbooks to the server and loading them. *Publishing* is the process of putting an Excel workbook in a location from which the server can load it (such as a SharePoint document library). On the server, the file gets downloaded to the ECS machine and then loaded into memory.

The ECS caches workbooks and other objects in memory to improve performance. You will explore the various settings that affect the caching and how those affect the behavior of the server.

You will also look at the basics of querying external data. The full details on this complex matter are in Chapter 5.

Next, you will learn about ways to scale out the server and to load-balance.

The discussion concludes with a look at how ECS threads are used to service requests.

Sessions

Any interaction that a user has with a workbook is done in the context of a *session*. A new session is automatically started every time a user opens a workbook. It may continue with additional user interactions, such as refreshing data or filtering a table, and it ends when the workbook is closed or after a timeout.

Opening a workbook is always done in the context of a new session. A user may open multiple sessions with the same workbook or with different workbooks. Each EWA instance on a Web Part Page will result in a separate session being opened. For example, if a user opens a Web Part Page with three EWA instances, two of them opening workbook A and the third opening workbook B, then three sessions will be opened. When the same user or a different user opens the same Web Part Page in a new browser instance, three more sessions will be opened.

Sessions provide isolation for the user. Changes performed in one session are not seen by any other session. For example, if two sessions are opened with the same workbook, and the user changes some workbook cell values in the first session, the user of the second session (be it the same user or a different one) will not see those changes in the second session. The best way to think of a session on the server is to imagine users opening workbooks in read-only mode in Excel. Each of those instances of Excel is a session, and changes made in those sessions are kept within them until they are saved.

The session is closed when the workbook is closed, either explicitly through the API or when a new workbook is opened in the EWA (depending on the EWA settings). In addition, sessions are automatically closed when a configurable timeout has expired after a period of user inactivity. After a session times out, the workbook continues to be displayed in the EWA, and the user is notified if he or she makes changes to the timed-out session that will be lost. A new session is then opened.

Session Settings

Each session consumes server resources, mainly memory and (when a request is being performed) additional resources such as a CPU and I/O. Administrators should configure the server for the right balance between preserving these resources and providing adequate service to their users.

Administrators can configure the maximum number of sessions a user is allowed to open at any time. By default, this is set to 25 sessions.

In addition, administrators can configure the session timeouts. There are two settings for timeouts. The *short session timeout* is used when the session has a workbook that was just opened (with no other operation performed on the workbook), and has a default value of 75 seconds. The *session timeout* is used after additional interactivity has been performed on the workbook, and has a default value of 5 minutes. In many cases, dashboards just display (open) workbooks without any additional interactivity, so setting a shorter timeout helps preserve server resources. You can change these timeout settings at the trusted location level. For more information about settings and trusted locations granularity, see Chapter 7.

Exposing the Session ID

The web service API exposes the session ID. It returns the session ID when a workbook is opened, and the session ID is passed as a parameter to the other API methods.

The EWA also exposes a JavaScript method that can be called to get the session ID from a running instance of the Web Part. You can extend the EWA to other controls on a page that interacts with its session through the API.

Session State

After each operation is finished, the session is left in a certain state. Operations on the session can change its state or query its state. Closing the workbook is a special operation that terminates the session.

Figure 3-8 shows the initial state of the session after the workbook is opened (State 1), followed by the states after two additional operations of setting values into cells are performed (State 2 and State 3).

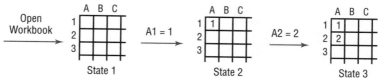

Figure 3-8

The session state is maintained in memory on the ECS machine. In a scaled-out configuration (when there are multiple ECS machines), all requests for a session will always be routed to the same ECS machine — the one that contains the session state.

Shutting down the ECS process causes all the users of that ECS machine to lose the session state. Therefore, you should not shut down the ECS process while there is activity on the system. Note that the ECS runs in the context of the IIS process, and, therefore, the IIS process recycling settings affect the ECS. Set IIS to recycle when there is no user activity.

When working with the EWA, the browser keeps the session ID and sends it to the server in every request, to identify the session that will process the request.

Workbook Operations

Operations are requests that the user performs on workbooks. Examples of operations are opening and closing workbooks, getting values from cells and setting values into cells, calculating the workbook, refreshing data, filtering and drilling a pivot table, filtering and sorting a table, and finding a value in the workbook.

The typical flow of a request is as follows:

1. The user sends the request from the client machine to the WFE, which forwards the request to the ECS.

2. The ECS performs the request, updates the state of the workbook in the session, and returns the result back to the WFE. In the case of the EWA, the result typically contains the new range to be displayed.

The ECS does not allow a user to perform more than one request per session at any given time, except for the following operations that can be performed in parallel in a session:

❑ Getting values from the workbook

❑ Getting charts from the workbook

❑ Closing the workbook

A user can cancel a request by sending a special cancellation request to the WFE and, from there, to the ECS. The cancellation request attempts to stop the operation that is being performed in the session to free system resources, and to enable the user to perform a new operation in the same session.

Request Settings

The ECS maintains a request timeout that can be configured by the administrator. If a request does not finish until the request timeout has expired, the ECS cancels the request. This prevents single requests from consuming large amounts of resources on the server.

Administrators can configure the request timeout. The default value of this setting is 5 minutes. You can change this setting at the trusted location level. For more information about settings and trusted locations granularity, see Chapter 7.

> *Although the ECS will attempt to cancel the request as described here, there are cases in which it might not succeed in doing so immediately. For example, if the request currently performs a data query and the data provider does not support cancellation, then the request will continue until the query is finished, and only then will it get cancelled. Most of the data providers support cancellation.*

Publishing and Loading Workbooks

This section examines how workbooks are published, stored, and loaded on the server.

Publishing

In the publishing process, the author creates the workbook and saves it to the server. The authoring is usually done in Excel or in another application that can generate a workbook. Excel Services supports both the Office Open XML (*.xlsx) file format and the Excel Binary (*.xlsb) file format.

> *Excel Services does not support file formats from older versions of Excel (such as *.xls) and macro-enabled files (such as *.xlsm). Chapter 4 provides more details about the file formats and Excel features supported by Excel Services.*

You can publish workbooks to a SharePoint document library or to a location outside of SharePoint. The latter can be either a Universal Naming Convention (UNC) path (such as a file share) or an HTTP address (such as a web folder). You can use a regular save operation to publish to the server at either of these locations. The Publish to Excel Services menu option allows a workbook author to specify the ranges to publish and workbook parameters, but it performs a regular save operation with the specified publishing information written into the file. When you publish ranges, the whole workbook is actually saved, and the published ranges are just notations in the file. The server does not do any processing on the file — it is kept in the storage location in the same form that it was published in.

> *Excel Services manages a list of trusted file locations, and allows loading files only from those locations. This is a security feature that is managed by the server administrator. If you publish the file to a location that is not trusted by the server, you will get an error when trying to load it on the server.*

Loading Workbooks on the Server

The ECS component loads the workbook file to Excel Services. It downloads the file from its storage location to the ECS machine, and then loads the file in memory. The security aspects (authentication and authorization) are discussed in Chapter 8.

The mechanism used to download the file depends on the storage location type. Files from SharePoint document libraries are downloaded using the SharePoint object model. Files from UNC and HTTP locations are downloaded using the appropriate protocol.

A downloaded workbook file is opened in read-only mode. A workbook author can make changes to the file while it is open on the server, but these changes will not affect existing sessions on the ECS. However, new sessions will get the updated file. The ECS allows for multiple versions of the same workbook to be loaded simultaneously in different sessions.

Figure 3-9 shows the process of publishing workbooks and loading them on the server.

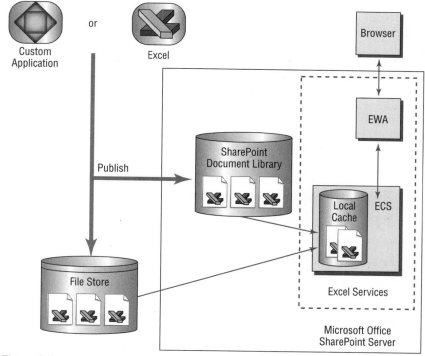

Figure 3-9

Workbook Disk Cache

In order to minimize the number of file downloads from the storage location, the ECS maintains a file cache on its local disk. Every time a user opens a file, the ECS verifies that he or she has permissions to open it (as detailed in Chapter 8) and that the file timestamp has not changed in its storage location compared to the cache.

The administrator can control several settings related to the disk cache. The maximum size of the disk cache has a default value of 40GB. The caching is turned on by default, and can be turned off if there is not enough local disk space. When caching is turned off, the files are still downloaded to the local cache location, but they are deleted after the session is closed instead of being kept in the cache.

By default, the location of the local cache is under the temporary directory of the ECS machine. Administrators should limit the permissions to the cache directory to the ECS process account so that users cannot go around the security of the storage locations by reading the files from the ECS cache. In addition, you should consider using Windows Encrypted File System (EFS) to provide encryption to this folder.

The maximum workbook size has a default of 10MB. Administrators can change this workbook to control if large files are allowed on the server. This setting can be configured for each trusted location. For more information about settings and trusted locations granularity, see Chapter 7.

Querying Data from External Databases

You can refresh all the data connections in a workbook or drill down in an Online Analytical Processing (OLAP) pivot table query data from an external database.

The ECS is the component that performs the data retrieval. It first determines the end-user credentials through single sign-on (SSO), the user and password embedded in the workbook, Kerberos-constrained delegation, or the ECS process account. The ECS then connects to the database by using those credentials and performs the query. The ECS updates the sheet with the results of the query, and calculates any dependent formulas before returning the result to the WFE.

Querying data from external databases is a very complex scenario in terms of the server architecture. Chapter 5 covers external queries in depth, including the following topics:

❑   The types of connections that are supported

❑   The protocols and databases that can be used

❑   The types of credentials and credential delegations that the ECS provides

❑   Connection pooling and data caching

❑   Asynchronous and parallel queries

❑   Refresh on open and periodic refresh

❑   Administrator settings for controlling and optimizing data queries

Caching and Memory Utilization

The ECS caches information in memory to improve performance. This section discusses those caches, and the settings available to control their impact on the overall memory footprint of the ECS.

The following table outlines an example of how a workbook is cached.

User Operation	Server Operation
User opens workbook A.	Session 1 loads and calculates the workbook.
User opens workbook A in a second session.	Session 2 reuses workbook calculated by session 1.
User closes session 1 and session 2.	The workbook is kept in the cache.

User Operation	Server Operation
User opens workbook A in a third session.	Session 3 reuses calculated workbook from cache.
User closes session 3.	The workbook is returned to the cache.
No activity.	The server frees resources, and the workbook is released.
User opens workbook A in a fourth session.	Session 4 loads and calculates the workbook.

Workbooks are kept in the cache so they do not have to be reloaded and recalculated for every new session.

Sharing Workbooks Between Sessions

There are some cases in which it is not possible to share a workbook. For example, to avoid disclosing personal information, if the workbook refreshes a data query that uses the end-user's credentials on open, the query results are not shared.

The following list shows some of the cases in which it is not possible to share a workbook state between sessions and require recalculation for each session:

❑   The user has performed some interactivity on the workbook (for example, the user has set some parameters values or has drilled down in a pivot table). In that case, the workbook state is private to the session and will not be shared.

❑   The workbook contains the results of a data query that was performed with different credentials. (For more details on external queries and their caching implications, see Chapter 5.)

❑   The workbook contains calls to user-defined functions (UDFs) that are marked as returning personal information.

❑   The workbook contains some volatile functions (for example =Now() or =Rand()) and the Volatile Function Cache Lifetime administrator setting does not allow for sharing the workbook state. This setting allows administrators to specify the maximum amount of time in which workbooks that contain volatile functions can be reused from the cache, in order to trade the accuracy of these volatile functions with performance and better caching. The default value is 5 minutes. This setting can be configured for each trusted location. (For more information about settings and trusted locations granularity, see Chapter 7.)

Managing Unused Objects

A workbook can be used by one or more sessions, or not used by any session. If the workbook is unused, then it may be kept in the cache as long as resources are available.

The ECS will free some of the unused objects if one of the following conditions is met:

❑   A memory allocation has failed.

❑   One of the administrator settings for the management of unused objects is exceeded.

The Memory Cache Threshold administrator setting determines the size of the ECS process that triggers freeing unused objects. When the size of the process goes above this limit, unused objects are freed to reduce the size of the process.

The Maximum Unused Object Age administrator setting determines how long objects can be kept unused before being freed. Unused objects older than this age are freed even if the process size is below the limit, in order to allow other processes on the machine to use the memory.

If the machine has only the ECS process on it, you can increase these settings to let the ECS take full advantage of the resources and maximize its performance. When other processes share the machine, you can reduce them to achieve the right balance.

The ECS decides which objects to free based on an algorithm that takes into account when the object was last used, how much it was used, how complex the object is, and how much memory it uses. It will first free objects that were not used recently, were not used much, are less complex, and use a lot of memory. These factors are weighted together to decide the order of freeing the objects when the process needs more memory.

Maximum Private Bytes

The administrator can set a maximum size for the ECS process. When this limit is reached, new requests will fail for this specific ECS machine, and might be redirected to another ECS machine if it is available. For example, this limit can be reached if there are no unused objects in memory. (Existing sessions use a lot of memory.)

This limit is called *Maximum Private Bytes*, and it can be set by the administrator. The limit you should set depends on how much memory is available on the machine, and if the machine is running other processes that require a lot of memory.

Figure 3-10 shows how the system behaves and frees memory, depending on the size of the process and the administrator settings.

Cached Objects

In the previous examples, the workbook instance was discussed as an object that can be shared between sessions, and that can be used or unused. The ECS manages the following objects:

- ❑ *The calculated workbook instance* — This was discussed earlier.
- ❑ *The results of a data query* — Data queries are a potentially expensive operation. The query results can be shared among those that use the same identity when connecting to the data source.
- ❑ *The loaded workbook* — This includes the cached workbook available on the local disk.
- ❑ *A saved workbook* — An example is a workbook that is generated when you start Excel, open a snapshot with the EWA, or call GetWorkbook with the API. If this cached object is available, performing the operation a second time brings the saved workbook from the cache instead of saving it again.

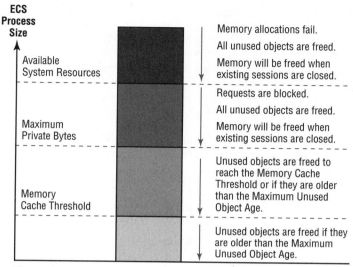

Figure 3-10

❑ *A generated chart image* — The process of generating the image is costly, so caching is used whenever possible.

❑ *A range of data for the EWA* — The EWA asks the ECS for the range it needs to display, and the ECS returns it from the cache if it is available. This range contains all the information needed for the EWA to render it.

Scaling to Multiple Machines

Excel Services supports multiple topologies. The most compact one is running all the components of the WFE and the ECS on the same machine. It can be used in relatively small, departmental, and evaluation deployments.

In larger installations, the WFE and the ECS can be deployed to separate machines. In addition to rendering the EWA Web Part, the WFE supports all SharePoint functionality.

Scaling Up and Scaling Out

To determine the best way to scale your system, you need to analyze your specific requirements. *Scaling up* means adding more resources to your machine. *Scaling out* means adding more machines to the farm.

You can scale up by using a multi-processor machine, adding more memory (preferably on the 64-bit architecture), and/or having faster network cards on your machine. As with any other performance analysis, you should start by understanding your bottleneck. For example, if your workbooks are calculation-intensive, adding more CPUs will help. If you load a lot of large workbooks, adding more memory will help. (Optimization of the CPU and memory is discussed in more detail later in this chapter.)

Scaling out is another alternative you should consider. Of course, you will need to factor in the price of the hardware and the maintenance and administration of the farm when you're determining the best way to scale out.

You can scale out the WFE and the ECS independently. For example, you can scale out the WFE if there is a lot of SharePoint front-end activity (such as displaying the SharePoint home page, browsing through lists and document libraries, and so on), as shown in Figure 3-11. Or you can scale out the ECS if there are a lot of Excel calculations being performed.

A combination of scaling up and scaling out is usually best. WFE machines are normally cheaper, so it would be most cost-effective to scale them out and scale up application server machines. (Chapter 6 discusses capacity planning for Excel Services.)

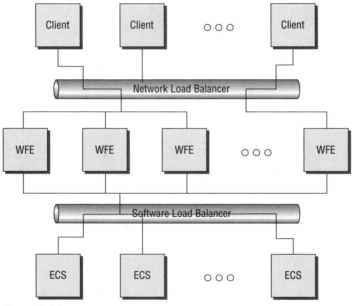

Figure 3-11

Load Balancing

When a client machine opens a connection to the WFE, the normal SharePoint load balancing (usually NLB) is used to choose the WFE machine that will service that request.

When the WFE opens a new Excel Services session on the ECS, it chooses the ECS machine according to the load-balancing scheme. This scheme is an administrator setting, and has the following values:

❑ *Local* — The WFE will attempt to use the ECS located on the same machine as the WFE. Choose this method if each machine in the farm contains both the WFE and the ECS.

❑ *Round Robin* — The WFE will choose the next ECS machine for every new session. You can use this method to better distribute the load between the ECS machines in some scenarios.

❑ *Workbook URL (default)* — The WFE will use a hash based on the workbook URL to determine the ECS machine. The same workbook will be serviced by the same ECS machine. This method reduces the memory consumption on the ECS machine, because each workbook will be opened only on one ECS machine. It does have the disadvantage of not using the CPU on the other ECS machines if the sessions all go to the same (or few) workbooks.

After the session opens and the ECS is chosen, all subsequent requests in the same session will be serviced by the same ECS machine (that is, the machine that contains the state of the session in its memory).

ECS Thread Management

Incoming requests to the ECS are queued by the IIS, and the next available request starts its execution when a thread is available. In the basic case, a request is taken out from the queue and assigned a thread that will execute it. After the request is done, the thread is returned to the thread pool to be used by a new request. The number of requests that get executed in parallel is the same as the number of available threads.

When a request performs an I/O or networking operation (such as fetching a file), its thread is not utilized. In some cases, the I/O or networking operation is performed asynchronously to avoid underutilization of the CPU on the ECS machine, and during this time, the thread is returned to the pool for use by another request. Not all I/O operations are asynchronous, so if your CPU is underutilized on the ECS while requests are queuing up, you should increase the number of available threads.

Queries to external data are performed in parallel on separate requests. For example, if a workbook has several pivot tables and the user refreshes them, the pivot tables will be executed in parallel to optimize for the total time. You can control the maximum number of queries that a request may run in parallel through the Maximum Concurrent Queries Per Session administrator setting.

Excel Services does not support multi-threaded recalculation (MTR). MTR is a new feature that was added to the Excel 2007 client, in which complex calculations are automatically broken down into multiple smaller parts that are run in parallel on multiple threads. In Excel Services, calculations are run serially in each request.

Charting

Charts are calculated and rendered in Excel as follows:

1. The EWA asks the ECS for a range that contains a chart.

2. The ECS calculates that range, including calculating the data on which the chart is based. This data could come from a sheet range or from a pivot table (in the case of pivot charts).

3. The ECS returns the range data along with the location and ID of the chart to the EWA.

4. The EWA generates the HTML for the range, which includes an `img` tag for each chart. These `img` tags are linked back to the WFE with the ID of the charts.

5. When rendering the page, the browser makes another call to the WFE for the chart image.

6. The WFE calls the ECS to generate the chart image.

7. The ECS generates the chart image, stores it on the local disk cache for future use, and returns it to the WFE. The ECS uses the Graphics Device Interface (GDI) to render the chart image. This operation allows only one chart to be generated at any time in an ECS process.

8. The WFE return the image to the browser, which displays it.

Charts can be rendered only through the EWA. The API does not support rendering charts.

Optimizing for Performance

This section analyzes the various architectural aspects of Excel Services from the performance point of view. You expect good performance and full utilization of your hardware. There usually is a trade-off between the response time and throughput, and the other aspects of the server such as security, data staleness, and functionality. Excel Services has a large number of ways to help the administrator and the author reach the balance that is best for them.

There are two major measurements for the performance of the server: response time and throughput. Response time expresses how the end user measures the performance of the server from the moment he or she performs an operation until the results come back and are displayed in the client. Throughput measures the capability of the system to perform a number of parallel requests from multiple users. It is measured in terms of requests per second that are actually performed.

The performance of the server depends on the optimal utilization of its resources, including load balancing, network, I/O, memory, and CPU. The following sections explain the various factors that impact the usage of each of these resources, and provide tips on achieving the right balance between performance and functionality.

Load Balancing

Excel Services supports the following three ways of load balancing the ECS machines when a new session is started:

❑ *Local load balancing* — The WFE opens the session on the ECS that exists on the same machine. Use this load balancing when each machine contains both the WFE and the ECS, and the expected request mix is mainly opening diverse workbooks. For this scenario, caching on the ECS is not relevant, so working with a local ECS ensures the most optimal load balancing by the NLB on the WFE, and no network communications is needed between the WFE and the ECS. On the other hand, if sessions are expected to have multiple requests, you should not use this configuration, because the requests after the first one might be served on a WFE that is located on a different machine than the ECS.

❑ *Round-robin* — The WFE picks a random ECS machine to open the session. This load balancing is best if there are a few workbooks (so they can all fit in the memory of each ECS) and they are not used uniformly. This method distributes the requests evenly, achieving good utilization of the

ECS CPUs, but not the best utilization of memory. If you have a lot of workbooks, you should not use this method, because each workbook will likely be opened in the memory of each ECS machine, will not have enough memory to be cached, and will therefore have an inferior performance.

❑ *Workbook URL* — This is the default load balancing. The WFEs will always open any workbook on the same ECS machine. Use this method when there are a lot of workbooks and requests on them. It will achieve a good utilization of memory, but might not achieve the best utilization of CPU. For example, if one workbook is accessed much more than the others, the ECS associated with that workbook will have a much higher CPU usage than the other ECS machines.

As you can see, each method had unique performance characteristics, and no method is optimal for all cases. Choose the one that best fits your scenario.

Network

Excel Services is a system distributed over multiple machines connected through the network in one of the following ways:

❑ Connection between the client machines and the WFE

❑ Connection between the WFE, the application server, and the database server

❑ Connection with other servers (such as external databases, SSO servers, or Active Directory servers)

Connection Between Client Machines and the WFEs

There are many factors that affect the performance of the connection between the client machines and the server. These include the network topology and speed, intranet versus extranet, HTTP versus HTTPS, firewalls, and load balancing. Some of these might be outside your control, but you should be aware of them because they impact the response time that your users will experience.

Loading one page of a workbook might require transmitting several hundred kilobytes over the network. As the designer of the workbook, you can impact this size as follows:

❑ You can reduce the number of rows and columns displayed. For example, a range of 75 rows by 20 columns will contain 1500 cells.

❑ Some features require larger amounts of data. Charts are sent as images to the browser, and the image size depends on the complexity and size of the chart. Some formatting features (such as conditional formatting) will send additional data for each relevant cell.

❑ A dashboard that has multiple EWA Web Parts on it will be as large as the sum of the Web Parts. To reduce the load time of the Web page, you could have a top-level dashboard that contains only the most important information, and use linked dashboards for additional details.

Secure connections (HTTPS) are slower because they must encrypt the communications. After you have complete your security analysis (for example, determining how sensitive the information passed over the network is, who your users are, and how secure the network is), you should balance it against the performance impact of using the HTTPS protocol.

When you're load balancing multiple WFEs, you can choose between hardware and software load balancers. This might impact the performance as well.

A firewall is normally a requirement when you're using the server in extranet scenarios, but it will slow down the communications. For extranet scenarios, the speed outside your internal network is much slower. Excel Services does not have a mode in which it sends smaller amounts of information for low network speeds.

You can configure IIS to use HTTP compression to reduce the size of the information sent over the wire. This is a tradeoff between CPU and network — enabling this setting will reduce the usage of the network resources, but it will require certain CPU usage (both on the server machine and the client machine) to compress and decompress the transmissions.

Connection Between the Office SharePoint Server Machines

In most topologies, the WFE, application server and database server machines are connected with a high-speed local network. You can ensure that the appropriate network speeds and network cards are used to connect the machines in the farm.

In some topologies, a firewall should be deployed between the WFE machines on one side, and the application server and database server machines on the other side to further protect the access to the workbook content. In addition, the administrator can require secure connections between the WFE and the ECS. As with the connections to the WFE, your specific needs should determine the right balance between security and performance.

The communication between the WFE and the ECS is through web service calls. These use TCP/IP ports that are freed after a certain timeout. To ensure that you do not run out of available ports on systems that perform a high amount of requests, you might need to increase the value of the following registry key on the WFE machines: `HKLM\SYSTEM\CurrentControlSet\Services\Tcpip\Parameters`.

Downloading files over the network from their storage location might be a significant performance hit. Excel Services uses a local cache to minimize additional downloads after the initial one. The ECS accesses the file storage location to check that the file has not changed, and that the user has permissions to access the file for every new session, even when the file is in the cache. If the file storage is in an external location (such as a UNC share or web folder), make sure that the storage is fast enough and does not become a bottleneck. For some very specific solutions that require a limited set of workbooks that do not change often, consider deploying the files locally to each ECS machine. The administrator can set the maximum workbook size setting to prevent extremely large files from affecting the overall performance of the server.

Connection with External Machines

Additional machines outside the farm are involved in some of the requests, especially the ones related to querying for external data. For example, to refresh a pivot table, the following servers might be accessed: the database that contains the data, the SSO server for getting credentials, the SharePoint database server for loading the connection information from a data connection library, and the active directory for certain credential types. Optimizing external data queries is a complex topic, and it is explained in detail in Chapter 5.

Memory

The WFE is a stateless machine, meaning that only the requests currently being executed require memory. The amount of memory that each request consumes depends on the size of the range being rendered. In most scenarios, memory is not a bottleneck on the WFE.

On the other hand, the ECS is stateful and keeps in memory the state of all the opened sessions. You can use the following formula to approximate the amount of data stored in ECS memory:

```
Total memory = (number of concurrent sessions * session size) + unused items cache
```

The amount of memory required depends on how much is used by the sessions, plus the size of the unused items cache kept in memory. Allowing for a larger ECS memory size will improve the ECS performance. The ECS memory size is limited by the available memory on the machine and by other processes that might need to use that memory. Each of the components that make up the ECS memory is discussed separately in the following sections.

Number of Concurrent Sessions

The number of concurrent sessions depends on the session length and the number of sessions opened per second.

Here are some tips on reducing the session length:

❑   Set the session timeout and short session timeout to values that are appropriate for your organization. The shorter you set these values, the fewer sessions will remain open, therefore reducing the memory footprint. For example, if you expect your users to only look at a dashboard without performing any interactivity, you could set the timeout values to 0. The downside of setting them to small values is that users might lose their work after a certain period of inactivity. Remember that after a session times out, the EWA continues to display the workbook, and users will get an error only if they try to perform an operation at a later time. You can configure the session timeout settings differently for each trusted location (see Chapter 7).

❑   When you're designing a web page that uses the EWA, consider configuring the EWA with the Close Session Before Opening A New One option enabled. When this option activated, users will not be able to navigate to the previous workbook by using the browser's Back button.

❑   When you use the API, explicitly call `CloseWorkbook` as soon as you don't need the session anymore. `CloseWorkbook` is an API method that closes the session.

Here are some ideas to reduce the number of sessions opened:

❑   As an administrator, you can control the maximum number of sessions that a user is allowed to open.

❑   As a web page designer, you can control the number of EWAs on a page. Remember that each EWA instance uses a separate session, even if they all display the same workbook.

❑   In the API, cache the session ID and use the same session for multiple method calls.

Session Size

As you learned earlier in this chapter, a session might share its state with other sessions, as long as they contain the same workbook information. When the session has a shared state, its size is very small. The size of a session that is not shared depends on the size of the workbook. To reduce the size of the session, use smaller workbooks. In addition, you can do the following to share as much state as possible between sessions:

❑ Use the same credentials for all users when accessing external data. This is appropriate for most scenarios, except when the query returns personal information that depends on the user opening the workbook.

❑ Use the External Data Cache Lifetime settings to determine how current you need your data to be. For example, if you know that your back-end data source is updated every 24 hours, there is no point in refreshing your query every 5 minutes. (For more details on optimizing external data, see Chapter 5.)

❑ Minimize the use of workbooks with volatile formulas and UDFs. Volatile functions return a different value on every calculation. You can use the Volatile Function Cache Lifetime administrator setting to determine how current your volatile formulas will be. The less current they are, the better the performance will be (at the expense of having them recalculate every time).

❑ Using UDFs that return personal information prohibits workbooks from being shared. Call these UDFs only where this is absolutely necessary.

❑ Performing operations (such as setting the value of parameters, drilling, filtering, and sorting) results in the workbook not being shared between sessions. As the designer of a web page, you can configure the EWA to not allow these operations.

Cache Size of Unused Items

You learned about the unused items cached earlier in this chapter. You can configure the size of the cache and how long items are kept there with the Maximum Private Bytes, Memory Cache Threshold, and Maximum Unused Object Age settings.

Increasing the number of items that can be cached so that future requests will reuse these cached items instead of recalculating them enhances the performance of the server. The downside of having more items cached is that it requires more memory to be available to the ECS process.

Available Memory

As with almost any process, the performance of the ECS is improved significantly if there is enough physical memory. The recommended configuration is a 64-bit machine, which allows for scaling up in terms of memory.

The ECS is designed to use memory for improved performance, and you should take that into consideration when tuning up your system. Depending on your specific needs, try to create a balance between reducing the memory consumption (following the tips presented earlier) and increasing the available memory.

As part of this equation, you should also take into consideration what other processes are running on the ECS machine and their memory requirements. When there are several SSPs running, keep in mind that each SSP has its own ECS process with its memory considerations and separate settings.

CPU

Operations such as loading files and querying external data consume I/O and network resources, and storing the session state requires memory. Operations such as calculating the workbook use the CPU on the ECS. The EWA and API on the WFE are not very CPU-intensive.

For many workbooks, the calculation is relatively fast (less than 1 second). Other calculations might require seconds, minutes, and — in some extreme scenarios — even hours. The following sections discuss ways of achieving your performance goals with both low-end and high-end workbooks.

Low-End Workbooks

The low-end workbooks are the majority. They might have tens or hundreds of formulas, and they calculate very fast when run by themselves on a machine. But you should still optimize these workbooks, because the server runs many of them in parallel. Here are some tips:

❑ Try not to use volatile formulas and UDFs in your workbooks (these are functions that return a different value on every calculation). The Volatile Function Cache Lifetime administrator setting determines how current your volatile formula will be. If you allow formulas to be less current, your performance will improve because the ECS will use cached results of previous calculations of these formulas.

❑ Remember that UDFs may consume CPU. Optimize your UDFs and the way they are called from the workbook (for example, you might use some caching in the UDF). Test the UDFs and install only those that are efficient.

❑ You can set the Workbook Calculation Mode setting to Manual to prevent some trusted locations from performing automatic calculations. This gives you control over which workbook authors can use the CPU, and enables you to focus your efforts on optimizing the workbooks that are allowed to perform calculations.

❑ Make sure your workbook authors optimize the workbooks they create. Start with the workbooks that are used the most, because improving them will have the largest impact on your server's performance.

❑ If the CPU is underutilized (the CPU is not close to 100 percent utilization, and yet the ECS has reached its maximum throughput), try increasing the number of available threads.

High-End Workbooks

You can use Excel Services to offload heavy calculations to the server. Relatively few workbooks with heavy calculations are calculated once or iteratively, usually via the API. A classic example is a Monte Carlo simulation (which tests the effects of various inputs over a model). Here are a few recommendations for best performance:

❑ Run high-end workbooks on dedicated hardware. You can do this by using a separate farm or by running it during the night when the normal end-user activity is at a minimum. Having dedicated hardware allows you to configure your server settings to optimize for this scenario. In addition, it provides predictable performance, because no other noise is running on the server.

❑ If your workbooks perform little to no external data queries, consider reducing the number of threads on the ECS to between 1 and 4 per CPU. This configuration will result in less context switching and better use of the CPU and memory.

❑ You might need to increase the Maximum Request Duration setting and the various IIS timeouts to ensure that requests are not aborted in the middle of their execution.

❑ Use a high performance computing (HPC) solution, such as Microsoft Windows Compute Cluster Server (CCS) to manage and balance your application.

❑ Excel Services does not support multi-threaded recalculation (MTR), which is a new Excel 2007 feature. MTR allows a complex workbook calculation to be split into multiple threads for parallel execution. On Excel Services, the calculation is executed serially on one thread. In some cases, you can achieve similar results by splitting your workbook into several smaller workbooks, and using your client application to call the individual workbooks and combine the results. You can also offload some of the calculation to UDFs that can be designed to run on multiple threads or even multiple machines.

I/O

The ECS uses the local disk to load workbooks from the disk cache. Loading workbooks is usually considered an expensive operation. One way to minimize the amount of workbooks loaded is to have enough memory so that the workbook is kept in the memory cache after its first load.

In addition, you can use the Maximum Workbook Size administrator setting to set a limit on the file size. This setting can have a different value for each trusted location, thus allowing the administrator to limit the amount of I/O some workbook authors are allowed to consume on the server. You can also ask the authors of the workbooks to design for smaller file sizes.

The ECS uses the local disk to cache chart images, calculated ranges, and saved workbooks. For example, when a chart image is generated on the ECS, it is saved in the cache. The next request for the same chart will return it from the disk cache rather than recalculating it. The assumption is that this operation is more effective than regenerating the chart.

The local disk is also used for logging, and the administrator can configure how verbose the logging is (see Chapter 7 for details). Logging can be very useful to investigate issues, but at high verbosity levels, it will cause a lot of I/O and might have a significant performance impact. Be sure to reduce the verbosity level according to your needs.

Given all the ways the disk is used, you should ensure that your disk is efficient. For optimal performance, you should use a local disk (as opposed to a remote share) and ensure that the disk is not fragmented.

Charting

Charting is expensive in terms of performance. It affects the network, CPU, and I/O in the following ways:

❑ Chart images could be large. They are sent over the network from the ECS to the WFE, and from there to the browser.

❑ Chart image generation can be CPU-intensive. More importantly, it uses GDI, which holds a global process-level lock and allows only one chart to be generated at any time by an ECS process.

❑ To reduce the number of charts that are generated, charts are cached on the local disk for future use. This increases the I/O consumption.

To reduce the resources consumed by charting, eliminate any unnecessary use of charts. In addition, you can use the Maximum Chart Size administrator setting at the trusted location level to limit how large the charts can be. The default value is 1MB.

Client Machine and Browser Speed

In addition to the client connection speed, the perceived responsiveness depends in part on the client machine and browser speed.

Workbooks can generate complex HTML and some JavaScript, which require client CPU cycles to render. Take into account that if a web page has several workbooks, they will all get rendered on the client machine, thus significantly reducing the perceived performance.

The client browser will cache some of the icons and JavaScripts, making the first browsing of a web page with EWA on it slower than the subsequent pages.

Although the client hardware is usually outside the server administrator's control, you should take it into account when estimating and analyzing the response time that your users are experiencing.

Summary

In this chapter, you learned about the architecture of Excel Services, its main components, and operational concepts, as well as how to configure it for best performance. Specifically, you learned the following:

- ❑ Excel Services is part of Office SharePoint Server, which has one or more web front ends (WFEs), application servers, and database servers. Shared Services Providers (SSPs) allow the hosting and managing of parallel logical application servers in a farm.

- ❑ The main components of Excel Services are the Excel Calculation Server (ECS), Excel Web Access (EWA) Web Part, and Excel Web Services API. The ECS is deployed on the application server and is the engine for loading and calculating workbooks. The EWA and the API are deployed on the WFE and provide the end-user interface and the programmatic interface, respectively.

- ❑ User activity is performed in the context of a session, which provides isolation. The session state is kept in the ECS memory and is not disclosed to other sessions.

- ❑ The ECS has caches of recently used objects in memory and on disk for improved performance. You can control the amount of memory used by the ECS and these caches.

- ❑ To achieve good performance and make the best use of your hardware, you should be aware of the various settings that Excel Services has. These settings allow you to tune the performance according to your needs. In addition, you can improve performance by controlling the way workbooks are authored and the web pages containing the EWA.

Chapter 4 discusses the Excel features that are not supported on Excel Services. Some workbooks are not supported on the server, and others are supported in a different way on the server and the client. You will learn about these features, and how to adapt your workbooks for the best experience on the server.

Part II
Working with Excel Services

Workbook Support

Excel Services loads, calculates, and displays Excel 2007 workbooks. There are a few differences between these two applications in terms of the level of support for Excel features.

Excel Services supports only the Office Open XML (*.xlsx) and the Excel Binary (*.xlsb) file formats. It does not support opening older file formats (such as *.xls) or workbooks containing code (such as *.xlsm).

There are some Excel features that are not supported on the server. The most important ones are query tables, images, shapes, and VBA projects.

Excel Services will not open a workbook that has unsupported features in it. After the server opens a workbook, there is full fidelity in the way the data is calculated. In some cases, there are relatively minor differences in the way the workbook is displayed in the browser. One of the most important differences is that three-dimensional charts are displayed as two-dimensional charts.

When the workbook is displayed, only a subset of the Excel functions can interact with the workbook.

This chapter describes the various Excel features that Excel Services supports, and the best practices for deploying successful workbooks to the server. The discussion provides valuable background about how some features are employed in Excel, examines which features are not supported in Excel Services, and presents possible workarounds for the unsupported features. Although this chapter focuses on the features that are not fully supported, Excel Services does support with full fidelity many of the important Excel features. Depending on your workbooks, you might need to perform additional steps to get them working on the server.

Supported File Formats

Excel Services supports only the Excel Workbook (*.xlsx) file format and the Excel Binary Workbook (*.xlsb) file format. You can author workbooks in these file formats with Excel 2007 or programmatically. In addition, you can install the Microsoft Office Compatibility Pack with Microsoft Office XP or Office 2003 to save workbooks in these file formats to the server.

The Excel Workbook (*.xlsx) file format is the default when you save a new file in Excel 2007. It is a ZIP-compressed file composed of several XML parts and uses the Office Open XML standard, which makes it easy to read and update programmatically.

The Excel Binary Workbook (*.xlsb) file format is similar to the Excel Workbook file format. It is also a ZIP-compressed file, but instead of XML parts, it has binary parts. The binary format is more efficient to load and save, so you should use it in scenarios in which the performance impact is important.

Excel 2007 has the following additional macro-enabled file formats, which might contain code:

- ❑ Excel Macro-Enabled Workbook (*.xlsm)
- ❑ Excel Macro-Enabled Template (*.xltm)
- ❑ Excel Add-In (*.xlam)

These formats are not supported by Excel Services. If you have a macro-enabled workbook that you want to port to the server, save it as an Excel Workbook or Excel Binary Workbook and remove the code from the file.

The Excel 2007 Template (*.xltx) file format is not supported on the server. If you use the template to create a new workbook, save it in one of the two supported file formats when publishing to the server.

None of the other older file formats are supported. These include the Excel 97-2003 Workbook (*.xls) file format, which was the default until Excel 2003, and the Web Page file formats (*.mht; *.mhtml; *.htm; *.html). When you are porting existing files that were authored with a previous version of Excel, save them with one of the new Excel 2007 supported file formats when publishing to Excel Services.

If you try to open a file with one of the unsupported file formats, you will get the error message shown in Figure 4-1.

Unsupported Features

You must use a supported file format to successfully open files in Excel Services. There are a number of Excel features that are not supported on the server, and they are detailed in this section. If a workbook has any of these features, the server will fail to open it.

The advantage of this behavior is that if a workbook successfully opens on the server, you know it will have fidelity with Excel. The disadvantage is that you cannot have a workbook with an unsupported feature and just have the server ignore it. For example, you might have VBA macros that are useful during the authoring of the workbook on the client and are not needed on the server. However, you will not be able to save the workbook to the server, because VBA macros are not supported. The workaround is to have two copies of the workbook, one with the macros that will be used on the client, and one without that will be published to the server.

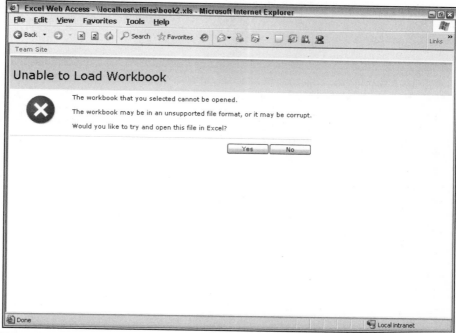

Figure 4-1

Most of the unsupported features can be categorized as follows:

❑ *Workbook security* — Settings such as restricted permissions, digital signatures, and workbook protection. SharePoint security can usually replace these features.

❑ *External data queries* — Features such as query tables, SharePoint lists, and links to other workbooks. Excel Services supports PivotTables.

❑ *Graphics objects* — These include pictures, shapes, SmartArt, and WordArt. Most chart types are supported on the server.

❑ *Code, macros, and solutions* — Extensibility features, such as VBA projects, ActiveX objects, and controls.

The following sections detail the unsupported features, and recommend workarounds in the cases where they are available.

When the server encounters one or more unsupported features, it displays an error message containing the full list of such features. In several cases, these features will be grouped together into one group of unsupported features, so it will not be straightforward to know, just by reading the error message, which features are not supported. You will have to scan your workbook for these features.

Figure 4-2 shows an example this type of error message. In this example, the workbook contains data validation and a shape. Graphics objects are not identified individually, so the error message contains the whole list of unsupported graphics objects.

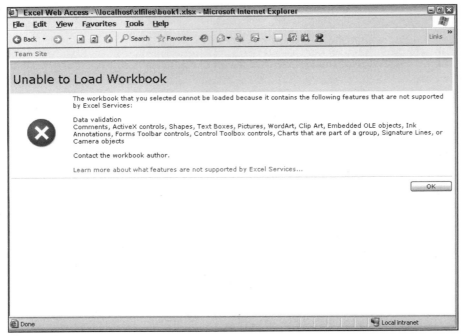

Figure 4-2

Workbook Security

Excel Services does not support opening workbooks that contain the following security and protection features:

❑   Files with restricted permissions

❑   Files with digital signatures

❑   Encrypted workbooks

❑   Workbook protection

❑   Sheet protection

Microsoft Office SharePoint Server and Excel Services provide a number of alternatives to secure and protect your workbooks.

Restricted Permissions

Files with *restricted permissions* allow you to specify which users are allowed to read, copy, print, edit, save, and programmatically access your workbook. This feature is also known as *Information Rights Management (IRM)*. Excel 2007 uses a server to authenticate users and decide which permissions (if any) a user is allowed to have on a workbook.

To set up restricted permissions, click the Office Button, and then select Prepare, Restrict Permissions, and Restricted Access. Figure 4-3 shows the Prepare menu in Excel 2007.

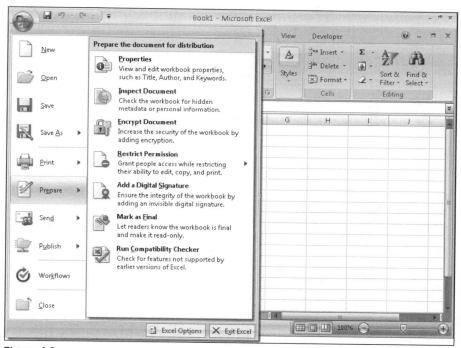

Figure 4-3

Excel Services does not allow users to open workbooks with restricted permissions. To publish a workbook to a server, choose Unrestricted Access from the Restrict Permission submenu, and use the SharePoint permissions model to grant access to the users. Here's how the SharePoint permissions map to the IRM permissions:

❑ *Read access* — To allow users to view the workbook in the browser, grant them the View Item right. To allow them to open the workbook in Excel and view the source of the workbook (including formulas and data connections), grant them the Open Item right. To prevent users from viewing the workbook, deny them both rights. The View Item right is available only when the workbook is saved in a SharePoint document library (not in a UNC or HTTP location).

❑ *Change* — To allow users to edit and save the workbook, grant them Write permissions to the document library or folder.

❑ *Copy and Print* — Copy and print permissions cannot be separated from the read access. Users who have only the View Item permissions can view the workbook in the browser, and copy and print the displayed range using the browser's copy and print functionality. Users who also have the Open Item right can open the workbook in Excel and use Excel's copy and print features.

❑ *Programmatic access* — You can restrict this by changing permissions on the API web service of the WFE.

You can also define Information Rights Management settings for document libraries on the SharePoint server. Excel Services does not allow users to open workbooks from these document libraries.

Digital Signatures

A *digital signature* identifies the originating author of a workbook, and signifies that the workbook has not been altered since it was signed.

To set up a digital signature in Excel, click the Office button, click Prepare, select Add a Digital Signature, and follow the instructions in the dialog box. Creating a digital signature marks the workbook as final and read-only, so no additional changes can be done on the workbook.

Excel Services does not support opening workbooks with digital signatures set on them. As long as the users open the workbooks on the server by using the EWA, the SharePoint security model is a good substitute for digital signatures. The administrator of the server should set up security in such a way as to limit who has permissions to upload files to the document library, and use the SharePoint auditing feature to keep track of who has changed a document. In addition, it is expected that the end user trusts the server and its administrator.

When you download the file from the server to the client, and then share it with other users, there is no digital signature to validate and authenticate the source of the workbook.

Document Encryption

You can use *document encryption* to specify a password that is required to open a document. These documents are encrypted using an encryption algorithm that you can specify when saving the file. Users opening the file will be prompted to enter the password before being allowed to see the document.

Depending on the strength of the encryption algorithm that you are using, it might be difficult for malicious users to break the encryption, but it might still be possible to do it using a brute-force attack.

To set up encryption in Excel, click the Office button, click Prepare, select Encrypt Document, and fill in the password.

Excel Services does not support opening encrypted workbooks. Instead, you should use the SharePoint security model to specify which users have permissions to the workbook. Users who have View Item rights are allowed to view the workbook in EWA, but cannot download it to the client. Users who also have the Open Item right can download the file and view it in the client.

Workbook Protection

With *workbook protection*, you can lock the workbook structure and windows. When the workbook structure is locked, users cannot add or remove worksheets or display hidden worksheets. When the windows are locked, users cannot change the size or position of workbook windows.

To set up workbook protection in Excel, click the Review tab, click Protect Workbook, and select Protect Structure and Windows. You can optionally specify a password required to remove the workbook protection.

Workbooks with structure or windows protection are not supported on the server. Excel Services will not open them, even if they don't have a password associated with the protection.

Excel Services does not have features to allow users to add or remove worksheets, display hidden worksheets, or change the size and position of workbook windows. Therefore, workbooks opened in EWA are implicitly protected, as long as they are viewed on the server.

Sheet Protection

By using *sheet protection*, you can limit the changes users can make to a worksheet. For example, you can lock certain ranges for modifications, as well as limit the insertion and deletion of rows and columns; the formatting of cells, rows, and columns; filtering; and sorting.

To protect a worksheet, click the Review tab, click Protect Sheet, and select the features you want to protect. You can optionally specify a password required to unprotect the workbook. When the worksheet is protected, any attempt to do any of the locked operations will result in an error in Excel.

A workbook with worksheet protection will fail to open in Excel Services, even if there is no password specified. Excel Services has a number of features to define the types of changes that users can make in the workbook.

By default, users cannot edit cells in EWA. You can specify workbook parameters when publishing a workbook to the server, and users will be allowed to modify only these parameters. Follow these steps:

1. Mark the cells that you want to allow users to modify as named ranges.
2. Click the Office button, click Publish, and select Excel Services.
3. Click Excel Services Options, open the Parameters tab, and click Add.
4. Use the parameters task pane of EWA to set the values of the parameters.

Several of the protected features are not supported on Excel Services, so they are implicitly protected. These are formatting cells, rows, and columns; inserting and deleting rows and columns; inserting hyperlinks; editing scenarios; and editing objects.

You can limit sorting and filtering and other interactivity features at the individual EWA instance by customizing its settings. In the browser, click Modify Shared Web Part from the Web Part menu, and check the relevant options.

Securing the Workbooks on the Server

Excel Services does not support the opening of workbooks with any of the security and protection features discussed here.

One of the main advantages of using the server in conjunction with the View Item right is to restrict who is permitted to view the workbook using the SharePoint security model. Only one version of the workbook is kept and managed centrally on the server, instead of having a number of versions distributed through e-mail or other means.

After a workbook is downloaded to the client, it is out of the server security model. Users who have only the View Item right are not permitted to download the file to the client.

Chapter 8 discusses the Excel Services security model in detail.

External Data Queries

Excel Services supports the use of PivotTables or Online Analytical Processing (OLAP) formulas for querying data from external databases. It does not support some types of PivotTables or other ways to query data (such as query tables, SharePoint lists, and links to other workbooks).

In most cases, you can work around the unsupported features by using PivotTables or user defined functions (UDFs). This section explains the limitations and workarounds for these features.

PivotTables

Most types of PivotTables are supported on the server, including the following:

❑ *OLAP* — PivotTables querying data from Analysis Services 8.0 or 9.0. Other OLAP providers that implement the same protocol could work, but are not formally supported.

❑ *Relational* — PivotTables querying data from a relational database, through the Object Linking and Embedding Database (OLEDB) or Open Database Connectivity (ODBC) protocols. These include SQL Server, Oracle, and DB/2, among others.

❑ *Excel list or range* — PivotTables querying data from a range in the current workbook.

For the PivotTable to work, the driver must be installed on the ECS machines. Chapter 5 discusses external data and supported data providers.

Some types of PivotTables are not supported by Excel Services, including the following:

❑ Multiple consolidation ranges

❑ Ranges from other workbooks

❑ Server-based page fields

PivotTables based on multiple consolidation ranges allow you to create one report based on several data ranges from multiple Excel sheets. This feature is not supported on the server. The workaround is to create in Excel one range that contains the consolidation of those smaller ranges, and base the PivotTable on the consolidated range.

In Excel, a PivotTable can be based on a range of data from a different workbook. This feature is not supported on the server. One workaround for you to consider is to unite these two workbooks into one. If that is not feasible, you could write a UDF that brings data from the second workbook into a range in the current workbook, and base the PivotTable on the results of the UDF.

PivotTables with server-based page fields are not supported on the server. In relational PivotTables, server-based page fields allow you to query the data for the current page field value. When this feature is on, every change of the filter value will query the database, but each of these queries will be smaller. To make these PivotTables work on the server, you can disable server-based page fields.

Query Tables

Query tables allow you to display the results of a relational database query in a tabular format. In addition, query tables allow you to add additional calculated columns (in the middle or to the side of the table) that grow as new rows are added to the table when the data is refreshed.

To create a query table, select the Data tab on the Excel Ribbon. Click From Other Sources, select From Data Connection Wizard, and create a new connection. After saving the connection, select the Table option in the Import Data dialog box to use the connection as a query table.

Excel Services does not support query tables. To create a relational PivotTable that behaves similarly to the query tables, follow these steps:

1. Create a relational PivotTable that uses the same connection as the query table.

2. Add all the relevant fields to the row labels.

3. In the Design tab of the Excel Ribbon, click Report Layout, and select Show in Tabular Form.

4. In the Options tab of the Ribbon, click Options, select the Display tab, and uncheck Show Expand/Collapse Buttons.

5. For each field, right-click the field, select Field Settings, and choose None for the subtotal.

By following these steps, you can create a PivotTable that has a very similar look and feel and functionality to a query table. However, you will not have the ability to create a calculated column that grows and shrinks with the table. You can approximate this behavior by using Excel formulas that return an empty value if the value in the respective row is blank. In addition, with the PivotTable, you will lose some of the sorting and filtering functionality that exists in the query table.

SharePoint Lists

With Excel tables based on SharePoint lists, you can query data from SharePoint directly into your Excel sheet. The easiest way to create this type of workbook is to open the SharePoint list in the browser, click Actions, and then select Export To Spreadsheet. In Excel, you can choose to display the data as a PivotTable or as a table.

Excel Services does not support PivotTables or tables based on SharePoint lists. However, you can write a UDF that brings the data from SharePoint into your workbook.

Web Queries

With web queries, you can have a sheet range that downloads data from a web page. To create a web query, select the Data tab in the Excel Ribbon, click From Web, and choose the part of the web page to download.

Excel Services does not support web queries. To work around this, you can write a UDF that queries the data from the web page.

Graphics Objects

Excel Services does not support most of the Excel graphics objects, such as pictures, Clip Art, shapes, and SmartArt. You cannot open a file with any of these features.

> *Excel Services does support charts, with some limitations. You will learn more about chart support later in this chapter.*

Although there is no direct workaround for the lack of graphics objects support, in most scenarios there is no significant functionality lost if these objects are removed from the workbook.

You can replace some of these objects with formatted text to get an approximation of the original feature. In most scenarios, you can replace text boxes, WordArt, signature lines, and pictures of the company logo with formatted text and maintain a good end-user experience.

The following unsupported features are available on the Insert tab of the Excel 2007 Ribbon (shown in Figure 4-4):

- ❑ *Picture* — An image from a file
- ❑ *Clip Art* — Drawings, movies and sounds from the Clip Art collections
- ❑ *Shapes* — Lines, rectangles, circles, arrows, callouts, and flowchart shapes
- ❑ *SmartArt* — A new type of illustration available in Excel 2007, including process, relationship, hierarchy, and pyramid diagrams
- ❑ *Text Box* — Allows text to be entered anywhere on the sheet
- ❑ *WordArt* — Various styles of decorative text
- ❑ *Signature Line* — A placeholder for a graphical signature
- ❑ *Object* — An embedded OLE object

In addition, the following graphics features are not supported in Excel Services:

- ❑ *Ink annotations* — Graphics entered from a Tablet PC with a tablet pen.
- ❑ *Comments* — Notes usually intended for reviewers of the workbook, available on the Review tab of Excel.
- ❑ *Smart tags* — If there are smart tags embedded in the workbook (which you enable on the Smart Tags tab of the AutoCorrect Options dialog box), the workbook will not be opened on the server. Smart tags that are not embedded will not be calculated dynamically on the server.
- ❑ *Grouped charts* — Charts are generally supported, but two or more charts that are grouped are not supported.

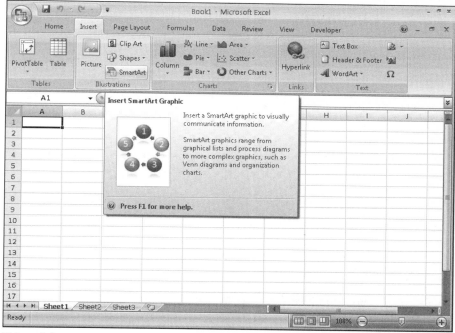

Figure 4-4

Code, Macros, and Solutions

There are a number of features that allow users to extend the functionality of Excel on the client but are not supported on the server.

Excel Services will not open a workbook that contains any of these features:

❑ VBA (Visual Basic for Application) code that is embedded in the workbook and recorded macros

❑ XLM (Excel macros)

❑ Embedded ActiveX controls

❑ Embedded OLE objects

❑ Forms toolbar and control toolbox items

❑ Custom toolbars

The recommended workaround for these features is to remove them before publishing the workbook to the server.

Other Features

Several other unsupported features do not fit in any of the previously mentioned categories, including the following:

- ❑ Data validation
- ❑ Shared workbooks
- ❑ Formula view mode

Data Validation

Data validation allows you to define valid values for certain cells and give users an error message when they enter invalid values to those cells.

To set up data validation, select the Data tab of the Excel Ribbon, and click Data Validation.

Excel Services does not support workbooks with data validation. This feature is relevant in the context of workbook parameters used to enter a value into a cell through the EWA. A partial workaround is to add a conditional formatting rule that will change the color of the parameter cell based on its validity. For example, red would mark an invalid value.

For API applications, you can add custom logic in the client application to validate the input.

Shared Workbooks

Shared workbooks allow multiple users to open and edit the same workbook in parallel.

To set up a shared workbook, select the Review tab of the Excel Ribbon, and click Share Workbook.

Excel Services does not support shared workbooks. There is no good workaround to allow multiple users to edit the same workbook at the same time on the server.

Show Formulas Mode

The Show Formulas mode in Excel displays the formulas in the worksheet instead of the results of the formulas. To set up this mode, you select the Formulas tab of the Excel Ribbon, and click Show Formulas.

Excel Services will not open a workbook that displays the formulas. If you need your users to see the formulas, a workaround might be to display them as text in a different cell in the sheet. In most server scenarios, you should not disclose the formulas to your server users, especially when using View Item rights.

Partially Supported Features

When a workbook is opened on the server, there should be full fidelity between the server and the client in terms of the data values that are calculated. In some cases, there are differences in the way the information is displayed in the browser. This section examines those visual differences.

> *Even if a feature is not fully supported on Excel Services, it will be loaded by the server, and saved back with full fidelity when the workbook is opened in Excel.*

Sheet Rendering

In most cases, Excel Services will display the sheet in a way that is very similar (and perhaps identical to) Excel. Usually you will find it difficult to distinguish between the two applications.

Because of some browser limitations, there might be minor differences in the way some advanced features are displayed. For example, the appearance of the following items may vary:

❑ Rich text

❑ Cells with various alignments

❑ Wrapped and shrink-to-fit text

❑ Rotated text

❑ Merged cells and gradients

In addition, diagonal borders are not displayed.

In Figure 4-5, you can see a side-by-side comparison of a sheet rendered in Excel and in Excel Services.

The following sections drill down into additional environmental settings that might affect the way the information is displayed in the browser.

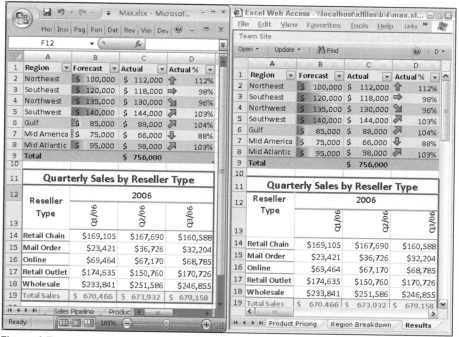

Figure 4-5

Installed Fonts

To get good display fidelity, the fonts used in the workbook should be installed both on the ECS machine and on the client machine. If a workbook contains special fonts that are not installed on the server and the client, there will be differences in the display.

The ECS requires the fonts to calculate the cell width and height when automatically resizing. It will substitute the font with the closest match if the font used in the workbook is not installed. This could cause lack of fidelity when the cell size is calculated, and might result in a cell displaying ### instead of the value of that cell.

The browser uses the fonts installed on the client machines to render the text in the cells. If the workbook font is not installed, the sheet might render differently for those fonts.

Browser Support

There are differences in the way various browsers interpret and display HTML. Excel Services is designed to work best with Internet Explorer 6.0 and above.

Different browsers are supported at various levels. Some browsers (such as Mozilla Firefox) have very good support, which is close to the support for Internet Explorer. Other browsers might provide only a basic display of the workbook without the visual fidelity, and yet others will not work at all.

If your organization uses browsers other than Internet Explorer, you should verify the level of support that Excel Services has for those browsers.

International Settings

The server uses the regional settings on the SharePoint site for rendering information such as currency and dates, not the settings of the client machine. If the SharePoint settings are different from the client settings, the workbook will be displayed differently.

Charts

Excel Services does not support three-dimensional charts, and will automatically downgrade any three-dimensional chart to its two-dimensional equivalent, as follows:

- ❑ Most three-dimensional chart types (such as three-dimensional columns, three-dimensional bars, three-dimensional lines, three-dimensional areas, and three-dimensional pies) have a natural equivalent.

- ❑ Three-dimensional cylinders, three-dimensional pyramids, and three-dimensional cone charts are downgraded to a two-dimensional column or two-dimensional bar chart.

- ❑ Surface charts are not supported at all, because they do not have a natural two-dimensional equivalent. When Excel Services opens a workbook with surface charts, the workbook will display in EWA, and there will be an error at the chart locations.

In addition, Excel Services does not support gradients and some of the advanced visual effects.

Figure 4-6 shows a side-by-side comparison of charts displayed in Excel and Excel Services. The top charts are almost identical. The bottom set of charts shows how three-dimensional charts are displayed as two-dimensional charts.

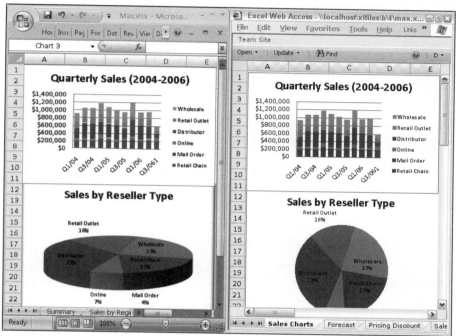

Figure 4-6

Calculation Extensibility

Excel allows several types of add-ins that can be invoked as part of the calculation formulas. Excel Services does not support any of these types, but does allow you to write managed UDFs.

If a UDF with the same signature is not installed on the server, then the server will not be able to calculate the workbook in the same way as the client. The behavior will be the same as when the UDF is not installed on the client machine (the cell will display the error #NAME?).

You should write managed UDFs that have the same signature and functionality as the client add-ins, either by writing new code or wrapping the client code in a managed UDF. Chapter 14 discusses Excel Services extensibility in detail.

Summary

Although Excel Services supports most of the Excel features, there are some important features that are either not supported, or supported with some differences. You should expect a certain overhead required from the authors of the workbooks to have them work correctly on the server.

In this chapter, you learned about the best practices for authoring existing or new workbooks for the server:

❑   Ensure that you publish in the correct file format. Excel Services supports only the *.xlsx and *.xlsb file formats.

❑   Familiarize yourself with the unsupported features described in this chapter. Take them into account when authoring a new workbook and when deciding if you can port an existing one.

❑   Consider alternatives and workarounds to the unsupported features.

❑   Publish the important workbooks to the server and test them before making them available to your end users.

The chapter also pointed out that after the workbook is opened on the server, there might be some visual differences.

Chapter 5 discusses querying data from external data sources. It examines setting up the server to enable external data connections, security, performance, and common configurations.

External Data

Excel Services queries data from external data sources such as relational and OLAP databases. This functionality is critical for a number of mainline scenarios such as reporting and business intelligence. It is also one of the most difficult areas to configure properly.

The complexity is caused by the need to synchronize the settings across the workbooks, the Data Connection Library (DCL), Excel Services, single sign-on (SSO), and the external data sources. These entities are owned by different groups of people who might have different (and, in some cases, even conflicting) goals:

❑ The external data sources are, in many cases, managed by a different group, such as the central IT department of the organization. Their goal is to keep these data sources running. They might not trust a specific application such as a deployment of Excel Services enough to give them special permissions to the data source.

❑ The goal of the administrator of Office Server is to ensure that Excel Services has high availability, is secure, and has high performance. To achieve that, the administrator might oppose connecting to certain data sources or allowing some types of authentication.

❑ Power users can author data connections and save them in a DCL for the benefit of other users creating workbooks with external data. They will usually manage a number of important connections to data sources, which might not satisfy the needs of all users.

❑ The end users want to create workbooks that query data and work both in Excel and on the server. They are usually not familiar with all the complexities of running queries to external data sources in a server environment, and just expect their workbooks to work.

In this chapter, you learn about creating data connections on the client, publishing them to the server, and how the server connects to external data. Then you learn about the security and performance implications of data on the server. The chapter concludes by summarizing several common usage patterns and server configurations for external data connectivity.

Connecting to Data

When the ECS receives a request to refresh one or more data connections (either by opening a workbook with an implicit refresh on open, or an explicit refresh operation coming from the user), it performs the following steps for each connection:

1. Determine which connection to use. The ECS might use a connection file from a DCL.

2. Determine the credentials to connect to the data (such as SSO credentials for a single sign-on).

3. Look for a cached version of the data queries that can be used. If so, the ECS will use it and not continue with the query.

4. Open a connection to the data source or use an existing connection from the connection pool.

5. Perform the query and store the results in the cache.

6. Continue calculating the workbook and returning the results to the WFE.

This sequence is a high-level description of the flow. The rest of this chapter will detail each of these steps. Figure 5-1 shows the components involved in external data queries.

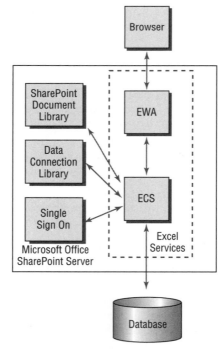

Figure 5-1

Data Connection Libraries

Data Connection Libraries (DCLs) are SharePoint document libraries that contain connection files to external data sources. A workbook can embed the definitions of external data connections or link to data connection files in any folder or SharePoint document library (such as a DCL).

Benefits

DCLs are central repositories of connections. A power user usually defines these for their group or organization. After data connection files are published to a DCL, workbook authors can use them to easily find connection definitions for their workbooks.

You can use DCLs to centrally manage all the connections. Changes in a DCL file propagate to all the workbooks that use them. As an example, consider a database that is moved from a test server to a production server. Instead of changing all the reports for that database, you could centrally update the data connection file in the DCL. Any workbook using that DCL file receives the updated connection to the new database server.

In addition, using connections from a trusted DCL allows for better security, because only a few trusted users have permissions to create these files.

Figure 5-2 shows an example of a DCL.

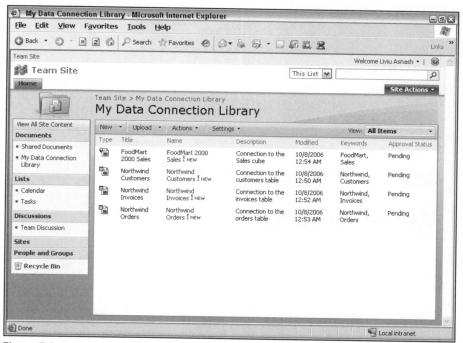

Figure 5-2

Creating Data Connection Libraries

To create a new DCL in SharePoint, open the Site Actions menu, select Create, and then click Data Connection Library. Fill in the Name, Description, and other properties of the document library.

In the Document Template field, select None. When you use the Report Center Web template to create a new site, a DCL is created by default on the site.

Creating Connections

There are two main ways to add connections to a DCL: uploading them through SharePoint and publishing them from Excel. Uploading is done in the same way as with any other file in a document library. Select Upload Document or Upload Multiple Documents from the Upload menu of the DCL, and then browse to the documents you want to upload.

From Excel, if you have sufficient permissions, you can publish an existing connection from a workbook to a DCL. In the Data Ribbon of Excel 2007, click Connections and select the connection you want to publish from the list. Click the Properties button to open the Connection Properties dialog box and select the Definition tab. Then, click the Export Connection File button to choose the DCL folder you want to publish to, and click Save. You can set the metadata properties of the file (such as its description and keywords) to allow users to find the right connection quickly. Figure 5-3 shows the Excel dialog boxes for publishing connections.

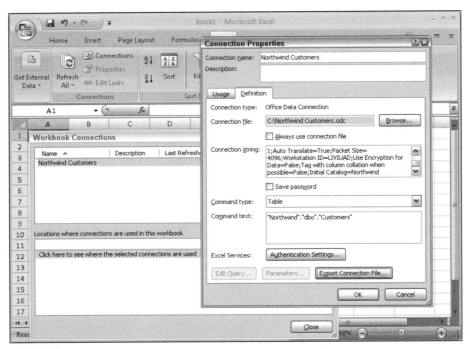

Figure 5-3

Depending on the permissions and other settings on the DCL, an approval workflow might be enabled on the DCL. In that case, new files will be usable only when approved by the authorized users.

There are multiple types of data connection files. Excel and Excel Services use Office Data Connection (*.odc) files. Other applications can use other file types with the DCL. For example, InfoPath uses Universal Data Connection (*.udc) files.

Using a Connection from Excel

One of the difficulties for end users when creating a new PivotTable or other external data object is to find the correct connection. Creating a new connection from scratch is a major obstacle for many users.

To work around this, you can browse to an existing connection in a DCL. From the Connections dialog box, click the Browse For More button, and browse to the DCL. Select the relevant data connection file and click Open.

Data Connections in Excel Services

Excel Services can use data connections from DCLs in order to benefit from central management and security of data connections. In addition, Excel Services can use data connections that are embedded in the workbooks.

Trusted Data Connection Libraries

Excel Services manages a list of trusted DCLs and allows users to open connection files from these trusted DCLs.

In a SharePoint farm, there might be many DCLs. To increase the server security, you should define only the DCLs that a small group of trusted individuals have permissions to manage.

Choosing the Connection

Workbooks can contain two variants for each connection: the embedded connection that is saved in the workbook file and the path to a linked connection file. Excel Services determines which connection to use based on two settings: the Always Use Connection File flag in the workbook and the Allow External Data setting of the trusted location of Excel Services.

To set or clear the Always Use Connection File flag, open the Data Ribbon of Excel 2007, click Connections, select the connection, and click the Properties button to open the Connection Properties dialog box. The flag is in the Definition tab.

You can configure the Allow External Data setting to one of the following values:

❑   *None* — No data connections are allowed from workbooks in that trusted location. All data operations (such as refreshing a PivotTable or opening a workbook with refresh on open or periodic refresh) will fail and return an error to the user. Use this value if, for security or performance reasons, you do not want to allow workbooks from certain locations to access external data.

❑ *DCL Only* — The ECS will first check that the connection file path the workbook contains points to a trusted DCL, and will try to load and use the connection from that file. If it fails to load the file from the DCL, the ECS will return an error to the user, and will not try to use the embedded connection information. Using the DCL Only value ensures that only trusted connections will be used by Excel Services and is best from a security point of view. However, it does have a performance impact, because the ECS will need to download the connection file from the SharePoint document library.

❑ *DCL And Embedded* — Excel Services will check the Always Use Connection File flag of the workbook. If the flag is set, it will try only the DCL connection and ignore the embedded connection. If the flag is not set, the ECS will first try to connect using the embedded data connection information, and if that fails, it will fall back to the DCL connection.

Linked Connection Path

As discussed in the previous section, Excel Services may download and use a file from a DCL. The workbook can contain a path to a DCL file instead of the embedded connection information.

This path is an absolute path. Therefore, you can move or copy the workbook to a different location and it will continue to work against the same DCL file. On the other hand, moving the connection file from the DCL will result in the workbook failing to connect (except when using the embedded connection information).

This becomes a problem if you have one or more data connections and workbooks on a test server and you want to move them to a production server. The only solution is to update all the workbooks (either manually or by using script) to use the path to the DCL on the new server.

Trusted Data Providers

Excel Services manages a list of trusted data providers. The ECS only executes queries to data sources that have been deemed safe and added to this list.

The server is installed with a default list of trusted providers, and the administrator can add or remove providers from the list. Figure 5-4 shows the administrator page for managing the list of trusted data providers. By default, the following data providers are supported:

❑ Microsoft SQL Server:

    ❑ SQLOLEDB and SQLOLEDB.1

    ❑ SQL Server ODBC and ODBC DSN

    ❑ SQLNCLI and SQLNCLI.1 OLEDB drivers

    ❑ SQL Native Client ODBC and ODBC DSN

❑ Microsoft OLAP Services:

    ❑ MSOLAP

    ❑ MSOLAP.2 (Microsoft OLE DB Provider for OLAP Services 8.0)

    ❑ MSOLAP.3 (Microsoft OLE DB Provider for OLAP Services 9.0)

- ❑ Oracle:

    - ❑ OraOLEDB.Oracle.1 (Oracle Provider for OLE DB)

    - ❑ Oracle ODBC driver for Oracle 9.2

    - ❑ Oracle ODBC DSN driver for Oracle 9.2

- ❑ IBM:

    - ❑ IBMDADB2 (IBM OLE DB Provider for DB2)

    - ❑ IBM DB2 ODBC Driver

    - ❑ IBM DB2 ODBC DSN Driver

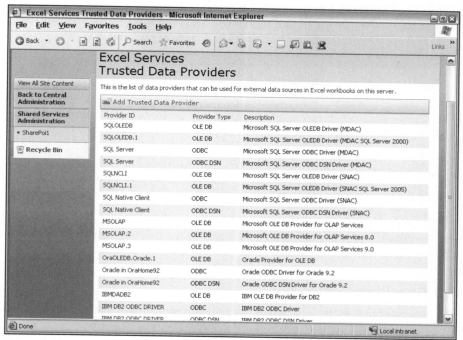

Figure 5-4

Installing the Driver

In addition to having the provider in the trusted providers list, the driver itself must be installed correctly on all the ECS machines. Most of the drivers listed earlier are not installed by default with Windows.

When installing a driver, ensure that you install the correct version and platform (32 bit versus 64 bit). If ECS is running as 64 bit, the driver must also be 64 bit, because it runs in process with the ECS. Some drivers (such as MSOLAP.2) do not support 64 bit and cannot be used with Excel Services on 64 bit deployments.

In addition, some drivers require special steps for installation on a server. For example, the Oracle drivers might require granting special permissions to certain registry keys. Read the relevant support documentation and Knowledge Base articles for those drivers.

Finding a Trusted Provider

To determine whether or not a provider can be trusted, find out the following information from the manufacturer of the driver or from a dependable source:

❑ *Security* — Can the provider be trusted to handle security and authentication properly? For example, verify that the driver cannot be used to launch an attack against Excel Services or the external data source, and that it respects the privacy of the users (such as handling passwords and not revealing the queries of one user to other users).

❑ *Reliability* — Is the provider designed and tested to work reliably in a multithreaded environment? Some drivers are designed to work in a single-threaded client environment, and might crash, deadlock, or return incorrect results in multithreaded environments. You should also verify that the driver can run in unattended mode (for example, it will not launch any UI when it fails or needs additional information).

❑ *Performance* — Does the driver provide the performance that is required for your application? Look at aspects such as running multiple queries in parallel, driver memory consumption, caching of data, network resources consumption, and running queries asynchronously.

❑ *Features* — Excel Services takes advantage of certain features of the drivers if they exist. These are the types of authentication (such as passing the username and password on the connection string), the ability to define a timeout for the connection, and the ability to cancel the connection when the request is cancelled or times out.

Because external data drivers run as part of the ECS process, any security, reliability, or performance issues that the driver might have can impact the whole ECS. Therefore, be very careful when deciding which drivers can be trusted.

MSOLAP.2 Considerations

Many BI and other scenarios use SQL Server Analysis Services. Analysis Services 9.0 is the latest version, but many deployments still use the Analysis Services 8.0 (MSOLAP.2) version.

The MSOLAP.2 driver is in the list of trusted data providers, but it has a number of important limitations when used with Excel Services:

❑ It does not support 64-bit systems. It can be used only on 32-bit systems.

❑ It does not efficiently support multiple locales from the same ECS process. This has limitations in multinational companies that use different regional settings against one ECS and one Analysis Services server.

❑ It does not support PivotTable grouping.

Supported Data Objects

Excel Services supports the use of PivotTables or OLAP formulas for connecting to external data. This version does not support any other data objects, including the following:

❑ Query tables

❑ PivotTables based on data ranges from other workbooks

❑ PivotTables that have server-based page fields

❑ SharePoint lists

❑ Web queries

❑ Links to other workbooks

❑ Dynamic Data Exchange (DDE) links

❑ RTD formulas

To be able to open workbooks on the server, replace the listed features with equivalent supported features, such as PivotTables, OLAP formulas, or equivalent UDF assemblies.

Chapter 4 provided information about supported and unsupported features in Excel Services.

Using UDFs to Query External Data

One way to query additional data sources that are not supported natively by Excel Services is to write your own UDF. The UDF can take in parameters, perform the query, and return a value or a range of values.

When writing this type of UDF, design for security and performance. Excel Services does not provide any tools to help with these tasks — you, as the writer of the UDF, must handle the external data authentication and optimize the performance by other means, such as caching.

When allowing a UDF to run on the server, the administrator must verify that the UDF developer has written it in such a way that it will not undermine the overall security and performance of the server, especially with UDFs that connect to external data.

Security

Implementing a server solution that accesses data from a source external to that solution in a secure way is a challenging task. In today's world of increased security risks, protecting the data is critical.

In this section, you learn about the security threats related to accessing external data. You also explore the various solutions that Excel Services provides to support securing the data access. There is no silver bullet to solve this complex problem, but you can combine a number of tools and techniques to achieve the results that are best for your unique situation.

Security Threats

Security between two parties is achieved, in part, by each party knowing who the other party is and trusting the other party. In external data scenarios, there are many parties involved, including the workbook author, the DCL file author, the end users, Excel Services, and the external database. Each of these might intentionally try to disclose data it does not have access to, or add, change, or destroy the information in the database.

The following sections explain the most important security threats.

Unauthorized Read Access

Databases protect the information that they manage by enforcing a set of permissions. Depending on the credentials of the users accessing a database, they might be permitted or denied read or write access to the database, a table, or some other information. It is the database's job to protect itself against unauthorized access, and it is Excel Services' job to use the correct credentials when connecting to the database.

Excel Services must first be able to correctly authenticate the end user who tries to access external data. Chapter 8 explains in detail how the user identity is determined.

Excel Services has several ways to decide which credentials to use. It can delegate to end users credentials in certain topologies, use different credentials that the user is mapped to through SSO, or use some fixed predefined credentials. Later in this chapter, you learn more about these methods.

When configuring Excel Services, be very careful which credentials the ECS will use to connect to external data. Using a fixed set of credentials is equivalent to the ECS administrator knowing a user and password for that database connection, and giving them to all users of that instance of Excel Services. It is fine to do that if the administrator knows and trusts the users, or wants to give them all the same permissions to the data.

Correctly configuring Excel Services to collaborate with the database owner ensures that only the authorized end users will have permissions to read the data they have permissions to.

Reading Other Users' Data

Excel Services must ensure not only that users will not be able to query data they are not authorized to, but also that end users will not have access to queries performed by other users (with different credentials). The ECS caches external data to improve performance, but it shares those caches only between users who have identical data credentials and permissions. That way, end users will only get the data they have access to. These performance optimizations are described in the "Performance" section, later in this chapter.

Another security threat is that end users will see external data that the workbook author has saved. Workbook authors usually have higher permissions to the database than some of the end users. Data returned from queries that the author makes when authoring the workbook is saved in the workbook. When opening a workbook with refresh on open, the ECS performs the query with the credentials relevant for the end user. The security risk exists if the refresh-on-open query fails for any reason. In that case, Excel Services might completely fail to open the workbook, as opposed to displaying the data that was saved in the workbook. You can control this feature with the Stop When Refresh On Open Fails administrator setting.

Malicious Author

The workbook author is the one who controls which query is performed. A malicious author can construct a query that, when executed by another user, can either steal data or change the information in the database. Here's how it works:

1. A malicious user creates a workbook that performs a query to an external data source that changes the database. For example, it might insert, update, or delete some records in a table. The user doesn't need to have permissions to the database.

2. The malicious user creates a SharePoint page containing an Excel EWA Web Part that opens the workbook, which may have refresh on open.

3. The malicious user then sends the link to the page to a user who has permissions to the database.

4. When the second user accesses the page, the ECS opens the workbook and performs the malicious query using the second user's permission.

In order to steal data, the malicious user can create a query that reads data from the database and stores the query results into another database (to which the malicious user does have access).

For certain trusted locations (for which only very few trusted authors can publish workbooks), the administrator can allow external data access with embedded connections. It is assumed that these trusted authors will not to create malicious workbooks.

For the other less-trusted locations, the administrator should only allow external data using predefined connections in trusted DCLs, or even no external data access at all. The assumption is that the connections defined in a trusted DCL are safe. In addition, the administrator can turn on the Warn on Data Refresh setting for the less-trusted locations. When this setting is on, the end users are warned that a potentially risky data access will be performed (using their credentials).

The attacker cannot perform this by creating his or her own farm. Therefore, the external database owner should not allow the non-trusted user to delegate Kerberos-constrained users' credentials through its farm.

Chapter 7 provides more details about trusted locations. Warn on Data Refresh and Kerberos-constrained delegation are explained later in this chapter.

External Attacker

Attackers who are not farm users can try to steal information by using various means. For example, they can try to use cross-site scripting to listen to messages sent over the wire, read files on the ECS machine, or gain administrative rights to the farm. In addition, they could try to stage a denial of service attack by using the server's resources such as the network, CPU, or memory.

These attacks are not specific to external data queries. Their mitigations are described in Chapter 8.

Security Mitigations

This section describes the various security features that Excel Services uses to mitigate threats.

Trusted Locations

By using trusted locations, the administrator can limit which workbooks may be opened by Excel Services. Each trusted location has settings that depend on the level of trust the administrator has about giving the authors permissions to write to that location. For example, a trusted location that points to a document library to which only a few trusted authors have write permissions will be very trusted.

The administrator can control the Allow External Data, Warn on Data Refresh, and Stop When Refresh on Open Fails settings for each trusted location (see Figure 5-5).

Allow External Data

By using the Allow External Data setting, the administrator can choose not to allow external data queries at all for locations that have a large number of authors (and, therefore, cannot be trusted), to allow only data queries with connections coming from a trusted data connection library, or to allow all external data queries.

Warn on Refresh

With the Warn On Data Refresh setting activated, users who try to refresh data from an external source receive a warning about the potential security implications. From a security point of view, you can turn off the warning if only a small number of trusted authors are permitted to author workbooks in the trusted location.

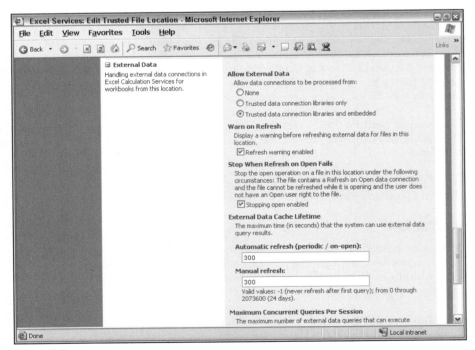

Figure 5-5

Stop When Refresh on Open Fails

Normally, if a workbook doesn't have refresh on open, or the refresh on open fails, the workbook displays the cached values from the sheet. When the query results depend on the user's credentials, the author's query results that were saved in the file are displayed to the other users if the query fails. When this setting is turned on, Excel Services returns an error instead of displaying the saved values when the refresh on open fails.

Trusted Data Providers

Trusted data providers were described at the beginning of this chapter. They allow the administrator to limit the queries only to data providers that were deemed safe.

Trusted Data Connection Libraries

By using trusted DCLs, the administrator can further limit which connections are allowed in the system.

Credentials Delegation

In the previous sections, you learned about the flow of data connections and their security limitations. This section examines the credentials that are used to connect to data.

One Hop

On a client application such as Excel, the user is logged in on the client machine. When Excel establishes a connection to the database machine, the underlying operating system passes the user's credentials to the database server. Figure 5-6 shows the connection from the client to the database server.

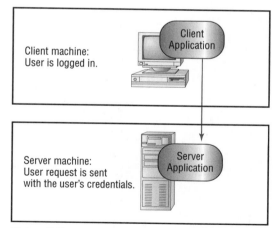

Figure 5-6

Because the operating system performs this delegation of credentials between two machines at a low level, the database server can trust that the request was indeed initiated by someone logged in with the credentials of the user. This is called a *one-hop topology*, because the credentials need to hop over the network once between the client machine and the database machine.

The credentials that the database server uses to determine permissions are called *integrated* credentials. Some databases (such as Microsoft SQL Server) also support *database* credentials. The username and password are passed on the connection string, and the database uses them to determine permissions.

Multiple Hops

In most Excel Services topologies, there is more than one hop between the client machine and the database machine. Figure 5-7 shows the *two-hop* and *three-hop topologies*.

The main issue with delegating the user's credentials in multiple hops is that those credentials may pass through one or more applications with malicious or security issues. As opposed to the one-hop topology, the operating system does not ensure that the end user who is logged in and the application in the middle are using the credentials appropriately.

Excel Services solves this problem with the following:

❑   One-machine topology

❑   Kerberos-constrained delegation

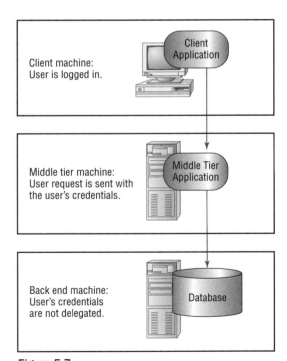

Figure 5-7

❑   Single sign-on (SSO)

❑   Workbook-embedded credentials

❑   Unattended account

Each of these has its advantages and disadvantages. None of them is a silver bullet, and you should use the methods that work best for your specific configuration and needs. The following sections detail how to set up the workbooks and the server for each of these options, and when to use them.

Authoring the Workbook

Excel Services can support multiple credentialing options at the same time. When you're authoring a connection in Excel, define the credentials you want to use to connect to data on the server.

In the Workbook Connections dialog box in Excel, select a connection and click Properties. In the Connection Properties dialog box, switch to the Definition tab and click the Authentication Settings button. Select from one of the following settings:

❑   *Windows Authentication* — Select this to use the end user's credentials. This setting works in a one-machine topology or when Kerberos-constrained delegation is enabled.

❑   *SSO* — Select this to use the end user's SSO credentials. This requires you to define the SSO application ID.

❑   *None* — When you select this setting, the end user's credentials are not delegated. You can embed a user and password in the connection string. If there is no such user and password, predefined server credentials are used to connect to the database.

One-Machine Topology

In this topology, the WFE, the ECS, and the database server are on the same machine, as shown in Figure 5-8. Because there is only one hop, the credentials are delegated.

The major advantage of this topology is that it is extremely simple to set up and secure. The disadvantages are as follows:

❑   It will work only against databases that you own and can deploy to the same machine. You cannot connect to any other databases in your organization.

❑   In terms of performance, you are limited by how much you can scale up your machine. You will not be able to add machines to the farm and scale out.

❑   Some of the optimizations described later in this chapter in the "Performance" section will not work. Each user has a separate connection with different credentials and therefore potentially different results, so query results are not shared between users. When connecting to Analysis Services, a separate optimization can allow different users to have the same roles for sharing query results.

This topology is great if you want to build a full solution that has Excel Services and a database, and you own and control both pieces.

To make this work, you must set the workbook connection to use Windows Authentication. In addition, you need to set up the access model between the WFE and ECS to Delegation (see Chapter 8 for details).

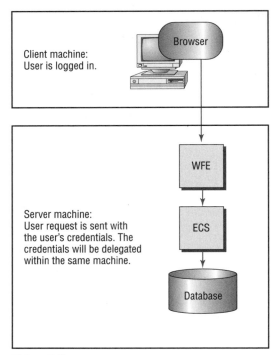

Figure 5-8

Kerberos-Constrained Delegation

You can use Kerberos-constrained delegation with Windows Server 2003 Active Directory to allow multiple hops. When enabling the delegation, the network administrator defines a level of trust between two services on different machines. One service (in this case, a database) trusts another service (in this case, an Excel Calculation Service instance) to correctly pass the correct end-user credentials.

The main advantage of this configuration is that the correct end-user credentials are passed to the database. The disadvantages are as follows:

❑ It requires the central IT of the organization to set up the delegation in the Active Directory.

❑ It usually limits the trust to cases in which both the database and the Excel Services deployment are owned by the same group (usually the central IT). An organization's central IT department usually does not trust a small departmental Excel Services deployment to delegate its credentials to a central database, because it has no control over the security of this type of deployment.

❑ The performance optimizations described previously in the "One-Machine Topology" section will not work.

To set up Kerberos-constrained delegation, contact your central IT organization. The trust will need to be set up between the ECS and each of the databases to which you want to connect using this type of delegation. In addition, the access model between the WFE and the ECS should be set to Delegation. If the WFE and the ECS are on separate machines, the central IT department will need to set up delegation between the WFE and the ECS as well. The workbook author will have to set the connection to use Windows Authentication.

Workbook Embedded Credentials

The workbook author can save in the workbook specific credentials to be used when connecting to a database. Then all users who open that workbook can use the credentials.

The main advantage of this method is its simplicity. The author can publish a workbook to the server and allow all other users to connect to any database that supports database credentials. In addition, it is very good in terms of performance, because everyone uses the same credentials, which enables them to share the cached query results.

The main disadvantage is that all users who can view the workbook receive permissions to perform the query from the database. This method is almost equivalent to sending these credentials to all users. It is good for cases in which those credentials would normally be known to everyone in the organization.

Anyone who has access to the workbook can get the password that is stored in the file. You can limit this disclosure by saving the workbook into a document library to which only the author has open rights and all other users have only view rights.

To specify that a connection should use embedded credentials, set the Server Authentication to None, write the user and password to the connection string, and select Save Password.

The ECS will log in as the unattended account when creating the connection to the database. The query will fail if the unattended account is not defined correctly.

Unattended Account

The administrator can define a special account to be used when the author defines a connection with the authentication type set to None. This account is called the *unattended account*. The unattended account is defined in the External Data section of the Excel Services Settings (see Figure 5-9).

Connections with a None authentication type will fail if the unattended account is not defined and/or if the user or password is incorrect.

If the unattended account is defined correctly, the ECS logs in as the unattended account when creating a None connection type. The ECS then passes the connection string, which may or may not contain a database username and password, to the database. If the database does not find any user and password on the connection string, it works as the unattended account. (The previous section described what happens when there is a database user and password.)

To increase the security of your system, either don't define the unattended account or define it as an account with very low privileges and no access to the databases. When you use a low-privilege account, the ECS is allowed to use embedded workbook credentials, but it cannot use the unattended account to connect to a database.

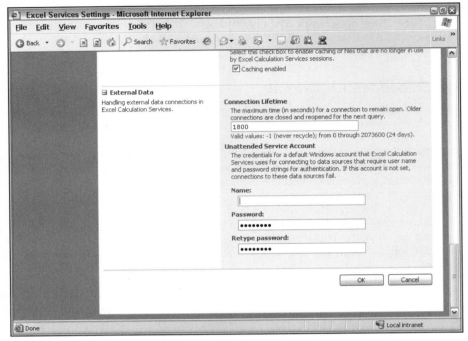

Figure 5-9

If you use an account with more privileges, a workbook that has None as the authentication method can be opened with that account.

The main advantage to this method is similar to the workbook-embedded credentials. Everyone has the same username and password to connect to the databases. In addition, the password is saved securely in the server settings, so users cannot access it by getting the workbook.

The main disadvantage is that all users have the same credentials to all the databases when the author sets the authentication to None. There is no way to limit this feature to certain databases.

Single Sign-On

Single sign-on (SSO) is a technology that provides credentials to access certain enterprise applications. In the case of Excel Services, the enterprise application should be a database. For this type of application, an administrator gives credentials to each user or group of users.

Microsoft Office SharePoint Server has a default SSO provider. It also allows you to plug in third-party providers that implement a certain interface.

To use SSO, the workbook author must set the connection authentication method to SSO and specify the enterprise authentication. When opening this type of connection, Excel Services gets the credentials for the current user and the given application from SSO, and then uses those credentials to connect to the database. If the specified application is not defined in SSO, or the current user is not mapped to any credentials, the connection will fail.

SSO credentials can be defined as integrated or database. When retrieving *integrated credentials*, the Excel Calculation Server uses them to log in, and then it connects to the database while being impersonated with those credentials. When retrieving *database credentials*, the Excel Calculation Server adds them to the connection string, and uses the unattended account (if it is defined) to connect to the database.

The main advantage of SSO is that it allows different credentials to be used for each user or group of users without requiring Kerberos-constrained delegation. In other words, it provides the SSO administrator with flexibility in defining the credentials.

The main disadvantage is that it requires additional overhead to define and maintain the credential mappings.

Performance

The previous section covered the various aspects related to external data security. This section discusses issues related to performance. In many cases, there is a tradeoff between security and performance, because increased security often comes at the expense of performance.

External data queries can be extremely expensive. They may require connecting to another machine to get the connection file from a DCL, get the credentials from SSO, and perform the actual query from the database. Depending on the query and the database, this might take a long time, consume resources on the database machine, transfer a lot of data over the network, and require memory and CPU resources on the ECS machine to process the results.

Excel Services has a number of optimizations for caching data query results and connections, and for sharing them between users. The net result is that, in many cases, the performance of Excel Services with many users querying data from a few workbooks is much better than the performance of the same users connecting to the database from Excel. Because of the caching of the results sharing, it puts much less strain on the database itself.

The following sections describe how you can configure Excel Services for optimal performance.

Caching and Sharing

After performing a query, the ECS will cache each query result for up to the cache lifetime setting that is defined for the trusted location. As long as the cache lifetime for that query has not expired, the ECS will use the cached results instead of performing a new query.

The cache will be shared with other users who have the same credentials. When using workbook-embedded credentials or the unattended account, the cached results will be shared with all the other users, because all users have the same credentials. When using SSO, the cached results will be shared with all the other users who are mapped to the same SSO credentials. When using Kerberos-constrained delegation, the cached results will not be shared, because each user has individual credentials.

Time	Operation	Result
12:00	User A refreshes a connection.	The connection is not in the cache. ECS performs the query and saves the result in the cache. The cache will expire at 12:05.
12:01	User A refreshes the same connection.	The cache is not expired. The ECS reuses the connection the cache.
12:02	User B (who has the same credentials as user A) refreshes the connection.	The credentials match. The ECS reuses the same connection from the cache.
12:03	User C (who has different credentials) refreshes the connection.	The ECS performs the query with the new credentials and caches the new results. These cached results will expire at 12:08.
12:06	User A refreshes the connection.	The cache entry for user A is expired. The ECS performs the query again.

Cache Lifetime Settings

Two settings define the external data query cache expiration. The Automatic Refresh Data Cache Lifetime setting is used when a workbook is opened with refresh on open and for periodic refresh. The Manual Refresh Data Cache Lifetime setting is used when a connection is explicitly refreshed.

The default value for both settings is 5 minutes. You can change this setting from the administration pages for each trusted location. Various databases have different update schedules. Some may update once a week or once a day; others may have new data every hour, every minute, or even close to real time. In addition, even if the database updates frequently, each workbook will need data refreshed on a different schedule. For example, a workbook could use a data query to create an historic quarterly report, so it won't need up-to-date data. Other workbooks could be used to perform operational decisions based on the most current information.

When you're setting these values, balance the performance of the server with the user's need for up-to-date data. In many cases, there is no conflict, because workbooks don't need the latest information or the database itself doesn't update that often. The default values for these settings are relatively low, and, in most cases, you should increase them to achieve better performance.

In addition, the workbook author has an impact on the performance. If the workbook refreshes on open or has periodic refresh, it will potentially perform more queries than a workbook with no automatic refresh. The actual periodic refresh period will be the maximum between the one defined in the workbook and the Automatic Refresh Data Cache Lifetime setting. For example, if the periodic refresh defined in the workbook is 10 minutes but the cache lifetime setting is 1 hour, the workbook will refresh automatically only once an hour.

Having a separate setting for manual refresh allows for better granularity. For example, an administrator might have a relatively high automatic cache lifetime to improve the server performance for most cases, but will have a lower manual cache lifetime to provide more up-to-date data for users who need it, and manually refresh. Alternatively, an administrator can set the manual refresh cache lifetime setting to a high value to discourage manual refreshing and to keep the automatic refresh schedule prescribed by the author.

SQL Server Analysis Services

Excel Services shares query results between users only if they are using the same credentials to connect to data. In the case of Windows authentication, each user has his or her credentials delegated to the database, resulting in no sharing and a significant performance impact.

Many databases have a role model that maps multiple users to the same security roles, so it would be safe (from the security point of view) to share query results between different users who are mapped to the same database roles. Excel Services has an optimization specific to SQL Server Analysis Services 9.0. When the ECS uses Kerberos to connect to Analysis Services 9.0 (or later versions), it will first verify that the Analysis Services security roles of the current user are the same as those of any of the cached results. If they are, it will reuse the cached results, resulting in improved performance with no security hit.

Connection Pooling

To improve performance, the ECS keeps a pool of connections. It reuses those connections if their settings match, rather than creating a new external data connection for every request.

The Connection Lifetime setting limits the maximum amount of time that a connection can be kept in the pool. For security reasons, the connection is closed after this period of time. The default value for this setting is 30 minutes.

Parallel and Asynchronous Queries

To improve the end-user response time and to maximize the resource utilization, the ECS executes multiple queries in parallel. For example, if a workbook has multiple query tables and the user refreshes all of them, the server uses several threads to execute the queries.

The Maximum Concurrent Queries Per Session setting determines the maximum number of threads that will be used. The default value for this setting is five parallel queries. You can change this setting separately for each trusted location. Although increasing this setting might result in better response time for an end user, it will degrade the performance of the whole machine. If there is one trusted location that has a few critical workbooks with multiple queries that should get priority, you can increase this setting for that trusted location.

OLAP Formulas

Excel 2007 issues queries for OLAP formulas asynchronously. It can run several of these types of queries in parallel, one for each data connection in the workbook.

As opposed to PivotTables, Excel Services does not have this performance optimization for OLAP formulas. The ECS issues the OLAP formulas queries synchronously during the calculation of other workbook formulas.

Excel Web Access

In the previous sections, you learned about external data and focused mainly on the ECS and the administrator's experience. This section looks at the Excel Web Access (EWA) and the end user's experience.

External data queries may occur when the user opens the workbook, explicitly when the user refreshes the data or interacts with a PivotTable, and implicitly as part of periodic refresh. The following sections examine each of these cases.

Refresh on Open

When opening a workbook with refresh on open, the data will refresh automatically. The user might get a message asking for confirmation to perform the data query, as shown in Figure 5-10.

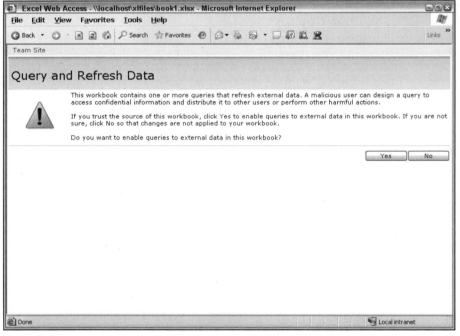

Figure 5-10

Interactivity

After you open a workbook with external data, you can refresh it and perform interactivity.

From the Update entry in the EWA toolbar, you can refresh all data connections in the workbook or only a selected connection. To refresh only one connection, select it by clicking anywhere within the data range and choose Refresh Selected Connection from the toolbar. Figure 5-11 shows the Refresh entries on the Update toolbar.

In Excel Services, you can perform the following operations on the rows, columns, and filter fields of a PivotTable (see Figure 5-12):

❑ Press the plus (+) and minus (-) controls to expand and collapse members in a hierarchy.

❑ Sort in ascending or descending order.

❑ Filter the labels or values by selecting from a list of members, or by choosing from a list of options (such as equals, less than, greater than, and between).

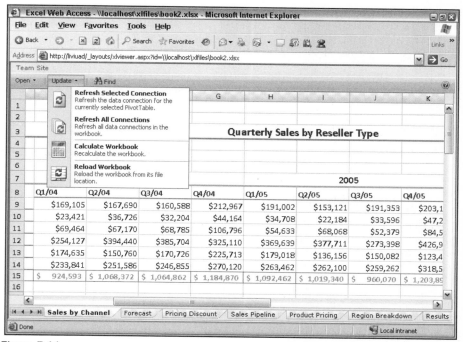

Figure 5-11

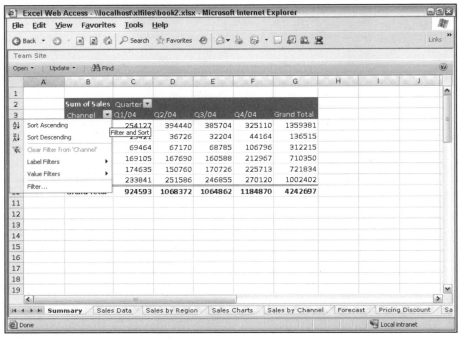

Figure 5-12

Controlling Interactivity

When you're designing a web page, you can use the EWA settings to turn off some of the interactivity features.

From the Web Part menu, click Modify Shared Web Part to open the EWA tool pane. Scroll to the Toolbar and Title Bar section to control the Refresh operations on the toolbar. You can uncheck the Refresh Selected Connection, Refresh All Connections setting to remove the Refresh entries from the Update toolbar. In addition, you can change the Type of Toolbar setting to remove some of the entries from the toolbar, or to completely remove the toolbar. Figure 5-13 shows the EWA tool pane.

To disable pivot interactivity, scroll down to the Navigation and Interactivity section. You can uncheck the Sorting, Filtering, or All Pivot Interactivity settings to disable some or all the PivotTable functionality.

Periodic Refresh

The author can configure a workbook connection to automatically refresh at predefined time intervals. On the server, this feature is mostly used for dashboards that constantly display the latest data from one or more databases.

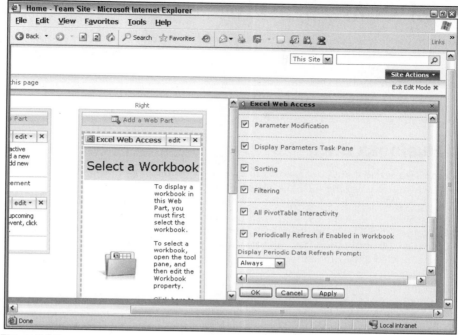

Figure 5-13

EWA enables you to control how periodic refresh is performed. To disable periodic refresh, uncheck the Periodically Refresh If Enabled In Workbook setting in the EWA tool pane. If the above setting is checked, periodic refresh will be enabled.

EWA can perform periodic refresh in one of three ways. Use the Display Periodic Data Refresh Prompt to choose from the following:

❑ *Always* — Selecting this option tells EWA to notify users when the periodic refresh interval has expired. You are given the option to refresh the connection once and show the notification again the next time it has expired, or to never show it again. Use this option when you want to notify users and do not want the data to automatically refresh without user intervention.

❑ *Never* — Selecting this option means that the notification will never be displayed. The data is automatically refreshed every time the periodic timeout has expired, without any notifications to the users. Select this option in unattended dashboard scenarios.

❑ *Optionally* — Selecting this option is similar to selecting Always. It tells EWA to notify you when the periodic refresh timeout has expired. The notification bar has an additional option that allows you to switch to the automatic mode that performs the refresh without displaying the notification bar.

Common Configuration

In this chapter, you learned about the various external data features of Excel Services as well as their security and performance implications. This section shows a few common cases of accessing external data and the recommended configuration for each case.

The common cases described here are generic cases that might not fully correspond to your situation. Adapt these configurations to your specific needs.

Line of Business Data

In this example, assume that your organization has one or more line of business (LOB) applications such as enterprise resource planning (ERP) or customer relationship management (CRM). You want to build a number of reports that can be accessed through your SharePoint portal.

To do this, you set up SSO in your SharePoint farm to map the credentials of the users to the account used to connect to the LOB application. You might need to install the relevant drivers to the ECS machine and define them as trusted data providers.

When authoring the reports, you define the authentication settings to be SSO. On the server side, you create a trusted location to which these workbooks will be published. You set up the trusted location with a value of DCL and an Allow External Data setting of DCL And Embedded. You should give write permissions to this trusted location to only a few trusted authors. If you want to allow other users to create their own reports, you can create additional trusted locations and allow the users to publish reports in those libraries.

In addition, you can allow access to some of these reports on your extranet, for customers or partners. You should allow only view item rights to the users outside of your firewall, so that they will not have access to the data connection information or the calculation model of the workbooks.

Reporting on Restricted Data

In this example, assume that the central IT department of a large organization manages an Analysis Services database that contains restricted data that can be accessed only by certain users. In addition, various users will get different views on the data. For example, managers will get only the data for their departments.

The IT organization wants to add a number of reports for those managers in the organization's SharePoint portal. To build the solution, you define Kerberos-constrained delegation between the ECS and the Analysis Services machine.

When authoring the reports, you define the authentication settings as Windows Authentication. You create a trusted location to which these workbooks will be published. This trusted location should have a value of DCL, an Allow External Data setting of DCL And Embedded, and the Stop When Refresh on Open Fails setting turned on. You should limit the write permission for this folder to a few trusted authors, but you can give the read permission to a larger set of users, because the database will restrict the data access.

Business Intelligence Portal

For this example, assume that you manage an OLAP database containing the business results of your organization. You want to provide a number of predefined reports and key performance indicators (KPIs) that summarize the health of the business. In addition, you want to allow users in various departments to add their own reports and analysis.

You can deploy a dedicated standalone SharePoint farm that has the OLAP database on the same box as the WFE and the ECS. If you want to make the information in the OLAP database available to all the users in your organization, you can use the unattended account (the workbooks will specify None in the authentication settings). In this case, the unattended account should have low privileges and be allowed to access only this OLAP database.

If there are security restrictions on the data in the database, use the one hop, one machine configuration and set the workbook authentication to Windows Authentication.

Publish your predefined reports in a special trusted location. Give only a few trusted authors write permissions to ensure that the reports representing the state of the business are common and consistent across the organization. To maintain authenticity, allow only view item rights to this trusted location to everyone except the authors. Synchronize the cache lifetime settings to the frequency at which the OLAP database gets updated.

These reports will be exposed through one or more dashboards, which can also contain SharePoint KPIs based on the same workbooks or directly on the database. You can set up a report on the home page of the portal, with refresh on open and periodic refresh.

In addition, you can create one or more additional trusted locations to allow other users to publish their own reports of the data. The DCL will contain the connection information to the OLAP database.

Summary

In this chapter, you learned about the Excel Services features related to accessing external data:

- ❑ Various people are involved in running workbooks with external data on the server: the author, the power user (who manages connections), the administrator of the server, and the owner of the external data source. They often have different (and even conflicting) agendas.

- ❑ DCLs provide central repositories for data connections, making it easy for authors to find connections and author reports, and allowing central management of connections. Both the Excel client and Excel Services can use connections for a DCL.

- ❑ Excel Services has a list of trusted data providers to ensure that only safe drivers are used.

- ❑ Excel Services supports only a subset of the external data features of Excel: PivotTables and OLAP formulas.

- ❑ A large number of security threats are related to accessing external data. Excel Services mitigates some of them by limiting which workbooks, connections, and data providers it trusts. A trusted location defines a set of workbooks to be trusted and their settings.

❑   The credentials that should be defined for connecting to a database depends on your configuration and requirements. Excel Services supports a number of authentication settings. Kerberos-constrained delegation uses the end user's credentials. SSO has a mapping of groups or users to database credentials. In addition, a predefined unattended account can be used to connect to a database.

❑   Excel Services uses caching and sharing results between users with the same credentials in order to increase performance. You can configure your server for optimal performance.

❑   The EWA has a number of settings to control how data is refreshed in dashboards.

This chapter has also provided a number of recommended configurations to solve a few common scenarios. Each situation is different, and you can tune the server to best fit your needs.

Chapter 6 discusses capacity planning for Excel Services. It examines the hardware needed for your deployment. When planning your configuration, you should take into account various factors, such as the number of users, types of workbooks and requests, and usage patterns.

Capacity and Deployment Planning

Chapter 2 provided guidance for installing the Evaluation Server and some example Excel Services scenarios. This chapter shows what is possible through other, more advanced deployments. The topic of capacity planning for Excel Services is covered in the second half of this chapter.

In this chapter, you do the following:

- ❏ Learn about various Excel Services topologies
- ❏ Discover how Excel workbooks can affect system capacity
- ❏ Learn how authors and consumers of workbooks can impact capacity
- ❏ Identify the focus points behind capacity-planning decisions
- ❏ Learn about Excel Services capacity-planning concepts
- ❏ Learn about configuration settings that impact capacity

Choosing a Deployment Topology

A Microsoft Office SharePoint Server (MOSS) deployment consists of three essential server roles: database, front-end, and application. Both the front-end and the application server roles can be further subdivided by the MOSS services typically comprised by each role. The supported topologies are, for the most part, characterized and distinguished by the distribution of the three roles across the computers in the deployment. The capacity expectations could dictate that all that is needed is a single server to host all of the roles. The other extreme is possible where multiple servers will be used to support each of the roles.

You must consider a number of factors when deciding which type of deployment to pursue. The focus of this chapter is on Excel Services, but your deployment may also need to take into consideration the other services being provided by MOSS, as well as the effect those services will have on your topology. The performance and capacity of an Excel Services deployment will be affected by how you intend to leverage it. The "Capacity Planning" section of this chapter explores the factors that you need to consider when deploying Excel Services.

The following sections outline the core deployments and describe the progression from a single-server topology to a multiserver topology. The deployments noted here provide an opportunity to discuss the differences between the deployment types, but they don't represent a finite set of the allowed topologies. The actual topology you end up with may be a hybrid of a farm type discussed in this chapter. One valuable point to take away is that you can scale a MOSS deployment in different ways to meet your specific needs for Excel Services.

Single-Server Topology

Different terms are used when referring to a single-server topology. An *evaluation server* and a *standalone server* both refer to a single-server topology. In this topology, a single server supports all three roles, and all MOSS components are installed on a single computer. For Excel Services, this includes both the Excel Services front-end web components and the application server Excel Calculation Services (ECS) components. The SQL Server Express Edition of SQL Server 2005 is installed on the machine, and the configuration and content databases reside on the server. Installing an evaluation server is discussed in Chapter 2. Figure 6-1 shows a single-server topology.

You cannot add more MOSS servers to this deployment. The single server is all you get with this topology, and there will not be any opportunity to scale this farm out by adding servers to take on any of the roles, like Web Front-End (WFE) or application server. If there is even the chance that scaling out is a possibility in the future, then consider starting with a small farm topology (discussed later in this chapter).

This topology is the easiest and quickest way to install and get Excel Services up and running. This type of deployment is also referred to as a *one-click install* because it really doesn't require much effort to get it installed and working. Excel Services is configured right out of the box to load workbooks, whereas all other types of deployments require additional post-setup steps to enable Excel Services to load workbooks.

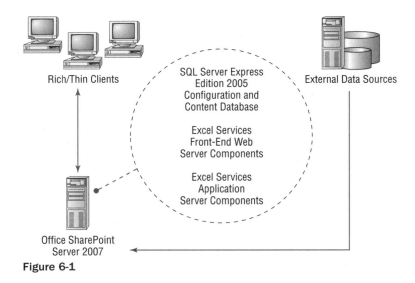

Figure 6-1

The single-server topology is a useful deployment for evaluating Excel Services. It is the cheapest way to get Excel Services deployed and for discovering the many features offered by Excel Services.

A single-server topology may also be sufficient to satisfy the needs of an Excel Services production deployment. This type of deployment is best suited for a work group or business unit. Because this deployment uses SQL Server Express, the database associated with this deployment is limited to a maximum size of 4GB.

Small Farm Topology

The *small server farm topology* typically consists of two computers. The *database server* is used to host SQL Server 2005 (or SQL Server 2000), along with the configuration and content databases. A *single front-end server* is configured as both the web server and the application server. For Excel Services, this means the front-end server contains the Excel Services WFE components, and the application server contains the ECS components. The WFE server may also support other MOSS services, such as search and indexing. Figure 6-2 shows a small server farm topology.

As mentioned previously, a single-server topology can be used in a production environment, but the small farm is considered the entry-level production topology. This type of deployment is best suited for a workgroup or business unit. One immediate advantage to this topology over the single-server topology is that the 4GB size limit of the configuration and content database is no longer present because the small farm is using SQL Server. The small farm deployment allows servers to be added (or removed), which keeps your options open should you ever want to perform actions such as increase the capacity of the farm or take a server offline.

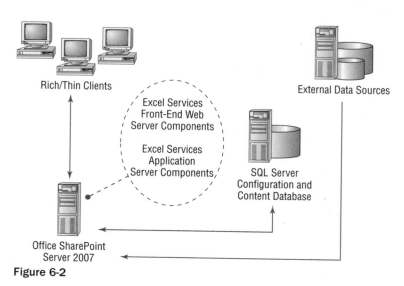

Figure 6-2

Medium Farm Topology

The *medium server farm topology* typically consists of three or four computers. The medium farm will contain a *database server*, an *application server*, and one or two *WFE servers*. The database server is used to host SQL Server 2005 (or SQL Server 2000), along with the configuration and content databases. The WFE servers contain the Excel Services WFE components and may host the search service. The application server contains the ECS components, and may host the indexing service. Figure 6-3 shows a medium farm topology.

The medium farm represents a shift away from a single server hosting all Excel Services components. With the medium farm, the Excel Services WFE components are now separated from the ECS application server components. The addition of a second WFE server (also containing the Excel Services WFE components) is common in a medium farm, and represents a move toward scaling out Excel Services.

The medium farm offers more Excel Services functionality than the small farm. If the workbook characteristics are going to remain constant, the medium farm can provide support for higher concurrent Excel Services users, provided the ECS application server component was not already the bottleneck.

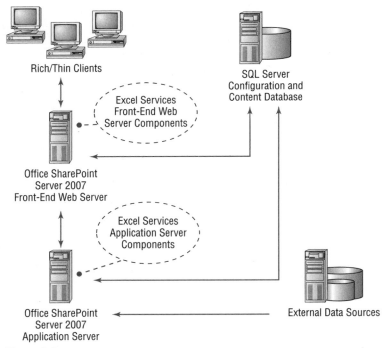

Figure 6-3

Large Farm Topology

The *large server farm topology* typically consists of six or more computers. The large farm contains two *clustered database servers*, multiple *application servers*, and multiple *WFE servers*. Each WFE server hosts the Excel Services WFE components. Each application server hosts specific MOSS services. This means that the ECS components are hosted on one or more application servers, depending on the capacity expectations of the system. The search and indexing services can also be hosted on separate application servers. Figure 6-4 shows a large farm topology.

In a large farm topology, you can essentially customize Excel Services to address the infinite combinations of concurrent users, calculation intensity, and workbook complexity. One or more application servers exist specifically to host the Excel Calculation Services components. By scaling out the ECS, opportunities now exist to provide support for a high number of concurrent users simultaneously with a high number of unique workbooks. Even long-running calculation operations in calculation-intensive workbooks and large external data queries can be supported.

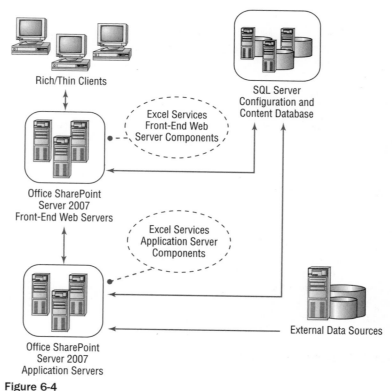

Figure 6-4

Single-Server and Farm Topology Comparison

There are no hard-and-fast rules as to how an Excel Services topology must be used. The combination of operations and workbook features that you want to use will, for the most part, dictate the type of deployment you need. The following table compares the single-server, small farm, medium farm, and large farm topologies.

Criteria	Single-Server	Small Farm	Medium Farm	Large Farm
Concurrent users for Excel Services	Low	Low	Medium	High
Workbooks	Not calculation-intensive	Not calculation-intensive	Not calculation-intensive	Calculation-intensive
Number of unique workbooks loaded by Excel Services	Low	Low	Low	High
Workbook external data queries	Can return small data sets	Can return small data sets	Can return small data sets	Can return large data sets

Intranet and Extranet

Figure 6-5 shows an example of Excel Services in an intranet topology. The Excel Services applications servers are behind a firewall separate from the front-end servers, SQL Server configuration, and content database. This provides an additional security layer for the ECS located within the intranet, as well as the external data sources that are isolated behind an additional firewall.

Figure 6-6 shows an example of Excel Services in an extranet topology. In this example, the Excel Services application servers, SQL Server configuration, content database, and front-end servers are together behind the perimeter firewall.

High-Performance Computing

Windows Compute Cluster Server (CCS) 2003 and Excel Services can be deployed together to take advantage of the ability of CCS to run parallel, high performance computing (HPC) applications to solve complex computations. In this topology, the installation of MOSS looks a lot like a small farm, where each compute cluster node contains both the Excel Services WFE components and the application server Excel Calculation Services components. A collection of compute cluster nodes creates a CCS compute cluster. All of the nodes share a SQL Server 2005 configuration and content database. A separate server (referred to as the *CCS head node*) hosts the compute cluster scheduler, which will schedule and load balance jobs across the nodes in the CCS compute cluster. Figure 6-7 shows an HPC topology.

A CCS deployment with Excel Services is best suited for scenarios where calculation-intensive operations can be performed in parallel. Each ECS on the compute cluster nodes works in isolation on the jobs it receives from the scheduler. You can find more information about Windows CCS 2003 at www.microsoft .com/windowsserver2003/ccs/default.mspx.

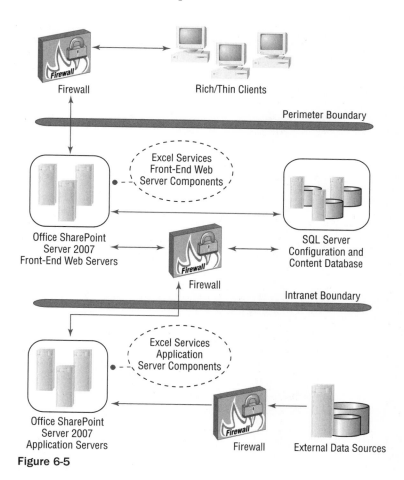

Figure 6-5

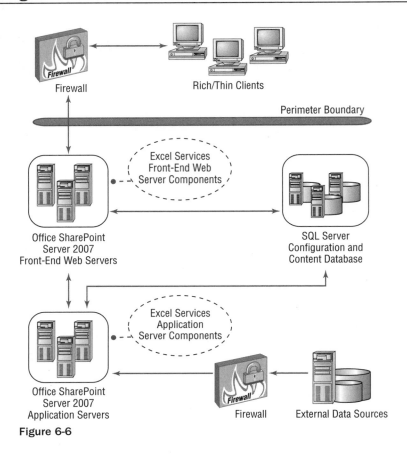

Figure 6-6

Capacity Planning

Capacity planning is a process where the minimum server hardware is identified to support the expected load on the system. The goal of the capacity planning exercise is to deploy a system that can support the Excel Services' operations in terms of throughput, response time, and availability of the system. In this section, the capacity planning discussion focuses specifically on the Excel Services system, and not on the other services installed by MOSS.

You need to consider a number of factors when addressing capacity planning for Excel Services, including the number of concurrent users, the number of active sessions, the number of workbooks, and even the characteristics of the workbooks. The challenge in capacity planning is coming up with the inputs. How well is the expected Excel Services usage understood? Existing deployed systems may hold answers that can assist you. For example, there may be Excel workbooks intended for Excel Services in a SharePoint site or in various file shares.

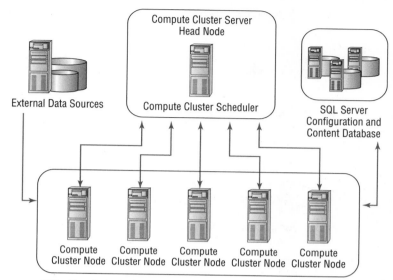

Figure 6-7

This discussion cannot specify the exact hardware requirements that will support your expected Excel Services load. However, you can use the information contained here as a guide when you're thinking about capacity planning for Excel Services. There are no magic rules and formulas where capacity planning answers are provided after a question-and-answer session.

> *To get the proper understanding of how your scenarios will be handled by MOSS (and, specifically, Excel Services), you should use an actual Excel Services deployment to try out a representative sample of the load to be supported by your targeted system.*

Considerations

The performance of Excel Services depends on how the system is used. Because there is such a wide range of usage patterns for Excel Services, you should evaluate and understand each area that will affect the capacity of Excel Services.

Begin by asking yourself the following questions about the areas that will impact Excel Services capacity:

❑   What are the characteristics of the workbooks to be loaded by Excel Services? This includes file format, size, quantity, content formatting, features (such as conditional formatting), and how often the workbook changes.

❑   How many users will Excel Services serve at peak?

❑   How many sessions will be active at peak?

❑   What types of operations are users of Excel Services performing? This includes user roles (permissions), actions being performed (such as PivotTable drill operations), and interactivity.

❑   How much throughput is needed from Excel Services? What are the response time expectations for Excel Services?

Addressing the capacity requirements of the system may require that Excel Services be scaled out, scaled up, or possibly both. The direction your system takes will come down to the answers to the previously noted capacity questions. The following sections discuss how the answers affect capacity.

For Excel Services, to *scale out* implies adding additional servers to the farm to benefit Excel Services. You can either add front-end servers where the Excel Services front-end web components are located, or add application servers where the ECS components are located.

In Excel Services, to *scale up* commonly applies to increasing system memory, but it could also apply to increasing available processors. You can scale up an ECS by replacing an existing four-processor server with an eight-processor server.

The administrative controls provided by Excel Services, as well as the best-practice implementation directed at workbook authors and consumers, can also affect Excel Services capacity. Ask yourself these questions:

❑   Which security model will be used for accessing external data? How many different sets of credentials will be used when querying results from a data source? Will the use of trusted data connections be enforced? Will ECS data cache lifetimes be long or short?

❑   Will SharePoint roles be used extensively, or will most users be operating with elevated privileges? How much interactivity will the typical user perform when using the EWA? Will EWA toolbars be customized and tailored to expose only relevant and necessary functionality?

❑   How many dashboards will be used with the EWA? How many sessions will each dashboard generate? How long will a typical dashboard session last? How often will sessions be private instead of shared? How many concurrent active sessions will each user be allowed to create?

❑   Will authors create calculation intensive workbooks? Will UDFs be used? How often will volatile functions be used, and will the volatile function cache lifetime setting be long or short?

❑   Will the Excel Services Web Service be available to a large part of your workforce? Will code authors consistently close sessions and be responsible users of the API?

Affecting Capacity

One of the main areas you need to focus on when capacity planning is the amount of memory consumed by the ECS process. The second area is CPU usage. The ECS is a memory-intensive service. The ECS can also be CPU-intensive, but that is typically isolated to performing heavy calculation operations. If you are not accustomed to seeing a process size grow beyond 1GB, then you may be a bit alarmed when you see the ECS process size after servicing requests for a while. In a 64-bit environment, the process size is allowed to grow even more, provided system resources are available to the process.

The following sections provide background on what contributes to the ECS process size, as well as what can contribute to the CPU usage. Understanding the ECS architecture discussed in Chapter 3 will help you apply the concepts discussed here.

ECS Process Size

Excel Services was designed to cache workbooks and other objects in memory to improve performance. The ECS process size can (and most likely will) become one of the larger (if not the largest) process executing on the application server. Consequently, the process becomes a focal point during capacity planning and performance discussions.

Disk Size

Excel Services loads workbooks that are saved in either the .xlsx (Excel Workbook) or the .xlsb (Excel Binary Workbook) file format. The Excel Workbook file format is the Excel 2007 default, and is an XML-based file format. As the name implies, the Excel Binary Workbook file format is a binary format. Workbooks saved by previous releases of the Excel client are not loaded by Excel Services.

The workbooks saved in either of the two supported file formats have a disk size that is significantly different when compared to the Excel 11 file disk size for the same workbook. Both the Excel Workbook and the Excel Binary Workbook file formats typically consume less disk space than the same file saved in an Excel 11 file format. The size difference depends on the workbook characteristics.

The following table provides a comparison of three workbooks and their file size on disk. The primary difference between the workbooks is the used range for each: A1:J5000, A1:AD8500, and A1:AN12500. Each workbook consists of numbers populated in each cell in the used range with no cell containing more than 11 characters. Ten percent of the cells contain formulas and 70 percent of the cells contain number formatting or cell formatting. These workbooks are a simple example, and every workbook that is compared in this manner will show different ratios between the two file formats, depending on the contents and characteristics of the workbooks.

Workbook	.xlsb Size (Bytes)	.xlsx Size (Bytes)
F1	196,608	425,984
F2	294,912	1,736,704
F3	589,824	3,342,336

Each workbook loaded by Excel Services is written to the ECS local workbook disk cache for the ECS loading the workbook. If the workbook disk cache feature is disabled, then the workbook is removed from the workbook disk cache when the associated sessions are closed. You can configure the size of the workbook disk cache through the Excel Services administration page, which is covered in Chapter 7. The amount of disk space consumed by each workbook written to the workbook disk cache depends on the workbook's contents and characteristics. However, there is nearly a 1:1 ratio of the workbook's size when it is saved to disk and when it is saved to the workbook disk cache.

When the ECS saves a copy of the workbook to the local workbook disk cache, the workbook disk size is essentially the same size as when the Excel client saved the workbook to disk.

Each ECS requires a workbook disk cache. The quantity and size of the workbooks being loaded by the ECS dictate how much physical disk space is required to support all of the workbooks. As workbooks get updated by workbook authors, new versions of the workbooks are saved to the workbook disk cache. The outdated versions of the workbooks remain in the workbook disk cache until evictions are triggered by the ECS, which occurs when the maximum size of the workbook disk cache is reached or the ECS process is restarted.

Memory Size

Each ECS has an associated w3wp.exe process, also referred to as the *ECS process*. The size of the ECS process is indicated by the w3wp.exe private bytes performance counter. You can use the Windows Task Manager or Performance Monitor to see the size of the ECS process in real time. The Memory Usage column in the task manager represents the ECS process size.

Follow these steps to use the Task Manager to view the ECS process size:

1. Use the Windows tasklist.exe utility to identify the w3wp.exe process that is associated with the ECS. From a cmd.exe window, enter **tasklist /FI "MODULES eq xlsrv.dll"**.

    The output will look like this:

    ```
    Image Name                    PID Session Name       Session#    Mem Usage
    ========================= ======== ================ =========== ============
    w3wp.exe                     3232 RDP-Tcp#3                   0     95,440 K
    ```

2. Click Start ➪ Run.

3. Enter **taskmgr** and click OK.

4. Select the Process tab and then click the Image Name column to sort the list of processes.

5. Scroll the list to locate the w3wp process ID (PID) that was returned by the `tasklist` command you executed in step 1. (In the output shown as an example in step 1, the w3wp PID associated with the ECS was 3232.)

In addition to saving a copy of the workbook to the ECS workbook disk cache, the ECS also loads the workbook into memory. This is the w3wp process memory that you can monitor by watching the private bytes, as described in the previous steps. Each workbook that gets loaded into memory impacts the ECS process size, and after the workbook is loaded into memory, it is referred to as the *base workbook*.

Consider the workbooks listed in the previous table, and assume that the workbooks do not yet exist in the ECS workbook memory cache (the base workbook does not yet exist). When the open workbook call is made for each workbook, the size of the ECS process increases as the workbook gets loaded into memory.

The following table shows the amount of ECS memory consumed by each of the three base workbooks as a percentage of the workbook's disk size. The amount of memory needed for workbooks depends on the content of the workbook, which encompasses data, formatting, and the Excel features contained in the workbook.

	Workbook F1	Workbook F2	Workbook F3
.xlsb 32-bit server	200 percent	375 percent	350 percent
.xlsb 64-bit server	290 percent	560 percent	540 percent
.xlsx 32-bit server	85 percent	65 percent	60 percent
.xlsx 64-bit server	124 percent	96 percent	92 percent

This table demonstrates that the size of the base workbook in memory is typically less than the size of the xlsx workbook on disk, but more than the xlsb workbook on disk. The xlsx F1 workbook is an exception. A key point to be made here is that there isn't a clear method of predicting how much ECS process memory will be needed for a workbook, even if the disk size is known. Ideally, you can use the ECS to load workbooks that are representative of a broad set of workbooks used by your organization so you can accurately determine how your workbooks will affect the ECS process size.

The ECS process memory needed to load the same workbook in either the Excel Workbook or the Excel Binary Workbook file format is essentially the same. However, the use of the Excel Binary Workbook file format will significantly improve ECS throughput and response times.

Excel Services successfully loads only workbooks that do not contain unsupported features. If an unsupported feature is encountered during the loading process, the operation and open workbook call fail. Excel Services is designed to release the memory associated with loading a workbook in the event of a failed load operation. Avoid loading workbooks that contain unsupported features, because it unnecessarily consumes server resources with no benefit. (Chapter 4 discussed the unsupported features that can cause a workbook to fail when loaded.)

The three example workbooks used in this chapter are shared by all users after the workbook is loaded into memory. This is because the workbooks do not contain any features that would cause a private state to be created when the workbook is opened. (Chapter 3 discussed workbook states.)

Each of the workbooks is configured for manual calculation and each contains the use of a volatile =Rand() function. When a manual calculation operation is invoked for the workbook and the ECS performs the calculation, the size of the ECS process increases. This is because the workbook state changes and the current user's workbook is no longer shared between sessions. The session that performed the manual calculation now has a private copy of the workbook in memory. This increase in ECS memory size is incurred for anyone who subsequently manually calculates the workbook and creates a private copy in memory.

Performing an operation on a workbook that changes the workbook state to private results in a corresponding ECS memory size increase that is roughly equivalent to 50 percent of the base workbook memory size.

In addition to calculation, other types of interactivity can cause a private copy of the workbook to be created in memory. Examples include pivot drill operations, using parameters, and refreshing external data connections where the credentials for accessing the external data source are not shared.

Workbook Characteristics

Having a good understanding of the types of workbooks that will be loaded by the ECS increases the effectiveness of capacity planning. In most cases, settling for a pretty good understanding or even being able to rule out certain types of workbooks will be about all you can hope for. Unless you have very narrow use for the ECS, or already possess the majority of the workbooks to be used by the ECS, almost all of the Excel features supported by the ECS can be used for workbook authoring, provided, of course, that you configure the server to support them.

The following sections describe a few of the features that you should consider during capacity planning.

External Data

Here are a few areas to consider for external data:

❑ *The size of the data* — The size of the result set returned by a data query impacts the ECS process size as well as the CPU of the application server. As rows and columns in the result set expand, the amount of memory used to cache the data increases. The ECS also consumes more CPU as the result set grows, because it takes more processing time and power to work with the larger number of rows and columns of data. Generating the HTML to send to the EWA is also more expensive as the EWA grid becomes more populated with data. Of course, the time necessary to stream the response to the EWA is closely tied to the size of the package.

❑ *Data cache sharing* — The number of unique credentials used for the data queries impacts the amount of memory devoted to caching the query results. The memory consumed specifically for caching of data query results increases in relation to the number of different credentials used for querying the available data sources. This is because there is less sharing of the query results that are cached by the ECS. (Chapter 5 provided a detailed discussion of external data.)

❑ *The refresh frequency of the data source* — Knowing the frequency at which data sources return updated results for the data sources that will be trusted by the ECS allows you to optimize the ECS External Data Cache Lifetime setting for maximum efficiency. If, for example, the external data source will have new data every 60 minutes, you should configure the External Data Cache Lifetime to use ECS cached query results for approximately 60 minutes. Allowing the cache to be updated more often isn't going to provide the workbooks with any newer data, yet the ECS is expending resources refreshing the data cache. The more often the results can be retrieved directly from the ECS data cache, the better the performance will be.

❑ *The data cache timeout frequency* — Each workbook author can set a refresh rate for the workbook, which could have the workbook configured to refresh the data when the workbook is opened by the ECS, or to refresh at a set frequency after it is opened. The ECS External Data Cache Lifetime setting determines when the data source gets queried.

Calculation

Evaluate workbooks for their calculation intensity. Consider the following during your capacity planning:

❑ Calculating workbooks on the ECS can be a CPU-intensive operation. Pay special attention to workbooks that have long calculation times. This will help you account for the increased time at potentially high CPU when these workbooks are calculated. The ECS can continue to successfully respond to other requests while the calculation operations are in process, but throughput will most likely degrade during those periods.

❏ In addition to using the built-in Excel functions, the ECS supports user defined functions (UDFs). The trusted UDF-managed assemblies are custom code called from workbooks. You should have an understanding of how each UDF can impact server resources. (Chapter 14 provides further information about the UDF feature.)

❏ Workbooks can be authored to calculate in automatic or manual mode. An automatic calculation workbook is very convenient, but it may also perform unnecessary calculation operations. You might want to set the calculation mode to manual for workbooks with longer calculation times. This can serve as a real convenience to workbook consumers, because they won't have to wait for a calculation operation to finish unless they initiate the operation themselves. The ECS also provides an administration feature that allows you to set the calculation mode at the trusted file location level, overriding the workbook's calculation mode. (Chapter 7 provides additional details.)

❏ You can further control the behavior of the automatic calculation mode for workbooks with the Volatile Function Cache Lifetime setting for each trusted file location. You can allow workbooks to use the automatic mode for calculations, and allow multiple users of the same workbook to share the calculation results. (Chapter 7 provides additional details.)

Formatting

The amount of formatting applied to the workbook and its contents can increase the size of a workbook as well as the CPU usage. Consider the following:

❏ Formatting increases the size of the response, which must be sent to the client when rendering a workbook using the EWA, or when providing a formatted data response to an API `getrange()` call, for example.

❏ By default, the EWA Web Part renders 75 rows and 20 columns. You can configure the number of rows and columns for each EWA. As the grid size increases, so does the response time, and the effect of the formatting becomes more evident. Additional load will be present on the WFE as the grid size increases.

❏ Conditional formatting that must be evaluated by the ECS has a direct impact on the capacity of the ECS in terms of CPU.

Updates

Another aspect of the workbooks to consider is the frequency with which the workbooks will be modified in the ECS trusted location. When the ECS gets an open workbook request, the workbook in the trusted location is checked to determine if it is newer than the copy in the ECS workbook disk cache. Any time an update is found, a new copy of the workbook is loaded into the workbook disk cache and into the memory of the ECS process.

Take into consideration not only how often workbooks will get updated, but also how frequently they will be used. For example, users shouldn't be updating a workbook that is used by a dashboard as a home page for a large number of users during periods of high traffic.

User Actions

The designers and consumers of the workbooks should play a big role in your capacity planning. The more you can learn about their intentions, the more you will be able to plan your deployment to meet the capacity expectations for your system. By proactively using the various administrative configuration options for Excel Services (discussed in detail in Chapter 7), the actions allowed by the designers and consumers of the workbooks can be somewhat controlled, which translates into more control over the anticipated capacity of Excel Services.

Each EWA Web Part creates a session when a workbook is opened and subsequently rendered. As Share-Point sites, pages, and dashboards are created, the number of EWA Web Parts added to each page should be monitored closely. The ECS process size can grow and get out of hand very quickly when each visitor to a site is creating many sessions. By default, the EWA will not explicitly close a session. Instead, the session life is controlled by the trusted location's session timeout setting, which could be up to 5 minutes from the last user action if the default settings are still in effect. You can configure each EWA embedded in SharePoint to reduce the session lifetime, which helps minimize the number of sessions opened by each user at any point in time. To do this, use the Close Session Before Opening A New One property exposed through the EWA Modify Shared Web Part feature.

A session is more controllable when you use the Excel Services Web Service. Every API open workbook call should eventually be followed by a close workbook call. This provides the best session-management practice because the session will end immediately, thereby releasing ECS resources promptly.

Determining the right amount of EWA functionality for site visitors can go a long way toward getting more out of the available ECS and WFE resources. You can configure an EWA Web Part to support various levels of functionality. For example, you can hide the EWA toolbar, which prevents the site visitor from performing any of the operations that would otherwise be available (such as a calculation or open operation in Excel). If removing the toolbar completely isn't appropriate, then leave the toolbar, but remove specific toolbar menu commands. You can also curtail navigation and interactivity within the grid to suit the needs of the specific EWA use. You can access these and other features through the EWA Modify Shared Web Part.

Maybe reducing EWA functionality for all visitors to a site is a bit too drastic. Instead, you may want to use SharePoint permissions to control the functionality allowed by the site users. Using this method, you can ensure that a certain class of users on the site has less impact on the ECS and WFE because their permissions restrict the type of operations they can perform when interacting with the EWA.

Concurrent Users

Another aspect of capacity planning for Excel Services is to determine how many users will be accessing Excel Services concurrently. The term "concurrently" has a couple of different meanings that should be understood.

The first meaning refers to how many users could be accessing the WFE at the same time, such as when an e-mail is sent to a large distribution list with a link to a workbook on Excel Services and many recipients of that e-mail click the link simultaneously (or nearly so). Will the WFE be able to handle the concurrent client connection load at that point in time? Or do the availability expectations of the system dictate that it is okay to be unable to service all requests in this type of situation?

The second meaning refers to how many active users could be using the system at the same time. This scenario targets the day-to-day peak activity of Excel Services. In this context, all users have at least one session that is active or has not timed out because of inactivity. For this scenario, the concurrent client connection load on the WFE remains a point of interest. The ECS is of interest as well, because the number of sessions available to support the peak activity will impact the ECS process size and CPU as it responds to the various requests.

Mitigation

Eventually, the Excel Services capacity planning results will start to come into focus and the capacity limitations for the system will become evident. Scaling is one available option to alleviate capacity bottlenecks. A second option is to ensure that the system is optimally configured for the load being applied.

Adding Resources

The primary bottleneck specific to Excel Services is the ECS process size or CPU utilization on either the WFE or the application server. A few external components could possibly be limiting as well, and you can fix some of those by adjusting the configurable settings.

High CPU utilization on the WFE is a signal that additional WFE servers may be needed in the farm. For example, you may encounter high CPU utilization on the WFE because of a large number of concurrent users, expensive EWA-rendering operations, or other SharePoint activity. You can add WFE servers to scale out, thereby increasing the capacity of the WFE servers. Monitor the SQL server hosting the configuration and content database to ensure that it is capable of supporting the requests being generated by the WFE servers.

The ECS may encounter high CPU utilization when performing calculation operations or when initially loading workbooks. A high volume of concurrent user activity can also contribute to high CPU usage. You can add ECS application servers to scale out the farm and alleviate both CPU and memory limitations. You can also increase available memory on an ECS application server to address ECS process size limitations.

It is important to note that the ECS load-balancing scheme may contribute to higher CPU and memory utilization on one ECS, while others in the farm appear to be underutilized. The Workbook URL load-balancing scheme can lead to this condition. The Workbook URL load-balancing scheme uses a hash based upon the workbook URL to determine which ECS will service the request. The scheme does not factor in the existing load on the ECS, so load may not be balanced across all available ECS servers.

Configuration

There are two types of configuration options: the Excel Services provided configuration settings, and the configuration settings for components on which Excel Services is dependent. The available Excel Services configuration settings are discussed in Chapter 7, and the various configuration settings that could affect capacity are discussed throughout this chapter. The following sections describe configuration settings that are external to Excel Services, but can provide a positive impact on capacity under some circumstances.

Application Pools

Each application pool has a few properties that you can use to maintain a healthy environment. The application pool associated with the ECS is SharedServices1. You can configure it in a few different ways to control the size of the ECS process.

The setting for recycling worker processes lets you specify a time when the application pool for the ECS will be recycled. This releases all memory, and affects system performance because all of the ECS-cached objects have been released and the ECS is essentially starting from a clean state.

Another point to consider is that any sessions that are active when the process recycles will lose their state. Anyone actively working with a workbook on Excel Services will be forced to reload the workbook and begin anew.

Follow these steps to locate the setting to recycle the process:

1. Click Start ⇨ All Programs ⇨ Administrative Tools ⇨ Internet Information Services (IIS) Manager.

2. Locate the IIS Manager tree and click the plus sign (+) next to the server name.

3. Click the plus sign (+) next to the Application Pools folder.

4. Right-click the SharedServices1 object in the tree, and then click Properties.

5. On the Recycling tab of the ShareServices1 Properties dialog box, locate the "Recycle worker processes at the following times" control. Specify the time when you want the ECS process automatically recycled.

Memory Fragmentation

A system that has experienced a high volume of requests over an extended period of time could wind up in a state where requests for memory are failing, even though indications are that the system should have sufficient memory to operate. This condition may occur more readily on 32-bit systems, given that less memory is available on these systems when compared to 64-bit systems. The `HeapDecommitFreeBlockThreshold` registry key should only be used on systems with greater than 1GB of RAM. See `http://support .microsoft.com/kb/315407` for additional information.

Available Connections

The WFE server may not be able to communicate with the ECS under periods of intense stress. Failures of this nature may occur when HTTP requests are opening and closing connections at a rate high enough to consume all of the available connections. Even though the connection is closed and is no longer being used, it is not immediately returned to the pool of available connections, and the available connections can become exhausted.

An IIS configuration setting allows you to increase the connections available in the pool, which will make this problem less prevalent. See `http://support.microsoft.com/kb/925714` for additional information. Use `regedit.exe` to create and set the registry entry for `MaxUserPort`. For example, the following registry entry represents a `MaxUserPort` setting of `20000`:

```
[HKEY_LOCAL_MACHINE\SYSTEM\CurrentControlSet\Services\Tcpip\Parameters]
"MaxUserPort"=dword:00002710
```

A second setting that is closely related to the `MaxUserPort` setting is `TcpTimedWaitDelay`. You can use this setting alone or in conjunction with `MaxUserPort` to make more connections available. The `TcpTimedWaitDelay` setting determines how long the sockets wait in the TIME_WAIT state, with lower values signifying less wait time. A lower `TcpTimedWaitDelay` setting makes the closed connections available sooner because they spend less time in the TIME_WAIT state.

Use `regedit.exe` to create and set the registry entry for `TcpTimedWaitDelay`. For example, the following registry entry represents a `TcpTimedWaitDelay` setting of 15:

```
[HKEY_LOCAL_MACHINE\SYSTEM\CurrentControlSet\Services\Tcpip\Parameters]
"TcpTimedWaitDelay"=dword:0000000f
```

HTTP Two-Connection Limit

Requests from the WFE to the ECS may time out. This behavior may be seen during periods when the ECS request response times are high. The issue here is that the ASP.NET threads have all been consumed, and the waiting threads are timing out while waiting for a thread to become available. You can allow more calls by increasing the `maxconnection` attribute on the `<ConnectionManagement>` element in `Machine.config`. The default setting is 2. A side effect to increasing the `maxconnection` attribute is increased CPU utilization, because more requests come into the ECS. If the increased response times are a result of already high CPU utilization, then this change would not be suitable.

To modify the `maxconnection` attribute, insert the following code into the .NET v2 `Machine.config` file. The example shown here sets the `maxconnection` limit to `10`:

```
<system.net>
<connectionManagement>
 <add address="*" maxconnection="10"/>
</connectionManagement>
</system.net>
```

Long Running Requests

After a long running request is successfully completed by the ECS, the WFE may fail the request because the thread is aborted. This situation may arise for any request that does not finish before the ASP.NET request execution timeout setting is exceeded. The default setting for the ASP.NET request execution timeout setting is 110 seconds. An ECS request, such as `RecalcAll`, may require more than 110 seconds to complete. The ECS will successfully complete the request, but the failure can occur when the response is propagated through the WFE proxy.

Increasing the ASP.NET timeout setting will prevent the operation from failing. Use the following steps to change the ASP.NET request execution timeout setting on the WFE server:

1. Click Start ⇨ All Programs ⇨ Administrative Tools ⇨ Internet Information Services (IIS) Manager.

2. Locate the IIS Manager tree and click the plus sign (+) next to the server name.

3. Click the plus sign (+) next to the Web Sites folder.

4. Click the plus sign (+) next to the SSP object (such as SharedServices1).

5. Right-click the ExcelCalculationServer folder in the tree and then click Properties.

6. Click the Edit Configuration button on the ASP.NET tab of the ExcelCalculationServer Properties dialog.

7. Locate the Request Execution Timeout input field on the Application tab of the ASP.NET Configuration Settings dialog box. Use this control to change the timeout value.

Summary

This chapter outlined the Excel Services topologies, from the single-server to the large farm. A couple of other deployments were called-out as well, including the high-performance computing solution.

This chapter also examined Excel Services capacity planning. The primary concerns for capacity planning were outlined. Configuration and scale options were noted to assist with alleviating bottlenecks, or minimizing their impact on the system.

You should now have a good grasp of the following:

❏ Excel Services topologies

❏ The ways that Excel workbooks can affect system capacity

❏ How authors and consumers of workbooks can impact capacity

❏ The primary Excel Services areas that affect capacity planning

❏ The configuration settings that impact capacity

Chapter 7 discusses Excel Services administration and examines each of the configuration settings.

Administration of Excel Services

In Chapter 2, you learned how to set up and deploy Excel Services. You learned that very few administrative changes are necessary to render basic workbooks with Excel Web Access (EWA). To get the most out of your system, you need to be aware of the myriad of settings available to optimize the system for the scenarios that you ultimately want to support. Monitoring your system will become more important as the reliance on your Excel Services deployment increases. This chapter describes the administrative and monitoring features that are available to you. The international administration point of view is also covered.

In this chapter, you learn about the following:

- ❑ Excel Services Administration Pages
- ❑ How to use Administer Excel Services
- ❑ Key components of Unified Logging Service (ULS), including trace logs and event logs
- ❑ The Diagnostic Logging Page and how to administer ULS
- ❑ How to use performance counters to monitor Excel Services
- ❑ How to use language packs to extend Excel Services international support
- ❑ How to use the Data Culture to control workbook data formatting

Configuring

Your first administrative task in Excel Services will most likely be to create a Trusted File Location. This is very predictable because it is the only Excel Services property with a default setting that actually prevents Excel Services from working after you complete the Microsoft Office SharePoint Server (MOSS) setup. (One exception is the evaluation version of MOSS, which will automatically create one trusted location for you.) The rest of the Excel Services settings are exposed through the Central Administration Web interface or through the command-line interface. You use these settings to enable additional features and/or tune your deployment.

This section introduces all of the Excel Services administration settings that can be configured through Central Administration. A collection of web pages provides the interface for working with these Shared Service Provider (SSP) configuration settings.

The discussion continues with the Excel Services administration settings by covering the command line equivalent to the web page administration of Excel Services.

This section focuses primarily on Excel Services settings and not the shared settings found elsewhere in Central Administration, or as part of a SharePoint site (such as SSO or document library properties). Although the shared settings can have an impact on Excel Services, they are not the focus of this section, and are discussed throughout this book as the topics present themselves.

Using Central Administration

The administration pages devoted specifically to Excel Services have been separated into five key areas:

❑   Excel Services Settings

❑   Trusted File Locations

❑   Trusted Data Connection Libraries (DCLs)

❑   Trusted Data Providers

❑   User-Defined Function (UDF) Assemblies

To get to these areas, you use a browser on the Shared Services Provider (SSP) administration page. You access this page through Central Administration.

Excel Services Settings refers to the collection of properties that you can access through the Shared Services Administration's ExcelServerSettings.aspx page. Collectively, the five top-level pages noted here can also be referred to as the Excel Services Settings. To keep all of this clear, the term "Excel Services Settings" is used in this chapter to refer to the properties presented on the ExcelServerSettings.aspx page.

Each SSP has its own set of configuration values for each of the Excel Services properties. The settings captured by the Excel Services Settings administration area are scoped to the SSP. Additional settings are available through the Trusted File Locations administration area, and they are scoped to the trusted location within the SSP.

Editing Excel Services Properties

Follow these steps to navigate to the area of Central Administration where you can access each of the five Excel Services administration pages:

1.   Start Central Administration by clicking Start ➪ All Programs ➪ Microsoft Office Server ➪ SharePoint 3.0 Central Administration.

2.   From the Central Administration default page (see Figure 7-1), navigate to the Shared Services Administration page for the SSP you want to configure. The left side of the Central Administration home page contains links to each SSP that exists in your farm. Click the SSP that you want to configure. (If you performed a default installation, the only available SSP is SharedServices1.)

The home page for Shared Services Administration (see Figure 7-2) of your SSP should now be displayed. The Excel Services Settings section on the right side of the page contains links to the five key areas mentioned earlier. These five links represent the entry points to the Excel Services administration pages.

You need to create a trusted location to really get started with Excel Services, so the administration of trusted file locations is covered next.

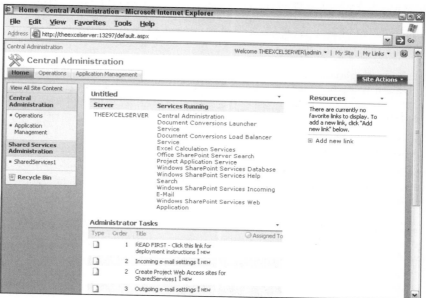

Figure 7-1

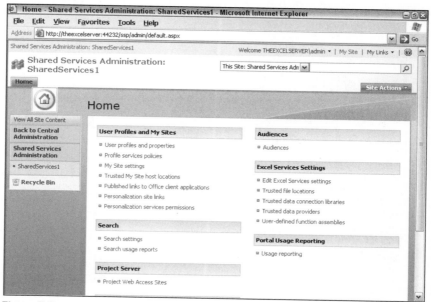

Figure 7-2

Trusted File Locations

Excel Services loads workbooks only from locations that have been explicitly added to the Trusted File Locations list. This list is empty by default. You must create at least one trusted location to begin using Excel Services. The scope of trusted file locations is limited to the SSP under which they are created.

After you get past the hands-on learning stage and are ready to consider deploying a production server, some amount of trusted location planning would be beneficial. For some deployments, you may want to create a top-level trusted location of `https://` and then one-off trusted locations for the few scenarios where additional control is necessary. The other extreme is to avoid the use of `https://` as a trusted location and commit to many trusted locations to meet your needs.

Something else to keep in mind as you start working with trusted locations is the permissions associated with each of the trusted locations where you will be storing your workbooks. You need to apply the proper rights and roles to the trusted locations to ensure that your workbooks are as accessible only as you intended them to be.

Trusted Location Properties

Follow the directions provided previously in this chapter to navigate through Central Administration until you arrive at the SSP home page. Then click the Trusted File Locations link in the Excel Services Settings section on the right side of the page.

The ExcelServerTrustedLocations.aspx page is displayed (see Figure 7-3). You can use this page to add a trusted location, edit an existing trusted location, delete an existing trusted location, or simply see the properties for the existing trusted locations.

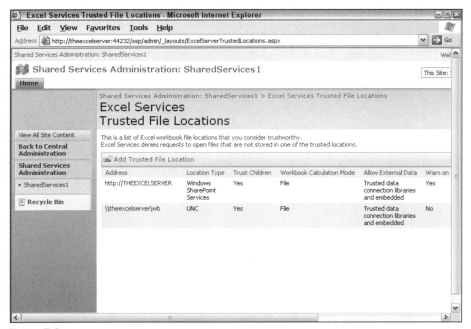

Figure 7-3

To edit or delete an existing trusted location, open the edit control block (ECB) menu associated with the corresponding trusted location entry in the list, and select the operation you want to perform. To create a new trusted location, use the Add Trusted File Location link at the top of the trusted locations list.

Location

As shown in Figure 7-4, the Location section of the page contains settings for the following trusted file location properties:

- ❏ *Address* — This is the full path to the trusted location and can be a SharePoint site or document library, UNC path, or web folder. Entries such as `http://` or `https://` are supported as valid addresses and indicate to Excel Services that all content in the Windows SharePoint Services (WSS) content database is to be trusted. You cannot enter a local folder path (such as E:\TheWorkbooks) as the address. Following are examples of valid addresses for a trusted file location:

    - ❏ \\TheServer\TheShare\TheWorkbooks
    - ❏ http://TheExcelServer/TheSite
    - ❏ http://TheExcelServer/TheSite/TheDocLib

- ❏ *Location Type* — Use this to identify the storage type for the trusted location. You have three options: Windows SharePoint Services, UNC, and HTTP. If the syntax of the Address field does not correspond with the Location Type field, the trusted location Save operation will return an error.

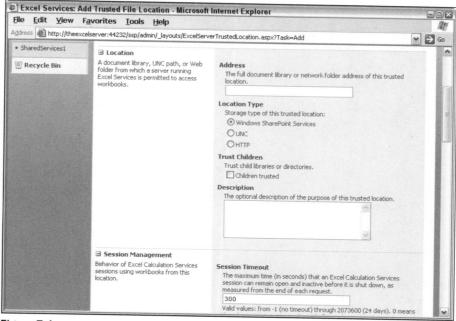

Figure 7-4

❑ *Trust Children* — If you want to trust the children (sites, libraries, or folders) of your trusted location, select the Children Trusted check box. The default setting is to not trust children.

❑ *Description* — This is an optional field that you can use for documentation of the trusted location.

Session Management

As shown in Figure 7-5, the Session Management section of the page contains settings for the following trusted file location properties:

❑ *Session Timeout* — The maximum amount of time (seconds) that a session remains active before it is timed out, as measured from the end of each request using the session. The default value is 300 seconds. This timeout value becomes applicable following the first interactive request for the session (such as a PivotTable drill operation or calculating the workbook). The Short Session Timeout (which is explained next) is the applicable session timeout value when a workbook is initially loaded and before any user interactivity occurs. The Session Timeout property can have the following values:

    ❑ 0 — The session will expire immediately upon completion of the request.

    ❑ -1 — The session will never timeout.

    ❑ 1 through 2073600 (24 days) — The session will expire after this number of seconds.

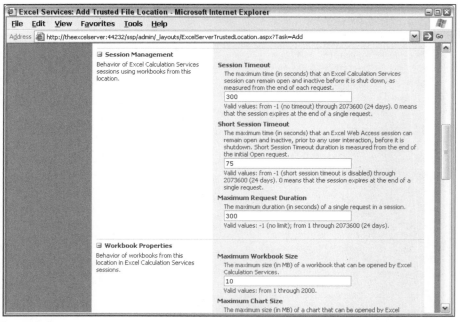

Figure 7-5

❑ *Short Session Timeout* — The maximum amount of time (seconds) that a session remains active, as measured from the end of the EWA request. The timeout is measured from the end of each subsequent request in the session. The Excel Services Web Service does not use the Short Session Timeout. The Short Session Timeout is only until an interactive request is made, and then the Session Timeout setting is used for the duration of the session. The default value is 75 seconds. The valid values for the Short Session Timeout property are the same as the valid values for the Session Timeout.

❑ *Maximum Request Duration* — The maximum amount of time (seconds) that a request can execute without finishing before the Excel Calculation Server attempts to cancel the request. The default value is 300 seconds. The Maximum Request Duration property can have the following values:

  ❑ -1 — No maximum duration is placed on a request.

  ❑ 1 through 2073600 (24 days) — The session will expire after this number of seconds.

Workbook Properties

As shown in Figure 7-6, the Workbook Properties section of the page contains settings for the following trusted file location properties:

❑ *Maximum Workbook Size* — The maximum size (MB) of a workbook that the ECS will load. The default value is 10. Valid values for the Maximum Workbook Size property are 1 through 2000.

❑ *Maximum Chart Size* — The maximum size (MB) of a chart within a workbook that the ECS will load. The default value is 10. The value must be a positive integer.

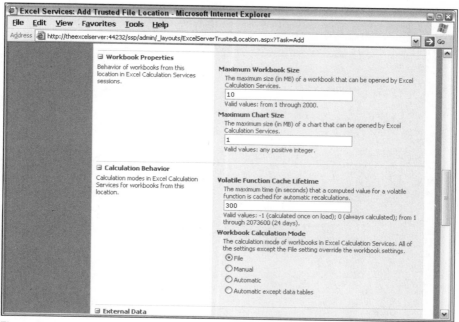

Figure 7-6

Calculation Behavior

As shown in Figure 7-7, the Calculation Behavior section of the page contains settings for the following trusted file location properties:

❑ *Volatile Function Cache Lifetime* — The maximum amount of time (seconds) that a computed value for a volatile function will be cached for automatic recalculations. This setting has no bearing if the workbook is loaded in manual calculation mode. The default value is 300. You can set the following values for this property:

  ❑ -1 — Calculated once when the server initially loads the workbook. Everyone receives this version and the values from the calculation that occurred when the workbook was first loaded by the server. You can still cause the workbook to calculate again, but you will be the only one who sees the results.

  ❑ 0 — Calculated when the server initially loads the workbook and each time someone asks for the workbook.

  ❑ 1 through 2073600 (24 days) — Calculated when the server initially loads the workbook. The server calculates the workbook on subsequent requests for the workbook if the cache lifetime is exceeded. New requests for the workbook receive this version.

❑ *Workbook Calculation Mode* — This setting determines how the ECS calculates workbooks when loading them. You have the following four options for this setting:

  ❑ *File* — This is the default. It uses the calculation mode specified by the workbook.

  ❑ *Manual* — Overrides the workbook's calculation mode. Only manual calculation is supported, so the workbook will never calculate when loaded by the ECS.

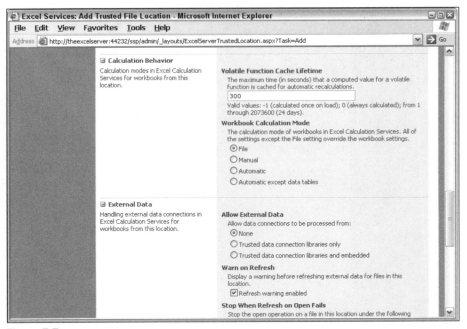

Figure 7-7

❑ *Automatic* — Overrides the workbook's calculation mode. Only automatic calculation is supported, so the workbook is always calculated when loaded by the ECS.

❑ *Automatic Except Data Tables* — Overrides the workbook's calculation mode. Only automatic calculation is supported, so the workbook is always calculated when loaded by the ECS. The one exception is that data tables are not calculated.

External Data

As shown in Figure 7-8, the External Data section of the page contains settings for the following trusted file location properties:

❑ *Allow External Data* — This setting determines where the workbook's external data connection information can be retrieved. You have three options for this setting:

❑ *None* — This is the default. External data connections will not be used.

❑ *Trusted Data Connection Libraries Only* — External data connection information must be retrieved from a trusted DCL.

❑ *Trusted Data Connection Libraries and Embedded* — External data connection information can be retrieved from a trusted DCL, or from the connection information contained in the workbook.

❑ *Warn On Refresh* — Select this if you want a confirmation dialog box displayed before external data can be refreshed. The default setting is to display the confirmation dialog box.

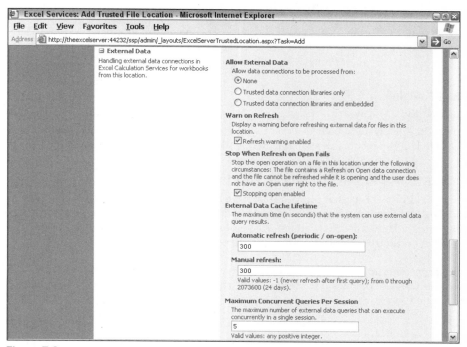

Figure 7-8

❑ *Stop When Refresh On Open Fails* — This setting ensures that the workbook loads only after the data refresh operation succeeds. When you select this check box, users see an error message if the workbook they attempt to open cannot refresh. You may want to use this setting to prevent workbooks from loading if the data isn't current. The default setting is to stop opening the workbook if the following criteria are met:

  ❑ The workbook contains a refresh on open data connection.

  ❑ The data cannot be refreshed during the open operation.

  ❑ The person opening the workbook does not have the open right to the file. When you have the right to open a workbook, you can download it from the document library and view it in the client.

❑ *External Data Cache Lifetime* — The maximum time (seconds) that the external data cached by the ECS can be used. If the lifetime value is exceeded, then the external data source is queried for the data. If the lifetime value is not exceeded, then the cached external data is used to satisfy the request. Two cache lifetime settings exist: one for automatic refresh operations, and one for manual refresh operations. Automatic refresh is used when a connection is configured to use either periodic or refresh on open operations. Manual refresh is when a user forces the data refresh to occur. The default setting for both Automatic and Manual refresh is 300. The External Data Cache Lifetime property can have the following values:

  ❑ -1 — Never refresh again after the first refresh operation.

  ❑ 0 through 2073600 (24 days) — If the cache lifetime setting is exceeded, the ECS issues a new external data request and updates the cached results. If the cache lifetime is not exceeded, the request is served results from the cache.

❑ *Maximum Concurrent Queries Per Session* — The maximum number of external data queries that can execute concurrently for a session. The default value is 5. The Maximum Concurrent Queries Per Session property must be a positive integer.

User-Defined Functions

As shown in Figure 7-9, the User-Defined Functions section of the page contains one trusted file location property setting. The Allow User-Defined Functions setting enables workbooks in the trusted location to make calls to UDFs. The default setting is to not allow UDFs in the trusted location.

Command-Line Options for Trusted File Locations

You can also administer trusted file locations from the command line. The command-line interface supports adding and removing trusted locations for each SSP in your farm. Unlike the web page interface, which inherently knows the SSP that the trusted location belongs to, you must specify the SSP name when working with trusted locations through the command line.

Two operations are supported for working with trusted locations through the command line: Add and Remove. Use the Add operation to create a new trusted location. Use the Remove operation to delete an existing trusted location.

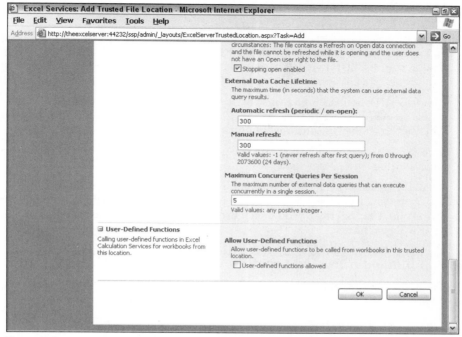

Figure 7-9

There is no specific command-line operation for modifying existing trusted locations. To use the command line to make changes to an existing trusted location, you need to do the following:

1. Remove the existing trusted location.
2. Add the new updated trusted location.

Executing the `add-ecsfiletrustedlocation` statement on an existing trusted location does not affect the existing trusted location, and returns an error message such as the following:

```
Add-EcsFileTrustedLocation: Cannot add this entry to the list. An entry corresponding
to this key already exists, and duplicate entries are not supported.
```

The trusted location command-line feature does not support reading an existing list of trusted locations or trusted location properties. If you want to view the existing trusted locations and their property values, use the SSP's Trusted File Locations administration page.

In order to work with trusted locations through the command line, you need to know the location of the stsadm.exe file. This executable is installed on each MOSS server as part of setup, and the file is located in C:\Program Files\Common Files\Microsoft Shared\Web Server Extensions\12\bin\, for example.

The syntax for working with the command line is fairly standard. It uses the following argument types:

❑ *User input required* — An argument that requires you to enter custom information contains < and > to represent where you need to enter information, and includes a description of the information you need to provide. For example, -Location <URL|UNC> indicates that you need to provide either a URL or a UNC value for the Location property of the trusted location.

❑ *Optional* — The optional arguments are surrounded by [and]. For example, [-SessionTimeout <time in seconds>] indicates that SessionTimeout is not required, but can be included if you want to set the Session Timeout property for the trusted location.

❑ *Required* — Any arguments that don't begin with [must be included. For example, you must always include -Ssp <SSP name>.

❑ *Restricted values* — Some arguments require a value to be set, but the valid values are fixed. For example, -LocationType SharePoint|Unc|Http indicates that the only valid value is SharePoint, Unc, or Http. If you do not use one of these values, the operation will fail and an error will be returned.

Try It Out   Adding a Trusted Location

In this example, you create a SharePoint trusted location in the SharedServices1 SSP. As a result, the ECS will open workbooks up to 15MB in size.

Follow these steps:

1. Open a command window and navigate to the directory containing the stsadm.exe file.

2. Enter the following to create the trusted location:

```
stsadm -o add-ecsfiletrustedlocation -Ssp SharedServices1 -Location
http:// -LocationType SharePoint -IncludeChildren True -MaxWorkbookSize 15
```

The following code shows the supported command-line arguments for working with trusted file locations:

```
stsadm -o add-ecsfiletrustedlocation

    -Ssp <SSP name>
    -Location <URL|UNC>
    -LocationType SharePoint|Unc|Http
    -IncludeChildren True|False

    [-SessionTimeout <time in seconds>]
    [-ShortSessionTimeout <time in seconds>]
    [-MaxRequestDuration <time in seconds>]
    [-MaxWorkbookSize <file size in Mbytes>]
    [-MaxChartSize <size in Mbytes>]
    [-VolatileFunctionCacheLifetime <time in seconds>]
    [-DefaultWorkbookCalcMode File|Manual|Auto|AutoDataTables]
    [-AllowExternalData None|Dcl|DclAndEmbedded]
    [-WarnOnDataRefresh True|False]
    [-StopOpenOnRefreshFailure True|False]
    [-PeriodicCacheLifetime <time in seconds>]
    [-ManualCacheLifetime <time in seconds>]
```

```
        [-MaxConcurrentRequestsPerSession <number of requests>]
        [-AllowUdfs True|False]
        [-Description <descriptive text>]

stsadm -o remove-ecsfiletrustedlocation

        -Ssp <SSP name>
        -Location <URL|UNC>
        -LocationType SharePoint|Unc|Http
```

For a detailed description of the supported trusted location properties on the SSP Trusted File Locations administration page, refer to the "Trusted Location Properties" section earlier in this chapter.

Excel Services Settings

The properties on the Excel Services Settings administration page affect all workbooks opened from any trusted location for the SSP. Additionally, all Excel Calculation Servers in the SSP are affected by these properties. If you envision scenarios where one setting isn't going to work for this broad scope, consider alternative configurations for your deployment, such as creating additional SSPs.

Excel Services Settings Properties

Follow the directions provided previously in this chapter to navigate through Central Administration until you arrive at the SSP home page. Then click the Edit Excel Services Settings link in the Excel Services Settings section on the right side of the page.

The ExcelServerSettings.aspx page is displayed. You can review the existing values or edit the settings to fit your specific requirements. Keep in mind that these properties can impact every ECS contained in the SSP and every workbook opened through the SSP.

Security

As shown in Figure 7-10, the Security section of the page contains the following Excel Services settings:

❑ *File Access Method* — This setting determines the authentication method used by the ECS to get workbooks from trusted file locations other than SharePoint document libraries. You have two options for this setting:

   ❑ *Impersonation* — This is the default. The end-user account is used to access the workbooks.

   ❑ *Process account* — The ECS process account will be used to access the workbooks.

❑ *Connection Encryption* — This setting determines if the communication between clients and the WFE components of Excel Services are required to be encrypted. You have two options for this setting:

   ❑ *Not Required* — This is the default. Encryption is not required.

   ❑ *Required* — Encryption is required.

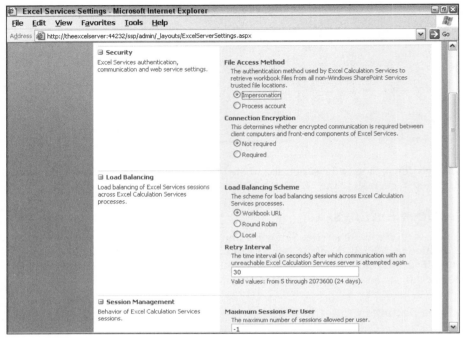

Figure 7-10

Load Balancing

As shown in Figure 7-11, the Load Balancing section of the page contains the following Excel Services settings:

❑ *Load Balancing Scheme* — This setting determines the scheme for load-balancing sessions across the available ECS processes. You have three options for this setting:

❑ *Workbook URL* — This is the default. The WFE uses a hash based on the workbook URL to determine the ECS machine. The same workbook is serviced by the same ECS machine. This method reduces the memory consumption on the ECS machine, because each workbook will be opened on only one ECS machine. The disadvantage of this method is that it does not use the CPU on the other ECS machines if the sessions all go to the same (or few) workbooks.

❑ *Round Robin* — The WFE chooses the next ECS machine for every new session. You can use this method to improve the load distribution between the ECS machines in some scenarios. Over time, all available ECS processes should see the same approximate number of open workbook requests.

❑ *Local* — The WFE attempts to use the ECS located on the same machine as the WFE. Use this method if you have a topology in which each machine in the farm contains both the WFE and the ECS.

❑ *Retry Interval* — The time interval (seconds) after which communication with an unreachable ECS is attempted again. A server can be marked unreachable when the Excel Services proxy component encounters problems connecting with the ECS. When an ECS is designated as unreachable, it is not included in the load-balancing scheme (no more requests are sent to the unreachable ECS). After the retry interval elapses, the proxy attempts to communicate with the ECS to determine if it is responsive and, therefore, can be included in the load balancing scheme again. Valid values for the Retry Interval property are 5 through 2073600 (24 days). The default setting is 30.

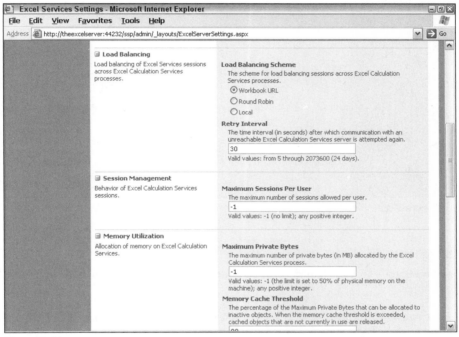

Figure 7-11

Session Management

As shown in Figure 7-12, the Session Management section of the page contains one Excel Services setting. Maximum Sessions Per User determines the maximum number of active sessions allowed for each user. The default setting is 25. You can set this property to either of the following:

❑ -1 (no session limit)

❑ Positive integer

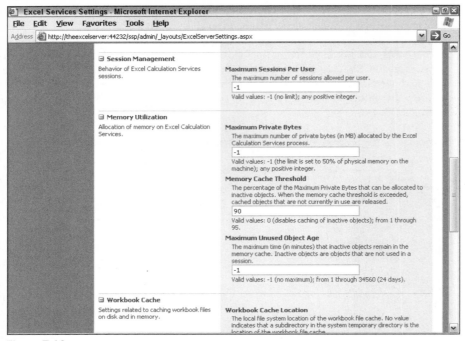

Figure 7-12

Memory Utilization

As shown in Figure 7-13, the Memory Utilization section of the page contains the following Excel Services settings:

❑ *Maximum Private Bytes* — This setting determines the maximum number of private bytes (MB) that can be allocated by the ECS process. When this limit is reached, the ECS stops processing requests until the size of the process is reduced below the limit. You can set this property to either of the following:

    ❑ -1 — This is the default. It sets the maximum size to 50 percent of physical memory on the ECS.

    ❑ Positive integer

❑ *Memory Cache Threshold* — This setting determines the percentage of the maximum private bytes that can be allocated to inactive objects. When this limit is reached, the inactive objects are released from the memory cache (objects not associated with an active session). The default setting is 90. You can set this property to either of the following:

    ❑ 0 — Disables caching of inactive objects.

    ❑ 1 through 95

❑   *Maximum Unused Object Age* — This setting determines the maximum time (minutes) that inactive objects will remain in the memory cache. You can set this property to either of the following:

    ❑   -1 — This is the default, which is no maximum age for inactive objects.

    ❑   1 through 34560 (24 days)

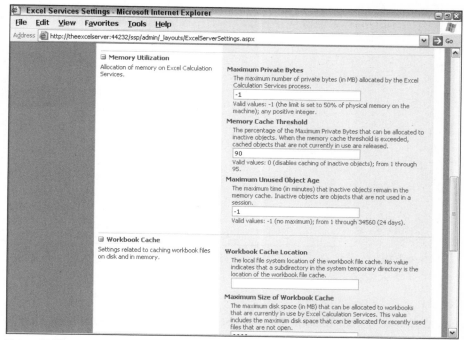

Figure 7-13

Workbook Cache

As shown in Figure 7-14, the Workbook Cache section of the page contains the following Excel Services settings:

❑   *Workbook Cache Location* — This setting determines the workbook file cache location on the local file system. Each workbook loaded by the ECS will be written to this cache location. Additional cache folders will be created at this location as well to support caching of charts, ranges, and saved workbooks. The default setting is %SystemRoot%\TEMP\Excel Server\FileCache\ <Ssp Name>.

❑   *Maximum Size Of Workbook Cache* — This setting determines the maximum amount of disk space (MB) that can be allocated to workbooks currently being used by the ECS, plus any recently used workbooks that are not being used by an active session. The default setting is 40960. The valid value for this property must be a positive integer.

❑   *Caching Of Unused Files* — Select this if you want to allow the ECS to cache workbooks that are no longer being used by an active session. The default will allow caching of unused files.

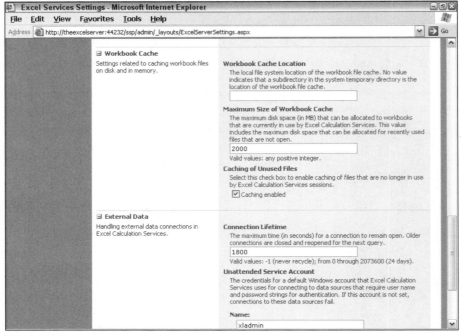

Figure 7-14

External Data

As shown in Figure 7-15, the External Data section of the page contains the following Excel Services settings:

❑ *Connection Lifetime* — This setting determines the maximum time (seconds) for an external data connection to remain open. When the Connection Lifetime is exceeded, the connection is closed, but it opens again when needed by the next query. Memory associated with a connection can be released by the ECS after the connection is closed, which may be more relevant for connections that are used infrequently. You can improve the reliability of the connections in the pool by allowing connections to close periodically, because this removes any connections that are in a less-than-optimal state. The default setting is 1800. You can set this property to either of the following:

    ❑ -1 — Immediately closes the connection and never reuses a connection.

    ❑ 0 through 2073600 (24 days)

❑ *Unattended Service Account* — This setting determines the default Windows account that ECS uses to connect to data sources that require a user name and password string for authentication. You must provide the following:

    ❑ *Name* — Enter the account name in the form of domain\username.

    ❑ *Password* — Enter the password for the account name in both the Password and Retype Password fields.

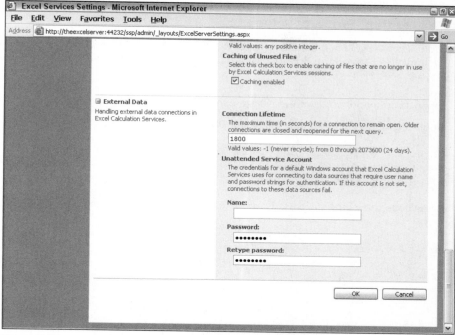

Figure 7-15

Command-Line Options for Excel Services Settings

You can also administer Excel Services Settings from the command line. The command-line interface supports setting a value for each of the Excel Services Settings properties for the SSP in your farm. Unlike the web page interface for managing Excel Services Settings, which inherently knows which SSP is being administered, you need to specify the SSP name when working with this collection of properties through the command line.

The Excel Services Settings command-line feature does not support reading the current property values. If you want to view the current property values, use the SSP's Excel Services Settings administration page.

To work with this collection of properties through the command line, you must know the location of the stsadm.exe file. This executable is installed on each MOSS server as part of the setup, and the file is located in C:\Program Files\Common Files\Microsoft Shared\Web Server Extensions\12\bin\, for example.

The syntax for working with the command line is fairly standard. See the "Command Line Options for Trusted File Locations" section earlier in this chapter for an overview.

Try It Out   Setting Property Values

This example sets the ECS Load Balancing scheme to Round Robin, Maximum Sessions Per User to -1 (no session limit), and Maximum Private Bytes to 10GB. The settings will be applicable to only the SharedServices1 SSP.

1. Open a command window and navigate to the directory containing the stsadm.exe file.

2. Enter the following to set new values for three of the properties:

```
stsadm -o set-ecsloadbalancing -Ssp SharedServices1 -Scheme RoundRobin
stsadm -o set-ecssessionmanagement -Ssp SharedServices1 -MaxSessionsPerUser \-1
stsadm -o set-ecsmemoryutilization -Ssp SharedServices1 -MaxPrivateBytes 10000
```

The following code shows the supported command-line arguments for working with Excel Services Settings:

```
stsadm -o set-ecsexternaldata

    -Ssp <SSP name>

    [-ConnectionLifetime <time in seconds>]
    [-UnattendedServiceAccountName <account name>]
    [-UnattendedServiceAccountPassword <account password>]

stsadm -o set-ecsloadbalancing

    -Ssp <SSP name>

    [-Scheme WorkbookUrl|RoundRobin|Local]
    [-RetryInterval <time in seconds>]

stsadm -o set-ecsmemoryutilization

    -Ssp <SSP name>

    [-MaxPrivateBytes <memory in MBytes>]
    [-MemoryCacheThreshold <percentage>]
    [-MaxUnusedObjectAge <time in minutes>]

stsadm -o set-ecssecurity

    -Ssp <SSP name>

    [-FileAccessMethod UseImpersonation|UseFileAccessAccount]
    [-AccessModel Delegation|TrustedSubsystem]
    [-RequireEncryptedUserConnection False|True]
```

```
stsadm -o set-ecssessionmanagement

    -Ssp <SSP name>

    [-MaxSessionsPerUser <number of sessions>]

stsadm -o set-ecsworkbookcache

    -Ssp <SSP name>

    [-Location <local or UNC path>]
    [-MaxCacheSize <storage in Mbytes>]
    [-EnableCachingOfUnusedFiles True|False]
```

For a detailed description of the supported Excel Services Settings properties on the SSP's Excel Services Settings administration page, see the "Excel Services Settings Properties" section earlier in this chapter.

Trusted Data Connection Libraries

By using trusted DCLs as a repository for data connection files, you add a layer of security to your deployment of Excel Services. You can configure the library to restrict contributors, which gives you control over the data sources used by all workbooks that Excel Services loads. You can configure each trusted location to load connection information from only trusted DCLs.

Like trusted file locations, trusted DCLs have a scope that is limited to the SSP under which they are created. The actual DCL has a scope that makes it available to multiple SSPs.

You must create the DCL separately, which you can do with the SharePoint site administration feature or from the command line.

Trusted Data Connection Library Properties

Follow the directions provided previously in this chapter to navigate through Central Administration until you arrive at the SSP home page. Then click the Trusted Data Connection Libraries link in the Excel Services Settings section on the right side of the page.

The ExcelServerTrustedDcls.aspx page is displayed (see Figure 7-16). You can use this page to add a trusted DCL, edit an existing trusted DCL, delete an existing trusted DCL, or simply see the properties for existing trusted DCLs.

To edit or delete an existing trusted DCL, open the ECB menu associated with the corresponding trusted DCL entry in the list, and select the operation you want to perform. To create a new trusted DCL, use the Add Trusted Data Connection Library link at the top of the trusted DCLs list.

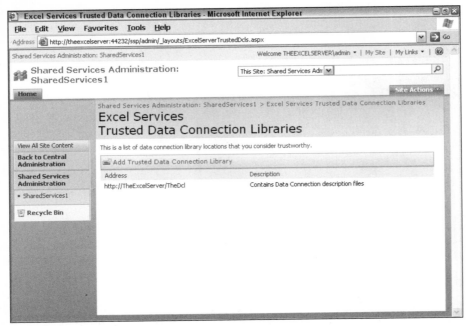

Figure 7-16

Location

As shown in Figure 7-17, the Location section of the page contains the following settings for the trusted DCL properties:

- ❑ *Address* — The URL of the SharePoint DCL to be trusted.
- ❑ *Description* — An optional field that you can use for documentation of the trusted DCL.

Command-Line Options for Trusted Data Connection Libraries

You can also administer trusted DCLs from the command line. The command-line interface supports setting a value for each of the trusted DCL properties for the SSP in your farm. Unlike the web page interface for managing Trusted DCLs, which inherently knows which SSP is being administered, you must specify the SSP name when working with this collection of properties through the command line.

The trusted DCL command-line feature does not support reading the existing list of trusted DCLs or the property values. If you want to view the existing trusted DCLs and their current property values, use the SSP's Trusted Data Connection Libraries administration page.

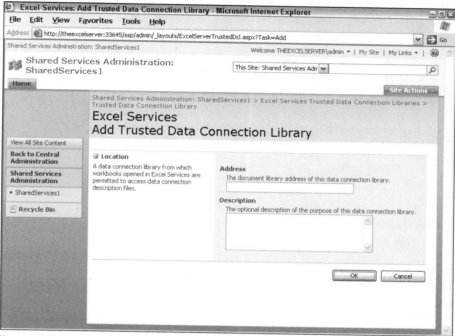

Figure 7-17

To work with this collection of properties through the command line, you must know the location of the stsadm.exe file. This executable is installed on each MOSS server as part of the setup, and the file is located in C:\Program Files\Common Files\Microsoft Shared\Web Server Extensions\12\bin\, for example.

The syntax for working with the command line is fairly standard. See the "Command Line Options for Trusted File Locations" section earlier in this chapter for an overview.

Try It Out   Adding and Removing a Trusted DCL

The first statement in this example creates a trusted DCL that points to a data connection library named TheDcl and scopes to the SharedServices1 SSP. The second statement deletes the Trusted DCL.

1. Open a command window and navigate to the directory containing the stsadm.exe file.

2. Enter the following to create the trusted DCL:

```
stsadm –o add-ecstrusteddataconnectionlibrary -Ssp SharedServices1 -Location
http://TheExcelServer/TheSite/TheDcl
```

3. Enter the following to delete the trusted DCL:

```
stsadm –o remove-ecstrusteddataconnectionlibrary -Ssp SharedServices1
-Location http://TheExcelServer/TheSite/TheDcl
```

The following code shows the supported command-line arguments for working with trusted DCLs:

```
stsadm -o add-ecstrusteddataconnectionlibrary

    -Ssp <SSP name>
    -Location <URL>

    [-Description <descriptive text>]

stsadm -o remove-ecstrusteddataconnectionlibrary

    -Ssp <SSP name>
    -Location <URL>
```

For a detailed description of the supported trusted DCL properties on the SSP's Trusted Data Connection Libraries administration page, see the "Trusted Data Connection Library Properties" section earlier in this chapter.

Trusted Data Providers

Excel Services does not query an external data source unless the data provider for the query is considered a trusted data provider. Trusted data providers have a scope that is limited to the SSP under which they are created. The following table describes the trusted data providers that Excel Services provides by default.

Provider ID	Provider Type	Description
SQLOLEDB	OLE DB	Microsoft SQL Server OLE DB driver (MDAC)
SQLOLEDB.1	OLE DB	Microsoft SQL Server OLE DB driver (MDAC SQL Server 2000)
SQL Server	ODBC	Microsoft SQL Server ODBC driver (MDAC)
SQL Server	ODBC DSN	Microsoft SQL Server ODBC DSN driver (MDAC)
SQLNCLI	OLE DB	Microsoft SQL Server OLE DB driver (SNAC)
SQLNCLI.1	OLE DB	Microsoft SQL Server OLE DB driver (SNAC SQL Server 2005)
SQL Native Client	ODBC	Microsoft SQL Server ODBC driver (SNAC)
SQL Native Client	ODBC DSN	Microsoft SQL Server ODBC DSN driver (SNAC)

Provider ID	Provider Type	Description
MSOLAP	OLE DB	Microsoft OLE DB Provider for OLAP Services (MSOLAP)
MSOLAP.2	OLE DB	Microsoft OLE DB Provider for OLAP Services 8.0
MSOLAP.3	OLE DB	Microsoft OLE DB Provider for OLAP Services 9.0
OraOLEDB.Oracle.1	OLE DB	Oracle Provider for OLE DB
Oracle in OraHome92	ODBC	Oracle ODBC Driver for Oracle 9.2
Oracle in OraHome92	ODBC DSN	Oracle ODBC DSN Driver for Oracle 9.2
IBMDADB2	OLE DB	IBM OLE DB Provider for DB2
IBM DB2 ODBC DRIVER	ODBC	IBM DB2 ODBC Driver
IBM DB2 ODBC DRIVER	ODBC DSN	IBM DB2 ODBC DSN Driver

Properties for Trusted Data Providers

Follow the directions provided previously in this chapter to navigate through Central Administration until you arrive at the SSP home page. Then click the Trusted Data Providers link in the Excel Services Settings section on the right side of the page.

The ExcelServerSafeDataProviders.aspx page is displayed (see Figure 7-18). You can use this page to add a trusted data provider, edit an existing trusted data provider, delete an existing trusted data provider, or simply see the properties for existing trusted data providers.

To edit or delete an existing trusted data provider, open the ECB menu associated with the corresponding trusted data provider entry in the list, and select the operation you want to perform. To create a new trusted data provider, use the Add Trusted Data Provider link at the top of the trusted data provider list.

Figure 7-18

Provider

As shown in Figure 7-19, the Provider section of the page contains the following settings for the trusted data provider properties:

❑ *Provider ID* — The unique provider identification for this data provider. For example, the MSO-LAP.3 provider ID is associated with Microsoft Object Linking and Embedding (OLE) DB Provider for OLAP Services 9.0.

❑ *Provider Type* — Identifies the data provider type for this data provider, and determines the driver that the ECS uses when accessing the source. The default selection is OLE DB. You have three options for this setting:

  ❑ *OLE DB* — The data provider accesses an OLE DB data source using a driver installed on the ECS.

  ❑ *ODBC* — The data provider accesses an ODBC data source using a driver installed on the ECS.

  ❑ *ODBC DSN* — The data provider accesses an ODBC data source using a system DSN defined on the ECS.

❑ *Description* — An optional field that you can use for documentation of the trusted data provider.

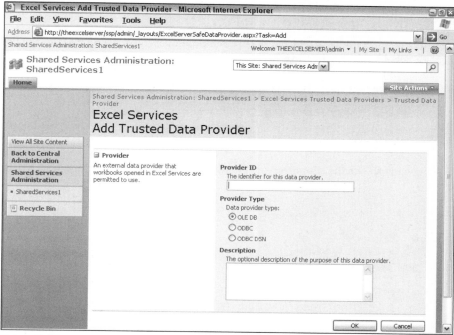

Figure 7-19

Command-Line Options for Trusted Data Providers

You can also administer trusted data providers from the command line. The command-line interface supports setting a value for each of the trusted data provider properties for the SSP in your farm. Unlike the web page interface for managing trusted data providers, which inherently knows which SSP is being administered, you must specify the SSP name when working with this collection of properties through the command line.

The trusted data providers command-line feature does not support reading the existing list of trusted data providers or the property values. If you want to view the existing property values, use the SSP's Trusted Data Providers administration page.

To work with this collection of properties through the command line, you must know the location of the stsadm.exe file. This executable is installed on each MOSS server as part of the setup, and the file is located in C:\Program Files\Common Files\Microsoft Shared\Web Server Extensions\12\bin\, for example.

The syntax for working with the command line is fairly standard. See the "Command-Line Options for Trusted File Locations" section earlier in this chapter for an overview.

Try It Out   **Creating a Trusted Data Provider**

In this example, you create a new trusted data provider with an ID of MDrmSAP for the SharedServices1 SSP. You also include a description for this trusted data provider.

1.   Open a command window and navigate to the directory containing the stsadm.exe file.

2.   Enter the following to create a trusted data provider:

```
stsadm -o add-ecssafedataprovider -Ssp SharedServices1 -ID MDrmSAP -Type
oledb -Description "SAP OLAP OLE DB Provider"
```

The following code shows the supported command-line arguments for working with trusted data providers:

```
stsadm -o add-ecssafedataprovider

    -Ssp <SSP name>
    -ID <data provider id>
    -Type Oledb|Odbc|OdbcDsn

    [-Description <descriptive text>]

stsadm -o remove-ecssafedataprovider

    -Ssp <SSP name>
    -ID <data provider id>
    -Type Oledb|Odbc|OdbcDsn
```

For a detailed description of the supported trusted data providers properties on the SSP's Trusted Data Providers administration page, see the "Properties for Trusted Data Providers" section earlier in this chapter.

User-Defined Function Assemblies

A UDF enables you to call custom functions from your workbooks, with syntax similar to how you would make a call to an intrinsic Excel function. You must enable UDFs on each trusted location that needs to support a UDF; otherwise, each call to a UDF from a workbook in the trusted location will return #NAME to the calling cell in the workbook.

UDFs have a scope that is limited to the SSP under which they are created. You can use the actual managed UDF assembly across multiple SSPs, provided those SSPs are configured to use the UDF assembly.

As you start planning your deployment, take into consideration how you want to leverage UDF assemblies. The UDF assembly must be available to each ECS in the SSP.

Properties for User-Defined Function Assemblies

Follow the directions provided previously in this chapter to navigate through Central Administration until you arrive at the SSP home page. Then click the User-Defined Function Assemblies link in the Excel Services Settings section on the right side of the page.

The ExcelServerUserDefinedFunctions.aspx page is displayed (see Figure 7-20). Use this page to add a UDF assembly, edit an existing UDF assembly, delete an existing UDF assembly, or simply see the properties for existing UDF assemblies.

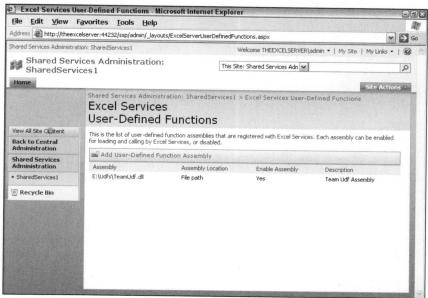

Figure 7-20

To edit or delete an existing UDF assembly, open the ECB menu associated with the corresponding UDF assembly entry in the list, and select the operation you want to perform. To create a new UDF assembly, use the Add User-Defined Function Assembly link at the top of the UDF assembly list.

Assembly Details

As shown in Figure 7-21, the Assembly Details section of the page contains the following settings for the User-Defined Function Assembly properties:

❑ *Assembly* — Either the strong name or the full path for the managed UDF assembly. This location determines how you reference the assembly. If the assembly is in the Global Assembly Cache (GAC), provide the strong name for your assembly. Otherwise, provide the full path, which must include the name of the assembly. For example:

    ❑ *Strong name* — Company.Department.TeamUdf

    ❑ *File path* — E:\Udfs\TeamUdf.dll or \\TheServer\TheShare\Udfs\TeamUdf.dll

❑ *Assembly Location* — Identifies the location type for the assembly. You have two options for this setting:

    ❑ *Global Assembly Cache* — This is the default, .NET Global Assembly Cache.

    ❑ *File Path* — This is the local or UNC path.

❑ *Enable Assembly* — Select this if you want to enable this assembly and allow the ECS to load and use it. The default setting is to disable the UDF assembly. This feature gives you the option of disabling a UDF assembly without needing to actually remove the UDF assembly from the list of UDF assemblies.

❑ *Description* — An optional field that you can use for documentation of the UDF assembly.

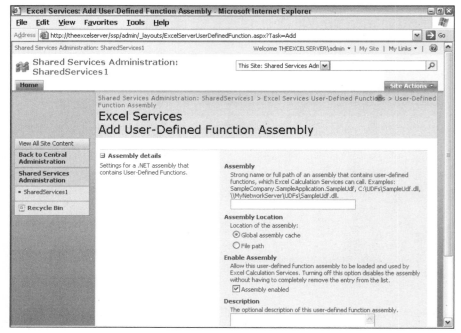

Figure 7-21

Command Line Options for User-Defined Function Assemblies

You can also administer UDF assemblies from the command line. The command-line interface supports setting a value for each of the UDF assembly properties for the SSP in your farm. Unlike the web page interface for managing UDF assemblies, which inherently knows which SSP is being administered, you must specify the SSP name when working with this collection of properties through the command line.

The UDF assembly's command-line feature does not support reading the existing list of UDF assemblies or the property values. If you want to view the existing property values, use the SSP's User-Defined Function Assemblies administration page.

To work with this collection of properties through the command line, you must know the location of the stsadm.exe file. This executable is installed on each MOSS server as part of the setup, and the file is located in C:\Program Files\Common Files\Microsoft Shared\Web Server Extensions\12\bin\, for example.

The syntax for working with the command line is fairly standard. See the "Command Line Options for Trusted File Locations" section earlier in this chapter for an overview.

Try It Out   **Creating a UDF Assembly**

In this example, you create a UDF assembly for the SharedServices1 SSP. You use the assembly's strong name, Company.Department.TeamUdf, as the assembly location type.

Follow these steps:

1.   Open a command window and navigate to the directory containing the stsadm.exe file.

2.   Enter the following to create the UDF assembly:

```
stsadm -o add-ecsuserdefinedfunction -Ssp SharedServices1 -Assembly
Company.Department.TeamUdf -AssemblyLocation GAC
```

The following code shows the supported command line arguments for working with UDF assemblies:

```
stsadm -o add-ecsuserdefinedfunction

    -Ssp <SSP name>
    -Assembly <strong name|file path>
    -AssemblyLocation GAC|File

    [-Enable True|False]
    [-Description <descriptive text>]

stsadm -o remove-ecsuserdefinedfunction

    -Ssp <SSP name>
    -Assembly <strong name|file path>
    -AssemblyLocation GAC|File
```

For a detailed description of the supported UDF assembly properties on the SSP's User-Defined Function Assemblies administration page, see the "Properties for User-Defined Function Assemblies" section earlier in this chapter.

Monitoring

Monitoring the MOSS is a necessary task for any administrator. Understanding the monitoring resources at your disposal can certainly help you respond to problems, but it also increases your awareness of how Excel Services is functioning. This section explains how to monitor Excel Services transactions and overall health, as well as how to exert some control over the available monitoring for MOSS.

The first section, "Unified Logging Service (ULS)," explains the core architectural component used by MOSS for server logging. The options available that allow for configuration of ULS are also discussed here.

The "Windows Event Logs" section takes you through this familiar interface and shows how it can provide much of the same information available through the ULS logs.

The "Performance Counters" section explains the performance objects that are available to further assist you with monitoring Excel Services.

Unified Logging Service (ULS)

This section explains the primary logging system used by MOSS and explores the various configurable properties. It also describes the data that is provided through ULS and how you can leverage this information to assist with administering your Excel Services enterprise deployment.

The ULS is an API used by the MOSS applications, including Excel Services. The ULS interface allows the applications to send notifications to the event and trace logs, feed data to performance counters, and use the error reporting system that collects information related to hardware and software problems.

ULS is enabled and functional out-of-the-box. In fact, the MOSS setup process does not prompt you to make any decisions related to monitoring. Default settings are in place to ensure proper operation of ULS upon completion of your farm's setup. Immediately after setup, ULS trace logs, event log entries, and performance objects are available for your use.

ULS Trace Logs

The ULS trace logs are primarily intended to be used by Product Support after you report a problem and share the logs with them. A number of tools have been developed within Microsoft to assist with searching, filtering, and reading the ULS trace logs, but unfortunately they have not made their way into public-release channels. However, the logs are tab-delimited text files that you can read with your favorite text editor. You can use Excel's filtering functionality to work with large trace logs.

Each server in the farm has its own ULS trace logs that contain only trace entries specific to the events for the MOSS applications running on that server. By default, the trace logs are written to the C:\Program Files\Common Files\Microsoft Shared\Web Server Extensions\12\LOGS directory on each of the servers in your farm. When you navigate to the logs folder, you can readily identify the ULS trace log files by the naming convention associated with them, as follows:

- ❑ ULS trace log file name mask — ServerName-YYYMMDD-HHMM.log, where
    - ❑ ServerName is the computer name for this server.
    - ❑ YYYMMDD is the date the log was created.
    - ❑ HHMM is the time the log was created, in 24-hour format.
- ❑ ULS trace log file name — TheExcelServer-20060711-1124.log, for example.

The volume of trace events present in the log is mostly a factor of the chosen logging level and the activity level associated with the server. A new sequential trace log is created every 30 minutes from the time when the Windows SharePoint Services Tracing service is started (see Figure 7-22). The service is automatic, so it is always running and requires no manual administration.

With events being written to the trace logs around the clock, the ULS trace log directory becomes crowded if left unchecked and requires some disk management. A total of 96 ULS trace logs are allowed to accumulate in the trace log directory before log cleanup is automatically initiated. A first-in, first-out methodology is applied when determining which log to permanently delete from the ULS trace log directory.

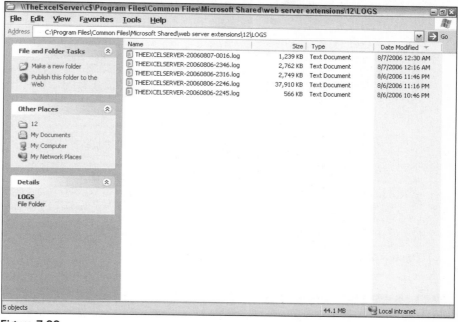

Figure 7-22

So far, you've seen a few of the settings and characteristics of the ULS trace logs without actually taking a peek inside a ULS trace log and examining the settings that directly affect the content of the logs themselves. You know the default settings that dictate where the logs are written, the log naming convention, the frequency at which a new log is created, and how many logs are allowed to exist at any one time. Now it's time to explore the ULS trace log content.

The ULS trace log, at its most basic form, is nothing more than a tab-delimited text file consisting of nine columns of data. Figure 7-23 shows an example of the ULS trace log content. You can use notepad.exe if you just want to read smaller logs and don't need to perform any analysis on them. However, if you want to work with larger logs and/or do some analysis, use the Excel client feature set designed for this purpose.

You may even get the opportunity to try out Excel 12's support for more than 1 million rows.

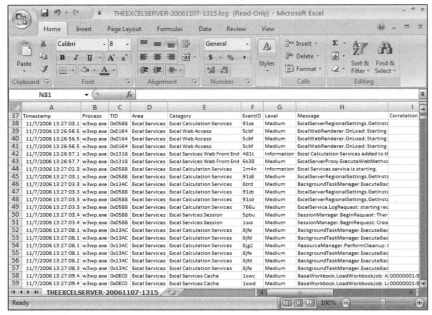

Figure 7-23

The ULS trace log event fields are described in the following table. Not all traces have all nine fields populated.

Field Name	Description
Timestamp	The date and time this trace enters the ULS interface.
Process	The name of the executable responsible for generating the trace.
TID	The thread identification number.
Area	The MOSS application name that is responsible for generating the trace.
Category	Each area is further broken down by categories.
EventID	This is a unique four-character ID for this type of trace.
Level	This gives an indication of the trace type and its importance.
Message	This is the text information that is to be conveyed to the log reader for this trace.
Correlation	Related traces have commonalities within the correlation identification number.

The ULS trace event level, in conjunction with the category, determines if the trace gets written to the log. The MOSS default setting is the same for all categories, and writes all trace events except for those with a Verbose level. The following table shows a breakdown of the 11 levels supported by the ULS, with the most-critical level (Unassigned) described first and the least-critical level (Verbose) described last.

Level	Description
Unassigned	This is used if one of the other levels is not assigned to the trace event.
Critical	Events of type `Error` map to this level.
Warning	Events of type `Warning` and `FailureAudit` map to this level.
Information	Events of type `Information` and `SuccessAudit` map to this level.
Exception	This is used for traces where an exception has occurred.
Assert	This is used for any trace where an assert has occurred.
Unexpected	This is used for any trace where something unexpected occurs.
Monitorable	This is used for any trace where an Office Web Service wants something to be monitored.
High	This is used for high-level user actions and to relay high-level functional information.
Medium	This is used for medium-level user actions and to relay medium-level functional information.
Verbose	This is used for low-level user actions and to relay low-level functional information. It includes technical details to assist with troubleshooting.

Changing the ULS Trace Logging Configuration

There may come a time when you want to make adjustments to the ULS trace event logs. The remainder of this section explores the configuration settings that you can change through the SharePoint 3.0 Central Administration site. The Try It Outs show you how to locate the settings within the Central Administration site and its pages, followed by a discussion of the various settings.

Try It Out   Locating the Central Administration Site

You can access the SharePoint 3.0 Central Administration site using any of the following methods, depending on where you happen to be when you need to do so:

❑   Select Start ➩ All Programs ➩ Microsoft Office Server ➩ SharePoint 3.0 Central Administration. This launches the browser and loads the Central Administration site.

❑ Select Start ➪ All Programs ➪ Administrative Tools ➪ Internet Information Services (IIS) Manager, and then expand the tree control under the Internet Information Services text in the left window until you see the Web Sites node. Expand that folder as well. Locate the SharePoint Central Administration V3 node, and then right-click the node. Click Browse from the context menu. This loads the Central Administration site on the right side of the Microsoft Management Console session you already have running that is hosting the IIS Manager. Figure 7-24 shows a view of the Central Administration site when it is loaded within the IIS Manager.

❑ After you become familiar with your farm, you can simply launch a browser and enter the URL to get to the Central Administration site. Start Internet Explorer and enter the URL as `http://<server running Central Administration>:<TCP port>/default.aspx`.

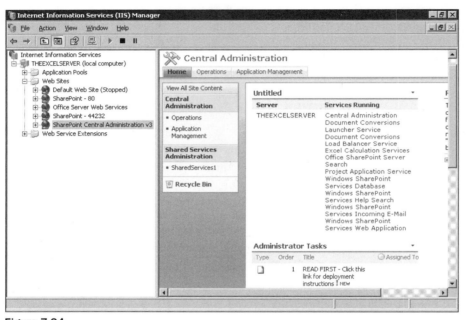

Figure 7-24

Try It Out   Locating the Operations Page

After you load the Central Administration site, you need to open the Operations page (see Figure 7-25). You can do this using either of the following methods:

❑ Click one of the links to the Operations page from the Central Administration site.

❑ Access it directly at `http://<server running Central Administration>: <TCP port>/_admin/operations.aspx`.

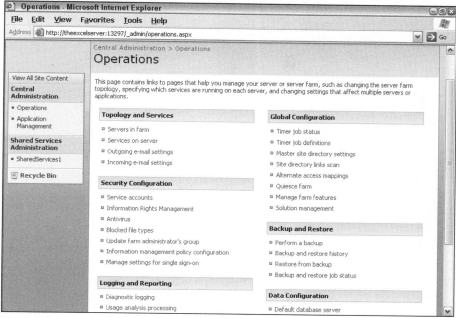

Figure 7-25

Locating the Diagnostic Logging Page

The Diagnostic Logging page (metrics.aspx) exposes the ULS trace log directory path, the number of log files to retain, and the number of minutes to use each log file (see Figure 7-26). This page also provides the controls to adjust the logging level for each of the logging categories.

Use either of the following methods to open the metrics page:

❑ Locate the Logging and Reporting section on the Operations page. Within that section, click the Diagnostic Logging link.

❑ Access it directly at `http://<server running Central Administration>: <TCP port>/_admin/metrics.aspx`.

Trace Log

The Trace Log section of the metrics page contains the following ULS trace log configurable properties:

❑ *Path* — You can use this setting to change the directory for the ULS trace logs. Keep in mind that this setting affects the trace log directory on each server in the farm. It is a farm-wide ULS configuration setting. The path you use must exist on each server in the farm. The default setting for this property is C:\Program Files\Common Files\Microsoft Shared\Web Server Extensions\12\LOGS.

175

❑ *Number of Log Files* — This setting determines how many log files are retained in the trace log directory. You can enter any value between 1 and 1024. The default setting is 96.

❑ *Number of Minutes To Use A Log File* — This setting determines when a new log file is created. You can enter any value between 1 and 1440. The default setting is 30.

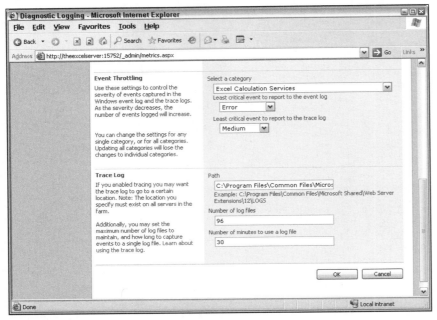

Figure 7-26

Event Throttling

The Event Throttling section of the metrics page contains the settings that control the severity of events logged to both the event log and the trace log. This is determined by associating a logging level with each of the categories. There are more than 250 categories to choose from for all of MOSS. The following are the eight Excel Services categories.

❑ Excel Calculation Services

❑ Excel Services Administration

❑ Excel Services Cache

❑ Excel Services External Data

❑ Excel Services Session

❑ Excel Services Web Front End

❑ Excel Web Access

❑ Excel Web Services

Each ULS trace event is mapped to a single category. The Excel Services categories are representative of the major components, and all Excel Services trace events use one of the eight categories. As mentioned earlier, the information contained in the ULS trace event log is intended to be used by support personnel, so the categories provide an opportunity for filtering, sorting, and narrowing the focus of an investigation into a customer-reported problem.

The default configuration specifies that all categories are logged at the Medium level.

As previously mentioned, the ULS is aware of 11 trace logging levels. The 11 levels represent the exclusive list of values that can be displayed in the ULS trace log level field. The ULS trace level throttling interface does not expose all 11 to you as options for throttling. Instead, seven choices are presented from which you can choose. You can choose the least-critical events that you want to see in the ULS trace log. (The trace logging levels were shown in a previous table, with the most-critical level appearing first in the list.)

You can set a specific logging level for each ULS trace category. The first entry in the list of categories is ALL and, as its name implies, it allows you to set a common ULS trace logging level for all MOSS categories. This is particularly helpful when you want to get all of the MOSS categories back to a known logging level without having to go through the entire list.

If you choose to set a logging level for specific categories instead of using ALL, keep in mind that you can select only one category in the list. The task of setting a level for individual categories is tedious, because you have to apply the change for one category, reload the metrics page, apply the change for the next category, reload the metrics page, and so on.

The Diagnostic Logging page also contains the following drop-down category, event log, and trace log throttling controls (as previously shown in Figure 7-26):

❑ *Select A Category* — Use this control in conjunction with either of the following two controls to select the category for which you want to change event throttling. When this control has focus, you can quickly navigate it by typing the first character of the category you are looking for. For example, type an **E** to put focus on the eApproval item in the list. This control does not support multiselecting.

❑ *Least Critical Event To Report To The Event Log* — This control allows you to set the logging level for the Windows event log (discussed in the next section). The setting you choose for this control is applied to the selected category in the previous control. The default value for the All category is Success.

❑ *Least Critical Event To Report To The Trace Log* — This control allows you to set the logging level for the ULS trace log. The setting you choose for this control is applied to the selected category in the previous control. The default value for the All category is Medium.

Windows Events

The Event Viewer provides another view of the ULS Logging System output. The ULS trace logs are targeted toward Product Support, and the Event Viewer logs are for the administrator. The volume of events seen in the Event Viewer is a fraction of the traces that appear in the ULS trace logs. The Event

Viewer doesn't contain the technical details found in the ULS trace logs, but it contains a good trail of the Excel Services activities that occur on the server. Figure 7-27 shows an example of an event that is logged for a successful `OpenWorkbook` operation.

Figure 7-27

Try It Out   **Locating Excel Services Events**

You can launch the Event Viewer application using either of these methods:

❑   Select Start ➪ Run, type **eventvwr**, and select OK.

❑   Select Start ➪ All Programs ➪ Administrative Tools ➪ Event Viewer.

When the Event Viewer is running, select Application from the left frame of the Event Viewer window. MOSS event traces have a Source value of Office SharePoint Server. The Category field maps to the ULS trace log categories discussed previously.

MOSS also provides a way to monitor the event traces through Central Administration. Select Start ➪ All Programs ➪ Microsoft Office Server ➪ SharePoint 3.0 Central Administration ➪ Operations ➪ Server event logs. This loads the event viewer at `http://<server>:<port>/_admin_EventLog.aspx`.

The Central Administration's viewer for the event traces allows you to choose a server in the farm, and then view any of the event logs for that server (such as Application, Security, or System). You can sort entries in the view by column title, but the view is restricted to 25 entries at a time.

Making Configuration Changes to Event Logging

Excel Services event traces are written to the application event log as defined by the Event Throttling properties. As described previously, the Diagnostic Logging page (metrics.aspx) exposes the three drop-down event log and ULS trace log throttling controls: the category, event log level, and trace log level selectors. The event log selector controls the events that ultimately get logged to the Event Viewer's Application log.

Performance Counters

Excel Services provides performance counters that are available on each MOSS server by default. All three Excel Services performance objects are available on each server, regardless of the role of that server in the farm. This simply means that the role of the server dictates which performance counters actually return data for activity on the server. For example, trying to use a WFE performance counter on an Application Server will prove fruitless because the WFE components are not used on that server.

Try It Out   **Using an Excel Services Performance Counter**

Launch the Performance Monitor application by selecting Start ⇨ Run. Type **perfmon** and select OK.

When PerfMon is running, add Excel Services performance counters by following these steps.

1. Click the Add button (or press Ctrl+I), which opens the Add Counters window.

2. Ensure that you are working with the expected Excel Server. Use the top input field to type the server name (in the format of \\serverName).

3. Using the Performance Object control, select one of the following three objects for Excel Services:

    ❑ *Excel Calculation Services* — This object is relevant for the application server where the ECS is installed.

    ❑ *Excel Services Web Front End* — This object is relevant for the WFE where Excel Services is installed.

    ❑ *Excel Web Access* — This object is also relevant for the WFE where Excel Services is installed.

A list of the counters that correspond to your selection is displayed. For example, if you select the ECS object, the counters list looks like Figure 7-28.

4. Select a counter from the list and click Add.

5. Click Close to return to System Monitor view, and notice that the Excel Services performance counter has been added.

The ECS performance object consists of 11 performance counters that provide data on the ECS activities. The following table describes each of the ECS performance counters.

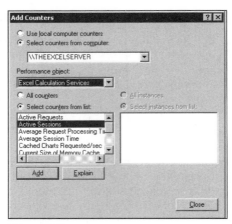

Figure 7-28

Counter Name	Counter Description
Active Requests	The number of active requests being processed on ECS at the time the sample is taken.
Active Sessions	The number of active sessions on ECS at the time the sample is taken.
Average Request Processing Time	The average time to process a request on ECS between samples.
Average Session Time	The average duration (in seconds) of a session on ECS between samples.
Cached Charts Requested/Second	The number of charts requested per second that are delivered from a cached chart image by ECS.
Current Size Of Memory Cache	The size (in bytes) of the ECS unused items manager.
Excel Calculation Services Workbook Cache Size	The size (in bytes) of the ECS workbook cache.
Rendered Charts Requested/Second	The number of chart requests per second on ECS.
Requests Received/Second	The number of requests received per second on ECS between samples.

Counter Name	Counter Description
Requests With Errors Per Second	The number of requests that are returned with errors per second on ECS between samples.
Sessions/Second	The average number of sessions created per second on ECS between samples.

The Excel Services WFE performance object consists of three performance counters and provides data on the WFE (Excel Services proxy component). The following table describes each of the Excel Service WFE performance counters.

Counter Name	Counter Description
Active Requests	The number of active requests being processed on the Excel Services WFE at the time the sample is taken.
Average Request Processing Time	The average time to process a request on the Excel Services WFE between samples.
Requests Per Second	The number of requests received per second on the Excel Services WFE between samples.

The EWA performance object consists of three performance counters that provide data on the WFE (EWA component). The following table describes each of the EWA performance counters.

Counter Name	Counter Description
Average Chart Image Request Time	The average time taken (in seconds) by EWA to respond to a request for a chart image.
Chart Image Requests/Second	The number of chart image requests per second handled by EWA.
Excel Web Access Request Time	The average time to process a request on EWA between samples.

Microsoft Operations Management Pack

This section provides a brief introduction to a monitoring platform available from Microsoft. The Microsoft Operations Manager (MOM) is a Microsoft product that can help you monitor your system. A Management Pack is a MOM add-on that provides rules and knowledge specific to an application.

MOM 2005 is available for purchase separately from MOSS. The MOM Pack for MOSS is supported only by MOM 2005. Neither MOM 2000 nor MOM 2007 are supported. To find out how to obtain MOM 2005, visit www.microsoft.com/mom.

The Excel Services MOM Pack provides built-in rules support for a subset of the Excel Services events. The following table briefly describes each of the Excel Services MOM Pack event rules.

Event Rule Name	Summary
Memory Allocation Failed	This error indicates that ECS attempted to allocate memory, but the memory allocation failed.
Incorrect URL for Excel Calculation Services	Components of ECS that run on front-end web servers use URLs to communicate with ECS. These URLs are specified in the configuration database, and vary depending on which servers are enabled with the ECS role in Central Administration.
Workbook disk cache is full	ECS uses the workbook disk cache to store workbooks previously opened by user requests. This cache is created on the hard disk of each computer running ECS.
Unable to establish a connection with Excel Calculation Services	ECS can be installed on each front-end web server, or on a separate application server. Regardless of where ECS is installed, all front-end web servers must be able to establish a connection with ECS.
Unauthorized attempt to access a session	When a user attempts to hijack another user's session, ECS denies requests made by the user who does not own the session, and logs an event in the Windows NT event log.
Unable to delegate credentials	ECS is configured to use delegated credentials. This error indicates that the front-end web server was unable to delegate end-user credentials to ECS.
SSL is required but is not configured	ECS is configured to use Secure Sockets Layer (SSL), also referred to as HTTPS, but SSL is not configured. This results in client requests being denied by ECS.

Event Rule Name	Summary
Workbook disk cache cannot be created	ECS uses a disk cache to store workbooks. This disk cache is used for loading workbooks in ECS. The location and size of this disk cache is configured on the ECS pages in Central Administration.
Error communicating with Excel Calculation Services	This error occurs when the front-end web server attempts to establish a connection to ECS, but a communication error occurs.
Maximum memory configured for Excel Calculation Services has been exceeded	ECS provides a configurable setting for Maximum Private Bytes that is used by the application pool in which ECS runs. When the number of private bytes used by the application pool process exceeds the value of the Maximum Private Bytes setting, ECS stops processing requests for new sessions, and processes only navigation and find requests on existing sessions.
Single Sign-On failure	The Microsoft SSO service is a mechanism used to authenticate a user only once to allow the user to gain access to all computers and systems. Excel Services uses SSO for authenticating with external data sources.
Excel Calculation Services not available	In order for a front-end web server to use ECS, this service must be running on either the front-end web server or on another server in the farm. This alert indicates that ECS is not running on any computer in the farm.
Invalid Session ID in the request	There is an invalid session ID in the request.
Excel Calculation Services is not running locally	ECS provides a set of load-balancing schemes from which the administrator can choose. When the load-balancing scheme is configured as Local, the Excel web components running on the front-end web server always send requests to ECS running on the local computer.
Invalid File Access method configured	ECS provides a setting for configuring the file access method that is used for UNC and HTTP trusted locations. If the file access method is configured as impersonation, ECS must be able to delegate the end-user credential for accessing files.

After an Excel Services rule is defined in MOM, you can then further refine the rule to perform a responsive action when the rule event fires. For example, you could execute a script that triggers e-mail notifications, pages your IT staff, or even runs code to remedy the condition.

International Deployments

This section focuses on a few different aspects of the Excel Services international administration options. The discussion starts with the Excel Services setup, progresses into language packs, and finishes with WSS configuration settings that directly affect workbooks and how data is presented. You should make the majority of the international decisions up front, when you are building out your farm and getting it ready for the users of the system.

Setup

One of the first international decisions you need to make is which language of MOSS to install. Your MOSS deployment should be an environment in which you are comfortable working. From an international perspective, this means choosing a language that you can read, understand, and communicate with using a keyboard. The MOSS installation language you choose does not have to match the language of the Windows Server 2003 operating system on the farm.

The setup wizard for installing MOSS shows content using the language that you have chosen to install. Chapter 2 provides more detail about the steps to set up MOSS.

After setup is finished, the SharePoint 3.0 Central Administration site is rendered using the language of the MOSS installation. It is very important to understand that after SharePoint creates a site, you cannot change the site language ID (UI culture). SharePoint 3.0 Central Administration is a site, and because it is created at setup, the site language ID of the site matches the MOSS installation language used to set up the farm server hosting the Central Administration service.

Other Excel Services features use the MOSS installation language as well, including the default UI culture for both the EWA and Excel Services web service, user assistance (help context), performance counters, event logs, and ULS logs.

Language Packs

You can extend the international support for your MOSS deployment by installing Office server language packs. You can install a *single language pack* (SLP) to support a single additional language. You can install as many individual SLPs as you need to support your deployment. The SLP must be installed on each WFE and application server that hosts Excel Services components.

> *WSS language packs aren't discussed here, but it might be helpful to point out that an Office server language pack contains the WSS language pack content. By installing the Office server language pack for a given language, you also get the WSS language pack functionality for that language.*

By installing an SLP, you can create sites using a language other than the MOSS installation language. For example, if a French SLP is installed on a German MOSS installation, then an administrator can create new sites that would ultimately have either a French or a German site language ID (UI culture).

When you add the EWA Web Part to a site, the UI culture is used to determine the language for menus, drop-down lists, toolbars, and error messages. Essentially, all of the EWA Web Part properties use the UI culture of the site. Remember, after a site is created, you cannot change the UI culture.

It is worth noting that there is clear separation of the EWA Web Part properties and the workbook being rendered by the Web Part. The Web Part properties are sensitive to the UI culture, but the workbook content is not. The UI culture of a site does not affect the workbook content. Error messages often seem to span the boundary between Web Part and workbook, so don't be surprised if you see the error messages displayed using the UI culture of the site. The site's data culture affects the workbook content, and that relationship is discussed further in the upcoming "Cultures and Workbooks" section of this chapter.

The Excel Services web service can also leverage any SLPs that are added to your system. The Excel Services web service uses the UI culture when reporting messages back to the caller. The caller of an Excel Services web service method can specify the UI culture of the SKU language or any installed SLPs. For more detailed information on using the Excel Services web service, see Chapter 14.

Installing an SLP

You can install most SLPs on a MOSS server simply by running the applicable setup executable, because their prerequisites were already met when you installed MOSS on the server. However, there are a couple of exceptions.

Some language packs may fail to install and display a message that says "The language of this installation package is not supported by your system." What this message is referring to is that your server's operating system does not have language support installed for the SLP language.

To satisfy the language support prerequisite for the SLP, determine if the language falls into the category of East Asian languages or Complex Scripts languages. Then perform the following steps:

1. Select Start ➪ Control Panel ➪ Regional and Language Options.

2. On the Regional and Language Options dialog box, select the Languages tab.

3. Scan down to the Supplemental Language Support section, and select the check box to Install Files for the languages that correspond to the SLP you are going to install.

   The installation wizard for an SLP uses the SLP language for the user interface. The installation is nothing more than a click-through with no input required, so don't be discouraged if you cannot read the installation wizard UI.

4. Rerun the SharePoint Products and Technologies Configuration Wizard, using the default settings. To perform this operation, click Start ➪ All Programs ➪ Administrative Tools ➪ SharePoint Products and Technologies Configuration Wizard.

You can also install SLPs through the command line, which can be very useful when you need to install many SLPs and/or you want to install the SLPs on multiple MOSS servers. All you need to do is pass the path of the configuration xml file that you have created to the SLP setup.exe, like this:

```
Setup.exe /config <pathToConfigXml>
```

The xml file contains the following lines:

```
<Configuration>
        <Logging Type="verbose" Path="%temp%" Template="Office Server Language Pack
Setup(*).log"/>
        <Display Level="basic" CompletionNotice="no" />
        <PIDKEY Value="<Pid Key Here>" />
</Configuration>
```

The Display Level can have a value of none, which prevents the setup wizard from displaying. This is probably the desired behavior if you are using the command line.

Removing an SLP

You can remove an SLP through Add or Remove Programs in the Control Panel. You can also repair the SLP. In addition, you can use the command line to remove or repair the language pack.

Cultures and Workbooks

As mentioned earlier, the WSS site language ID is equivalent to the Excel Services UI culture. The site language ID is set when the site is created and cannot be changed. The Excel Services UI culture cannot be changed for a given site either. Each site also has an associated locale (or *data culture* as it is called in Excel Services) that is set at site creation to correspond with the UI culture. You can change the locale after a site has been created.

The site's locale can be set by either the web administrator or by the users of the site. The web administrator locale setting affects all users of the site and is considered the default or the *web setting*. When users first visit a site, they use the web settings, and they can continue to use those settings unless they explicitly make changes to their My Settings properties.

You can change the web administrator locale settings by following these steps:

1. Navigate to the site where you want to make the locale change.

2. Select Site Actions ⇨ Site Settings ⇨ Regional Settings.

3. Locate the Locale setting on the Regional Settings property page. The drop-down control provides an extensive list of available locales from which to choose. Pick the locale that meets your needs.

   When you make changes to a site's locale, the site's sort order also changes to remain in sync with the locale and to give the users of your site the best experience possible.

4. Select OK to apply your changes to the Regional Settings properties.

As a consumer or user of a site, you can change your locale settings by following these steps:

1. Navigate to a site and click the Welcome <your name> link at the top of the page.

2. Click the My Settings option from the drop-down control.

3. On the User Information page, click the My Regional Settings link.

4. On the Regional Settings page, locate the Locale setting. By default, this setting is disabled. Uncheck the Follow Web Settings check box if you want to make changes and deviate from the web administrator's settings for these properties.

5. The Locale drop-down control provides an extensive list of available locales from which to choose. Pick the locale that meets your needs.

6. Click OK to apply your changes to the Regional Settings properties.

Excel Services uses the data culture when formatting numbers, currencies, and dates within a workbook. As the author of a workbook, you can control rendered formatting of the workbook's content. When you are creating the workbook, you can use Excel's cell formatting features to explicitly set a format and force Excel Services to render the cell content exactly as you have specified, or implicitly set a format and then let Excel Services format the content by taking into consideration the data culture of the site where the workbook is being rendered.

Try It Out   Applying Explicit and Implicit Cell Formats

In this exercise, you create a workbook that contains dates and times, and apply a mix of implicit and explicit formatting to the values in the workbook. Then you load the workbooks on a site first as the administrator (using the default web settings), and then as yourself (using your own custom locale).

First, create a workbook and publish it to your existing deployment of MOSS as follows:

1. Start Excel 12 and begin with a blank workbook.

2. Use the information provided in the following table to populate and format the three cells. The Value is the information you type in the cell noted in the first column, the Category is the number formatting to be applied, and the Type is the specific format to be applied. Figure 7-29 shows how Excel displays the workbook in an English environment after the formatting has been applied.

Cell	Value	Category	Type
B3	9/30/2006	Date	*3/14/2001
B4	8/31/2006	Date	*Wednesday, March 14, 2001
B5	15:30	Time	1:30:55 PM

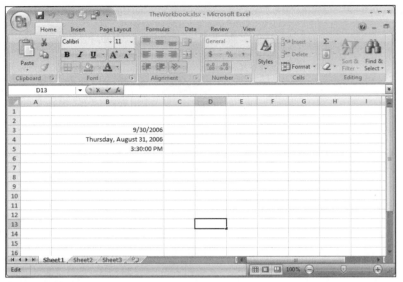

Figure 7-29

3. To publish the workbook, click the Office button and select Publish ⇨ Excel Services. This opens the Save As dialog box.

4. In the File Name field, enter the path to the Documents folder at the root of your portal (such as http://TheServer/Documents/TheWorkbook.xlsx). The Open in Excel Services check box is selected by default — leave it checked for this scenario.

5. Click Save to put the workbook in the Documents folder. Your browser automatically starts and loads the workbook using the Excel Services feature, which allows you to render workbooks without requiring the EWA Web Part to be embedded on a WSS page.

The EWA rendering shown in Figure 7-30 is for a site with a UI culture of English and an English data culture. The formatting for cells B3 and B4 use the formatting that is applicable to the site's data culture (English). Cell B5 uses explicit formatting, and so the formatting for that cell won't change, regardless of the data culture.

Follow these steps to change your data culture and reload the workbook in Excel Services:

1. Use the same browser session and click the Home link in the upper-left corner of the browser.

2. Select Welcome <your name> ⇨ My Settings ⇨ My Regional Settings.

3. The Regional Settings property page loads. Unselect the Always Follow Web Settings option and set the locale to German. Save your settings by clicking OK.

4. Navigate back to `http://TheServer/Documents` and locate TheWorkbook.xlsx.

5. Hover over the workbook name to make sure the ECB control is activated. Click the down arrow to see the available options for the workbook. Click View in Web Browser to load the workbook using EWA.

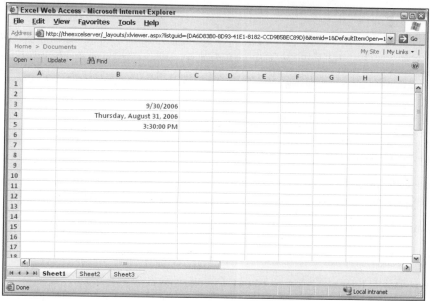

Figure 7-30

Compare the formatting of the cells shown in Figure 7-31 with the formatting previously shown in Figure 7-30. The formatting for cells B3 and B4 now uses the German data culture, but cell B5 is unchanged and continues to use the explicit number formatting applied by the author of the workbook.

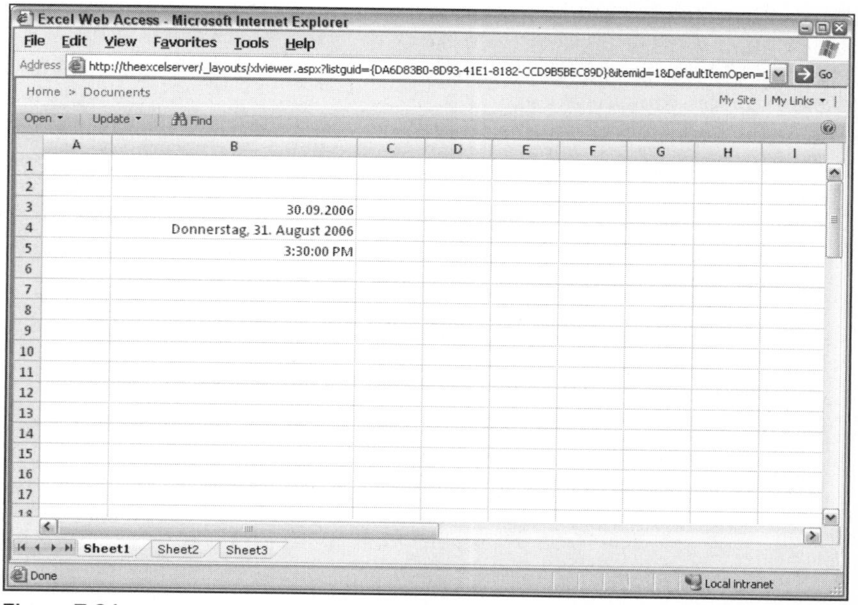

Figure 7-31

Summary

In this chapter, you learned about each of the five administration pages devoted to Excel Services. You navigated your way through Central Administration to reach Excel Services administration pages and learned about each of the properties presented on those pages. The stsadm command-line interface was introduced, and you used this feature to make administrative changes to Excel Services.

You were able to locate the key components of ULS on your system. You successfully loaded the Diagnostic Logging page, where you identified the administrative controls for ULS that affect both the event and trace logs. Additional monitoring features were discussed, and you were able to add an Excel Services performance counter to the Performance Monitoring application.

The chapter concluded by introducing you to the international administration features for Excel Services. You were able to add a language pack to your system and witnessed the benefits first-hand. The use of a data culture was explained, and then you created a workbook using both implicit and explicit data formatting to see how the data culture is used for that formatted data.

To summarize, you should now know how to do the following:

- ❏ Use each of the Excel Services administration pages
- ❏ Use the stsadm command-line interface to administer Excel Services
- ❏ Use the key components of ULS, including trace logs and event logs
- ❏ Use the Diagnostic Logging Page to administer ULS
- ❏ Use performance counters to monitor Excel Services
- ❏ Use language packs to extend Excel Services international support
- ❏ Use the data culture to control workbook data formatting

Chapter 8 covers a wide range of methods that enable you to secure your environment while using Excel Services to support your scenarios.

Security

When thinking about security in the context of Excel Services, you might consider some of the following aspects:

❑ Workbooks and information queried from external data sources are shown only to users with appropriate privileges.

❑ There are ways to limit which parts of the workbooks are displayed.

❑ Excel Services is not used by a malicious user to attack innocent end users.

❑ The server is robust against attacks meant to take it down.

❑ Excel Services can help with corporate compliance regulations.

These and other aspects are part of security. The Excel Services security is based on SharePoint, which provides the platform for authenticating the users, setting permissions on files, auditing, groups, roles, and the administration model.

Excel Services adds security features to SharePoint that are specific to Excel workbooks and querying data from external sources.

In this chapter, you learn about the various aspects of Excel Services security. The first part covers how users are authenticated and how their permissions are used to limit what they are allowed to see. The second part covers the various ways you can protect the server against malicious attacks.

Protecting the Workbook

You can use Excel Services to limit the information that is given to users based on their privileges. Chapter 11 provides step-by-step instructions for controlling this information.

Authentication

In order to protect the information, the user needs to be identified. This process is called *authentication*. Excel Services support Windows authentication, forms authentication, and anonymous users.

Windows Authentication

Windows authentication is the default mode for SharePoint. The authentication is done through IIS on the WFE machines. IIS maps the user to a Windows domain account. Windows authentication gives you the following options:

❑ *Windows Integrated* — This is the default configuration for IIS. It authenticates the user through the username that he or she logs in on the client machine. This is the most common setting for intranet scenarios within an organization.

❑ *Digest* — This option allows the user to enter the username and password. The password requires Active Directory for encryption. This setting is useful for browsers that do not support Windows integrated authentication and in extranet scenarios.

❑ *Basic* — This option is similar to Digest, except that the password is sent in clear text over the network. In general, it is not recommended, except if the connection is secure.

In all these options, IIS handles the authentication on the WFE. If the authentication is successful, SharePoint and Excel Services use the Windows username that was authenticated to check the authorization for opening the workbook.

You can use Windows credentials with Excel Services to access external data, through SSO or if Kerberos-constrained delegation is enabled. For more details about accessing external data, see Chapter 5.

Forms Authentication

Forms authentication is an alternative way of authenticating credentials that are not Windows credentials. ASP.Net provides a pluggable infrastructure to allow users to design their own authentication mechanism. Usernames and passwords are stored in a system such as a SQL database, Lightweight Directory Access Protocol (LDAP), or other identity-management systems. After users log in and the system authenticates them, a cookie is used on the client side to identify them in future requests in the same session.

Forms authentication is useful in extranet or Internet configurations, in which the users are not part of the domain of the server.

You can use forms authentication with Excel Services to ensure that users have permissions to open workbooks from a SharePoint document library.

You use Kerberos-constrained delegation for forms authentication, because it is not a Windows account. Connecting to an external data source through SSO works only for SSO providers that support forms authentication. You can use the None authentication setting to query external data work, because it uses the Unattended Account. Chapter 5 describes the Kerberos, SSO, and None authentication methods.

Anonymous Users

You can set up IIS to allow anonymous access. In that case, the end user is not authenticated, and a predefined account is used. This configuration is useful when there is no need to differentiate between users — all users are given the same permissions. When you use this setting, you won't know which end user is really logged in.

With anonymous users, SSO and Kerberos delegation do not work if the predefined account for all users is a local account on the WFE machine (this is the default in IIS). You can change the anonymous user to a domain account instead of a local user, or use the None authentication setting, which connects to external data as the Unattended Account.

> *With anonymous access, the limit of maximum sessions per user applies to all the users together (because all of them use the same account). By default, this limit is set to 25 sessions per user, but you can increase the limit with the Excel Services administration settings.*

Opening Workbooks

Now that you know how users are authenticated, the next step is to examine the *authorization* process for opening workbooks.

Excel Services allows workbooks to be opened from SharePoint document libraries, UNC folders, and HTTP locations. You can define a trusted location for each such library or folder, or use the Include Children option to define a root folder and all its subfolders. When you set up a trusted location, you define its type (SharePoint, UNC, or HTTP). Chapter 7 discusses the administration of Excel Services and setting up trusted locations.

The authorization process depends on the type of trusted location.

SharePoint Document Libraries

When a user opens a workbook from a SharePoint location, Excel Services uses SharePoint to determine if he or she is authorized to do so.

When Kerberos-constrained delegation is set up between the WFE and the ECS, or both of these components are running on the same machine, the ECS is impersonated as the end user. SharePoint uses these end user credentials to authorize the workbook to be opened.

In the other configurations, the ECS is not impersonated as the user. When the request to open the workbook is processed on the WFE, Excel Services gets a token from SharePoint that identifies the user who was authenticated. The WFE sends the token to the ECS component, which then passes it to SharePoint when opening the workbook.

Even though the ECS caches workbooks for performance reasons, it still checks the permissions for every request to open a workbook.

UNC and HTTP Locations

Excel Services has two ways of determining which credentials to use to authorize the user against a UNC or HTTP workbook. You can set the File Access Method in the Security section of the Excel Services administration settings to determine the credentials used.

When you set the File Access Method to Impersonation (as shown in Figure 8-1), the ECS uses the impersonated user's credentials to open the file. Impersonation is the default option for this setting. When you use Impersonation, the authorization is done by the UNC or HTTP location, based on the user's permissions to those files.

Figure 8-1

Use this option if the end user's credentials are delegated from the WFE to the ECS. This is done when the WFE and the ECS are deployed to the same machine, or Kerberos-constrained delegation is used between the WFE and the ECS. If the end user's credentials are not delegated to the ECS, attempting to use Impersonation to get the workbook fails.

When you set the File Access Method to Process Account, the ECS opens the file using its own process account. The file opens if the account under which the ECS process is running has permissions to read the file, regardless of the end user account. This option is less secure, so you should use it only in cases when you want to allow all authenticated users access to certain UNC or HTTP files.

Protecting the Workbook Content

Some workbooks may contain sensitive information or intellectual property that you do not want to disclose to various users. Excel, SharePoint, and Excel Services have a number of features designed to protect the content of a workbook. Unfortunately, not all of the features work seamlessly across Excel client and Excel Services.

In this section, you learn about the various ways that you can protect the workbook content with Excel Services, and also about the features that are not supported by Excel Services.

View Only Permission

SharePoint distinguishes between Open permissions and View Only permissions to a workbook. When you have the right to open a workbook, you can download it from the document library and view it in the client. When you have only the right to view a workbook, you can view it in Excel Services, but you can't download it to Excel.

The View Only permission is designed to protect the workbook model while allowing you to view the calculated result of the workbook. You don't see the formulas or the data sources to which the workbook connects, but you do see the calculated data. When a workbook is protected with View Only permission, you cannot open the workbook in Excel from the Excel Web Access (EWA) Web Part or perform a `GetWorkbook` call with Excel web services. You can, however, open Snapshot because they save only the data, not the model.

Excel Services provides the Viewers group out-of-the box. You can use this group to give only View permission to the relevant users. When it is important to protect the content of the workbook, you can give the Open permission to a few trusted authors, and the View Only permission to all the users that you want to see the workbook data.

You can also use the View Only permission when you want to ensure that there is only one version of the workbook (the one published to the document library). This way, users cannot download it and have their own versions of the workbook.

> *View Only permission works only with workbooks in SharePoint document libraries. Workbooks in UNC or HTTP locations have only the Open permission, because this is a feature specific to SharePoint. It is one of the reasons that SharePoint document libraries are the preferred storage location for Excel Services workbooks.*

Published Items

You can limit which workbook items can be published to the server. You can choose between publishing the whole workbook, a set of worksheets, or specific objects in the workbook. These objects can be named ranges, PivotTables, and/or charts. Excel Services displays only those published objects, hiding all other areas of the workbook.

Even though Excel Services displays only the published items, the workbook still contains all the other parts of the workbook. A user who has permissions to open the workbook sees the parts that were not published.

To fully protect parts of the workbook, you should use published items in combination with the View Only permissions. When View Only permissions are applied, a user cannot download the workbook to the client, and Excel Services displays only the published items.

Unsupported Protection Features

As you learned in Chapter 4, Excel Services does not support a number of other protection features. The server will not open workbooks that contain any of the following features:

❑ *Workbooks with restricted permissions or protected by Information Rights Management* — These can restrict which users are allowed to read, print, copy, edit, and save the workbook.

❑ *Digital signatures* — Allows you to verify that the workbook has originated from the author who has signed it, and that it has not been changed since it was signed.

❑ *Document encryption* — Requires a password to decrypt the document and show its content.

❑ *Workbook and sheet protection* — Limits the changes that users can make to a workbook.

The recommended alternative with Excel Services is to use SharePoint Open and View Only permissions, and to publish only part of the items in the workbook.

Configuring and Delegating Credentials

In the previous sections, you learned about how the user is authenticated and how you can use permissions to protect the workbook and its content. This section describes how the user's credentials are delegated between the various server components.

A client application is executed in the context of the user's credentials. For example, the Excel process runs as the user who is logged on to the machine. Loading a file from a SharePoint document library into Excel or querying data from a database is done as the user, because the operating system delegates the user's credentials to any other machine. This *one hop* of credentials over the network was described in detail in Chapter 5.

In a server environment, there are multiple components running on multiple machines: the WFE, the ECS, the SharePoint content database, or other file-store and external databases. Each of these processes might run under different credentials, and delegating the user's credentials between these components is a complex process. Excel Services supports several ways of doing this.

Opening a Workbook on the ECS

When opening a workbook, the ECS needs the user's credentials to verify the user's permissions to the file. There are two ways of sending the credentials from the WFE machine to the ECS machine: delegation and trusted subsystem.

The credentials can be passed through *delegation* if the WFE and the ECS are on the same machine, or if Kerberos-constrained delegation is configured between the WFE and the ECS. In either case, the credentials of the user who has connected to the WFE are delegated to the ECS.

If it is not possible to use delegation, a *trusted subsystem* is created between the WFE and the ECS. With this method, the WFE makes the requests to the ECS under the credentials of a special user, and passes the ID of the end user to the ECS as part of the request. The ECS trusts that special user to pass in the correct end-user ID.

> *The default when setting up Office Server is to use delegation for single-box installations and a trusted subsystem for multiple-box installations. You cannot change the setting with the administration UI. The only way to change it is to run the command-line administration tool as follows:*

```
stsadm.exe -o set-ecssecurity -AccessModel Delegation
stsadm.exe -o set-ecssecurity -AccessModel TrustedSubsystem
```

When opening a workbook from a SharePoint document library, the ECS must pass the correct end-user credentials to the SharePoint object model. The ECS uses delegation or a trusted subsystem to the SharePoint object model to pass the credentials it has received from the WFE. SharePoint uses those credentials to find out if the user has Open or View Only permissions to the file.

When a workbook is opened from an UNC or HTTP location, the way the credentials are delegated depends on the access model between the WFE and the ECS (delegation or trusted subsystem), and the file access model (impersonation or process account). The following table shows the various combinations.

Delegation	Trusted Subsystem	
Impersonation	The end user's credentials are delegated to the ECS via Kerberos-constrained delegation, or if the WFE and the ECS are on the same machine. These credentials are used to open the file.	This option fails to load the file, because impersonation requires the end user's credentials to be delegated.
Process account	The ECS process account is used to open the file. Using the process account is less secure (because all the users get the same credentials), and therefore is not recommended when using delegation.	The ECS process account is used to open the file. Using the process account is less secure (because all users get the same credentials), but it is the only way to load UNC and HTTP files when using a trusted subsystem.

External Data

The issue of delegating the end user's credentials to the database in order to check permissions gets more accentuated when querying data from an external database. The database might be on a separate machine, creating one more hop.

Excel Services has multiple ways to define which credentials to use to connect to a database. This must be done by the workbook author in the Authentication Settings dialog box. In addition, the administrator of the server must set up the server correctly to support these authentication settings.

The first way is through the use of Windows Authentication. To allow this method, the access model between the WFE and the ECS must be set to Delegation. In addition, the database must be on the same machine as the ECS, or the administrator must enable Kerberos-constrained delegation between the ECS and the database. When using this method, the end user's credentials are delegated to the WFE, the ECS, and then the database.

The second way is to use SSO. To allow this method, SSO must be set up on the server, and the user must be given certain mapped credentials for this database in SSO. The ECS asks SSO for those credentials, and uses them to connect to the database.

The last way is to not use any credentials that are related to the end user. Rather, a predefined Unattended Account is used to connect to the database, optionally passing in a username and password that were saved in the workbook on the connection string. You can set the Unattended Account username and password in the External Data section of the Excel Services administration settings.

Protecting Against Attacks

In the first part of this chapter, you learned how to set up the server to allow users to see workbooks and the data contained in them according to their permissions. This was based on a normal working scenario, in which the permission limitations were set because of various business rules.

In addition to functioning in normal scenarios, security must be able to protect against malicious attacks. In today's world of cybercrime, security and protection against such attacks play an ever-increasing role.

Threats

There are many types of possible attacks against the server. One way to categorize them is by what they are trying to achieve. In this section, you learn about the various categories of threats, the features that Excel Services has to protect against those threats, and additional recommendations on how to configure and administer the server in a secure way.

The following threat categories are addressed in this section:

❑ *Spoofing* — Impersonating another user in an unauthorized way.

❑ *Tampering with data* — Changing data in a database or data that is displayed in a malicious way.

❑ *Repudiation* — Doing something (usually a bad thing) without a way for the system to know and prove it.

❑ *Information disclosure* — Stealing private information.

❑ *Denial of service* — Reducing the availability of the server, possibly by overloading it.

❑ *Elevation of privilege* — Gaining access to higher privileges than were intended for the user.

Spoofing

Spoofing means impersonating another user in an unauthorized way, or pretending to be someone else. An example related to Excel Services could be if user A tries to trick the server into believing that he or she is user B in order to access the workbook and data results that user B is allowed to see.

Securing the Passwords

To protect against spoofing, you need to ensure that the users of your system do not disclose their passwords, and that there is no way for a malicious user to find out those passwords. Here are some tips:

❑ Educate your users to keep their passwords private. They should not share the passwords with any friends or coworkers.

❑ Change the passwords at an interval that you determine best for your needs.

❑ Ensure that the complexity requirements for the passwords are enough to prevent a malicious user from figuring them out by a brute-force attack.

❑ Changing the passwords too often or having them too complex for users to remember them might have an opposite effect: users may write them down.

❑ Ensure that every user has individual credentials to the system, rather than shared credentials for a group of people.

Basic Authentication

If you use basic authentication, the username and password are sent in clear text over the network. A malicious attacker listening to the network communications may use these usernames and passwords to log in to the system. Therefore, you should not use basic authentication except if you have a way to ensure that the network traffic is secure from eavesdropping.

Trusted Subsystems

One of the ways of transmitting data between the WFE and the ECS is over a trusted subsystem. With this method, the WFE sends the request on behalf of a user. The ECS trusts the special account that the WFE is using to send the requests to the ECS to send the correct user.

A malicious attacker who obtains this trusted subsystem account and is able to send requests to the ECS directly can pretend he or she is the WFE, and trick the ECS into executing requests on behalf of any user.

Following are possible mitigations against this threat:

❑ Protect the credentials of the trusted subsystem account.

❑ Use delegation instead of a trusted subsystem between the WFE and the ECS. You can do this by either having the WFE and the ECS on the same machine, or by enabling Kerberos-constrained delegation between these components.

❑ Install a firewall between the WFE and the ECS to prevent users outside the organization from calling the ECS directly. Some users will still be able to access the ECS directly, but because they are behind the firewall, the threat is reduced.

Passwords in Data Connections

Excel allows a username and password embedded in a connection string to be saved. This username and password are used to connect to an external data source, when the authentication settings are configured to None.

The password is saved in clear text, so anyone who can open the workbook can read those credentials. As a general rule, do not use this feature except if these credentials are well known. If you have to use the feature, make sure you limit the number of users who have Open permissions to the workbook, and give only View permissions to the other users. Users who have only View permissions cannot download the workbook to read the credentials.

Process Account

Excel Services allows the process account to be used to read workbooks from UNC or HTTP locations. Although this is not a classic spoofing threat, the result is similar: users are allowed to read a workbook, even though they might not have permissions to it.

You should use SharePoint document libraries rather than UNC or HTTP locations to ensure that the end user's credentials are used to verify the permissions. For UNC and HTTP locations, you should use impersonation rather than the process account. Using impersonation requires setting up Kerberos-constrained delegation to the UNC or HTTP server, which makes this deployment more difficult.

If you must use the process account, ensure that it is acceptable for all authenticated users to have permissions to those files.

Unattended Account

When the authentication settings for accessing external data are set to None in a workbook, the ECS attempts to use the Unattended Account to connect to the external database. It optionally passes on a username and password if they were specified as part of the connection string. While this is not a classic spoofing attack, it results in all users using the same account.

The Unattended Account is not set by default, disabling this threat. If you do set up an Unattended Account, use an account with very low permissions, so that it is useful only when a username and password are defined on the connection string, or only against databases that contain public information.

Tampering with Data

Tampering with data means changing data in a malicious way. Following are examples related to Excel Services:

❑ Through Excel Services, a user adds, changes, or deletes data in a database that he or she would not have permissions to otherwise.

❑ A malicious attacker changes the information that is displayed to a legitimate user of the system, tricking him or her into believing that the data of the workbook is different from what it actually is.

Client to WFE Communications

An attacker could interfere with the communications that are returned from the WFE to the client and replace the transmitted data with different data. For example, the attacker could change certain financial information, tricking an end user into certain actions such as buying or selling large amounts of stocks based on incorrect price assumptions.

The way to mitigate this threat is by securing the connection between the client machine and the WFE. IPSec and HTTPS are the most common ways to secure the connection within the intranet. For extranet or Internet scenarios (which has the highest risk for this threat), the main way is HTTPS. Enabling HTTPS is done when configuring the IIS on the WFE.

Excel Services has a setting called Connection Encryption. When you set this to Required, the request to the ECS fails if the WFE is not configured to require HTTPS connections.

Server Components Communications

The threat of an attacker tampering with the data sent over the network exists for the communications between any two server components that reside on different machines. Following are examples of such communications between components:

❑   The data returned from the ECS to the WFE could be altered so that the workbook information is different, in a similar way that the data sent from the WFE to the client can be changed.

❑   The data returned from a database to the ECS can be tampered with.

❑   The workbook returned from the SharePoint content database might be fuzzed.

To avoid these problems, you can secure the communications by using protocols such as IPSec or HTTPS.

Tampering with a Database

A malicious user might build a workbook that contains commands that change the content of a database, by adding, updating, or removing rows, or by changing the structure of a database. That attacker could trick another user into viewing the workbook, which will trigger the attack with the second user's credentials.

Excel Services offers a number of ways to mitigate this threat.

The feature set that exists in this version of Excel Services does not allow execution of random commands. However, features such as query tables might be added in future releases, so the following mitigations are still relevant to offer several layers of defense.

❑   Limit which users have permissions to author workbooks. Only trusted users should be allowed to author workbooks that connect to external data sources. You can achieve this by having several trusted locations: some that don't allow external data and are accessible by more users, and those that do allow external data are accessible by a small number of trusted authors. You could also add a middle layer to allow only data from trusted data connection libraries, and to limit them to a small list of DCLs that only a small number of users are allowed to publish to.

❑ The Warn On Data Refresh setting on a trusted location prompts the user before doing the operation. Although turning on this setting allows users to confirm that they really trust the workbook author before refreshing the data, it is not a good user experience and most users just click the Yes button to allow the refresh.

❑ As much as possible, use credentials that have only read-only access to databases when setting up the Unattended Account and the SSO accounts. With read-only access, it is not possible to execute this attack.

Repudiation

Repudiation means that a user or a malicious attacker can perform an action or attempt an attack on a system (regardless of whether or not the attack is successful), without of a way for the system to prove that the action or attack have happened. Non-repudiation means that all relevant transactions are tracked through logging or auditing.

Auditing

SharePoint audits certain operations such as accessing or changing files in a document library. Auditing is a feature added for certain compliance scenarios, and to track the operations done by users.

When Excel Services is used to open workbooks and auditing is turned on in SharePoint, all the open workbook requests are audited, including those served from the workbook cache.

Additional Logging

IIS, SharePoint, Excel Services, SSO, and databases all have their own logging to the event log, and some of them have additional trace logs. Although these logs do not have the formal structure of the auditing log, they can be used in the event of an attack to track the requests that have been sent.

Anonymous Access

Excel Services supports some level of anonymous access. One of the main disadvantages of anonymous access is that there is no way to know which user is doing the operations. Anonymous access is not recommended in most scenarios.

Information Disclosure

Information disclosure involves revealing private information to someone who is not supposed to have access to it. In the context of Excel Services, information disclosure might be any of the following:

❑ Listening to the network communications between the various components to get the data that is passed on the wire.

❑ Unauthorized reading of data from a database through a workbook.

❑ Using cross-site scripting to read data from a workbook.

Spoofing usually allows for information disclosure, because one user sees a different user's information. In addition to the recommendations in the "Spoofing" section earlier in this chapter, the following sections offer other ways to protect against information disclosure.

Secure Communications

One of the ways an attacker can try to get access to private information is to listen on the communication over the network between the various components of the server, or between the WFE and the client.

The way to mitigate this threat is the same as you learned in the "Tampering with Data" section: using a secure protocol such as HTTPS or IPSec between all the relevant components.

You can set Connection Encryption to Required to ensure that the communications between the WFE and the client are encrypted using HTTPS.

Limiting Access to the WFE Machines

In extranet and Internet scenarios, a firewall before the WFE machines limits the types of access that users from outside the domain have. In addition, you should lock down the IIS on the WFE machines to limit the attack surface and expose only the required functionality.

Limiting Access to the Excel Calculation Server

A significant advantage of separating the WFE and the ECS is the ability to further protect the ECS.

One way to do this is to insert a firewall between the WFE and the ECS, which protects the ECS from unauthorized access. This configuration is especially useful in extranet and intranet scenarios, when the users from outside the organization are less trusted.

The information that exists on the WFE is significantly reduced compared to the information on the ECS. The WFE never opens the workbook, and contains only one range of calculated results at a time. This is equivalent to the distinction between Open permissions and View Only permissions. The ECS has Open permissions, but the WFE has only View permissions. If the WFE is compromised, the important information that exists on the WFE is still safe.

Limiting Access to the File Cache

The ECS maintains a cache of workbooks and other calculated objects on the disk. If attackers gain access to the folder that contains the cache, they can read workbooks and other information that otherwise they do not have permissions to.

This cache is located by default under the temporary directory of the ECS machine. As an administrator, you should ensure that the permissions to the cache directory are limited to the ECS process account. In addition, you should consider using Windows Encrypted File System (EFS) to provide encryption to this folder.

Workbook Reading from Database

A potential threat is that of a malicious user building a workbook containing commands to read information from a database that the attacker does not have permissions to. The workbook can then write the information to another location that the attacker does have Write permission to. That attacker could trick another user into viewing the workbook, which would trigger reading the information from the database with the second user's credentials.

This attack is similar to the one described earlier in the "Tampering with Data" section, and the mitigations are similar. The main one is having only a limited number of trusted locations that allow querying external data, and limiting the Write permissions in these to a small number of trusted authors. In addition, you can use fewer trusted DCLs.

Cross-Site Scripting

A possible cross-site scripting attack is one in which the attacker reads data displayed in the workbook of another user. An attacker can build a web page that contains an EWA connected to a certain workbook, and a script running on the page that reads the data displayed in the workbook and stores it in some location that the attacker has access to. The attacker then invites a user to view this page. The workbook is displayed in the page under the credentials of that user. The script steals the information from the displayed range and sends it to the attacker.

Excel Services has a setting that allows or disables having EWA on a different domain than the workbook. By default, this setting is disabled. The Allow Cross Domain Access setting is available only from the following command-line administration:

```
stsadm.exe -o set-ecssecurity -AllowCrossDomainAccess True|False
```

To mitigate cross-site scripting attacks, use the following guidelines:

❑ Do not turn on the Allow Cross Domain Access setting, or if you need to allow access between domains and turn this setting on, ensure that the users on the other domains can be trusted.

❑ Limit the users who are allowed to upload script to web pages.

Denial of Service

Denial of service means reducing the availability of a server, usually by overloading it or causing it to crash. Following are examples related to Excel Services:

❑ Sending a lot of requests to the server trying to overload it.

❑ Loading a huge workbook that uses a lot of memory on ECS.

❑ Loading a complex workbook that causes it to use a lot of CPU on the ECS.

❑ Performing a large number of external data requests that cause denial of service on the database server or consume a lot of network resources to transfer the data.

The main types of mitigations are related to limiting the requests sent to the server and limiting the workbooks that are opened on the server. You can use the settings that limit the requests and workbooks to protect against denial-of-service attacks as well as to prevent a naïve user from overloading the server accidentally.

Web Front End

The first line of defense against denial-of-service attacks is at the WFE level. These types of defenses are generic to any type of web application, including Excel Services. In extranet and intranet scenarios, you should use a firewall to limit the protocols, ports, and the types of requests that can be sent to the WFE.

In addition, you should configure the IIS on the WFE to further reduce the denial-of-service attacks. Limit the attack surface by securing the web pages and web services that can be called. Use strong authentication to ensure that only real system users can get past this layer. Using anonymous access makes it more difficult to identify and track down such attacks.

IIS also has settings to limit the number of requests that can be made, and to log the requests to be able to track issues.

IIS on Excel Calculation Server

The guidelines for protecting the ECS are similar to those related to protecting the WFE:

❑   Set up a firewall between the WFE and the ECS, especially in extranet scenarios or when there is very sensitive information in the workbooks.

❑   Limit the attack surface on the ECS by opening only the required protocols and ports.

❑   Configure IIS to authenticate all requests.

❑   Set up IIS to limit the number of requests, the request timeout, and the memory size of the process.

Maximum Sessions per User

Usually, in a denial-of-service attack that goes beyond a brute-force attack on the WFE, it is difficult for the attacker to use multiple users, because the attacker needs the credentials for all users who are sending the malicious requests. The attacker might succeed in getting the passwords of only one or a few users.

Excel Services has a setting that limits the maximum number of sessions per authenticated user. The goal of this setting is to limit the amount of damage one user can do, and, therefore, reduce denial-of-service attacks.

Trusted Locations

Trusted locations define which workbooks can be opened on the server. Excel Services fails to open a workbook that is not from a trusted location. You should limit the trusted locations to folders over which you have some level of control. You should be able to trust that the authors who have permissions to write to these trusted locations will not attempt to take the server down. For a trusted location that has the Children Trusted flag set, make sure that all the folders below it inherit the same security settings.

In addition, you can use several settings on each trusted location to further lock it down. The less you trust the authors who are allowed to publish to a trusted location, the more you should limit the settings of that trusted location. This way, you can reduce the probability of any random user taking down the whole server.

You should set the following on each trusted location:

❑   *Session Timeout and Short Session Timeout* — These settings determine how long the workbook remains in memory after there is no activity in the session. The longer these settings are, the larger the impact on the memory footprint of the ECS. If you set these to large values and assume that the caller will explicitly close the session, an attacker might open workbooks without closing them, using all the memory of the ECS.

❑ *Request Timeout* — You can use this setting to limit how much time a request can run on the ECS. The default is 5 minutes. For a trusted location in which you do not want authors to be able to use too many ECS resources, you can set this value to a small number (such as a few seconds).

❑ *Maximum Workbook Size* — This setting limits the size of the workbook on disk that can be loaded to the ECS. A large workbook has an adverse impact on the ECS performance in terms of I/O, CPU, and memory consumption. The default size is 10MB. If you do not trust the authors of a trusted location, you should reduce this value.

❑ *Maximum Chart Size* — This setting limits the maximum size of a chart image. Resources on the ECS are used to create and cache large charts, and resources on the network between the ECS and the WFE, and between the WFE and the client, are used to transport them. You can reduce this setting to prevent a malicious user from publishing a workbook with huge charts.

❑ *Volatile Function Cache Lifetime* — Use this setting to prevent an attacker from creating a workbook with volatile formulas and complex calculations that are resource-intensive. The default is 5 minutes, which means that the workbook is not recalculated on open for 5 minutes, even if it has volatile functions such as NOW.

❑ *Workbook Calculation Mode* — Set this to Manual to prevent calculation of the workbook on open. This way, you can allow some users to publish static workbooks (which do not require calculation) to a trusted location. Static workbooks are relatively cheap in terms of resources, because they do not require calculation and they cache well. With this set to Manual, using settings in the Web Part properties that prevent interactivity in the Web Part, and limiting external data access, you can fully enforce static workbooks only.

❑ *Allow External Data* — Set this value to None to prevent workbooks in a trusted location from accessing any external data. Workbooks that access external data can use a lot of resources, both on the ECS and on the database server. A value of None prevents the attacker from using external data as a way to deny service. This setting can works well with the Manual workbook calculation mode to enforce static workbooks.

❑ *External Data Cache Lifetime* — Use this setting to prevent users from sending a lot of requests to refresh external data that are actually queries. Queries to databases are expensive and can result in a denial of service on Excel Services or the database. The default value for the external data cache lifetime is 5 minutes. This means that, by default, after a refresh has been performed, any refresh operation to that data object in the workbook within the next 5 minutes is returned from the cache.

❑ *Maximum Concurrent Queries Per Session* — Excel Calculation Services allows running multiple queries in parallel to improve the user response time. To prevent a malicious user from creating a workbook with a large number of data objects, all running in parallel, you should restrict the maximum number of concurrent queries. The default value is 5 parallel queries per workbook, and you can reduce this value further for less trusted locations.

❑ *Allow User-Defined Functions* — UDFs can run code on the server. When used inefficiently, this can result in a high usage of resources and denial of service. A malicious user can create a workbook that contains a lot of expensive calls to a UDF. Allow UDFs only for highly trusted locations.

To summarize this section, you should restrict the features and size of workbooks based on how much you trust the authors who have Write permissions to each trusted location.

Elevation of Privilege

Elevation of privilege means that users gain higher permissions than they should have. For example, a user tricks an administrator into getting more privileges.

This type of attack could be considered the worst kind, because someone who gains administrative access can perform any of the other types of attacks.

Trust the Administrators

SharePoint has several levels of administration. There is central administration of the farm, administration of the SSP level, and administration at the site level. When users have administrative powers, they can do anything within their scope of control. The system will not limit any activities.

You need to be able to trust your administrators. You should educate them and expect them to do the following:

❑ Not abuse their powers to perform any security attacks against the server.

❑ Configure the server in a secure way to limit the attacks that others might attempt to perform against the server.

❑ Grant administrator rights to only those users who are as trusted as they are.

Unattended Account

The general guideline is to not use an Unattended Account for external data access, and to define an Unattended Account with low privileges. If you need to define an Unattended Account with higher privileges, it is imperative that the account does not have permissions to the SharePoint content database.

If the Unattended Account has permissions to the content database, an attacker could create a workbook that queries data from the content database and runs under the Unattended Account. With this method, the attacker could work around the security model of the content database, possibly writing into it to elevate his or her own privileges.

Extensibility

The administrator of Excel Services can deploy code that extends the built-in functionality of Excel Services. The main types of extensibility are user-defined functions and data drivers.

UDFs are third-party code that can execute any commands. They run in the security context of the user who is opening the workbook. As such, they are extremely dangerous when used incorrectly.

UDFs are not a threat category by themselves, but they can result in a number of issues, such as the following:

❑ *Tampering* — A UDF can write data to a database with the credentials of the user who opened the workbook.

❏ *Information disclosure* — A UDF can read data off the workbook and send it to a malicious user who does not have access to that data. The data might be coming from a database.

❏ *Denial of service* — A UDF can use all the resources of the ECS machine, significantly lowering its resources. Excel Services does not enforce any limits in the amount of resources that a UDF consumes. It does not stop the UDF execution in the middle if the request timeout has expired.

For these threats to materialize, UDFs must either be malicious or be used in a malicious way.

In a similar way, data drivers are invoked as part of external data queries, and they can be malicious or be invoked in a malicious way.

Malicious User-Defined Functions

A malicious UDF is intentionally designed to harm the security of the server or its users by stealing information, changing data in an unauthorized way, or reducing the availability of the server.

To mitigate this threat, ensure that you fully control the executables that are deployed for the UDFs. Follow these guidelines:

❏ Deploy only UDFs that are developed by a trusted source. This guideline is the same as with any other software that you deploy on your machines, from an external vendor or a developer from your organization.

❏ Limit the access to the location that the UDFs are deployed to. Only administrators should have permissions to change the files deployed as the UDFs. UDFs deployed to the GAC are usually more secure, because the permissions to the GAC are more limited and it allows versioning and strong names.

❏ For UDFs written in managed code, use code access security to limit what the UDFs are allowed to do. For example, do not allow them to access the network or the disk if they do not need to.

Malicious Use of User-Defined Functions

A non-malicious UDF can be used in a malicious way with grim results. Here are a few examples:

❏ A UDF receives a range in the workbook as an argument and performs a complex mathematical calculation over that range. An attacker could craft a workbook that calls this UDF and passes a huge range of data as an argument, resulting in the UDF consuming a huge amount of CPU and memory.

❏ A UDF has a security defect that can be exploited to run arbitrary code. Altough the developer of the UDF did not intend a malicious exploit, an attacker could potentially take advantage of it to run some other code that results in a number of attacks.

❏ A UDF is designed to write data to a database. It receives as a parameter the database to write to, and the SQL command to execute. When used in a non-malicious way, such a UDF can have a positive business value. On the other hand, an attacker can use this UDF to tamper with any database that the user who opens the workbook has access to.

You can mitigate this threat by deploying well-designed UDFs and limiting who is allowed to author workbooks that have UDFs. Here are some guidelines:

❑ When evaluating the UDFs that you are going to deploy to the server, ensure that the developers use sound security practices. As with any other software product, deploy security patches to the UDF's code.

❑ Ensure that the UDFs are designed to minimize the chances of malicious use. For example, a UDF that executes mathematical calculations on a range might limit the maximum size of the range. The UDF that writes to a database might take the database name and table name from a configuration file or registry key, rather than any arbitrary SQL command passed in as input.

❑ Limit the trusted locations that are allowed to run UDFs. Each trusted location has a setting called Allow User-Defined Functions, which is turned off by default. Turn it on only in trusted locations that are limited to a small number of trusted authors.

Data Providers

Data providers are the drivers that the ECS uses to connect to external data. The malicious user could publish a workbook that queries data from that provider. An attacker could use data providers to create a denial-of-service attack by doing the following:

❑ Convince the administrator to install a malicious driver, that results in an attack when invoked. The attack could be denial of service, information disclosure, or tampering with data.

❑ Exploit a known security issue with the data provider, which could result in running arbitrary malicious code on the server in the security context of the user opening the workbook.

❑ Make calls to a data provider that is not well-designed for a robust server environment, which could use a significant amount of resources or lock the server threads and result in a denial of service.

As an administrator, you should do the following:

❑ Use the list of trusted data providers to limit which drivers can be called from Excel Services.

❑ As with any other software deployment, use only providers developed by trusted sources and install any relevant security patches.

❑ Limit the permissions to change these binaries to administrators.

Summary

In this chapter, you learned the following about Excel Services security:

❑ Users are authenticated via Windows Authentication (integrated, digest, or basic), Forms Authentication, or Anonymous.

❑ You can use SharePoint View Only permissions to allow viewing workbooks only on the server and prevent downloading them to the client. In addition to publishing only a subset of the items in the workbook, View Only permissions is a powerful tool for maintaining one version of the truth and protecting the intellectual property of the workbook model.

❑ Excel Services does not support opening workbooks with most of the client security-related features, including restricted content (Information Rights Management), digital signature, encryption, and workbook and sheet protection.

❑ The communication between the WFE and the ECS can be done through a trusted subsystem or credentials delegation.

❑ Files are loaded from SharePoint by checking the end user's permissions. Depending on the configuration, UNC and HTTP files can be loaded by using the process account.

❑ When loading data from external data sources, the credentials can be delegated through Kerberos-constrained delegation, be mapped to different SSO credentials, or use a predefined Unattended Account.

❑ Malicious users could try to attack the server or use the server to attack other machines (such as databases). You should configure the server in a secure way to prevent these attacks.

❑ Spoofing means pretending to be another user. The main prevention is to protect passwords and not send or store them in clear text.

❑ Tampering with data means changing data that the attacker should not be allowed to do. The main preventions are to secure communications between the components and limit write access to databases.

❑ Repudiation means that a malicious can get away with an attempt to perform something without a way to prove it. Auditing and logging are ways to track the user's actions.

❑ Information disclosure is a way for an attacker to steal information. Mitigations include secure communications over the network and limited permissions on critical resources.

❑ Denial of service means overloading a server in a way that reduces its availability. Limiting the attack surface and reducing trusted locations privileges are possible solutions.

❑ Elevation of privileges means gaining higher rights, such as those of an administrator. Education of the administrators and securing configuration of the server are critical.

The last part of this book contains step-by-step instructions for implementing the important Excel Services scenarios. Chapter 9 discusses publishing workbooks to the server. In Chapter 10, you learn about interacting with the workbook on the server. In Chapter 11, you find out about controlling those workbooks and the relationships with other Office Server features. Chapter 12 shows the Business Intelligence scenario, including dashboards. Chapter 13 explains how to use Excel Services to offload heavy calculations. In Chapter 14, you learn about extending Excel Services in programmability scenarios.

Part III
How-To Scenarios

Chapter 9: Sharing Workbooks with the Browser

Chapter 10: Interacting with Workbooks in the Browser

Chapter 11: Controlling Workbook Distribution

Chapter 12: Business Intelligence Solutions

Chapter 13: Offloading Workbook Calculation to the Server

Chapter 14: Building Custom Solutions

Sharing Workbooks with the Browser

Now that you have a good understanding of the scenarios Excel Services is designed for, how the server looks and works underneath the hood, and how to set up the server, this chapter focuses on sharing workbooks with the browser.

The remaining chapters in this book are designed to acquaint you with using the server's functionality. Though they present step-by-step instructions to using Excel Services features, this is not a replacement for the manual and online help provided with the product.

Using Excel Services to share workbooks with the browser consists of the following two steps:

1. Publishing workbooks to the server
2. Viewing workbooks in the browser

Publishing a Workbook to the Server

There are two basic steps to publishing a spreadsheet to Excel Services:

1. Saving the spreadsheet to a location that the server has access to and is a trusted location
2. Verifying that the server can load, calculate, and render the spreadsheet in the browser

The Simple Case

This section examines the most straightforward case for publishing a spreadsheet to the server and viewing it in the browser. In the following Try It Out, you use the sample workbook provided with this book, Sales Report.xlsx.

For the examples in this chapter and in the following chapters, you need Excel 2007 installed and a Microsoft Office SharePoint Server installed with Excel Services running. You also need to have at least one trusted location set up. In these examples, the entire server is trusted. You use the default Shared Documents document library under the root site. The server used in the step-by-step instructions and screenshots is called TheExcelServer. Replace the server name in the examples with your server name.

Try It Out   **Publishing a Workbook to the Server**

To publish a workbook to the server, follow these steps:

1.   Start Excel 2007 and load the Sales Report.xlsx workbook that is provided with this book.

2.   From the Office menu button, select the Publish option to display the Publish fly-out shown in Figure 9-1.

3.   Select the Excel Services option. The dialog box shown in Figure 9-2 is displayed.

4.   Enter the location where you want to save the workbook. This must be defined as a trusted location on the server. Save the workbook to `http://TheExcelServer/shared documents`.

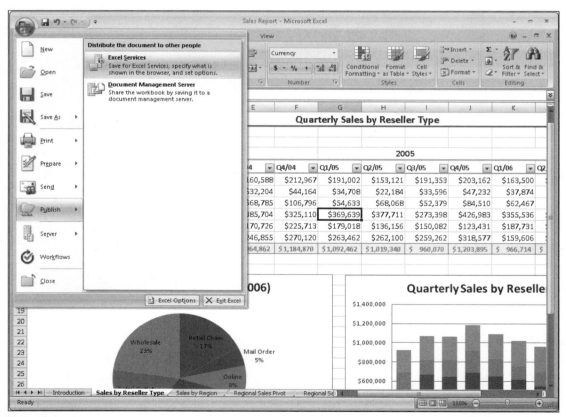

Figure 9-1

Figure 9-2

5.   Verify that the Open in Excel Services box is checked (which it is by default).

6.   Publish the workbook by clicking the Save button.

7.   A new browser window opens with the workbook displayed, as shown in Figure 9-3. Use the sheet tabs at the bottom of the display to view the different sheets in the workbook. (The toolbar at the top of the workbook is discussed later in the "Viewing Workbooks in the Browser" section, later in the chapter.)

8.   Close the browser window.

How It Works

The simple description of how this works is that the workbook is saved to the server, loaded by Excel Services, calculated, and then rendered in the browser as HTML.

Getting into more detail about what happened in this exercise, when you clicked the Save button, Excel simply saved the workbook to the location you specified. In this regard, you get the same results as when you use the Save or Save As features.

Next, because you used the Publish dialog box with the Open In Excel Services option checked, Excel opened a new browser window and passed the URL for the workbook you just saved to the Excel Viewer page as a parameter (more on this in the "The Excel Viewer Page" section later in this chapter).

The resulting page is not a "preview." It is the actual workbook loaded and rendered by the server. This is equivalent to saving the workbook and then manually opening a browser and navigating to that workbook on the server.

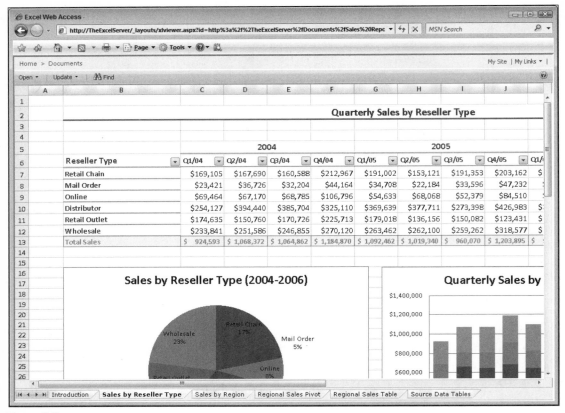

Figure 9-3

The Excel Viewer page contains the Excel Web Access (EWA) Web Part and it, in turn, called on the Excel Calculation Service (ECS). The ECS loaded the workbook, calculated it, and returned the updated workbook to EWA. EWA then created the HTML that represents the workbook and returned it to the browser. Finally, the browser rendered HTML on your desktop to give you an accurate representation of the workbook.

As the author of the workbook, you also have rights to view the workbook in the browser. The "Viewing Workbooks in the Browser" section later in this chapter goes into more detail on the rights necessary to view a workbook.

In the next section, you go back to the Publish dialog box in Excel and use the Show tab to control which parts of the workbook are visible in the browser.

Controlling What's Visible in the Browser

Excel Services gives you control over which parts of the workbook are accessible through the server when either viewed through the browser or accessed through the web services API. The benefits of having this control are as follows:

❑ You can simplify the browsing experience by displaying only the critical parts of a workbook. For example, you could display a final sales results report, but not all the data and scratch calculations used to come up with it.

❑ You can secure certain parts of the workbook from the readers. For example, you could display only an aggregated results table without providing access to all the detailed data on other sheets. You accomplish this by granting file access rights to the user (as described in Chapter 10).

As you saw in the first example, the entire workbook is visible in the browser by default. By using the Show tab in the Publish dialog box, you can limit access to specific sheets or specific items in the workbook. Items can be one or more of the following:

❑ Tables
❑ Charts
❑ PivotTables
❑ PivotCharts
❑ Named ranges (only consecutive named ranges are supported)

The following Try It Out shows you how to control which parts of the workbook are visible in the browser.

Try It Out   Controlling What's Displayed in the Browser

To control what's visible in the browser, follow these steps:

1. Start Excel 2007 and load the Sales Report.xlsx workbook that is provided with this book.

2. From the Office menu button, select the Publish option to show the Publish fly-out.

3. Select the Excel Services option.

4. If you are not continuing from the first example, enter a location where you want the workbook saved. This must be defined as a trusted location on the server.

5. Verify that the Open in Excel Services box is checked (which it is by default).

6. Switch over to the Show tab. By default, the Entire Workbook option is selected, and the list box below it is disabled.

7. In the drop-down menu, select Sheets. The list box is enabled and displays the available sheets in the workbook, as shown in Figure 9-4.

8. Select the Sales By Reseller Type sheet by checking the box next to it.

9. Publish the workbook by pressing the Save button.

10. A new browser window opens with the workbook displayed. This time, the workbook in the browser has only one sheet tab, Sales By Reseller Type, as shown in Figure 9-5. You cannot navigate to the other sheets. In fact, there is no way of knowing that the other sheets even exist.

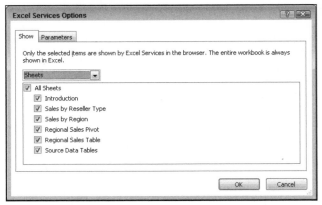

Figure 9-4

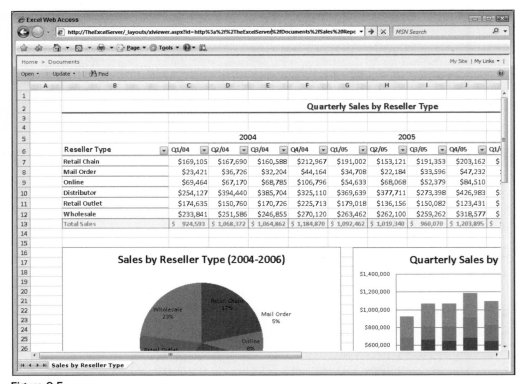

Figure 9-5

11. Close the browser window and return to Excel.

12. Open the Publish dialog box and select the Show tab again. This time, select Items In The Workbook from the drop-down menu, as shown in Figure 9-6. A list of available items in the workbook is displayed.

13. Select RegionalSalesTable by checking the box next to it.

14. Publish the workbook by pressing the Save button.

15. A new browser window opens with the workbook displayed. This time, the workbook in the browser displays only the RegionalSalesTable. The chart that was on the first sheet is not visible. The sheet tabs don't even exist, and you cannot view any other sheet or item in the workbook.

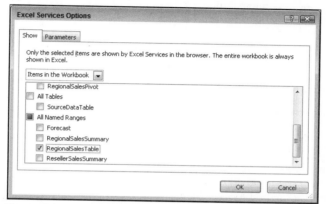

Figure 9-6

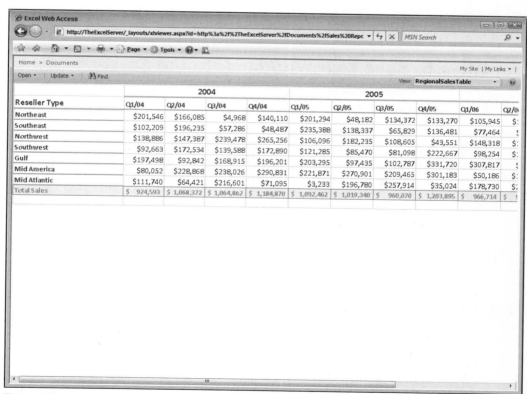

Figure 9-7

*There is now a new drop-down menu on the EWA toolbar. The menu has one entry, RegionalSalesTable.
If you had selected multiple items in step 13, they would all appear here. You would be able to toggle
between the various items (charts, tables, ranges, and PivotTables) by using this drop-down menu.*

How It Works

What's actually happening behind the scenes when you publish a workbook with only specific sheets or
items checked as visible? The most important thing to realize is that the entire workbook is saved to the
server. This is critical for the following reasons:

❑   The visible areas may refer to values and calculations in the nonvisible areas.

❑   It allows you to continue to develop and edit a single workbook file.

The workbook file you saved to the server contains the list of visible sheets or items you selected. When
the ECS loads the workbook, it reads this list and returns only those sheets and items to the EWA, which
renders them to the browser.

When you open the workbook in Excel (assuming you have permission to do so), the entire workbook is
displayed, including all the sheets and all the items. To see which sheets or items are visible when the
workbook is published, open the Publish dialog box or the Excel Services Options dialog box that is in
the Server Properties fly-out and look at the list in the Show tab.

*To completely secure the sheets and items in the workbook that you do not want to give access to, you
must limit the workbook users' rights.*

Other Ways to Save Your Workbook to the Server

There are a few additional ways to save a workbook to the server. Although using the Publish dialog box
is the most straightforward method, you may prefer one of the alternatives.

First, you can simply use the Excel Save or Save As function. There is no difference between a workbook
file saved to the server with the Publish option or one of these. They all load workbooks on the server,
which are then viewable in the browser. The Publish dialog box provides the additional functionality of
being able to set viewable sheets or items, define workbook parameters (discussed in Chapter 10), and
automatically open the browser page to view the published workbook. You achieve the same results by
saving the workbook the server using Excel's regular Save functionality, and then using the Excel Services
Options dialog box under the Server Properties fly-out. This dialog box lets you access the Show tab, as
well as set workbook parameters. However, it does not have an option for opening the workbook in the
browser — you have to do this manually.

You can also upload a workbook file to SharePoint from the SharePoint web UI.

Try It Out   **Uploading a Workbook to SharePoint**

To upload a workbook to SharePoint, follow these steps:

1.   Start your browser and navigate to the Office SharePoint Server home page of your server,
`http://TheExcelserver`.

2. Navigate to the document library into which you want to upload the workbook. For this example, go to `http://TheExcelServer/shared documents`.

3. In the toolbar for the document library, select the Upload option. A screen similar to Figure 9-8 appears.

4. In the Upload dialog box, select the workbook that you want to save to the server and then select OK.

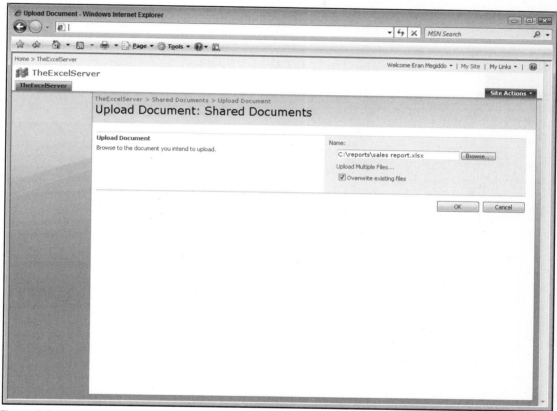

Figure 9-8

Common Issues with Publishing Workbooks

Problems will arise if you try to do the following in Excel Services:

❏ Publish a workbook to a location that is not accessible by the server and is not set up as a trusted location

❏ Publish a workbook that cannot be loaded by the server because it contains unsupported features or is in the wrong file format

- ❑ Publish a workbook that contains external data queries that cannot be refreshed on the server
- ❑ Use offline editing options and the server draft location when publishing a workbook

Trusted Locations

Excel Services can only load files from locations it has access to and that are defined as trusted locations. If you attempt to publish a workbook locally to your My Documents folder or to your desktop with the Open in Excel Services option selected, the browser window opens, but Excel Services fails to load the workbook. This is because, in most cases, the server does not have access to your local directories, nor are they defined as trusted locations. The error message shown in Figure 9-9 is displayed.

The simple remedy is to verify that the location to which you are publishing the workbook is, in fact, defined as a trusted location on Excel Services. Chapter 8 provides more information.

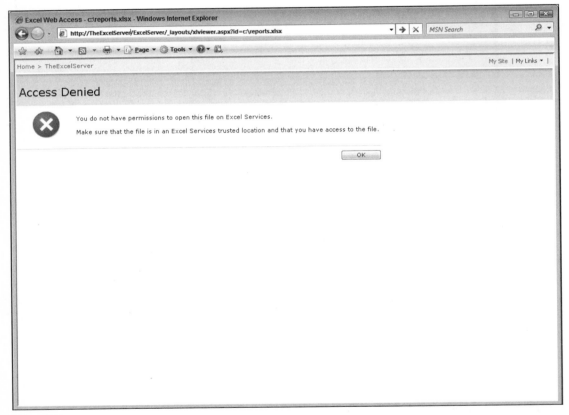

Figure 9-9

Unsupported Features or File Formats

Excel Services does not support all the functionality of the client. Therefore, a workbook that is working fine on the client may fail to load on the server, and the error message shown in Figure 9-10 is displayed. (Chapter 4 examined the features supported by Excel Services, as well as common workarounds for features that are not supported.)

To remedy this error, return to the Excel client, verify that you are saving the workbook in either Excel Workbook (*.xlsx) or Excel Binary Workbook (*.xlsb) format, and remove any unsupported features.

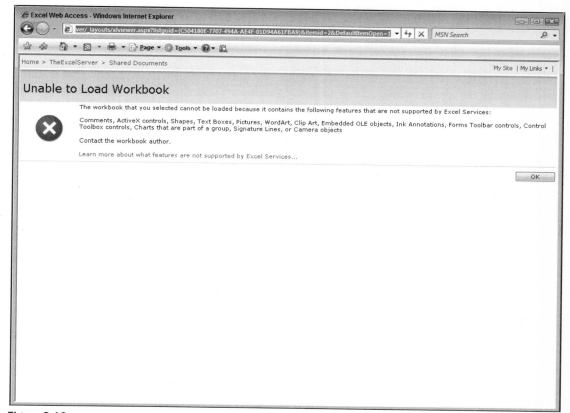

Figure 9-10

External Data Issues

Chapter 5 discussed how to work with external data and Excel Services. A common error is attempting to publish a workbook that contains a query to an external data source that the server does not have permissions for. If the server is set up to fail loading a workbook if the data refresh fails, you receive an error message (see Figure 9-11) and the workbook does not load.

To remedy this error, correct the server settings for the external data query (as described in Chapter 5).

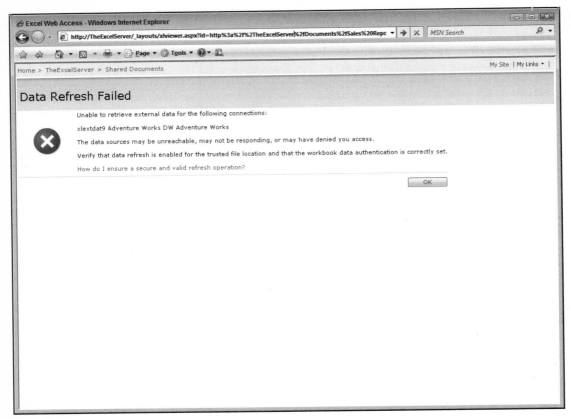

Figure 9-11

Offline Editing Options and the Server Drafts Location

Excel 2007 (as well as the other Office applications) has a new feature for the offline editing of documents stored in SharePoint. This feature works in conjunction with document library check-in and check-out features. When you check out a file from SharePoint for editing, a local copy is saved in a drafts folder. The file is saved to the original SharePoint location only when you check it back in.

If you are using offline editing options and trying to publish a workbook to Excel Services, you may receive an error message that says, "Unable to display the workbook in the browser. Unable to detect Excel Services." This error occurs when you are working on a workbook that is checked out. Publishing the workbook saves it locally to the drafts folder. When Excel attempts to open the workbook in the browser, it is unable to do so because the local folder is not on a server that Excel Services can reach. To actually publish the workbook to the server and view it in the browser, you must check the workbook back in.

If you want to view the workbook in the browser after publishing, and would rather not go through checking the workbook out and then in, you can turn the offline editing mode off through the Save options in Excel. By doing this, you guarantee that the workbook is saved directly to the server and can be opened in Excel Services.

Now that you have seen the various ways you can publish a workbook to the server, as well as how to control what is visible in the browser after a workbook is published, the next section describes how the consumers of your workbook find and view it in the browser.

Viewing Workbooks in the Browser

When you publish a workbook from Excel to the server, you can quickly and easily view it in the browser by selecting the Open in Excel Services option. But how do other users find out about your workbook and view it? This rest of this chapter describes a number of different options.

Viewing a Workbook from a Document Library

The most straightforward way to view a workbook in the browser is to navigate to the SharePoint document library that contains the workbook, and select the option to view the workbook in the browser.

Try It Out   **Viewing a Workbook from a Document Library**

To view a workbook from a document library, follow these steps:

1.   Open the home page of your server in the browser.
2.   Navigate to the document library where you saved your workbook in the previous exercise, `http://TheExcelServer/shared documents`.
3.   Hover over the workbook filename and open the drop-down menu.
4.   Select View In Web Browser from the drop-down menu.
5.   The workbook opens in the browser.

How It Works

When you selected the View In Web Browser option, the Excel Viewer page was loaded with the URL for the workbook passed to it. The workbook was loaded and calculated on ECS, and EWA rendered the workbook in the browser.

If you click on the workbook in the document library, it opens in Excel (the client application).

Next, you learn how to change the default click behavior of a document library to open Excel workbooks in the browser.

Changing the Default Click to View in Browser

You change the default behavior when a user clicks a workbook in a document library so it automatically opens in the browser.

Changing the Default Click Behavior

To change the default click behavior, follow these steps:

1. Navigate to the document library that contains the workbook, `http://TheExcelServer/shared documents`.

2. From the Settings menu, select Document Library Settings.

3. In the General Settings category, select Advanced Settings.

4. In the Opening Browser-Enabled Documents section on the right side of the page, select Display As A Web Page, as shown in Figure 9-12.

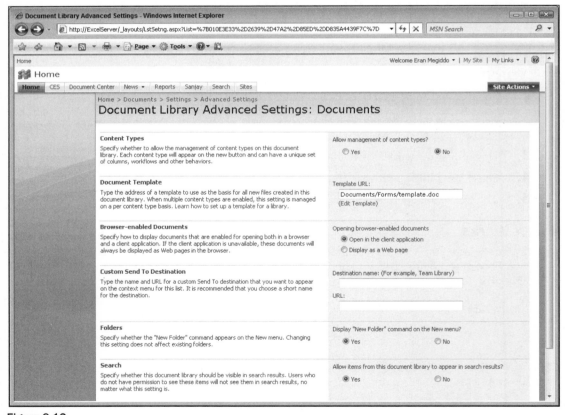

Figure 9-12

5. Click OK at the bottom of the screen.

6. Return to the document library by clicking its link in the My Links drop-down list at the top of the page.

7. Click the workbook name.

8. The workbook opens in the browser.

How It Works

The setting that you changed is not specific to Excel Services. It applies to any file type that has a File Handler for viewing files installed on SharePoint. You changed the default so that if a user clicks any file of this type in this document library, it is sent to the browser and not to the client application. No other file types are affected.

If you want to open the workbook in the Excel client (perhaps to edit it), hover over the workbook name and select Edit In Microsoft Office Excel from the drop-down menu.

The next section takes a closer look at the Excel Viewer Page.

The Excel Viewer Page

The Excel Viewer page provides the default out-of-the-box viewing experience for workbooks in Office SharePoint Server. It is designed to give maximum screen real estate to the workbook being viewed. The Excel Viewer is an ASP page that is installed by default with Office SharePoint Server. Every SharePoint site has an Excel Viewer page installed for each site in the layouts directory. The page has two elements: the SharePoint navigation crumb and the EWA control. The navigation crumb provides a link back to the location on SharePoint from which the user navigated to the Excel Viewer page. The EWA provides the browser-based interface to workbooks.

The Excel Viewer page takes a number of parameters on the query string. The most important of these is the URL for the workbook to be loaded and viewed in EWA, which is passed on the `id` parameter. You can use the `range` parameter to set the range or a named object to be displayed in the workbook.

You can customize the workbook viewing experience by creating your own Excel Viewer Pages and replacing the one installed by default.

Sending a Link to View a Workbook in the Browser

The previous examples assumed that the user who wants to view the workbook knows where it is, and navigates to the correct document library to view it. In the next Try It Out, you learn how you can send a user a link for viewing the workbook in the browser.

Try It Out   **Sending a Link to View a Workbook in the Browser**

To send users a link so they can view a workbook in the browser, follow these steps:

1. Navigate back to the document library that contains the workbook, `http://TheExcelServer/shared documents`.

2. Hover over the workbook name and open the drop-down menu.

3. Click the Send To menu option to open the fly-out.

4. Click Email A Link (see Figure 9-13).

5. Assuming you have an e-mail program installed, a new mail message with a link in it is created. For example:

```
http://TheExcelServer/_layouts/xlviewer.aspx?id=/shared documents/Sales
Report.xlsx.
```

If you or the e-mail recipient clicks the link in the e-mail message, the workbook opens in the browser if that is the default setting for files in this document library, or in the client if it is not.

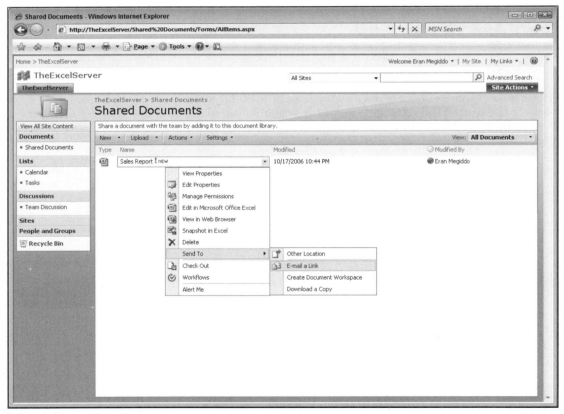

Figure 9-13

How It Works

The link that is generated is not the workbook URL. The link is to the Excel Viewer page with the workbook URL on its `id` parameter. This ensures that the workbook is, in fact, opened in the browser, assuming that this is the default setting for the document library.

> *If you simply use the browser's built-in Copy Shortcut functionality to capture the workbook URL and send that in an e-mail message, the link bypasses the Excel Viewer page and the workbook opens in the Excel client, regardless of the document library setting.*

Summary

This was the first of four chapters that take you through the user scenarios described in Chapter 1. This chapter dealt with the most basic use case of Excel Services: sharing workbooks through the browser.

The chapter began with a look at how to publish a workbook from Excel client to the server. It then looked at the scenario from the other side: viewing a published workbook in the browser.

In this chapter, you learned to do the following:

- ❑ Publish a workbook to the server
- ❑ Control which regions of the workbook are viewable in the browser
- ❑ View a workbook in the browser
- ❑ Change the default behavior for opening a workbook from a document library
- ❑ Send a link to a workbook published to the server

In Chapter 10, you learn how to navigate and interact with the workbook in the browser.

Interacting with Workbooks in the Browser

Excel Services allows you to not only view the workbook in the browser, but also interact with it. There are numerous things you can do within the workbook, starting with navigating within and between sheets all the way through exploring external data with a PivotTable.

The goal of the supported interactivity features is to allow you to explore the data in the workbook and use the calculation models within it. It is not to author or modify the saved workbook, so do not expect to be able to edit formulas, type in cells, or change the formatting of a chart, for example. You also won't find a Save button on the toolbar. It is assumed that you will be interacting with the workbook to find a number or perform a calculation, and that after you do, there will be no more interaction.

This chapter examines all the ways you can interact with a workbook in the browser, including the following:

- ❑ Navigating workbooks and hyperlinks
- ❑ Using tables to sort and filter data
- ❑ Using PivotTables
- ❑ Working with workbook parameters
- ❑ Interactivity and charting
- ❑ The EWA Toolbar
- ❑ Controlling EWA interactivity settings

Navigating Workbooks and Hyperlinks

When you view a workbook in Excel client, there are two primary ways to navigate within a worksheet and workbook:

❑ Scrolling within a worksheet

❑ Switching between sheets

When you view a workbook with Excel Services in the browser, the same is true, but the implementation is slightly different. In the first section, you learn the basic navigation of a worksheet and workbook in the browser. You then take a look at switching between items in a workbook, using hyperlinks to navigate workbooks, and expanding and collapsing grouped rows and columns.

Scrolling Within a Worksheet

By default, EWA displays only the first 20 columns and 75 rows of a worksheet in the browser. This is a performance optimization that minimizes the size of the HTML file transferred across the wire. Because of this, the scroll bars only let you scroll within the 20-by-75 region of the worksheet. If you want to scroll to a different area in the worksheet, use the page scrolling controls on the toolbar.

The page scrolling controls appear only when the worksheet has data in the range beyond the first 20 columns or 75 rows, in which case there is an arrow for each scroll direction: left, right, up, and down. If there is nowhere to scroll in a particular direction, then the corresponding arrow is disabled. Therefore, assuming you load the worksheet with the first row and column in the top-left corner, the left and up arrows are disabled. Because you cannot edit a cell in Excel Services, the *scrollable range* is defined as the used range within a worksheet.

Pressing the left or right arrows scrolls the workbook by 20 columns left or right. Pressing the up or down arrows scrolls the workbook to the next or previous 75 rows accordingly. Each of the arrow buttons is also a split-button, and you can use it to open a menu for scrolling explicitly by 500, 200, 100, 20, 10, 5, or 1 columns or rows. You can also scroll directly to the first or last column or row.

The default setting for how many rows and columns are displayed can be changed. The section, "Excel Web Access Interactivity Settings," later in this chapter, describes how to do this.

When you open a workbook in Excel Services, it displays the same worksheet that it was on when you saved it in Excel client, and with approximately the same range that was displayed on the client. For example, if you publish a workbook with an active cell in row 100 on worksheet two, it comes up in the browser with that cell in view.

Try It Out   **Navigating a Worksheet in the Browser**

To navigate a worksheet in the browser, follow these steps:

1. Open the original Sales Report.xlsx workbook in Excel client and publish it to the server. Ensure that you have the Open In Excel Services option checked so that the browser opens with the workbook displayed.

2. Use the scroll bar to scroll through the workbook. You can only scroll down to row 75 and across to column T.

3. Press the right arrow on the right side of the navigation toolbar to scroll 20 columns to the right.

4. Open the down arrow button menu and select Bottom Row (see Figure 10-1). Notice that the down arrow is disabled.

5. Open the up arrow button menu and select Top Row.

6. Open the left arrow button menu and select Left-Most Column to return to the beginning of the worksheet.

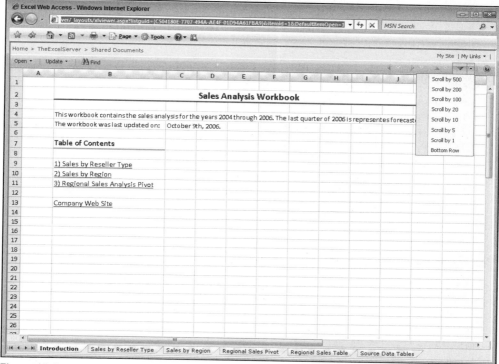

Figure 10-1

How It Works

When EWA is used to view a workbook, it requests a range of cells from the ECS. The size of this range is based on the settings for how many columns and rows to return. Each time you scroll within a worksheet using the arrow buttons, EWA requests the relevant range from ECS. In addition to the range, ECS also tells EWA whether there are additional used cells to the left, right, top, or bottom of the current range. The buttons on the toolbar are enabled or disabled accordingly.

Next, you learn how to switch between sheets in the browser.

Navigating Between Worksheets in a Workbook

Navigating between workbook sheets in Excel Services is very similar to the way you navigate in Excel client. You use the same worksheet tabs and controls to scroll the worksheet tabs. The only difference is that the server does not have the Insert Worksheet tab, because adding worksheets is not supported in Excel Services.

The sheet tabs appear only when you save a workbook and choose to show the entire workbook or specific sheets in the browser. If you choose to show only specific sheets in the browser, the sheet tabs for the other sheets are not displayed. If you choose to show only specific items in the browser, sheet tabs are not displayed at all.

If your workbook has more sheet tabs than can fit within the window, you can scroll through the sheet tabs just as you would in Excel. You have the option of scrolling or tabbing to the left or right, or moving to the first or last sheet tab.

Try It Out   **Switching Between Worksheets**

To switch between worksheets, follow these steps:

1. Open the original Sales Report.xlsx workbook in Excel client and publish it to the server. Ensure that you have the Open In Excel Services option checked so that the browser opens with the workbook displayed.

2. In the browser, select the tab for the second sheet, Sales by Reseller Type. Excel Services returns the second sheet in the browser.

Switching Between Items in a Workbook

So far in this chapter, you published the workbook with the entire workbook set to display in the browser. You can also publish the workbook with only specific items shown in the browser. When you do this, EWA displays the workbook in what is called *Named Item* view. In this view, you do not have access to the sheet tabs. Instead, there is a drop-down control on the toolbar that lets you switch between the various items you selected at publish. This mode is unique to Excel Services, and does not exist in the Excel client.

In the following Try It Out, you use the example workbook provided to publish the workbook with only certain named items visible. Then you view the results in the browser and toggle between the named items.

Try It Out   **Switching Items in a Workbook**

To switch items in a workbook, follow these steps:

1. In Excel, open the sample Sales Report.xlsx workbook provided with this book.

2. Open the Publish To Excel Services dialog box and click the Excel Services Options button.

3. In the Excel Services Options dialog box, select Items In the Workbook. A complete list of named items defined in the workbook is displayed, as shown in Figure 10-2.

4. Select the SalesByRegionChart, RegionalSalesPivot, and the RegionalSalesSummary items, as shown in Figure 10-3.

5. Click OK.

6. Provide a location and name for the workbook on your server and click Save. Ensure that the Open In Excel Services option is checked.

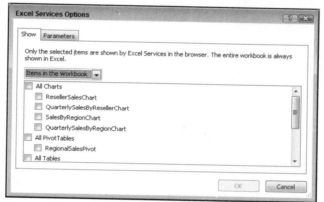

Figure 10-2

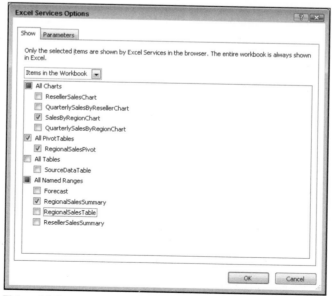

Figure 10-3

7. When the workbook opens in the browser, only the items you selected are displayed (see Figure 10-4). Even though the PivotTable is in the middle of the workbook, you cannot see any other cells around it. There are no sheet tabs at the bottom of the workbook.

8. On the toolbar, change from RegionalSalesPivot to SalesByRegionChart in the View menu.

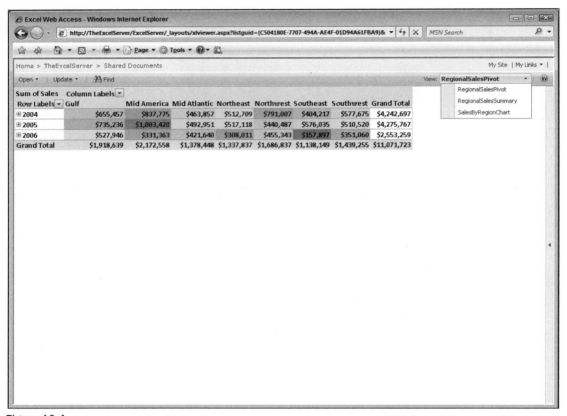

Figure 10-4

How It Works

As you learned in Chapter 9, tables, PivotTables, charts, and named consecutive ranges are each considered an item in the workbook that you can choose to show or hide when publishing to Excel Services. As soon as you choose to show only specific items in the workbook (in the Excel Services Options dialog box), the workbook is displayed in the browser in Named Item view. In this view, the sheets tabs are not available, and only a single named item is displayed at a time.

There are a couple of limitations worth noting. First, Excel (and, thus, Excel Services) supports only names that do not contain a space. Second, if you have more than one item with the same name (for example, two charts on different sheets can have the same chart name), you can view only one of them in the browser. If you try to publish the workbook and choose two items with the same name to be shown, you get an error message.

Working with Hyperlinks

Excel Services supports hyperlinks, as well as navigating within a workbook and to external workbooks or sites. This is very natural, given that you are viewing the workbook in the browser.

Hyperlinks are supported both when you display the entire workbook, as well as when you display only specific items in the workbook. In the latter case, if you try to click a link to a range or a cell in a range that is not defined to be displayed on the server, you receive an error.

A few types of hyperlinks are not supported by Excel Services. The server loads workbooks that contain these hyperlinks, but you cannot click them. Following are the hyperlinks that Excel Services does not support:

❑ Hyperlinks that directly link to another workbook or a cell within another workbook

❑ Hyperlinks that are relative to the workbook file path

❑ Hyperlinks that might contain malicious material (such as JavaScript)

Another discrepancy between the client and the server is that when you click a hyperlink to a range or column, the full column or range is not highlighted in the browser, as it is in Excel client.

Hyperlinks to the current workbook open within the same browser window and instance of EWA. Hyperlinks to external locations open in a new browser window.

In the following Try It Out, you learn how to use a hyperlink to navigate to a different location in the workbook, and to a web page that is outside of the workbook. For this example, use the sample workbook provided with this book.

Try It Out   **Working with Hyperlinks**

To work with hyperlinks, follow these steps:

1. Open Sales Report.xlsx in Excel client.

2. Publish the workbook to the server and ensure that the Open In Excel Services option is selected.

3. In the browser, switch to the Introduction sheet. The hyperlinks are displayed as shown in Figure 10-5.

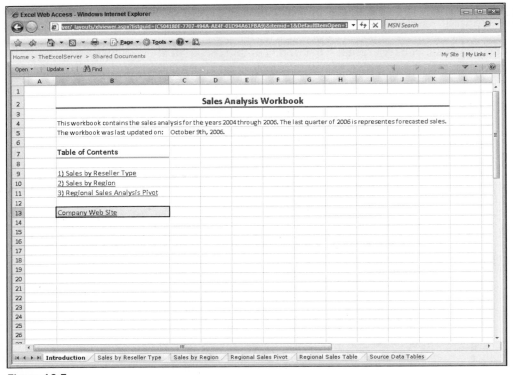

Figure 10-5

4. Click the Company Web Site hyperlink. A separate browser window opens, displaying the Microsoft site.

5. Click the Sales by Reseller Type hyperlink to go to that table.

You can also use hyperlinks to work around an Excel limitation. Excel supports hyperlinks to other places in the same workbook. Those places can be either named ranges or cell references. This does not include named items such as charts or tables. If you want to navigate to a chart or table item, create a hyperlink to a cell that is within that table, or on which the chart is placed. This hyperlink takes you to the specific item when you are viewing a workbook in the browser using Excel Services in Named Item view.

Working with Grouped Rows and Columns

Expanding and collapsing grouped rows and columns is sometimes called *outline mode* in Excel client. On the server, as on the client, you can expand and collapse any existing grouped rows or columns defined in the workbook. As with other features, you cannot change, add, or remove groupings from within the browser.

In the following Try It Out, you work with grouped rows and columns in the browser, using the example workbook as a starting point.

Try It Out   **Working with Grouped Rows and Columns**

To work with grouped rows and columns, follow these steps:

1. Open the original Sales Report.xlsx workbook in Excel client and publish it to the server. Ensure that you have the Open In Excel Services option selected so the browser opens with the workbook displayed. If you already published the workbook, you can simply open it in the browser directly from the document library on the server.

2. Switch to the Regional Sales Table sheet. This is the next-to-last sheet, so you may need to scroll to it. The sheet has the sales table grouped by region using Excel's grouping and subtotaling functionality.

3. Publish the workbook to the server and ensure that you have the Open In Excel Services option selected.

4. In the browser, you can expand and collapse the groups just like in Excel. Start by expanding the Northeast group. The details for that region are displayed, as shown in Figure 10-6.

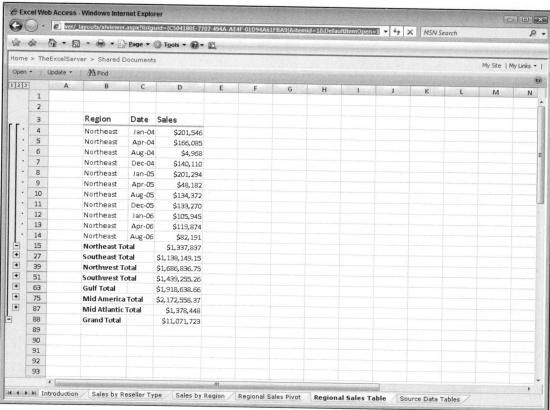

Figure 10-6

Using Tables to Sort and Filter Data

In Excel 2007, the primary way to sort and filter data is with tables. The Table feature is a continuation of the List feature introduced in Excel 2003. Tables offer more than just sorting and filtering, however — they are a new paradigm for working with tabular data in general, including structured formatting and naming within the table. Excel Services supports all aspects of the Table feature, but in the context of interactivity, the focus is on using the Table feature to sort and filter. Excel Services also supports autofilters, which enable you to sort and filter values in a sheet not in the context of a table.

Excel Services loads tables and filters them based on the settings in the workbook. You can also perform the following sort and filter operations directly in the browser:

❑ Sort ascending and descending within a column

❑ Use Excel 2007's new Number, Date, and Text filters (for example Equals, Above Average, Before, Next Week, and Begins With)

❑ Filter on specific values in a column (including Excel 2007's new automatic grouping of date values)

❑ Use custom filters

❑ Clear filters

Similar to Excel client, when a column is filtered, a filter icon is displayed in the column header.

In the following Try It Out, you use Excel Services to sort and filter the data in a table. For this exercise, you again use the sample workbook.

Try It Out   **Using Tables to Sort and Filter Data**

To use tables to sort and filter data, follow these steps:

1. Open the original Sales Report.xlsx workbook in Excel client and publish it to the server. Ensure that you have the Open In Excel Services option selected so that the browser opens with the workbook displayed. If you already published the workbook, you can simply open it in the browser directly from the document library on the server.

2. Switch to the Source Data Tables tab. (It is the last sheet in the workbook, so you may need to scroll to it.) This sheet has the Source Data table in it. You can sort and filter on each of the columns.

3. Select the sort-and-filter drop-down menu on the Region column. On the Text Filters fly-out menu, select Begins With, as shown in Figure 10-7.

4. In the Custom Filter dialog box, enter **North** as the Begins With text. This filters the table to show only the north regions, as shown in Figure 10-8. Your table should now look like the table in Figure 10-8. The sort-and-filter icon for the Region column drop-down menu is replaced with a filter icon, which signifies that the column is being filtered.

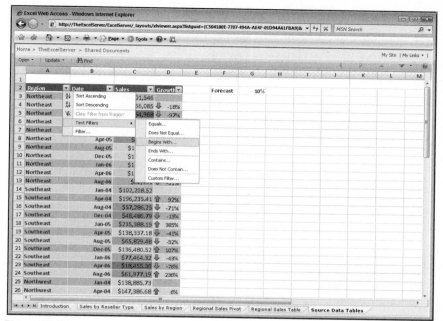

Figure 10-7

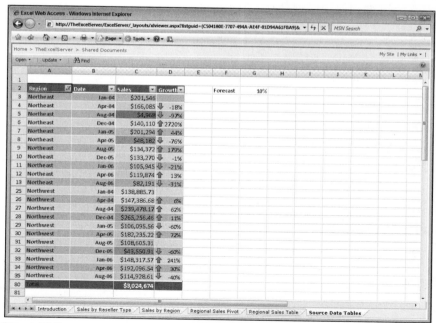

Figure 10-8

5. Select the Date column's sort-and-filter drop-down menu.

6. Select the This Year option on the Date Filter fly-out menu, as shown in Figure 10-9.

7. Click the check mark next to 2004 to filter those dates from the table.

8. Select the sort-and-filter drop-down menu on the Sales column.

9. Open the fly-out menu for Number Filters.

10. Select Top 10.

11. In the custom filter dialog box, change the value to show only the top five items.

12. Select the sort-and-filter drop-down menu on the Sales column.

13. Chose the Sort Ascending option to sort the values in the table by their sales.

14. Select the sort-and-filter drop-down menu on the Sales column.

15. Select the Clear Filter From "Sales" option to clear the filtering.

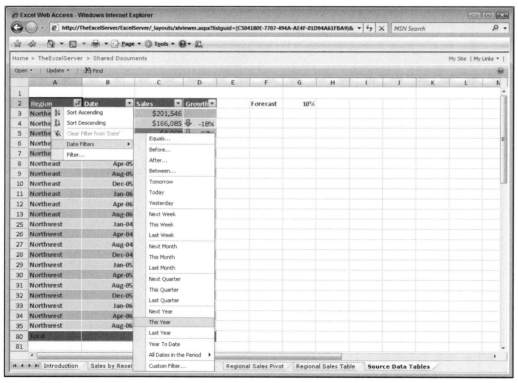

Figure 10-9

Using PivotTables

PivotTables play an important role in Excel Services. In addition to providing core interactivity, they are also the primary way to access external data that resides in databases and OLAP cubes. Excel Services supports most of the PivotTable sorting operations (as well as expanding and collapsing levels) to navigate through the data. You cannot, however, pivot fields in the browser, or add or remove fields to or from the PivotTable.

Excel Services supports PivotTables on data that resides inside the workbook, relational PivotTables connected to databases, and OLAP PivotTables connected to OLAP cubes. The basic interactivity option supported for all of these is refreshing the PivotTable so that it reflects the latest values. This could mean querying the database or cube for updated values, or refreshing against the source data in the workbook. The latter is relevant when the source data may change (for example, in cells containing volatile formulas such as RND or Time, cells that are hooked up to user-defined functions, or cells that are also workbook parameters).

In addition to refreshing the PivotTable, you can expand and collapse levels, and you can sort and filter the data, directly in the browser. However, some sorting and filtering options that are available in the client are not available on the server in the browser. The primary available features are as follows:

❑   Expanding and collapsing levels

❑   Sorting columns

❑   Filtering specific values

❑   Number, Name, and Date filters

❑   Custom filters

❑   Clearing filters

The browser does not support the Actions feature in OLAP PivotTables, or the Drill-Through feature in either OLAP or non-OLAP PivotTables.

In the following Try It Out, you use the sample workbook to interact with a PivotTable that is based on data in the workbook. You learn how to refresh, expand, collapse, sort, and filter PivotTable data while in the browser. First, you expand all the years in the PivotTable, then you filter to show only the first quarters for each year, and then you filter to show the top three regions in the first quarter.

In Chapter 12, you work with an OLAP PivotTable connected to SQL Server Analysis Services.

Try It Out   **Using PivotTables**

To use a PivotTable, follow these steps:

1.   Open the original Sales Report.xlsx workbook in Excel client and publish it to the server. Ensure that you have the Open In Excel Services option selected so that the browser opens with the workbook displayed. If you already published the workbook, you can simply open it in the browser directly from the document library on the server.

2.   Switch to the Regional Sales Pivot sheet shown in Figure 10-10.

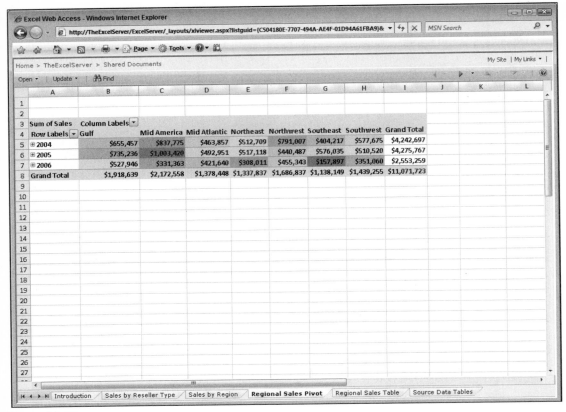

Figure 10-10

3. Expand the year 2004 by pressing the + sign next to it. The quarters in 2004 are now displayed, as shown in Figure 10-11.

4. Expand 2005 and 2006.

5. Select the Row Labels sort-and-filter drop-down menu.

6. Open the Date fly-out menu to filter based on quarters.

7. Select the Filter option.

8. In the dialog box, select qtr1 and click OK. The values for only the first quarter of each year are displayed, as shown in Figure 10-12.

9. Select the Column Labels drop-down menu.

10. Open the Value Filters fly-out menu and select Top 10.

11. In the "Top 10 Filter" dialog, change the value to **3** and click OK. The PivotTable is filtered to show only the Gulf, Northeast, and Southeast regions.

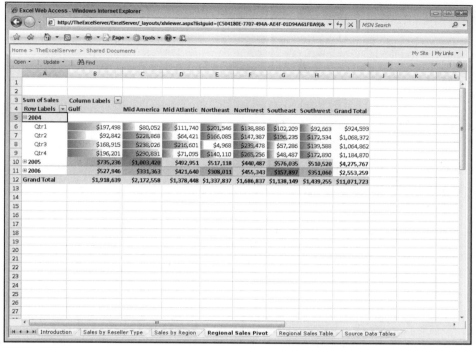

Figure 10-11

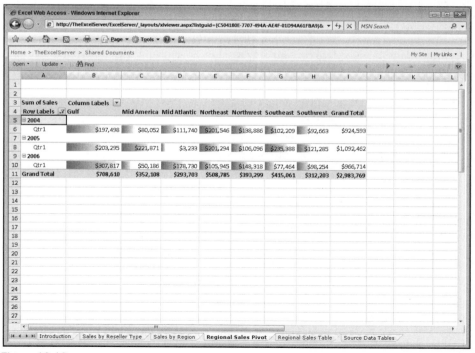

Figure 10-12

Working with Workbook Parameters

You've learned about various ways to interact with the workbook, but none of them let you change an actual value in a cell with user input. Because authoring workbooks in the browser is not a supported scenario for this release of Excel Services, you cannot simply type into the worksheet cells in the browser.

There are some scenarios, however, that require you to change a few select cells that serve as input into the workbook's calculation mode. Changing these values recalculates the workbook and returns the results. The workbook Parameters feature in Excel Services enables you to use the browser-based interface to interact with complex calculation models.

The Parameters feature lets you define certain cells in the workbook as parameters. You can change the values in these cells when you view the workbook in the browser. You can use workbook parameters to do the following:

❑ Create input for calculation models.

❑ Drive filtering in the context of a dashboard.

This section focuses on the first use case. The second is covered in Chapter 12.

There are two steps to working with Workbook Parameters:

1. Define the parameters.

2. Use the parameters through the Parameters task pane in the browser.

Defining Workbook Parameters

Workbook parameters are basically single cells that have been given a name and defined as parameters in the Excel Services Options dialog box. Not every cell can be used as a workbook parameter. The primary requirement is for the cell to contain only a value. Specifically, this means that the cell cannot contain a formula. There are a few more restrictions on which cells can be used as workbook parameters. Following are the primary ones:

❑ The cell can only contain a single value (not a formula).

❑ The cell cannot be inside of a table.

❑ The cell cannot be in the rows, columns, or data region of a PivotTable. (They can, however, be on the report filter, also known as the *PivotTable page field*.)

❑ The cell name must be a global in scope and not local (for example, sheet-specific).

In general, only those names that can be used as parameters are available in the parameter-definition dialog box.

> *A special type of parameter is one that is associated with a PivotTable page field. You learn how to use this parameter type in Chapter 12.*

To define a cell as a workbook parameter, you must first give the cell a name, and then add it to the workbook parameter list. You can do this through the Excel Services Options dialog box or using the Excel Object Model. In the following Try It Out, you use the sample workbook to define a workbook parameter.

Try It Out   Defining Workbook Parameters

To define a workbook parameter, follow these steps:

1. Open the original Sales Report.xlsx sample workbook in Excel client.

2. Switch to the Sales By Reseller Type sheet. Column N contains forecast numbers for Q4/06 sales. The forecast takes the values from the previous quarter and multiplies them by Forecast, an Excel name for the cell on the Source Data Tables sheet.

3. Open the Office menu and select Publish To Excel Services from the Publish fly-out menu.

4. Click the Excel Services Options button.

5. Switch to the Parameters tab, as shown in Figure 10-13.

6. Click the Add button. The list of available, valid named cells is displayed. As you can see in Figure 10-14, there is only one named cell available to be a parameter.

7. Check the Forecast box.

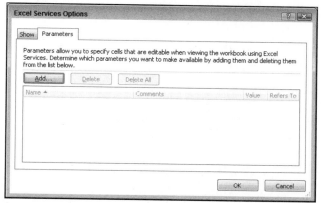

Figure 10-13

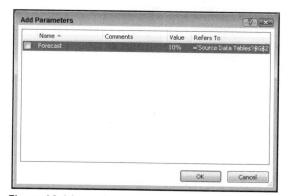

Figure 10-14

8. Click OK. Forecasts are now displayed in the list of workbook parameters, as shown in Figure 10-15.

9. Save the workbook to the server. Ensure that you have the Open In Excel Services option selected. (You use this workbook again in an upcoming Try It Out.)

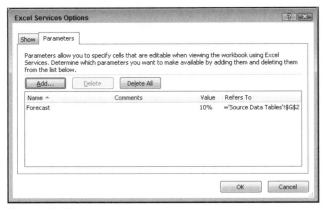

Figure 10-15

How It Works

When you chose to add a workbook parameter, Excel looked for all the available parameters to display in the list. The available parameters are those named cells that meet the criteria described earlier in the section. The list does not include any cells previously chosen to be workbook parameters. If no valid cells are available, the error message shown in Figure 10-16 is displayed.

Figure 10-16

Next, you use the newly created workbook parameter in the browser to change the discount percentage and see the effect on the discount price.

Changing Workbook Parameters in the Browser

When you publish a workbook that contains parameters to the server, it opens in the browser with the Parameters task pane visible. The Parameters task pane lists all of the workbook parameters and lets you change the value for each. You cannot edit the value directly in the cell grid. Though the Parameter task pane is displayed by default, you can minimize it to view more of the workbook.

When you change one or more parameters and apply the changes, the values are entered into their respective cells. If the workbook calculation mode is Automatic, the changes trigger a recalculation of the workbook and the updated results are displayed. Otherwise, you must manually choose to recalculate the workbook (see the "The Excel Web Access Toolbar" section, later in this chapter).

The Parameters task pane has of the following limitations:

❑ When you enter values in the task pane, you must include the relevant formatting. Thus, to specify 20%, you must type **20%**.

❑ Because names can't have spaces, the definition of the parameter can sometimes be cryptic to the user. To work around this, you can use the Name Manager to enter a comment for the defined name in Excel client. The comment is displayed as a tool tip when you hover over the parameter name in the task pane.

❑ Parameters in the task pane are displayed in alphabetical order by their names. You cannot manually sort them.

❑ You are limited to 255 workbook parameters per workbook.

❑ You do not need to enter values for every parameter before clicking Apply. Leaving a parameter blank means the value is unchanged.

❑ Because leaving a parameter blank means the value is unchanged, there is no way to clear a parameter cell.

❑ The only way to revert to the original value for a parameter is to reload the workbook using the toolbar, as described in the following section, "The Excel Web Access Toolbar." However, when you do this, any previous workbook interactions are lost.

In the following Try It Out section, you change the Forecast parameter in the browser and see the effect on the 2006 fourth quarter sales projections. Continue from the browser page that opened after you published the workbook at the end of the previous Try It Out (see Figure 10-17).

Try It Out   Changing Workbook Parameters

To change a workbook parameter, follow these steps:

1. Switch to the Sales By Reseller Type sheet if it is not already displayed.

2. In the Parameters pane, enter **20%** for the Forecast.

3. Click Apply. The workbook recalculates and the forecast sales for the fourth quarter in 2006 is updated.

4. To familiarize yourself with using the Parameters pane, minimize and maximize it by clicking the arrow bar along the left edge of the pane.

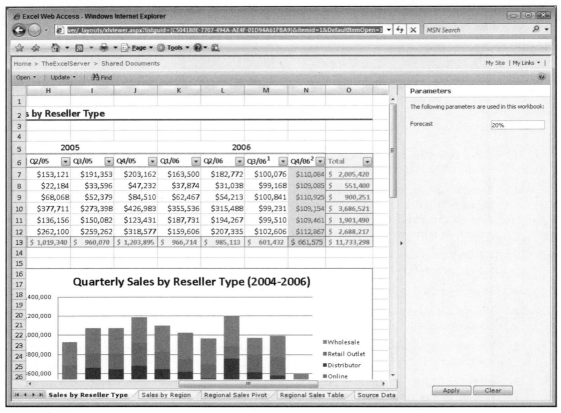

Figure 10-17

How It Works

When you entered 20% for the Forecast parameter and clicked Apply, Excel Services changed the value for the cell named Forecast in the workbook. Because the workbook is in automatic calculation mode, this triggered a calculation of the values in the sales forecast.

If you were publishing the workbook to display in Named Item mode, you would not even see the Forecast cell. You can use this mode to keep all of your parameters on a separate sheet in the workbook and not make that sheet visible on the server. This simplifies the experience for the user.

Interactivity and Charting

Excel Services does not support interacting directly with charts in the browser. For example, you cannot change the chart type or the formatting on an existing chart. In addition, you cannot interact with a PivotChart. However, charts are updated if the source data they use changes.

A chart or PivotChart is updated in Excel Services in the following cases:

- ❑ The chart or a PivotChart points to data in a PivotTable and you refresh or change that data.
- ❑ The chart points at data in a table and you use EWA to apply a filter to one of the columns in the table.
- ❑ The chart points at data that has a workbook parameter defined in it, or has calculations based on a workbook parameter in it, and you change that parameter.

The Excel Web Access Toolbar

You can use the EWA toolbar when you view a workbook in the browser through either the viewer page or the EWA Web Part directly on a custom page. The toolbar provides access to a number of features. As you have already seen, the toolbar contains the navigation controls for both navigating within a sheet and navigating between named objects. It also gives you access to the online product help. In addition, the toolbar includes the following functions:

- ❑ Opening the workbook in Excel
- ❑ Opening a snapshot of the workbook in Excel
- ❑ Refreshing the data sources in the workbook
- ❑ Refreshing the selected data source in the workbook
- ❑ Calculating the workbook
- ❑ Reloading the workbook file
- ❑ Finding data in the workbook
- ❑ Accessing help

Chapter 11 discusses opening a snapshot of a workbook. And you used the Refresh options on the toolbar earlier in this chapter, in the "Using PivotTables" section. This section focuses on the remaining features available in the toolbar.

Using the Toolbar to Open a Workbook in Excel

The first option on the toolbar is opening the workbook in Excel. This option is only available if you have permission to open the original workbook file. You should open the workbook in the client if you want to do the following:

- ❑ Save the state of the workbook, including any changes you may have made through interacting with it.

- ❑   Continue viewing and analyzing the workbook offline.

- ❑   Print the workbook. (Excel's printing capabilities are superior to printing from the browser.)

- ❑   Further change and analyze the workbook using features only available in the client (such as creating new charts, inserting additional fields in a PivotTable, and authoring new calculations).

When you choose to open a workbook from the EWA toolbar, you are not opening the original workbook file that was opened by the server. Instead, you are opening the current workbook as it exists in the server's memory. This means that any changes that were made to the workbook, either by refreshing external data or through user interaction (such as filtering a table), are reflected in the workbook you see in Excel client. It also means that if you choose to save the workbook from the client, by default you do not save over the original workbook file.

Opening workbooks in Excel client only works with Excel 2007. Even if you have the compatibility pack installed on previous versions of Excel, you cannot open the file within Excel. This is also true for opening workbook snapshots.

Using the Toolbar to Calculate a Workbook

So far, the exercises in this book assumed that you are publishing the workbook with the calculation mode set to Automatic. This is the default mode on the client. There are cases in which publishing a workbook in Manual calculation mode makes sense. For these cases, you can trigger a workbook calculation using the Calculate option on the toolbar. This is similar to clicking the Calculate button on the Ribbon in the client, or pressing the F9 key. The Calculate button on the toolbar in EWA calculates all the sheets in the workbook.

Assume you have a workbook that takes a significant time to calculate, and it contains both volatile data and input parameters. In this case, you would not want the workbook to calculate each time you open it in the browser and have to wait for the calculation to complete. Rather, you would want to give the user control to set the parameters first and then calculate the workbook. To do this, you set the workbook to Manual calculation mode in the client and publish it to the server. When the user opens the workbook in the browser, it does not calculate. The user can set the parameters in the workbook and then calculate the workbook using the Calculate option on the toolbar.

In the following Try It Out, you change the calculation mode for the example workbook to Manual and publish it to the server in this state. You then change the workbook parameters to verify that it does not calculate and update. Finally, you use the toolbar to manually trigger a calculation of the workbook and update the results.

Try It Out   Manually Triggering a Workbook Calculation

To manually trigger a workbook calculation, follow these steps:

1.   Open the original Sales Report.xlsx workbook in Excel client.

2.   Switch to the Formulas tab on the Ribbon.

3.   Select the Calculation Optons drop-down menu.

4.   Change the calculation mode to Manual, as shown in Figure 10-18.

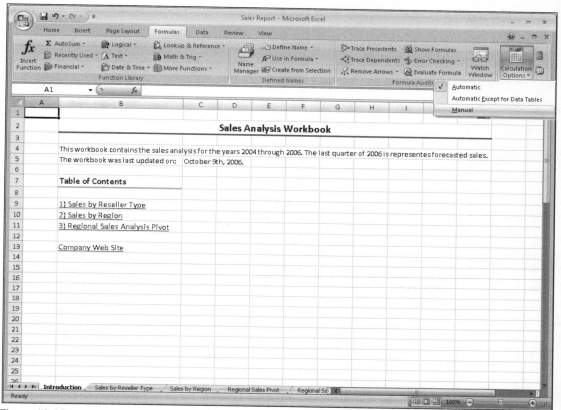

Figure 10-18

5. Open the Publish To Excel Services dialog box.

6. Click the Excel Services Options button to bring up the relevant dialog box.

7. Switch to the Parameters tab.

8. Click the Add button.

9. Select Forecast by checking the box next to it and clicking OK.

10. Click OK to exit the Excel Services Options dialog box.

11. Click the Save button to publish the workbook. Ensure that you have the Open In Excel Services option selected so that the browser opens with the workbook displayed.

12. View the workbook in the browser and switch to the Sales By Reseller Type sheet.

13. In the Parameter task pane, change the value for Forecast to **20%** and click Apply. The values for Q4/06 do not change, because the workbook is in Manual calculation mode.

14. Open the Update menu and select Calculate Workbook. The values in column Q4/06 are updated, because the workbook is calculated with the new parameter.

Reloading the Workbook File

As you learned earlier in the book, when you open a workbook in Excel Services, it is loaded into memory and a user session is created for you. This means that as long as you are working in the context of that session, you do not see any changes made to the original workbook file by the workbook author.

There may be cases in which you would like to load the latest version of the workbook to view any changes that were made. You can do this within EWA by using the Reload Workbook toolbar option. An important thing to keep in mind is that when you reload a workbook, you lose state information, including any previous workbook interactivity. The workbook is loaded in the state it was saved. Thus, if you expanded on a PivotTable or set parameters, those changes are lost.

In the following Try It Out, you first create and publish a simple workbook to the server. You then change the workbook using Excel client, while viewing it in the browser. After you save the workbook, you use the Reload Workbook option to view the changes you made.

Try It Out   Reloading a Workbook

To reload a workbook, follow these steps:

1. Open Excel client and start a blank workbook.
2. In cell A1, type **Hello World**.
3. Publish the workbook to your server and ensure that you have the Open In Excel Services option selected.
4. View the workbook in the browser.
5. Keeping the browser window open, return to the client and type **Goodbye** in cell A1.
6. Publish the workbook to your server again. This time, uncheck the Open In Excel Services option to deselect it.
7. Return to the browser. The workbook in the browser still shows Hello World in cell A1.
8. In the Excel Web Access toolbar, select Reload Workbook from the Refresh menu.
9. The workbook is loaded from the document library again and picks up the changes you made. Cell A1 now displays Goodbye.

If you had paged through the workbook or performed any interactivity, that state would have been lost when you reloaded the workbook.

How It Works

When you originally opened the workbook in the browser, Excel Services loaded the file from the document library into memory. Any operations you perform on the workbook in the browser from that point on are done on the workbook that is in the session memory. When you saved the workbook to the document library with the updated values, the workbook in memory is not affected. That is why you did not see any changes in the workbook. This is true even if you were to interact with the workbook or page through it. When you selected the Reload Workbook option, Excel Services closed the current session and cleared the workbook copy from memory. It then loaded the workbook from the document library again, and you saw the updated version.

Finding Data in a Workbook

The Find feature in Excel Services operates much like Find in Excel client. However, it is very limited when compared to the client. Excel Services supports only finding strings of text. It does not provide the broad range of functionality supported by the client, such as finding formatting or controlling the scope of the search.

When you use the Find function on the server, it searches within the active sheet, and only within ranges marked as visible on the server.

In the following Try It Out, you use the Find command on the toolbar to find a specific value in the sample workbook.

Try It Out   Finding Data in a Workbook

To find data in a workbook, follow these steps:

1. Open the original Sales Report.xlsx workbook in Excel client and publish it to the server. Ensure that you have the Open in Excel Services selected so that the browser opens with the workbook displayed. If you already published the workbook, you can simply open it in the browser directly from the document library on the server.

2. Switch to the Source Data Tables tab. (This is the last tab in the workbook, so you may need to scroll to it.)

3. Click the Find button on the toolbar. This displays the Find dialog box shown in Figure 10-19.

4. Type **south** in the Find What field.

5. Click the Find Next button. You are taken to the first entry for Southwest in the sheet.

6. Click the Close button to exit the dialog box.

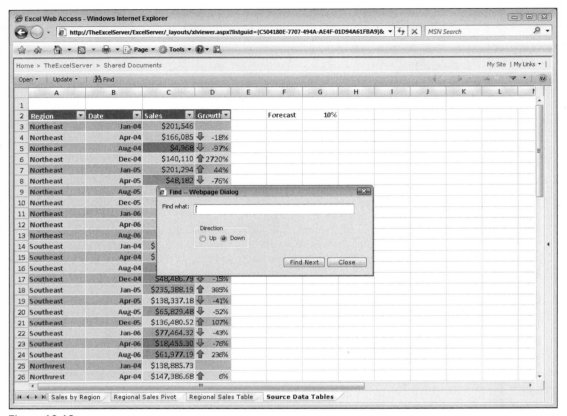

Figure 10-19

Excel Web Access Interactivity Settings

In this last section of the chapter, you explore the EWA settings that control interactivity within the Web Part. This section does not cover all the settings you will see for the Web Part. You have already covered a few of them in Chapter 5, and a few more are covered in proceeding chapters. For a complete reference to all available settings, check the online help in the product.

The settings that control interactivity are in the Navigation And Interactivity section of the EWA Web Part properties. There is a top-level setting that controls whether or not interactivity is allowed for this instance of the Web Part. If you do not allow interactivity, then the user viewing the workbook in the browser is limited to viewing only the data in the workbook as it was published. The user cannot perform such tasks as sorting and filtering the data. You can also enable and disable interactivity in more granular settings.

Using the EWA Web Part properties, you can enable or disable the following:

- ❏ Workbook navigation (including paging between sheets, as well as between objects)
- ❏ Hyperlinks
- ❏ All workbook interactivity (which disables all of the following options)
- ❏ Parameter modification
- ❏ Displaying the Parameters task pane (Chapter 12 describes cases in which it is relevant to hide the Parameters task pane but enable parameter modification.)
- ❏ Sorting (which disables sorting in AutoFilters, tables, and PivotTables)
- ❏ Filtering (which disables filtering in AutoFilters, tables, and PivotTables)
- ❏ PivotTable interactivity (which removes all other interactivity from PivotTables, such as expansion)
- ❏ Periodic refresh of external data (as discussed in Chapter 5)

You can also control whether the toolbar appears in its entirety, without the Find functionality, with only the item navigation controls (for both within a sheet and within objects), or not at all.

There are a number of different scenarios for which controlling the level of interactivity supported is important (as described in Chapter 12). These scenarios assume that users will be viewing the workbook in a custom Web Part page with the EWA part on them. The out-of-the-box Excel Viewer page has all interactivity options enabled. If you want to change the default viewing experience, you have to edit this page or replace it.

Summary

This chapter focused on interacting with a workbook in the browser. Excel Services is designed to enable users to view and interact in the browser with workbooks authored in Excel. The interactivity options supported are in line with this design point. You cannot edit a formula, change formatting, or start typing in any cell. You can, however, explore workbooks and the data in them, or the external data sources they are connected to. You can also use parameters to leverage calculation models defined in the workbook.

In this chapter, you learned to do the following:

- ❏ Navigate within worksheets, within workbooks, and using hyperlinks
- ❏ Use the Table feature to sort and filter data
- ❏ Use PivotTables
- ❏ Define and work with workbook parameters
- ❏ Use the EWA toolbar

❑   Use settings for controlling workbook navigation and interactivity in EWA

❑   Publish a workbook to Excel Services, and view and interact with it in the browser, enable the primary scenario of Excel Services: sharing and distributing workbooks using the browser.

Chapter 11 builds on these features and shows you how to use them in conjunction with additional Office SharePoint Server functionality to control and manage workbook distribution.

Controlling Workbook Distribution

In the previous two chapters, you used Excel to publish workbooks to the server, and then used Excel Services to view and interact with the workbooks in the browser. One of the key benefits Excel Services provides is allowing you to control and manage workbook distribution. In this chapter, you learn how to do this by using Office SharePoint Server's security, collaboration, and document management functionality, together with Excel Services functionality. The primary goal is to give the workbook author control over who sees the workbook and which version of the workbook they see. This control should put an end to the worries of having multiple versions of the truth caused by sending workbooks around in e-mails and copying them from file share systems.

There are two parts to controlling workbook distribution. First, you must control who can publish workbooks and provide ways to review workbooks prior to their being made available for others to see. Then, you must control who can see the workbooks. This chapter discusses the functionality that supports these two parts. In particular, you learn how to do the following:

❑   Control who can publish workbooks

❑   Use content approval and approval workflows to review workbooks

❑   Use check-in, check-out, and versioning

❑   Control who can view workbooks using the View Only Permission

❑   Use workbook snapshots

❑   Subscribe to alerts and RSS feeds to know when workbooks are updated

❑   Audit workbook use

Controlling Workbook Authoring

There are a number of reasons you may want to control workbook distribution. The primary one is verifying that all the recipients of a workbook are viewing the same, sanctioned workbook. By doing this, you eliminate having multiple versions of the workbook being viewed by different people, or people viewing out-of-date workbooks. A second reason is controlling who actually sees the workbook. To achieve this using Office SharePoint Server and Excel Services, you need to have a single, sanctioned version of the workbook and control who can view it. The first half of this chapter examines getting to a single, sanctioned version of the workbook.

First, you must control who can author a workbook and publish it to Excel Services. Then, you must enable approval and review of the workbook to ensure that this is the sanctioned version before making it broadly available.

In this section, you create a document library that is the official sales report repository. For the sake of demonstration, this is the location where your users go to see the sanctioned versions of sales reports. You learn how to control who can actually save workbooks into this library, and how you can control which workbooks are made broadly available through content approval and review workflows.

Controlling Who Can Publish Workbooks

To publish a workbook to Excel Services, the workbook author must have permissions to save the workbook to a location that is defined as an Excel Services trusted location. (Trusted locations were covered in depth in Chapter 8.) This is the first step towards controlling workbook distribution. It requires a SharePoint Shared Services Administrator to define which locations are trusted, and then it requires a Site Administrator to give permission to the workbook author to save workbooks into that location. A workbook author must have at least the Contribute permissions in SharePoint.

The following Try It Out assumes that you are either an administrator of the entire Office SharePoint Server (a Site Administrator), or have the permissions to create and control document libraries a site on the server. It is also assumed that the document library you are creating is defined as a trusted location either through inheritance from the entire site or server, or specifically. If you are the administrator and need to add the document library to the list of trusted locations, refer to Chapter 7 to see how this is done.

Try It Out   **Controlling Who Can Publish Workbooks**

To control who can publish workbooks, follow these steps:

1. Open a browser with the home page for your Office SharePoint Server installation. If you do not have permissions to create a document library at the root site, navigate to the site in which you do.

2. In the left navigation pane, click the View All Site Content link.

3. Click Create on the toolbar.

4. Click Document Library in the Libraries column.

5. In the Name field, type **Sales Reports**. (A description is optional.)

6. Leave the Navigation setting as Yes.

7. Leave the Document Version History setting as No.

8. Change the Document Template to Microsoft Office Excel Spreadsheet. The page should look similar to the one in Figure 11-1.

9. Click the Create button at the bottom of the page. Your document library is created.

10. On the document library toolbar, select the Document Library Settings option from the Settings drop-down menu, as shown in Figure 11-2.

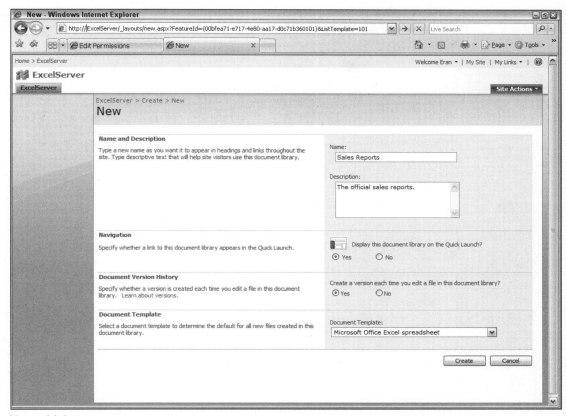

Figure 11-1

There may be additional users already listed on this page. This could be true if you are using an existing document library, or if the library is inheriting permissions from the parent site. If this is the case, and you want to ensure that only specific authors can save workbooks here, remove the unwanted users by checking the box next to their usernames and selecting Remove User Permission from the Actions drop-down menu.

13. On the Add Users page, type the usernames for the users who are your sanctioned workbook authors (those to whom you want to give permission to save workbooks into this document library).

There are two ways to give authors permission to save workbooks into this library. You can either give them a Contribute or higher (Approve, Manage Hierarchy, Design, or Full Control) right, or you can add them to a SharePoint User Group that has one of those rights. For the purposes of this example, give them the specific Contribute right.

14. In the Give Permission section, ensure that the Give Users Permission Directly option is selected.

15. Select the Contribute permission. The page should now look similar to Figure 11-3.

Figure 11-2

16. Click OK at the bottom of the page.

17. Use the breadcrumb links at the top of the page to return to the document library.

You now have a document library, Sales Reports, that is a trusted location, and you have given specific sanctioned workbook authors the right to save workbooks into it. Next, you learn how to use Content Approval to ensure that the workbooks the authors save are approved before they are made available for broad viewing.

Using Content Approval to Review Workbooks

In many cases, you may want to have someone review a workbook before it is made available for others to see. There are a couple of ways to do this using Office SharePoint Server. The first one discussed here is *content approval*.

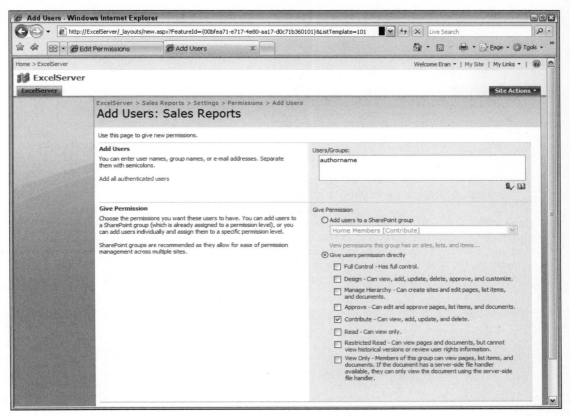

Figure 11-3

When a workbook (or any file) is saved to a document library in which content approval is required, it remains in Pending state until someone with the Approve permission assigns it the Approved status. As long as the workbook is in Pending state, it can only be viewed by the author and users who have Approve or higher permission (specifically, users who have the right to view drafts). Users who are the target readers of the workbooks do not have this permission and, therefore, do not see the workbook until it has been approved. This helps you use the server to guarantee that people are looking at the right, sanctioned workbook.

In the next Try It Out, you set up content approval on the Sales Reports document library. Continue from where you ended in the previous Try It Out, in the Sales Report document library.

Try It Out   Setting Up and Using Content Approval

To set up and use content approval, follow these steps:

1.   In the Sales Report document library, select Document Library Settings from the Settings drop-down menu.

2. On the Document Library Settings page, click Versioning Settings in the General Settings column.

3. In the Content Approval section of the Versioning Settings page, select Yes, as shown in Figure 11-4.

4. In the Draft Item Security section, leave the default "Only users who can approve items (and the author of the item)" option selected.

5. Click the OK button at the bottom of the page.

6. Return to the document library using the breadcrumb navigation link at the top of the page. The document library now has the Approval Status column added to it.

7. To see content approval in action, publish or upload a workbook into the document library. The approval status of the workbook is Pending, as shown in Figure 11-5.

As long as the state remains Pending, no one except the workbook author and users who have Approval permissions can view the workbook. In fact, no other users even see it in the list of files in the document library. A powerful aspect of this feature is that if the workbook author changes the workbook and saves an updated copy, the status is changed to Pending again, but the viewers still see and have access to the last approved version of the workbook. The updated workbook is available only after it has been approved.

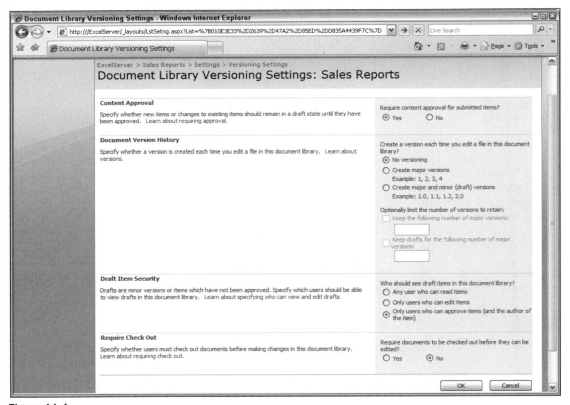

Figure 11-4

To see what it looks like for a viewer of the workbook who doesn't have authoring permissions, you have to switch to a different user. For now, follow these steps to see what it takes to approve a workbook, which you are able to do because you are the creator of the document library:

1. Drop down the menu on the name of the workbook you saved to the document library, as shown in Figure 11-6.

2. Select Approve/Reject from the drop-down menu. The screen shown in Figure 11-7 is displayed.

3. For the Approval Status, select the Approved option.

4. Enter a comment in the Comment section.

5. Click the OK button at the bottom of the screen. Now, anyone with viewing permissions can see the workbook.

You can use the Version History option for the workbook file to see who approved a workbook, when it was approved, and any comments entered. You use this option later in the "Using Check-In, Check-Out, and Versioning" section, later in this chapter.

Figure 11-5

Figure 11-6

Using content approval is a straightforward way to ensure that a workbook published to the server is reviewed prior to being broadly available. In the next section, you learn how to use the workflow features of Office SharePoint Server to drive more sophisticated approval processes.

Using Workflows to Review Workbooks

Chapter 1 introduced the workflows that are supplied out-of-the-box with Office SharePoint Server. In this section, you set up an Approval workflow on the Sales Reports document library. This workflow lets you create either a parallel or a serial approval process. You create tasks for the approvers, and they are notified by e-mail that they need to complete these tasks. After everyone has approved the workbook, the approval status state is changed from Pending to Approved, similar to the manual content approval process described in the previous section. Approvers also have the option of rejecting a document, requiring changes in it, or reassigning the approval task to someone else.

In the following Try It Out, you set the approval workflow to start any time a document is created or changed in the Sales Report document library. You give approvers one day to complete their reviewing task.

To use the e-mail notification functionality in a workflow, you must configure Office SharePoint Server to work with an existing e-mail server.

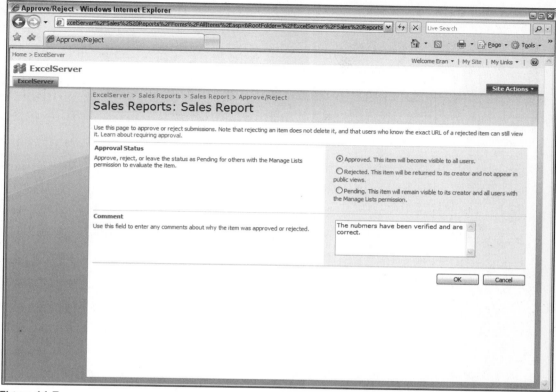

Figure 11-7

Try It Out   Setting Up and Using Content Approval

To set up and use content approval, follow these steps:

1. In the Sales Report document library, select Document Library Settings from the Settings drop-down menu.

2. On the Settings page, click Workflow Settings in the Permissions And Management column.

3. Select the Approval workflow (the default).

4. Give the workflow a unique name such as Sales Report Approval.

5. Select the Tasks list (the default) as the location for tasks assigned by the workflow to be stored.

6. Leave the default Workflow History (New) option selected as the location to store the workflow status.

7. Check the boxes next to "Start this workflow when a new item is created" and "Start this work-flow when an item is changed." Your screen should look similar to Figure 11-8.

8. Click Next at the bottom of the page.

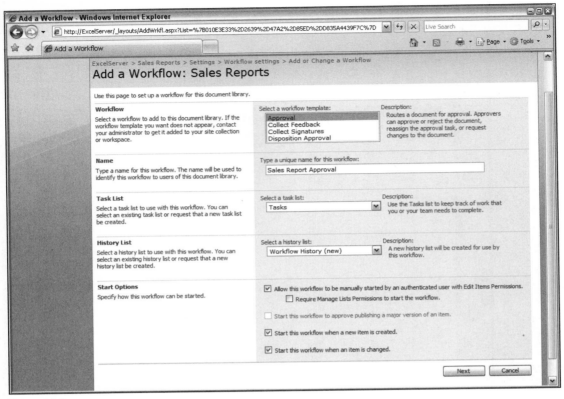

Figure 11-8

9. On the following page, leave the default options for Workflow Tasks. Keep this as a serial workflow and allow participants to reassign the task or to request changes.

10. Enter one or more valid e-mail addresses in the Approvers list. (You can use your own address to test this process.) Because you chose to keep this as a serial workflow, each approval is assigned a task and sent a notification e-mail only after the previous approver has completed the task.

11. Type a brief message to accompany the e-mail message that is sent out to notify an approver of the task that has been assigned.

12. Give each person one day to finish the reviewing task, as shown in Figure 11-9. (In a parallel workflow, you can assign a due date for everyone to complete their tasks.)

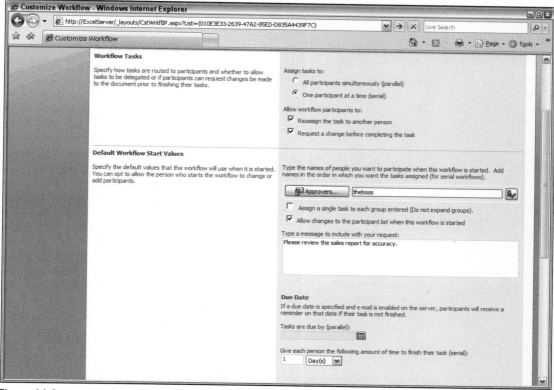

Figure 11-9

13. Leave all of the options unselected in the Complete The Workflow section, as shown in Figure 11-10. (This section enables you to cancel the workflow before the process is complete.)

14. In the Post-Completion Workflow Activities section, check the box to update the approval status. This ensures that the status of the workbook is changed to Approved after everyone has approved it as part of their workflow.

15. Click OK at the bottom of the page to save your settings. The Workflow Reports page is displayed, where you can view summary reports on each of the workflows you have set up. (You can access this page at a later time from the Document Library Settings.)

16. Return to the document library using the Go Back to Sales Reports link at the top of the page.

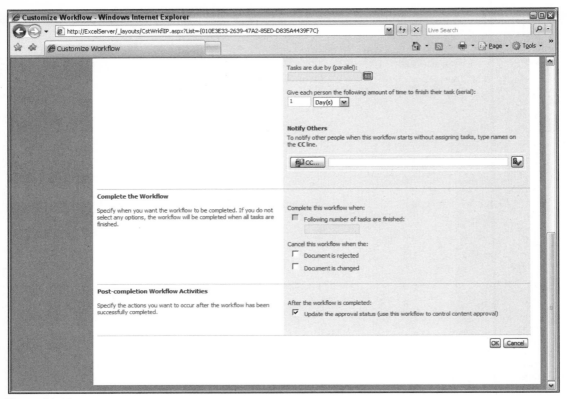

Figure 11-10

In the following Try It Out, you track workflows in progress to see their status. First, you trigger the workflow you just created on the Sales Report document library. Then, you check the status on this workflow.

Try It Out   Tracking Workflow Progress

To track workflow progress, follow these steps:

1. Return to the Sales Report document library.

2. To trigger a Sales Report Approval workflow, publish or upload a new workbook into the document library. This triggers the workflow, because you marked it to start when items are created and updated.

    The document library now has a Sales Report Approval column that tracks the status of this workflow for each item in the list.

3. Open the drop-down menu next to the workbook name and select Workflows. The Workflows page for the Sales Report document library is displayed, as shown in Figure 11-11. From this page, you can manually start a workflow, or track running and completed workflows. The Sales Report Approval workflow is displayed in the Running Workflows section.

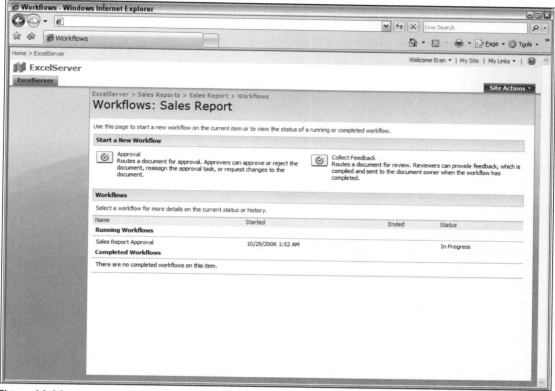

Figure 11-11

4. Click the Sales Report Approval link. This takes you to the status page for the specific workflow. The status page shows you which tasks are outstanding and what events have already occurred for the workflow, as shown in Figure 11-12. You can use this page to manage workflows that are in progress. For example, you can change reviewers or tasks, or cancel the workflow in progress. You can also access the workflow reports.

If you set up yourself as a reviewer in the previous Try It Out (to test the process), you should have received an e-mail notification requesting that you review the Sales Report for accuracy. You can approve a document as part of a workflow using these methods:

❑ Through the actual task created for it in the relevant task list. As shown in Figure 11-13, the task includes a link to the workbook and gives the option to approve, reject, reassign, or request a change in the file.

❑ Directly from within the client application (Excel in this case). When you open a workbook that has a workflow action associated with it, you are notified that you have a task pending. You have the same options to approve, reject, reassign, or request a change directly from with in Excel, as shown in Figure 11-14.

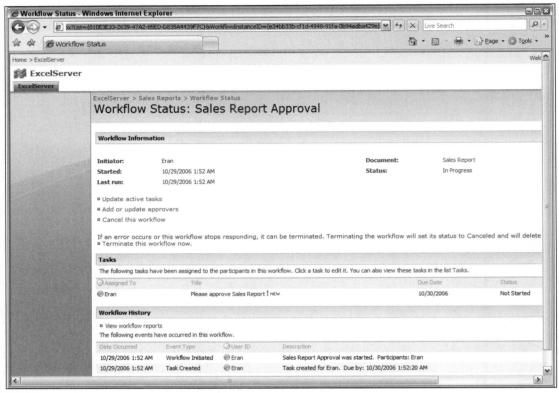

Figure 11-12

After all the approvers have approved the workbook, either in serial or in parallel (depending on how the workflow was set up), the workbook content approval status is set to Approved and everyone that has access can view it.

As you can see, between simple content approval and more advanced workflow capabilities, you can enforce review and approval of workbooks before they are made available for broad consumption. By combining this functionality with the ability to specify who can publish a workbook, you can control workbook distribution and know that the workbooks that are made available are indeed sanctioned.

In the next section, you learn how document versioning and check-in and check-out capabilities can help authors manage their workbooks and organizations maintain history and control.

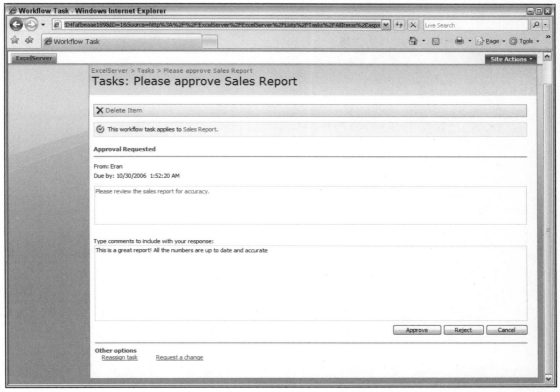

Figure 11-13

Using Check-In, Check-Out, and Versioning

To further enhance your ability to manage workbook distribution, you can use the version tracking features of Office SharePoint Server. You can track versions of workbooks as they are checked in, which gives you access to previous versions of a workbook so that you can review changes that made during multiphase or collaborative workbook authoring. It also lets you restore a workbook to a previous version if a mistake is made in a more recent edit.

In addition, with content approval, an author can make changes on a workbook while everyone else sees the previous approved version. With document versioning, authors are able to maintain numerous iterations of a workbook while making only the last approved major version available for everyone to see.

In the following Try It Out, you learn how to turn on versioning for a specific document library, work with major and minor versions of a workbook, and view the history of changes performed on a workbook.

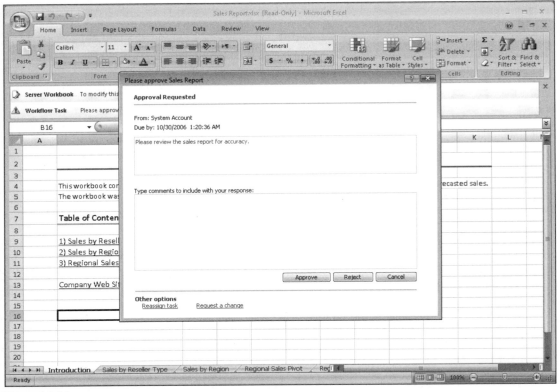

Figure 11-14

Try It Out   **Turning on Versioning**

To turn on versioning, follow these steps:

1. In the Sales Report document library, select Document Library Settings from the Settings drop-down menu.

2. On the Settings page, click Versioning Settings in the General Settings column.

3. Content approval should already be required from the previous exercise. If it is not, select Yes as the Content Approval option.

4. In the Document Version History section, select the option to create major and minor (draft) versions.

5. Require documents to be checked out before they are edited by selecting Yes for that option.

6. Leave the rest of the options at their defaults. Your page should look similar to Figure 11-15.

7. Click the OK button at the bottom of the screen.

8. Return to the document library by using the navigation breadcrumb link at the top of the page.

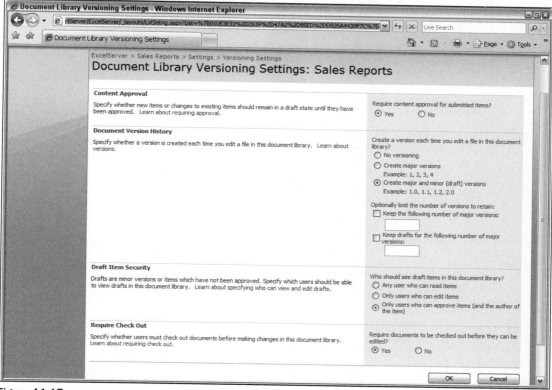

Figure 11-15

The Sales Reports document library is now set up to support versioning. Whenever a workbook is saved to the library, a version is created. A major version is created for every new workbook. A minor version is created implicitly on every subsequent save. The workbook author has control over whether a major or minor version is created when he or she explicitly checks it in.

You can also set up the document library to require authors to check out workbooks before they can edit them. This ensures that if multiple people are working on the same workbook, no conflicts occur. If someone tries to edit a workbook while it is being edited by someone else (and is therefore checked out), that person receives an error message and cannot access the workbook.

In the following Try It Out, you work with major and minor versions of the sample Sales Report and view the version history of the workbook.

Try It Out   **Working with Versions**

To work with different workbook versions, follow these steps:

1.   If you previously uploaded sales report.xlsx to the Sales Reports document library, delete the file from the document library by selecting Delete from the drop-down menu next to the filename.

2. Publish sales report.xlsx to the Sales Reports document library. When you do this, a minor version of the workbook is created and it is automatically checked out to you (the author).

3. In Excel, click the Office button, and select Check In from the Server fly-out menu, as shown in Figure 11-16.

4. The Check In dialog box lets you choose between checking in a major and minor version, as shown in Figure 11-17. Select the 1.0 Major Version (Publish) option to check in a major version of the workbook.

At this point, the major version has been checked in, but it hasn't been approved. Content approval is integrated with versioning. When both are set to work on a document library, a minor version is set as a draft of the file and does not require approval. It is also not broadly visible. When you check in a major version, it is considered a published file that requires content approval before it becomes broadly available. In the next step, you approve this version of the workbook.

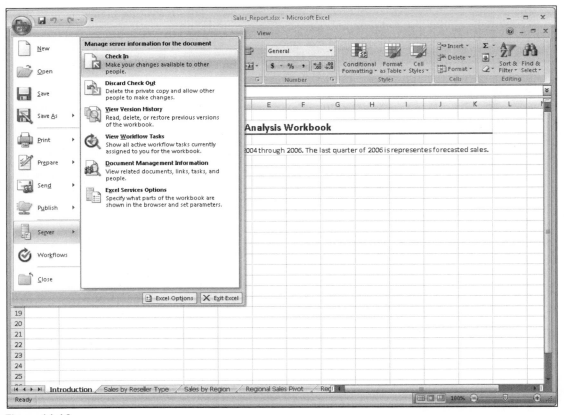

Figure 11-16

5. On the workbook name drop-down menu, select Approve/Reject and approve the workbook as before.

6. From the drop-down menu next to the workbook name, select Version History. In this view, you can see all versions (major and minor) created for the workbook. You can open any one of these, and you can restore the workbook to a specific version by selecting Restore from the drop-down menu in the date field, as shown in Figure 11-18. You can also access the version history directly from within the Excel client through the Server fly-out menu on the Office button.

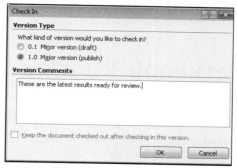

Figure 11-17

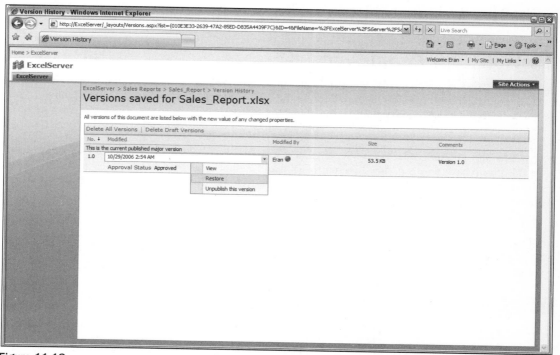

Figure 11-18

By working with versions, you can further control workbook authoring and publishing. Just as content approval is integrated with versioning, so is workflow. You can use the workflow to approve or reject publishing of major versions of a document.

This concludes the first part of controlling workbook distribution, namely the author's side. The focus has been on controlling who can publish a workbook for broad consumption, as well as on controlling the workbook itself by ensuring that it is approved prior to being broadly available and by maintaining version history. In the next section, you learn how to control who can view the workbook.

Controlling Workbook Viewing

The second part of controlling workbook distribution is controlling who can see workbooks and what they can do with them. Assume that you have a workbook that has been published to Excel Services. The workbook was published by an authorized author, because you gave the author at least Contributor permissions to the location on the server. In addition, the workbook itself has gone through an approval workflow and all the appropriate people have taken a look and approved that this is, in fact, the official copy.

If anyone can download the workbook and edit it, you are back to square one. You have multiple copies of the workbook, and you cannot guarantee that people are all looking at the same, sanctioned copy. What you need is the ability to limit access to the workbook and ensure that users are always looking at the sanctioned copy stored on the server.

The View Only Permission

As you learned in Chapter 8, the View Only permission is a new permission that limits users to viewing documents using server-side file handlers. In the case of Excel workbooks, this means using Excel Services. In the following Try It Out, you learn how to give the users who are viewing workbooks this permission only, so they are always viewing the latest sanctioned workbook copy on the server.

When you install Office SharePoint Server, a new user group is created for you: the Viewers group. Users in this group have only the View Item permission and cannot download or open files on the client. You can manage which users have View Only permissions to a site, document library, or specific file by either adding them to the Viewers group and verifying that the group has access to the resource, or by explicitly granting them permissions to the resource.

For this exercise, you must have access to a different user account than your own. You will be giving that user lesser permissions than what you have in order to demonstrate View Item permissions. If this isn't possible, either work with a peer, or follow the exercise through the accompanying figures.

Try It Out   Setting View Item Permissions

To set View Item permissions, follow these steps:

1. Open the Sales Reports document library in the browser and go to the Settings page by selecting the Document Library Settings option from the Settings drop-down menu.

2. On the Settings page, click the Permissions For This Document Library link under Permissions and Management.

3. On the Permissions page, select Add Users from the New drop-down menu on the toolbar.

There maybe additional users already listed on this page. This could be true if you were using an existing document library, or if the library were inheriting permissions from the parent site. If this is the case, and you want to ensure that only specific users can view the workbook and even fewer can open or edit the original workbook, remove the unwanted users by checking the box next to their corresponding usernames and select Remove User Permission from the Actions drop-down menu.

4. On the Add Users page, type in the usernames for the users to whom you want to give only the permission to view the workbook coming from the server.

There are two ways to give users permission to view workbooks into this library. You can either give them the View Only permission, or you can add them to a SharePoint user group that has only this permission. Out-of-the-box SharePoint has a Viewers group that is exactly that. This group isn't available on servers upgraded from previous versions.

5. In the Give Permission section, ensure that the Give Users Permission Directly option is selected.

6. Check the View Only permission. The page should now look similar to Figure 11-19.

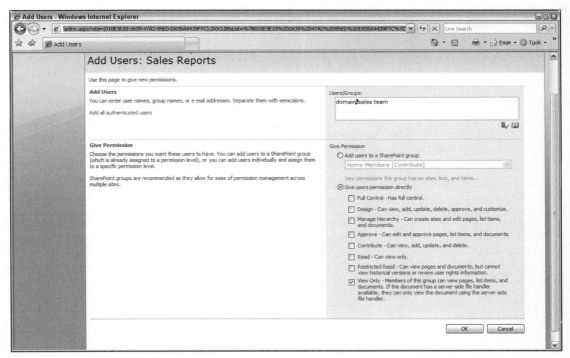

Figure 11-19

When users have the View Only permission, they cannot download or open the workbook in the client. This means that they see only the workbook as it is calculated by Excel Services and rendered in the browser. A number of options aren't available to the users in the interface, including the following options from within the document library:

- Edit in Microsoft Office Excel
- Edit Properties
- Managing Permissions
- Delete
- Check Out
- Sent To: Other Location, Create Document Workspace, and Download a Copy
- Workflows

When you view the workbook in the browser using Excel Services, the Open In Excel option is not available. You can see this in the following Try It Out. For this exercise, you must have access to a second user that has the View Only permission (as created in the previous exercise).

Try It Out   Viewing a Workbook with the View Only Permission

To view a workbook with View Only permission, follow these steps:

1. Log in to Office SharePoint as the user you created earlier who has View Only permission to the Sales Reports document library. You can do this by logging into Windows as this user, running the browser session as this user, or selecting the Sign In As A Different User option from the SharePoint drop-down menu (see Figure 11-20).

2. Open the drop-down menu for the Sales Report. As you can see in Figure 11-21, you only have access to server-side options.

3. Click the workbook name in the document library. You will get the Excel Services browser-based rendering of the workbook, even though the default for this library should be to open in the client. The default click is now View In Web Browser, because this is what you have permission to do.

4. Click Open on the toolbar. As you can see in Figure 11-22, you only have access to opening a snapshot (more on this in the next section). You cannot open the workbook in Excel client.

As you can see, you are confined to working with the workbook calculated and rendered on the server. This means that you do not have access to the original workbook file, to any of the sheets or ranges the workbook author did not make viewable on the server, or to the formulas behind the cells. This provides the security and control necessary to guarantee that users are viewing the sanctioned version of the workbook.

Figure 11-20

In the previous example, you granted the View Only permission for the entire document library. Using Office SharePoint Server's security features, you can grant this permission at the server, site, or specific workbook level as well.

Workbook Snapshots

In the previous exercise, you saw that a user with the View Only permission has the option of opening a snapshot of the workbook. This option exists both from within the document library and when you are viewing the workbook in the browser using Excel Services. The *workbook snapshot* lets the user take the values in the workbook to view offline or to print. The snapshot does not include the formulas behind the numbers, or the sheets or ranges that were not made viewable by the publisher. This is not the original workbook or even a copy of it.

Not all workbook features are rendered in the snapshot. For example, if the original workbook has conditional formatting, the snapshot does not.

Figure 11-21

In the following Try It Out, you create a workbook snapshot to see how it is different from the original workbook. This exercise assumes that you are logged in as a user with the View Only permission, although a user who also has full control of the workbook can also access the workbook snapshots feature.

Try It Out   Creating Workbook Snapshots

To create a workbook snapshot, follow these steps:

1. Log in to Office SharePoint as the user you created earlier who has View Only permission to the Sales Reports document library. You can do this by logging into Windows as this user, running the browser session as this user, or selecting the Sign In As A Different User option from the SharePoint drop-down menu (as previously shown in Figure 11-20).

2. From the Sales Report workbook drop-down menu, select Snapshot In Excel. (You can also access this functionality from the Open menu on the toolbar when viewing the workbook in the browser.) The workbook snapshot opens in Excel client.

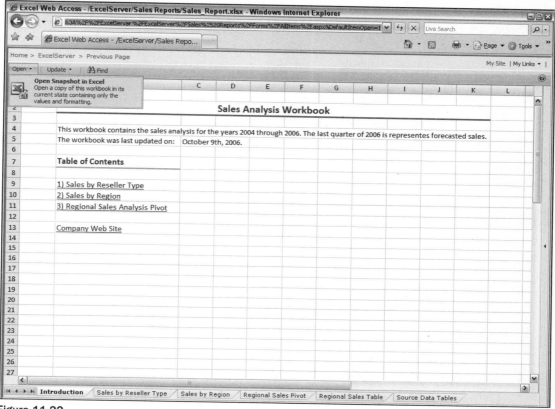

Figure 11-22

3. Step through the cells in the workbook, and notice that they contain values and formatting, but none of the formulas, from the original workbook.

4. Publish the workbook to the document library again and set only one of the sheets to visible. Repeat the exercise and notice that the workbook snapshot in the client has only that one sheet available to the user.

Alerts and RSS Feeds

After you set up a document library as the location for accessing a workbook, there are a couple of ways you can make it easier for the recipients of those workbooks to know when a new workbook is available, or when an existing workbook has been updated. This section examines the primary options for doing this.

The first option is to put the onus on the workbook author. The author can use the Send Alert To feature to create an e-mail message that notifies workbook consumers when a new workbook is available. The other options are more automated:

❑ *Workflow* — Notifies workbook approvers of an update to a workbook.

❑ *Alerts* — You can sign up to receive alerts from the server when a workbook has been added, deleted, or changed. Workbook consumers can either sign themselves up, or the workbook author can sign up the target audience to receive these notifications.

❑ *RSS feeds* — You can subscribe to an RSS feed from the document library that you are tracking.

In the next two Try It Outs, you use the alerts and RSS features to track workbook updates. For these features to work, you must have a valid e-mail server associated with the Office SharePoint Server installation.

Try It Out   **Using Alerts**

To use alerts, follow these steps:

1. Open the browser and navigate to the Sales Report document library you created earlier.

2. Select Alert Me from the Actions drop-down menu on the toolbar. The New Alert page is displayed, as shown in Figure 11-23.

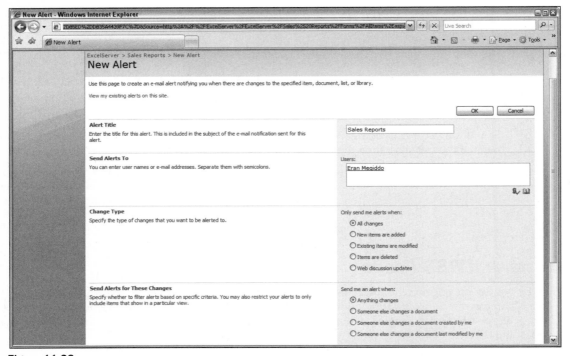

Figure 11-23

3. Leave the Sales Reports default in the Alert Title field.

4. Keep only your e-mail in the Send Alerts To box (this should be the default).

5. Keep the All Changes default option selected in the Change Type section. This allows you to select the granularity of changes from tracking only new items to tracking every modification made.

6. Keep the Anything Changes default option selected in the Send Alerts For These Changes section. This lets you track any changes to documents made by someone else as well as documents that you own or have worked on.

7. Keep the Send E-mail Immediately default option selected in the When To Send Alerts section.

8. Click OK at the bottom of the page.

   You will receive an e-mail message that you have successfully created an alert. The message will contain a link to the page where you can delete and manage alerts. You can also do this by returning to the document library and opening the Alert Me page again.

9. To test the alert feature, upload a new workbook into the document library. This triggers an alert e-mail to be sent out.

In the following Try It Out, you subscribe to an RSS feed from this document library. It is assumed that RSS feeds have been turned on for the server. If not, you (or the server administrator) need to do this on the Web Applications General Settings page in the Central Administration of the server.

Try It Out   Subscribing to an RSS Feed

To subscribe to an RSS feed, follow these steps:

1. Return to the document library page for the Sales Report library and select Document Library Settings from the Settings drop-down menu.

2. Select RSS Settings in the Communication Settings column. The Modify List RSS Settings page is displayed (see Figure 11-24), where you can set the various attributes of the RSS feed, including which columns to include in RDD description and whether or not to attach the documents or links to the document to the feed.

3. In the List RSS section, ensure that the RSS is allowed for this list (the default).

4. Leave the default settings in the RSS Channel Information section.

5. In the Document Options section, select the Link RSS Items Directly To Their Files option.

6. Leave the defaults in the remainder of the settings, and click OK at the bottom of the page.

You can choose to have the file attached to the RSS item, but this is only for users who have permissions to read and open the workbook file.

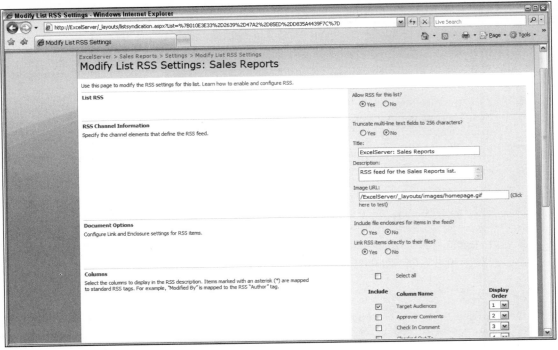

Figure 11-24

7. Return to the Sales Report document library using the navigation breadcrumb link at the top of the settings page.

8. Select the View RSS Feed option from the Actions drop-down menu. The RSS feed for this document library is displayed, as shown in Figure 11-25. You can either subscribe to the feed from here, or copy the feed URL to any RSS viewer application.

As you learned in this section, the Excel Services workflow, alert, and RSS feed features can help you manage workbook distribution. When workbook authors publish their files to sanctioned document libraries, users can be automatically notified about and can view updates. You can also use these features in collaborative authoring scenarios so that reviewers or people contributing the same workbook receive notifications whenever something has changed in the files they are interested in.

Auditing Workbook Usage

Auditing is another way to manage workbook distribution. Though you do not need to turn on auditing to control who can author and who can view workbooks, it provides you with the records of who did just that. This can be very useful in supporting compliance scenarios, and to verify that your current workbook-management solution is working.

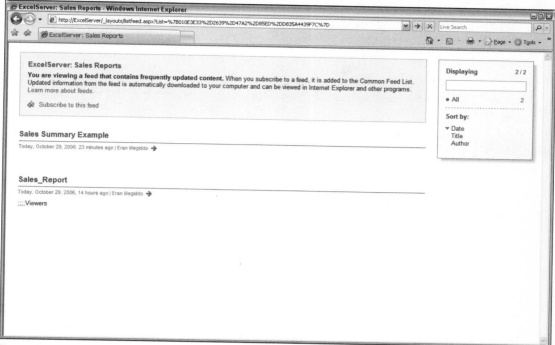

Figure 11-25

You must be a Site Collection Administer to set up and use audit logs. As such, you can define audit settings at the site level, define them as policies that can be applied to a document library, or define them specifically for a document library. This section focuses on the latter.

Auditing is defined as part of the information-management policy settings for a document library. When you set up a policy for a document library, you can enable auditing as part of that policy. You can audit the following events out-of-the-box:

- ❑ Opening, downloading, viewing items, and viewing item properties
- ❑ Editing items
- ❑ Checking out or checking in items
- ❑ Moving or copying items to another location in the site
- ❑ Deleting or restoring items

In addition, custom audit events can be programmed using the Office SharePoint Servers API. (That topic isn't covered in this book.)

After you specify which events to audit for the document library (or site), an audit log is generated and maintained by the server. You can then view a series of out-of-the-box audit reports. These reports include content activity reports such as who changed files; policy and security reports that provide information on changes to policy or security settings; and the ability to create a custom report based on the audit log. All the reports are in Excel format so that you can use Excel to view and analyze your audit log.

In the final two Try It Outs in this chapter, you set up an audit policy for the Sales Report document library and then view the associated audit reports. This exercise assumes that you are a Site Collection Administrator.

Try It Out   **Auditing Workbook Usage**

To audit workbook usage, follow these steps:

1. Open the browser and navigate to the Sales Report document library you created earlier.

2. On the document library toolbar, select the Document Library Settings option from the Settings drop-down menu.

3. Click the Information Management Policy Settings link in the Permissions And Management column.

4. Select the Define A Policy option and click OK.

5. Leave the sections for the policy name, statement, and labels as they are by default.

6. In the Auditing section, check the Enable Auditing option and select all five of the available events listed, as shown in Figure 11-26.

7. Leave the expiration and barcode settings off (this should be their defaults).

8. Click OK at the bottom of the page.

You have now created an audit policy for the Sales Reports document library. Every time a workbook is created, updated, deleted, or viewed, an entry is written in the servers audit log. Users do not know that this is happening, nor do they have a way of circumventing this.

Next, you look at the audit log reports for the document library. To make things interesting, you can view, upload, or delete one or more workbooks from this document library so that a few events are generated in the log.

Try It Out   **Viewing Audit Log Reports**

To view audit log reports, follow these steps:

1. Open the Site Actions drop-down menu, and then select Modify All Site Settings from the Site Settings fly-out menu, as shown in Figure 11-27.

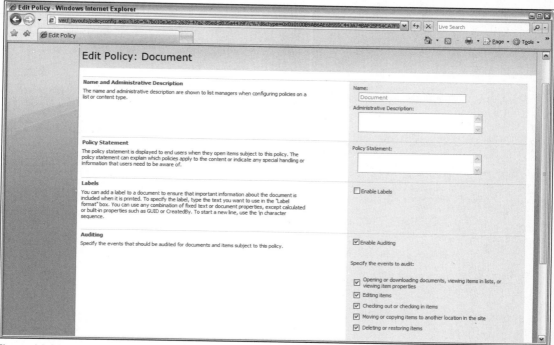

Figure 11-26

2. If you are not already at the top-level site of your site collection, click the Go To Top Level Site Settings link in the Site Collection Administration column.

3. In the Site Collection Administration column, click Audit Log Reports under. You are presented with a choice of predefined audit log reports or creating a customer report, as shown in Figure 11-28.

4. Select the Content Modifications report, save the file, and open it in Excel client to view the audit log analysis.

You can explore the other reports on this page. You can also choose to run a customer report. All of these reports build off of the audit log that is generated on the server. The detailed log is available on one of the sheets in the workbook, and a PivotTable is created off of the log table to facilitate analysis.

This completes the tour of the primary features you can use to manage workbook distribution. Next, you learn how to put it all together to provide a complete solution.

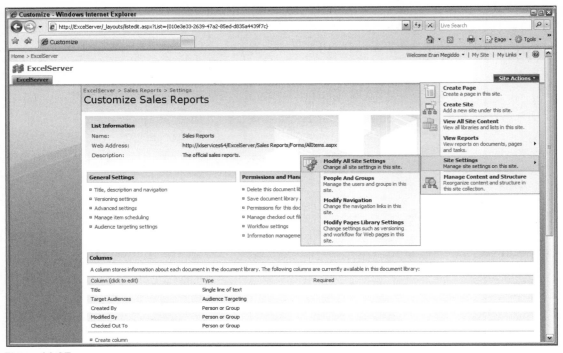

Figure 11-27

The End-to-End Scenario

Now that you have seen all the components for managing workbook distribution, you can set up a system that enables the end-to-end scenario. Not all workbooks need to be diligently managed and controlled, but for those that do, you can use a combination of features to manage their distribution. Do not distribute workbooks using the existing methods of sending workbooks through e-mail, placing them in file shares, or even simply placing them in document libraries. Instead, set up specific document libraries that are defined as trusted locations for your Excel Services. Then you can do the following:

❑ Control which users can author workbooks into these libraries.

❑ Control which users can access those libraries to read the workbooks, and ensure that they have View Only permissions to view the server-based workbooks.

❑ Set up content approval and/or approval workflows to ensure that the workbooks that are broadly accessible have been reviewed by the right people.

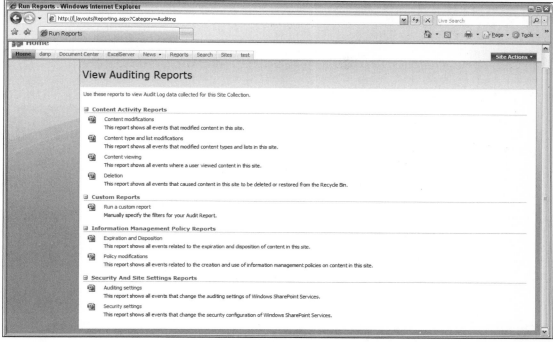

Figure 11-28

❑ Enforce document versioning so that workbook authors can work on draft versions without making them broadly available and so that you retain a version history.

❑ Set up alerts and feeds for users who want to be notified of workbooks added and updated in the document library.

❑ Turn on auditing for these documents so that you have an audit trail of who authored, changed, and viewed workbooks.

By following this process, you are ensuring that there is one location of the sanctioned version of any critical workbook. You are also ensuring that the users viewing these workbooks are looking at that sanctioned version. Because they can only access the workbook on the server, they users are always looking at the latest approved workbook.

There are a number of additional features that this book does not cover that can help you manage workbook distribution. You can learn more about these through Office SharePoint Servers online help or other reference material. A few specific features worth looking at are Policies, Document Expiration, Information Rights Management, and Usage Reports.

Summary

In Chapters 9 and 10, you learned how to publish a workbook to the browser and interact with it. In this chapter, you worked with the Office SharePoint Server features for document management, together with the Excel Services functionality, to gain control over workbook distribution. This is one of the key value propositions of the server. Understanding how to set up and use the server to achieve this is important. With the knowledge you gained in this chapter, you should be able to control workbook authoring, as well as consumption. To take advantage of these features, you must change the way workbooks are distributed in your organization.

This chapter discussed the following:

- ❑ Controlling who can publish workbooks
- ❑ Using content approval and approval workflows to review workbooks
- ❑ Using check-in, check-out, and versioning
- ❑ Controlling who can view workbooks using the View Only permission
- ❑ Using workbook snapshots
- ❑ Subscribing to alerts and RSS feeds to know when workbooks are updated
- ❑ Auditing workbook usage

Chapter 12 builds on everything you have learned so far, and shows you how you can use Office SharePoint Services with Excel Services functionality to create business intelligence portals and dashboards.

Business Intelligence Solutions

As discussed in Chapter 1, Excel is often used in business intelligence (BI) solutions. It is a primary tool for data analysis and reporting. In this chapter, you learn how you can use Excel Services with Office SharePoint Server features to build BI solutions that extend from the client to the server. To do this, you use Excel and Office SharePoint Server with Excel Services to build two primary BI constructs: reporting portals and dashboards.

This chapter discusses the functionality that supports building these BI solutions. In particular, you learn about the following:

❑ The Report Center
❑ Report libraries
❑ Key performance indicator (KPI) lists
❑ Building and using dashboards
❑ Building BI solutions outside of the Report Center
❑ Integration with SQL Server Analysis Services

Report Centers

Office SharePoint Server includes an out-of-the-box site template called Report Center. In fact, when you first install the server, a Report Center called Reports is provisioned for you as a top-level site. This template provides you with a great starting point for creating your BI portal. It includes the following common elements of such portals:

❑ A report library with templates for report and dashboard content type

❑   A Data Connection Library (DCL)

❑   A report calendar that is simply an Office SharePoint server calendar list and view, which you can use for such things as communicating report update schedules

❑   A reference library that is a document library in which you can place such things as report descriptions and meta-data glossaries

The Reports template also includes a sample report, key performance indicator (KPI) list, and dashboard. The rest of this section explores each of these elements and how they are used together.

First, although your default installation may already have created a Report Center, you create a new Report Center in the following Try It Out so that you can see how it's done. This exercise assumes that you have the permissions necessary to create a site on your server.

Try It Out   **Creating a New Report Center**

To create a new Report Center, follow these steps:

1.   Open a browser with the home page for your Office SharePoint Server installation, or the site under which you have permissions to create a new site.

2.   Select Create Site from the Site Actions menu.

3.   In the Site Creation page, type **Sales Report Center** in the Title field.

4.   Type **SalesReportCenter** in the URL Name field.

5.   In the Select A Template section, click the Enterprise tab.

6.   Select the Report Center template, as shown in Figure 12-1.

7.   Leave the rest of the selections at their default values and click Create at the bottom of the page. A new site is created, which should look similar to the one shown in Figure 12-2.

The home page for the site reflects what BI portals commonly look like. There is introductory text that explains how to use the site, a place for announcements, a place for upcoming events (which you can use to alert users of the data warehouse going down for upgrade, for example), a top-level view at a number of KPIs, a place for contacts for the primary owners of the reports and analysis in this site, and a place to highlight resources. You can customize each of these parts to make it relevant to your BI portal implementation. For the purposes of the following exercises, leave them with their default content.

Though you can store any document and content type in Report Centers, they are designed for reports and dashboards — the two primary building blocks of reporting portals.

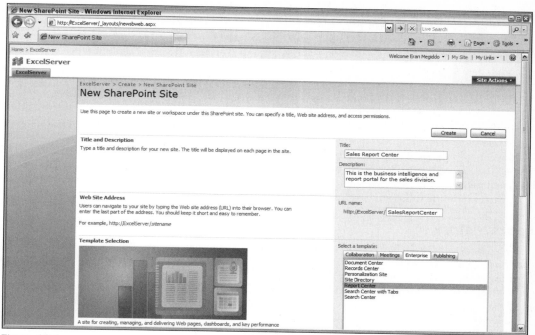

Figure 12-1

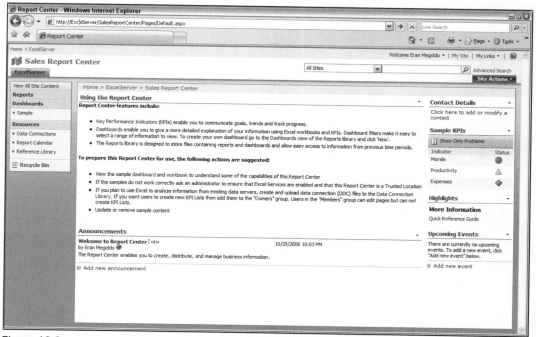

Figure 12-2

Report Libraries

Report libraries are a special type of document library that is optimized for reports and dashboards. The report library in the Report Center comes with a number of default views, content types, and columns. There is also a report viewer page. The following discussion shows all of these in action.

Content types are Office SharePoint features that allow you to group default metadata, templates, and information-management policies (for example, expiration policies, auditing settings, and workflows) as a specific content type. You can then associate that content type with any document library and, whenever and wherever an item of that type is created it abides by all those settings. This enables you to manage certain things such as policies not just hierarchically within your site, but also across sites, by content type. The Report Center template includes two content types: reports and dashboards. They are pretty basic in that they only include default metadata and a template. Nonetheless, they are useful, and you try them out in the following sections.

Report History

The primary difference between a regular document library and a report library is the concept of *report histories*. These are different from a document version history, which is also available in report libraries. Typically, a report is based on data that updates regularly (such as a monthly sales report or weekly inventory report). The report history feature lets you save each generation of such a report. You can then use the report versions (either major, or major and minor) to manage versions of the actual report definition or structure. In the case of a weekly inventory report, a copy of the report with each week's inventory numbers is created and stored as a report history. If you change the underlying report to include a new analysis, for example, you create a new major version of that report.

Try It Out   Working with Report Histories

To work with a report history, follow these steps:

1. Open a browser to the home page of the Report Center site you just created.
2. Click the link to go to the reports library created for you, Reports, in the left navigation menu.
3. On the Reports Library page, create a new report by selecting Report from the New drop-down menu on the toolbar, as shown in Figure 12-3.
4. Name the report **Weekly Sales Report**.
5. Select the Save To Report History option.
6. Enter a valid e-mail address for the Owner.
7. Your page should look like the one in Figure 12-4. Click OK at the bottom of the page to create the report.
8. Back in the report library, select Edit In Microsoft Office Excel from the drop-down menu next to the newly created report's name.
9. In Excel Client, enter **week 1 sales numbers** in cell A1 and save the report.

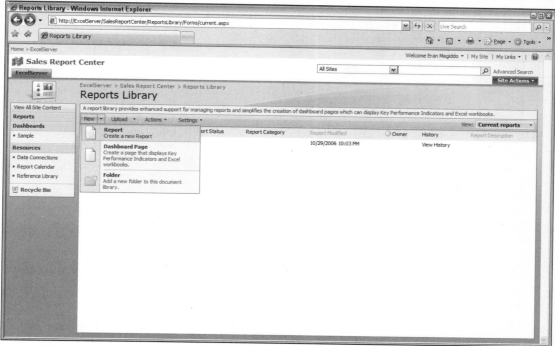

Figure 12-3

10. Enter **week 2 sales numbers** in cell A2 and save the report.

11. Return to the browser and to the reports library.

12. Click the View History link for the Weekly Sales Report you created. Figure 12-5 shows the various generations of the report. The latest report (the last one you saved) is represented by the actual top-level report that you can browse to from the document library itself. Therefore, it does not exist in the report history view, yet.

Separating the report history from the version history is especially useful when a report is created on a scheduled basis (either manually or programmatically). It helps organize the report library so that you do not have an endless list of reports, one for each period. Instead of having one entry for Weekly Sales Report – October 20, another one for Weekly Sales Report – October 27, and so on, you have one Weekly Sales Report item. That item always represents the latest report, and you can access all previous generations through the report history feature.

To see all instances of a report in the document library, toggle to the All Reports And Dashboards view. This view is different from the default Current Reports view in that it does not collapse report histories behind their latest instance.

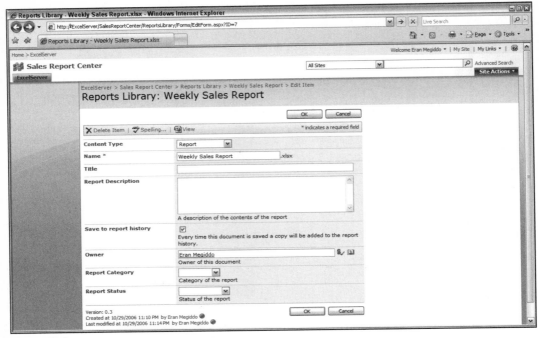

Figure 12-4

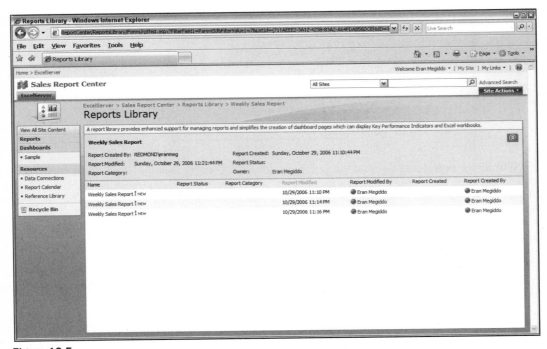

Figure 12-5

The Report Viewer Page

The Report Center template also installs a default report viewer page. For Excel reports, this is different from the regular Excel Viewer page. It includes some additional report metadata that is useful to have on hand when viewing a report. You can also collapse the metadata to make more room on the screen for the actual report, as you will see in the next Try It Out.

Try It Out   Working with the Report Viewer Page

To work with the report viewer page, follow these steps:

1. Return to the report library in the browser.

2. Click the SampleWorkbook link (or, if it doesn't exist, click the link for the Weekly Sales Report you just created). The report library is set to default to browser-based rendering, and the report is displayed on the report viewer page, as shown in Figure 12-6.

3. The metadata associated with this report, including the report creator, the create date, and so on, are displayed at the top of the report. Collapse this metadata view by clicking the up arrow icon on the right side of the pane.

4. Continue to explore the report library. Notice that there are a number of default columns that are part of the template, as well as default views on the library.

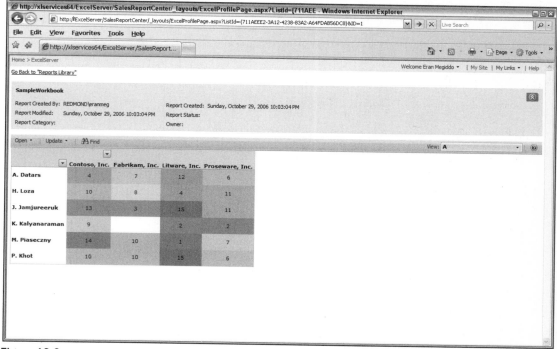

Figure 12-6

Other than the report history feature, a report library behaves just like any other document library on the server. The next section introduces another BI element: KPI in Office SharePoint Server.

Key Performance Indicators

Many BI solutions include some means for KPI tracking. This can be something as robust as a scorecard application, or as straightforward as an Excel workbook that tracks the key performance metrics for an organization. This book does not explain the methodologies behind KPIs and scorecards. Suffice it to say that KPIs track important metrics. They consist of a metric name and description, its current value and target, and warning values so that you know if you are on track or not. Office SharePoint Server includes functionality to create, track, and view KPIs. This section explores that functionality.

In Office SharePoint Server, you can use KPI lists to track indicators. These lists can contain any number of indicators from the following four supported types:

❑   Indicators that use data in SharePoint lists

❑   Indicator that use data in Excel workbooks

❑   Indicators that use data in SQL Server 2005 Analysis Services

❑   Indicators that use manually entered information

Because this book is about Excel Services, in the following Try It Out, you create an indicator using an Excel workbook. You can also experiment with the other indicator types on your own.

KPIs based on an Excel workbook take one or more of the value, goal, and warning numbers from it.

Try It Out   **Creating an Excel-Based KPI**

To create an Excel-based KPI, follow these steps:

1.   In the browser, return to the Report Center you created.

2.   Upload a copy of the Sales Report.xlsx workbook provided with this book to the report library. (You use this workbook to source the value for the KPI you create later in this exercise.)

3.   Click the View All Site Content link in the left navigation pane.

4.   Click the Create link at the top of the page.

5.   Click KPI List in the Customer Lists column.

6.   Name your list **Sales Metrics** and click Create.

7.   In the Sales Metrics list, select the Indicator Using Data In Excel Workbook option from the New drop-down menu on the toolbar. This loads the New Item form for defining metrics, as shown in Figure 12-7.

8.   Name the indicator **Total Sales**.

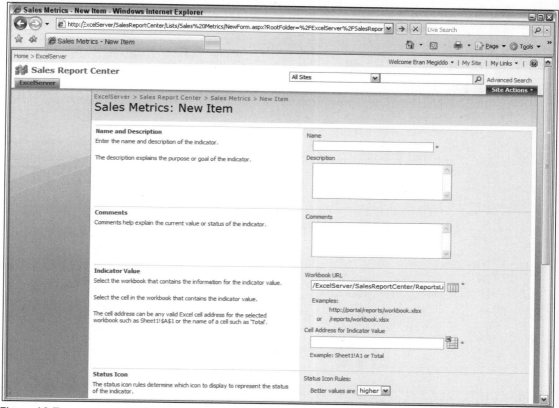

Figure 12-7

9. Click the icon to the right of the Workbook URL text box. This displays a file selector that lets you point at the workbook instead of manually typing in the URL.

10. The file selector opens with the Reports Library page. Select the Sales Report workbook you uploaded into the library and click OK.

11. Back in the New Item form, click the icon to the right of the Cell Address For Indicator Value text box. A pop-up window displaying the workbook in the browser opens, as shown in Figure 12-8.

12. Switch to the Sales By Reseller Type sheet.

13. Scroll to the total of all sales in the bottom right of the table and select cell O13.

14. Click the Set button to set the cell address for the indicator value (the top one of the three set buttons). You should see 'Sales By Reseller Type'!O13 in the text box.

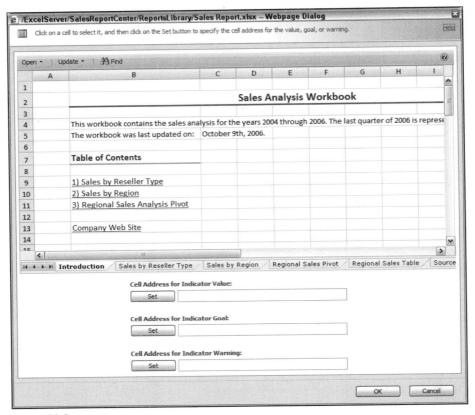

Figure 12-8

15. Click the OK button at the bottom of the page.

Next, you manually define the goal and warning values for the indicator. Had these values been present in the workbook, you could have taken them from there instead.

16. In the Status Icon Rules section of the New Item form, enter **10,000,000** for the goal and **8,000,000** for the warning, as shown in Figure 12-9.

17. Leave the rest of the options at their default settings and click OK at the bottom of the page. Your Sales Metrics indicator list now contains the Total Revenue KPI with the appropriate values, as shown in Figure 12-10.

How It Works

Every time you or any other user views this KPI list, the value for the Total Sales indicator is extracted from the Sales Report workbook. Behind the scenes, Excel Services calls the Web service interface to open the workbook and get the value from the cell you specified.

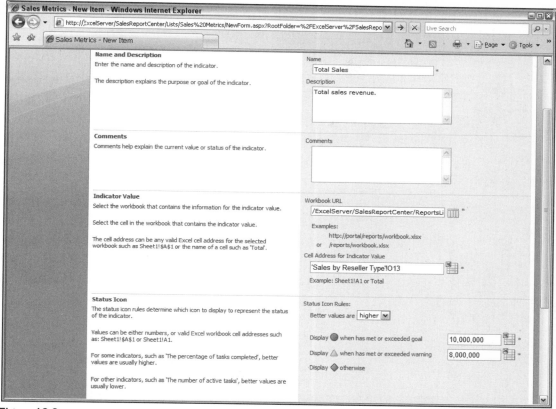

Figure 12-9

Because the indicator is extracted from the workbook every time the list is viewed, you are always guaranteed the latest value for the goal. This also means that the server must open and potentially calculate the workbook every time someone views the indicator list. You can also update the indicator value manually if you know when the workbook updates and will update the indicator with it, or if you do not want the indicator to update with every workbook change, but rather control when it does. This also reduces the load on the server, because the value is cached with the indicator and Excel Services must only open and calculate the workbook when you manually choose Update from the user interface.

Try It Out   Manually Updating an Indicator

To manually update an indicator, follow these steps:

1. In the KPI list you created, hover the mouse over the Total Revenue indicator name and select Edit Properties from the drop-down menu.

2. Scroll down to the Update Rules section and expand it by clicking the + sign icon.

3. Select the option to manually update the value, as shown in Figure 12-11.

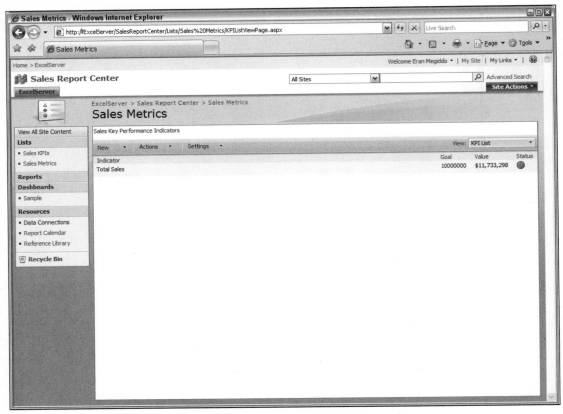

Figure 12-10

4. Click OK at the bottom of the page. In the KPI list, the indicator value is updated from the workbook. However, from this point on, the value is cached in the SharePoint list item and is not updated, even if the workbook changes.

When you chose to manually update the value for an indicator, the latest value from the workbook is stored in cache every time you select Update (and the first time you create it). This means that all users see this value, regardless of their permissions for the original workbook. This could be something that you do on purpose, or it could be seen as a security risk. If you need to protect the values in the workbook, be sure you keep it updating for every viewer automatically. This way, only viewers with access to the workbook and the specific cell in the workbook see the values in the indicator list.

5. To manually update the indicator value, select Update from the drop-down menu next to the indicator name in the list. (Note that the value has not changed in the workbook and, thus, won't actually change.)

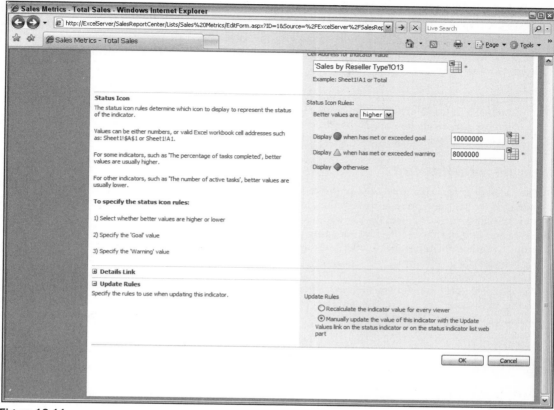

Figure 12-11

The KPI behaves much like any other SharePoint list. This means that you can use features such as alerts and RSS on this list. For a more specialized view of KPIs in Office SharePoint Server, use the KPI Web Part described in the next section.

Building Business Intelligence Dashboards

BI dashboards aggregate multiple views, data, and content to present a single complete picture. Using Office SharePoint Server's Web Part Pages and the various out-of-the-box Web Parts, you can easily create such dashboards. The Report Center template also includes both a sample dashboard that you can get started with, and a template for creating new ones. Following are the primary Web Parts you can use to build a BI dashboard:

❑ The Excel Web Access Web (EWA) Web Part to display Excel workbooks as part of the dashboard

❑ The KPI list Web Part

❑ Filter Web Parts that allow you to select values that the rest of the dashboard can use for filtering

In this section, you create a sales report based on the Sales Report.xlsx file provided with this book, with a dashboard that contains a couple of views on the sales data and a KPI that tracks total revenue. You then set up a filter part to define various levels for the forecast growth across all the views on the dashboard. To do this, you publish the Sales Report.xlsx workbook with the Forecast parameter. (Chapter 10 described how to set up parameters.)

The dashboard you create in this section is based on the template provided out-of-the-box with Office SharePoint Server. You can equally create a blank SharePoint Web Part Page, or edit an existing page (that you have rights to) and add the relevant Web Parts to it. The template is nothing more than a standard Web Part Page with some predefined content on it that helps get you started.

Creating a Dashboard

The dashboard template provided with the Report Center creates a SharePoint Web Part Page that is managed by the page-publishing functionality. This enables you to manage dashboards in a way that is very similar to how you manage workbooks (as discussed in Chapter 11). The primary idea is to let you create and edit dashboards while managing who can see drafts, manage versions, and require approval prior to making them broadly available. You can see these features in play as you go through the following examples.

The first step is to create the dashboard using the template defined for the dashboard content type. You do this in the next Try It Out. The template includes a couple of EWA parts, a KPI part, a Content Editor part, a Contact part, a list of links to related information, and a Filter zone into which you can add filter parts.

Try It Out   **Creating a Dashboard**

To create a dashboard, follow these steps:

1. Open the browser to the Report Center site you created earlier.

2. Click the Dashboards link in the left navigation pane. This opens the report library in the Dashboards view.

3. Select the Dashboard Page option from the New drop-down menu on the Reports Library toolbar. This displays a New Dashboard page, as shown in Figure 12-12.

4. In the Page Name section, enter **Sales Dashboard** in both the File Name and Page Title fields. Optionally, you can also enter a description for this dashboard.

5. In the Create Link In Current Navigation Bar section, leave the Yes option selected (the default). This makes it easier to navigate back to the dashboard later.

6. In the Dashboard Layout section, leave the Two Column Vertical Layout option selected (the default).

7. In the Key Performance Indicators section, select the option that allows you to select an existing KPI list later. (You are going to use the KPI list you created in the previous section.)

8. Click the OK button to save your settings and close the page.

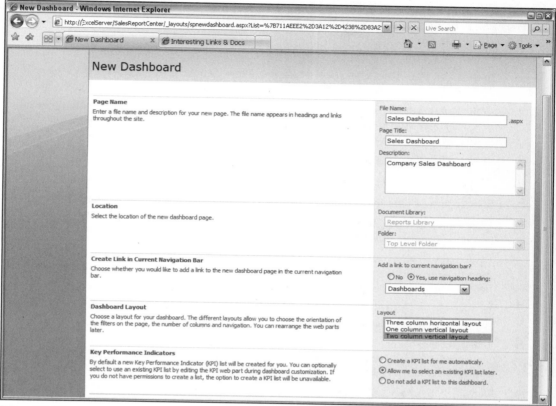

Figure 12-12

9. On the newly created dashboard, click Open The Tool Pane so you can add content at the top of the dashboard.

10. Click the Rich Text Editor button on the right side of the Web Part tool pane. Use the editor to type brief introductory text for the dashboard. For this example, type the following: **This is the sales dashboard for the company. Refer to the metrics and reports on this page for a complete picture of sales. Use this dashboard to see how the forecasts are helping us reach our targets**.

11. Click the OK button at the bottom of the Web Part tool pane to close it.

Adding Workbooks to a Dashboard

The next step is to start adding workbooks to the dashboard. The template sets up EWA Web Parts for you on the page. In the following Try It Out, you customize these Web Parts to show different sections of the Sales Report workbook. (You can use a different workbook in each Web Part instead, but this exercise is to show you how to configure Web Parts.)

Try It Out　　**Configuring Excel Web Access Parts**

To configure the Web Access Web Parts, follow these steps:

1. In the Excel Web Access Web Part on the left, Excel Web Access [1], click the Click Here To Open The Tool Pane link. The Web Part tool pane is displayed.

2. In the Web Part tool pane, click the icon with the three dots to the right of the workbook text box. This opens the asset picker dialog box where you can choose the workbook that you want to display in this Web Part.

3. Double-click Reports Library to open it.

4. Double-click Sales Report to select it. The workbook URL appears in the Workbook text box.

5. Select a named item to display by entering **RegionalSalesSummary** in the text box.

6. Click Apply at the bottom of the tool pane to verify that you have set up the workbook and item correctly. They should display in the Web Part.

   Now that you have selected a workbook and a named item to display in the Web Part, you modify a few additional settings on the Web Part to streamline the display for the dashboard in the remaining steps.

7. In the Toolbar and Title Bar section, choose Navigation Only. This enables paging through the named item, if necessary, but removes the rest of the toolbar.

8. In the Toolbar Menu Commands section, uncheck Named Item Drop-Down List to remove it from the toolbar. By doing this, you ensure that users cannot change named items, and you can control what the dashboard looks like.

9. In the Toolbar And Title Bar section, uncheck Autogenerate Web Part Title. (You give the Web Part a custom title in the next step.)

10. Expand the Appearance section by clicking the + icon.

11. In the Appearance section, change the title to **Regional Sales Summary**.

12. In the Navigation And Interactivity section, uncheck Display Parameters Task Pane. (You use the parameter in filtering.) This disables the task pane, which provides more room for the actual summary data and ensures that users can only change the value through the filter that you set up.

13. Click OK at the bottom of the tool pane. At this point, your dashboard should look like Figure 12-13.

14. Configure the second Excel Web Access Web Part to display a chart from the same workbook. To do this, repeat the previous steps, this time for the Excel Web Access Web Part on the right. Provide the same workbook. In step 5, replace RegionalSalesSummary with **ResellerSalesChart**. Change the title in step 11 to **Reseller Sales**. After you click OK in step 13, your dashboard should include the Regional Sales table and the Reseller Sales chart.

Next, you configure the KPI part, using the KPI list you created in the previous section.

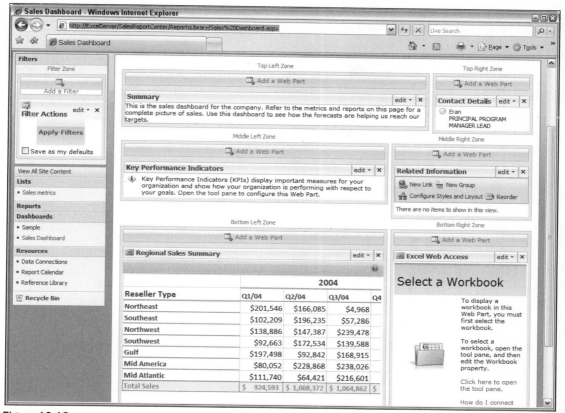

Figure 12-13

Configuring the Key Performance Indicator Part

To configure the KPI part, follow these steps:

1. In the KPI Web Part, click the Open The Tool Pane link.

2. In the tool pane, click the asset picker icon to the right of the indicator list text box.

3. Navigate to the top level of the Sales Report Center site by clicking the first link in the Look In options, SalesReportCenter, as shown in Figure 12-14.

4. Select the Sales metrics KPI list by clicking it, and then click OK.

5. Uncheck the Display Edit Toolbar In View Mode option.

6. In the Appearance section, change the Title to **Sales Metrics**.

7. Click OK at the bottom of the tool pane. Your dashboard now includes the Total Sales KPI, the sales table, and charts.

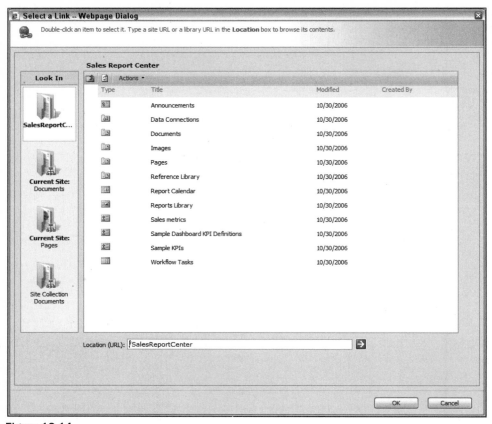

Figure 12-14

At any point, you can exit the page edit mode for the dashboard to see what your dashboard will look like when you finish editing it. You can do this by clicking the Save And Stop Editing button or the Check In button on the toolbar at the top of the page. To return to editing the page, select Edit Page from the Site Actions menu. This functionality is similar to the document management functionality you used to control workbooks. You can use similar concepts for check-in and check-out, approval work-flows, and so on, to manage dashboards.

Connecting Web Parts to a Filter

When you connect the EWA Web Parts to a filter, you can change the forecast numbers and see the effects on all the views. Office SharePoint Server includes a set of filter Web Parts. Their primary use is to filter other Web Parts in dashboards.

Each filter Web Part provides a different mechanism for selecting a value or values. You can then apply the values to other Web Parts on the same page using the part-to-part communication infrastructure.

On the other end, you must have a Web Part that can consume the values and apply them to the view or report, for example. The EWA Web Part can consume values from filter Web Parts. It lets you apply these values into workbook parameters, which in turn, change the values in the workbook. Using filter parts in conjunction with workbook parameters opens up many interesting scenarios.

In addition to Excel Web Access, a number of out-of-the-box Web Parts can consume filters. The KPI Web Part is one of these filters, which you explore in the "Working with SQL Server Analysis" section, later in this chapter.

There are two types of filter Web Parts: those that require the end user to select a value or values, and those for which a value is automatically set. The following filter Web Parts are shipped with Office SharePoint Server and require the end user to manually pick a value:

- ❑   *Text filter* — An edit box is provided where users type in text.
- ❑   *Choice filter* — A list of values to pick from.
- ❑   *Date filter* — The end user enters a date manually or with the calendar control.
- ❑   *SharePoint List filter* — The end user picks a value from a column in a SharePoint List.
- ❑   *Business Data Catalog filter* — Pick a value from a Business Data Catalog entity.
- ❑   *SQL Server 2005 Analysis Services filter* — Pick a value from an Analysis Services dimension.

The following filters are applied automatically:

- ❑   *Current user filter* — Provides the current user login name or a value from the SharePoint profile.
- ❑   *Page field filter* — Provides the value from a column in the SharePoint list that contains the page.
- ❑   *Query string (URL) filter* — Passes values from the query string on the URL.

You can place filter parts anywhere on the dashboard page, but there is also a special filter zone setup for them. It is in the navigation panel on the left-hand side of the page. You use this zone in the next Try It Out.

Filters require that you either include an Apply Filters control on the page or define the filter to be applied automatically. You should use the first method if you want to have a number of filters and let the user change more than one of them prior to having them applied and the page refresh. You can also save the current filter values as defaults. This lets you return to a dashboard page and have it prefiltered.

You can choose to hide filters, but still have them apply to the page. This is especially useful if you employ filters that are automatically set. For example, you can use the Current User Filter to automatically set a dashboard to filter to values for the current user. By hiding this filter Web Part, you guarantee that the user can't change the filter.

In the following Try It Out, you add a Choice List filter to provide three scenarios for forecasts: pessimistic, realistic, and optimistic. Each of these drives a different value into the workbook parameter for forecast, which, in turn, drives a calculation of a new forecast number.

Try It Out   Filtering Excel Workbooks on a Dashboard

To filter an Excel workbook on a dashboard, follow these steps:

1. With the dashboard still in edit mode, click the Add a Filter button in the Filter Zone in the upper-left corner of the page. This displays a list of the filter Web Parts that you can add, as shown in Figure 12-15. Only the filter Web Parts are listed because you are in a filter zone.

2. Check the Choice Filter box, and then click the Add button.

3. In the newly added Choice Filter Web Part, click the Open The Tool Pane link.

4. In the Filter tool pane on the right side of the page, type **Forecast Scenario** as the Filter Name.

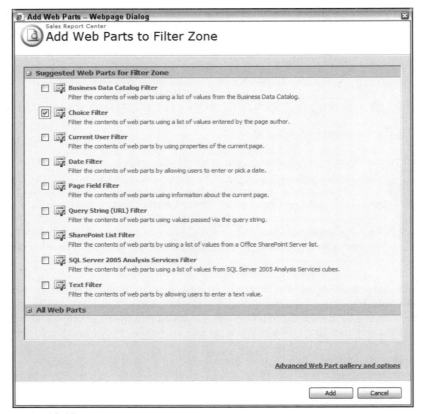

Figure 12-15

5. The choice filter uses a named-value pair list. In the choice text box, you enter each value and description with a semicolon between them (value;description) on separate lines. For this example, enter **-5%;pessimistic**, **5%;realistic**, and **10%;optimistic**, as shown on the right side of Figure 12-16.

You can expand the Advanced Filter Options to select a default value, but, in this case, the default is the value that is already in the workbook.

6. Click OK at the bottom of the tool pane.

7. Now you need to hook up the filter to the EWA Web Parts on the page. On the Choice Filter Web Part you just created, open the drop-down edit menu, and select Connections ⇨ Send Filter Values ⇨ Regional Sales Summary to send the values to the Regional Sales Summary EWA Web Part (see Figure 12-17).

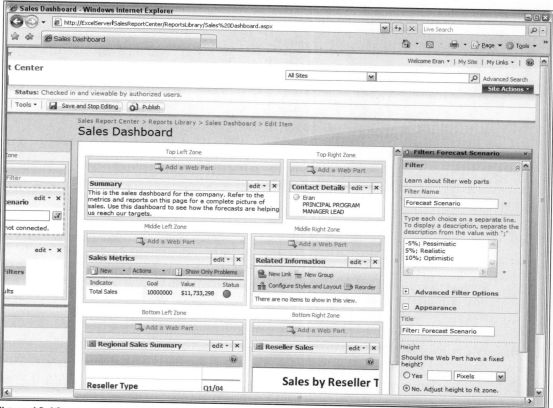

Figure 12-16

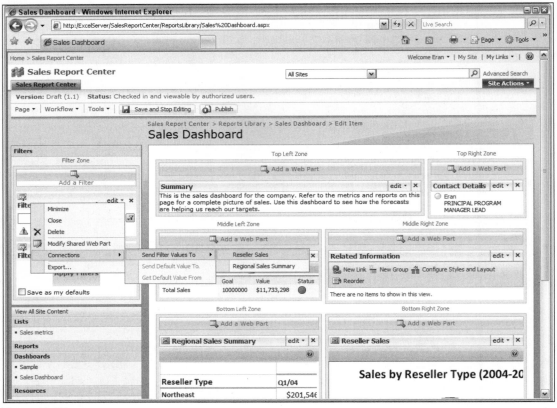

Figure 12-17

The Connection dialog box is displayed, which guides you through picking which Web Part property and workbook parameter to provide the value to. The drop-down menu presents three options: Get Workbook URL From, Get Named Item From, and Get Filter Values From. The first two options allow you to drive which workbook and which name item is displayed in the Web Part. You can set up a list of workbooks and/or named items and provide the user with a simple way of switching between workbooks and items without changing pages.

8. For the purpose of building the dashboard in this exercise, choose the Get Filter Values From option and click the Configure button to map the filter value to a specific workbook parameter.

9. Because there is only one workbook parameter, Forecast, it is already selected. Click the Finish button.

The Web Parts on the dashboard update to notify you of the connection. The filter Web Part shows that it is sending values to the Regional Sales Summary Web Part, and the Regional Sales Summary Web Part shows that it is receiving values from the Forecast Scenario filter.

10. Repeat the preceding steps to connect the Reseller Sales Excel Web Access Web Part. You only need to modify step 7 to select this Web Part from the Send Filter Values submenu.

11. Publish your dashboard so it is broadly available. To do this, click the Publish button on the toolbar at the top of the page. Your finished dashboard should look like Figure 12-18.

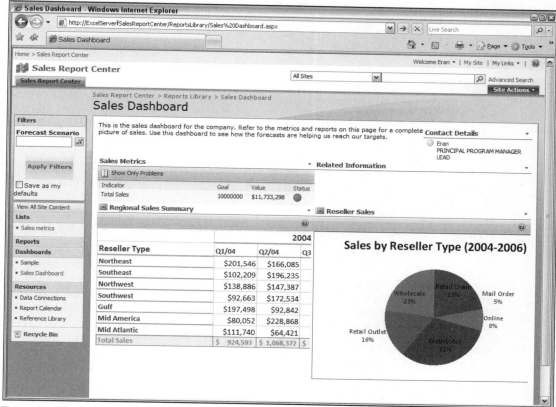

Figure 12-18

Next, you set the filter to change the forecast and view the results across the different views in the dashboard.

<table>
<tr><td>**Try It Out**</td><td>**Displaying Forecasts on Dashboards**</td></tr>
</table>

To configure a filter to display forecasts on your dashboard, follow these steps:

1. In the Filters pane on the left side of your dashboard page, click the Forecast Scenario filter icon (see Figure 12-18). This displays the list of values you defined.

2. Select Optimistic and click the OK button.

3. Click the Apply Filters button. The dashboard refreshes and the values in the two EWA Web Parts reflect a 10 percent increase in Q4 sales forecasts. (You may need to scroll the workbook to see this, depending on your screen resolution.)

You now have a working dashboard. The next section gives you a few tips on how to set up the Excel Web Part so it works well in a dashboard.

Tips on Working with Excel Web Parts

As you can already tell from setting up the dashboard, there are a number of design decisions you need to make when using the EWA part on dashboards. Use the following tips as a guideline when you need to set up Web Part properties in the tool pane (by choosing Modify A Shared Web Part from the Web Part edit drop-down menu):

❑ Set up workbooks to display specific items whenever possible. This way, you minimize the need to page within the dashboard, because you can use Named Item view to display the entire item instead of a small range of rows and columns.

❑ When you are displaying an item in the workbook, ensure that the user sticks with that item because it is integral to the dashboard. You can do this by turning off the Named Item Drop-Down List or disabling workbook navigation altogether. The latter also disables switching sheets and paging through the workbook.

❑ If you are using Sheet view or displaying the entire workbook, you can manually enter the number of rows and columns to return in the Web Part properties. This way, you can override the default settings to make the range smaller and fit better within the dashboard, or include an entire section of the sheet that you want displayed.

❑ Whether you are using Sheet view or Named Item view, consider publishing the workbook with grid lines set to Off. This gives your dashboard a cleaner look. If you are using Sheet view, consider turning row and column headers off as well. You can do both of these things from the Page Layout tab in Excel client.

❑ To maximize real estate for the actual workbook content, consider removing the toolbar, or at least using the summary or navigation-only toolbar. You can do both of these things from the Web Part properties.

❑ If you are using a workbook that has external data set to periodically refresh, consider turning off the prompt using the Web Part properties so that the dashboard can refresh without user intervention.

❑ To make the entire dashboard more readable, consider either removing the Web Part title bar, or changing it from the autogenerated title. To do the latter, uncheck the autogenerate Web Part title. Then, enter a custom title under Title in the Appearance section of the Web Part properties.

❑ You can control whether or not a user can link to the Excel viewer page to get a full-screen experience of the workbook. For example, you may want to do this to control where the link on the title bar goes to use a different viewer page, or to hide the complete workbook and toolbar (that appears with the viewer page). To do this, turn off the autogenerated title bar link in the Toolbar And Title Bar section and insert your own title bar in the Title URL box under the Advanced section in the Web Part properties. This also lets you further obfuscate the workbook URL.

So far in this chapter, you learned how to build BI solutions using sites created from the Report Center template. Equally (and perhaps even more) interesting is the fact that you can use all the features in any Office SharePoint Server site. The next section describes how to do this.

Business Intelligence Everywhere

You can create report libraries, DCLs, KPI lists, and dashboards literally anywhere that you can create regular lists and pages. Moreover, you can add the KPI Web Part or the EWA Web Part to existing pages (assuming you have the permission to edit them). The same can be done with the filter Web Parts.

The power of this is that you can embed BI functionality within your Web applications and sites. Your users do not need to go to a special site to see reports and dashboards. If your organization has an HR portal, for example, or if the Sales division already has a SharePoint Web site, you can add a report library with HR or sales reports within the respective site. You can also add a KPI list and place the associated Web Part on the home page of the sales division Web site. By embedding the functionality within the specific functional and team sites, you can spread the data and the derived value broader. Of course, if there is a need or preference for a standalone reporting site, you can always revert back to creating a Report Center from the template.

In the next Try It Out, you add the sales report to the home page of your Office SharePoint Server portal. This exercise assumes that you have the necessary permissions to edit the home page.

Try It Out   Adding Excel Web Access to the Server Home Page

To add EWA to the server home page, follow these steps:

1. Open the home page of your Office SharePoint Server.

2. In the Site Actions menu in the upper-left corner, select Edit Page.

3. Click the Add a Web Part button in the right zone of the page.

4. Show All Web Parts by clicking the + sign icon.

5. Select the Excel Web Access Web Part from the Business Data section.

6. Select a workbook by following the same steps as in the dashboard Try It Outs in the previous section.

7. Click the Publish button on the page editing toolbar to make the page available to everyone.

As you can see, the EWA Web Part is available from any Web Part Page on the server. The same is true for the KPI Web Part and the filter Web Parts you used earlier. Similarly, you can create a report library under any site and benefit from the features it offers.

The final section of this chapter delves into using Excel and Office SharePoint Server with Excel Services to connect to SQL Server Analysis Services, and creating a BI solution.

Working with SQL Server Analysis Services

The dashboard that you created earlier in this chapter is not bound to any external data. In many cases, you need to have workbooks and metrics bound to data that is changing and sourced from enterprise data systems such as your CRM or ERP applications. SQL Server Analysis Services provides a premium data source for BI scenarios for both Excel client and Excel Services. This last section of the chapter walks you through using Excel Services and SQL Server 2005 Analysis Services. For this section, it is assumed that you are familiar with Analysis Services and that you have them set up and running with the Adventure Works sample Unified Dimension Model (UDM) deployed. You also need to be able to access the UDM using either your username or some other username that you have available for this purpose.

To create a dashboard that is live against data in Analysis Services, you first need to set up a way for the server to get to external data in Analysis Services. To summarize from Chapter 5, you must be able to provide valid credentials when logging into Analysis Services. There are three primary ways of doing this:

❑   If Analysis Services is on the same box as the Excel Calculation Services (ECS), use integrated authentication.

❑   If Analysis Services and ECS are not on the same physical machine, set up a single-sign-on (SSO) account using Office SharePoint Server.

❑   If Analysis Services and ECS are not on the same physical machine, set up constrained delegation or Kerberos between the two machines.

A fourth option is also relevant for when you do not have the two services on the same box: use the browser on the same box as ECS. You can then use integrated authentication to connect to Analysis Services because your credentials only need to move one hop. However, this option is not a viable scenario for real-world use cases.

The rest of this example assumes that you have set up the SSO solution that is part of Office SharePoint Server. In addition, you must create an SSO application ID called SSO and map it to a user who has permission to access your SQL Server Analysis Services cube. If this is not possible, you can evaluate the functionality by working on the same box as the server.

For help on setting up SSO and an SSO application ID, refer to the Office SharePoint Server technical documentation.

This chapter also assumes that you are using an evaluation setup of Office SharePoint Server and, thus, have a trusted DCL in the Report Center. If you do not, you need to set up one. In addition, the trusted location to which you are saving your workbooks must support external data queries.

Connecting to Analysis Services from Excel

In this section, you create an Excel workbook that will be the basis for the dashboard. First, you create a data connection file and save it in the DCL on your server. This way, you can reuse that connection later to quickly author workbooks connected to the same data source. You also use this connection to create a KPI and a filter that are connected to Analysis Services.

In the following Try It Out, you use Excel to create the data connection file and save it to the server.

Try It Out   Creating a Data Connection Definition

To create a data connection file, follow these steps:

1. Open the Excel 2007 application.

2. Switch to the Data tab on the Ribbon.

3. Create a data connection to Analysis Services by selecting From Analysis Services on the From Other Sources drop-down menu, as shown in Figure 12-19.

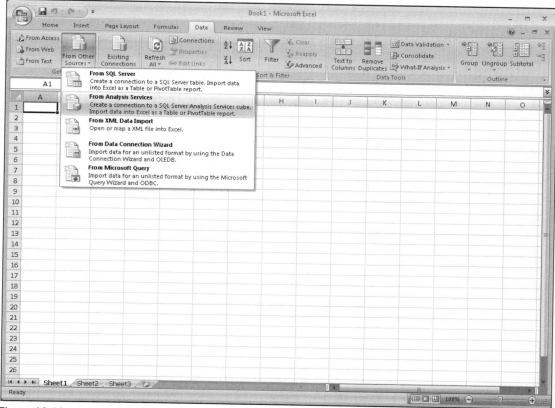

Figure 12-19

4. Enter the name of your Analysis Services server. In this example, it is **SQLAS**.

5. Keep the default Use Windows Authentication option selected. This is the authentication used by Excel client to connect to Analysis Services. It is assumed that you have the rights to connect to it.

6. Click the Next button in the wizard.

7. In the drop-down menu for the database, select Adventure Works DW. This is the default sample database that ships with SQL Server 2005 Analysis Services.

8. Ensure that the Connect To A Specific Cube Or Table option is selected.

9. Select the Adventure Works cube in the list.

10. Click the Next button in the wizard.

11. Click the Browse button to save the data connection file on your server.

12. In the file dialog box, navigate to the Data Connections Library on the Sales Report Center you created earlier. In this example, this library is located at `http://excelserver/salesreport-center/data connections`.

13. Enter the filename **Adventure Works.odc**.

14. Click the Save button. (The data connection file is not saved yet — this just lets you pick your destination location and filename.) The filename should be http://excelserver/salesreportcenter/data connections/adventure works.odc. The server name and Report Center URL should be specific to your deployment.

15. Enter a description to help users understand what this data connection provides. For this example, type the following: **This is the Adventure Works corporate data.**

16. In the Friendly Name text box, enter **Adventure Works**.

17. Select the option to always attempt to use this file to refresh data. This ensures that Excel client always uses the data connection file you save to the server when connecting to Analysis Services, and that you can update the file on the server if the data connection information changes. Any workbook that uses this file will have the updated connection information (for example, if the server name changes after an upgrade). Your screen should look like Figure 12-20.

18. Click the Excel Services Authentication Settings button to set up server authentication for this workbook.

19. Change the authentication type to SSO.

If you are not using SSO and have Analysis Services on the same box as Excel Services, are working with the browser on the same box as Excel Services, or have Kerberos set up, select the Windows Authentication option.

20. Enter the SSO-ID you created earlier: **SSO**.

21. Your settings dialog box should look like the one shown in Figure 12-21. Click the OK button.

22. Click the Finish button on the wizard to create the data connection file and connect the workbook to Analysis Services. The Web File Properties dialog box is displayed.

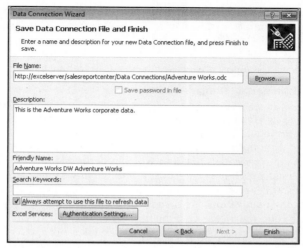

Figure 12-20

Figure 12-21

23. Enter the title **Adventure Works Data**. You can keep the rest of the settings as they are, or you can change the keywords to make it easier for users to find this data connection.

24. Click the OK button to close the dialog box. An Import Data dialog box appears, prompting you to select how you want to view the data in the workbook. You select this in the next Try It Out, so just leave the dialog box open for now.

You now have a data connection file, Adventure Works.odc, stored in the DCL on your Sales Report Center. This data connection file can be reused the next time you or another user wants to connect a workbook to analyze data in the Adventure Works cube.

In the next Try It Out, you create two PivotTable reports, each showing different data from the Adventure Works cube. You then publish them to the server. The first thing you do is define the report to refresh on open. This is an important step. It means that every time the workbook is opened, the PivotTable reports in it are refreshed and new data is retrieved from Analysis Services. This serves two purposes:

❑ It guarantees that if the data in the cube changes (for example, new sales data is loaded into it), the users viewing the report always see the most up-to-date values.

❑ It is potentially important from a security point of view.

When Excel creates the PivotTable, it saves the latest data queried from Analysis Services with the workbook. There may be cases in which different users have different permissions to the database or cube. In these cases, you do not want users to open the workbook and see the cached values. These values may have been queried with the credentials of a user who has permission to different data. For example, you may have two managers and each may have the permission to see only the salary data for their organization. The Human Resources analyst creating the report for them may have permission to see all the data. The values for both organizations are saved with the workbook (because the analyst's credentials were used to query the cube and create it). If the first manager creates a workbook, it contains the cached results of his or her organizations salary data. If the workbook is not set to refresh on open, then either manager viewing the workbook on the server sees all salary information for all employees.

To provide a solution to this problem, the workbook author must set the workbook to refresh on open. The workbook is then published to the server and the two managers are given View Only permissions so that they see only the server-based workbooks. In addition, the server administrator must ensure that the server is configured to fail when it attempts to open workbooks if the data query in the refresh on open fails. Now, when one of the managers tries to view the workbook on the server, the query to Analysis Services is performed on open, and the data that is returned is based on that manager's permission level only. If there was a problem querying the data, the workbook is not displayed at all. And, because the manager cannot open the actual workbook file, but only view the server-based workbook, the manager never sees the salary information for employees who are not in his or her organization.

You begin this Try It Out from where you left off in the previous one, with the Import Data dialog box open.

Try It Out   Creating a PivotTable on Analysis Services Data

To create a PivotTable on analysis services data, follow these steps:

1. Ensure that the PivotTable Report option is selected (the default).

2. Click the Properties button to set the report to refresh on open. This guarantees that the data is up-to-date when the dashboard is viewed.

3. Click OK to finalize the properties.

4. Click OK to create the PivotTable. You should have a blank PivotTable on the sheet and the PivotTable Field List should open.

5. Scroll down the Field List to show fields related to Internet Sales (in the drop-down menu).

6. Check the Internet Sales Amount measure to place it in the PivotTable values.

7. Scroll down and check Customer Geography to place it on the PivotTable rows.

8. Scroll down, right-click Product Categories, and select Add to Column Labels to place them on columns.

9. Scroll back up to the Date dimension and expand the Calendar folder.

10. Right-click Date.Calendar and select Add to Report Filter to place it on the report filter.

11. In the PivotTable Options tab on the Ribbon, change the PivotTable Name to **Internet Sales**.

12. Select the All Periods cell for the PivotTable Report Filter value.

13. Use the Name Box on the formula bar to name the cell **Date**. (You use this as a workbook parameter to filter the dashboard later.) Figure 12-22 shows the completed workbook.

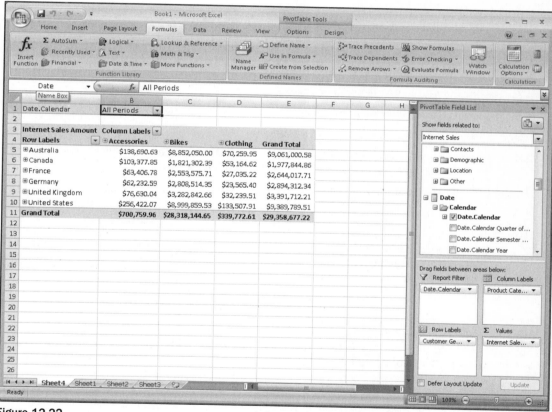

Figure 12-22

Before you can publish the workbook to the server, you must define a workbook parameter that you can use to filter the workbook on the dashboard. You also need to hide the actual Report Field on the PivotTable so that the only way users can change the date is through the filter on the dashboard.

Try It Out **Defining a Filter Parameter**

To define a parameter to filter the workbook on the dashboard, follow these steps:

1. In the workbook you created in the previous Try It Out, hide the row that contains the PivotTable report field and the row below it. Assuming you placed your PivotTable on A1, these should be rows 1 and 2.

2. Open the Publish dialog box by selecting Office ⇨ Publish ⇨ Excel Services.

3. Click the Excel Services Options button.

4. In the Excel Services Options dialog box, select Show Items In This Workbook.

5. Select the Internet Sales PivotTable.

6. Switch to the Parameters tab.

7. Click the Add button to add a parameter.

8. Select the Date parameter and click OK to close the Add Parameter dialog box.

9. Click OK to close the Excel Services dialog box.

10. Locate the report library in the Sales Report Center that you created earlier and save the workbook there. Name the workbook **Adventure Works Sales.xlsx**.

11. Click the Save button to save the workbook.

12. Leave the Document Type as Report and click OK.

13. The workbook should open in the browser (assuming you kept the option for opening with Excel Services checked). Depending on the settings in on your server, you may be prompted to allow the external data query to occur. If so, click OK. (This happens as soon as the workbook opens on the server because you set it to refresh on open.)

You now have a workbook that connects to and queries Analysis Services data on the server. You should be able to drill and filter the data in the browser. Each time you do this, Excel Services queries Analysis Services and the PivotTable is updated. Next, you place this workbook in a dashboard and hook it up to a filter part.

Building a Data-Bound Dashboard

The dashboard you are going to build will include the workbook you authored in the previous section, a KPI that takes data from the same Analysis Services cube, and a filter part for filtering both the KPI and the workbook based on the data period. In the first Try It Out in this section, you create the dashboard in the Sales Report Center site that you have been using and add the workbook to it.

Try It Out   Creating a Data-Bound Dashboard

To create a data-bound dashboard for your workbook, follow these steps:

1. Open the browser and navigate to the report library in the Sales Report Center.

2. In the New drop-down menu, select Dashboard to create a new dashboard page.

3. On the New Dashboard page, enter the **AdventureWorks** filename for the dashboard.

4. Enter the title **Adventure Works Sales** and optional description.

5. In the Dashboard Layout section, select the One Column Vertical Layout option.

6. Ensure that the option to create a KPI list automatically is select (this is the default).

7. Click OK to create the dashboard. Next, you add the workbook you just created to this dashboard.

8. Click the Open Tool Pane link on the Excel Web Access toolbar.

9. Click the button to the left of the workbook text box to open the asset picker. Navigate to the report library and select the workbook you created in the previous section, Adventure Works Sales.xlsx, and click OK.

10. Uncheck the Autogenerate Web Part Title option.

11. For the Type Of Toolbar, select None.

12. Expand the Appearance section and enter **Adventure Works Sales** in the Title field.

13. Click OK at the bottom of the tool pane to add the workbook to the page.

In the next Try It Out, you create a new KPI. This time, you use the Analysis Services cube as your data source, and connect directly to a KPI defined in the Adventure Works cube.

Try It Out   Connecting to a KPI

To create a new KPI and connect it to the cube, follow these steps:

1. In the KPI Web Part, select Indicator From SQL Server 2005 Analysis Services in the New drop-down menu.

2. You must select a data connection file to connect the KPI with the Adventure Works cube. To do this, click the icon to the right of the Data Connection text box to open the asset picker. This opens the DCL. Select the Adventure Works data connection that you created earlier and click the OK button.

3. Keep the All KPIs selected as the display folder, and select Internet Revenue from the KPI list, as shown in Figure 12-23.

4. Enter the name **Internet Revenue** for the KPI.

5. Click the OK button at the bottom of the page to create the indicator.

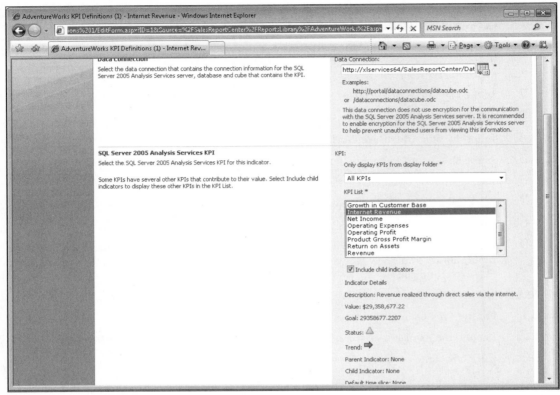

Figure 12-23

Next, you create a filter part so that you can connect both the KPI and the workbook to it. The filter also sources the filter options directly from the Analysis Services cube's Data dimension.

Try It Out   Creating the Filter Part

To create a filter part to which you can connect the KPI and workbook, follow these steps:

1. In the left pane of the dashboard page, under the Filter Zone, click Add A Filter.

2. Select the SQL Server Analysis Services Filter option in the Add Web Parts dialog box. Click Add.

3. Configure the filter part by clicking Open The Tool Pane link on the newly added part.

4. Enter the name **Date** for the filter.

5. To pick a data connection for the filter part, keep the default, which uses the same data connection as the KPI List Web Part that is on the page. This automatically connects the part to filter the list. (Alternatively, you can select the Adventure Works data connection file from the DCL.)

6. Select the Date dimension in the Dimension drop-down menu.

7. Select the Calendar hierarchy in the Hierarchy drop-down menu.

8. Change the title to **Calendar Date**.

9. Click OK to finish configuring the filter part.

In the last Try It Out, you connect the filter part to the workbook.

Try It Out   Connecting the Filter Part

To connect the filter part you just created to your workbook, follow these steps:

1. On the filter part, open the Edit drop-down menu and select Connections ⇨ Send Filter Values To ⇨ Adventure Works Sales (which is the name you gave the Excel Web Access Web Part displaying the workbook on the dashboard), as shown in Figure 12-24.

2. Select Get Filter Values From in the Connection Type drop-down menu.

3. Click the Configure button.

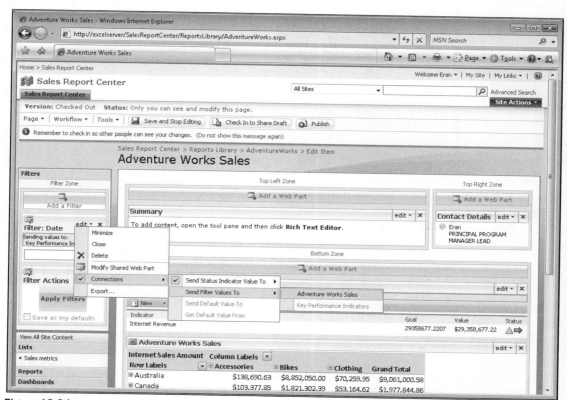

Figure 12-24

4.   Make sure Date is selected for the Filtered Parameter.

5.   Click the Finish button to create the part-to-part connection.

6.   Either edit the Summary Web Part and type in introductory text, or delete it from the page by clicking on the x icon in the upper-left corner of the Web Part.

7.   Click the Publish button on the toolbar at the top of the page to make the dashboard available for users to see. The completed dashboard is shown in Figure 12-25.

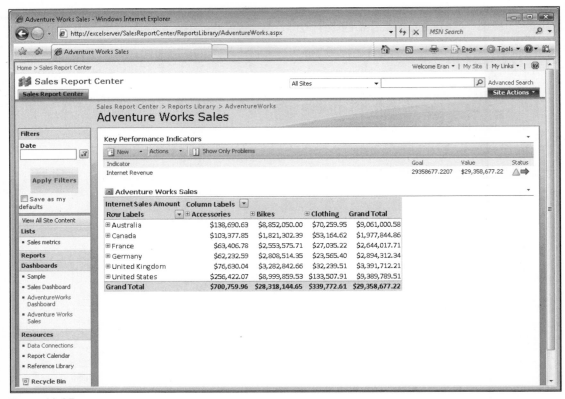

Figure 12-25

8.   To filter the dashboard, click the filter icon on the Date filter part. The values are loaded from the Analysis Services Data dimension and displayed.

9.   Select the CY 2004 value and click OK.

10. Click the Apply Filters button. Both the KPI and the workbook are filtered to present sales values for only calendar year 2004.

The Excel workbook you created has a Date parameter that drives a value in the report filter of the PivotTable. The Report field must have a valid Analysis Services member to filter the PivotTable.

Because you hooked up the filter Web Part to the same `Date` dimension in Analysis Services, the filter part passes a fully qualified member name to the report filter in the workbook.

You now know how you can use Excel and Office SharePoint Server with Excel Services to create a complete BI dashboard. By combining the various filter Web Parts that are shipped with Office SharePoint Server together with different views into Excel workbooks on the same dashboard page, you can create very powerful BI solutions.

Summary

Excel is often used as a BI tool. Excel Services and the rest of Office SharePoint Server's functionality enable you to extend your BI applications to the server, and provide report portals and dashboards that contain reports and analysis authored in Excel. You can do this using the out-of-the-box BI portal template, or by embedding the functionality directly within existing sites and Web applications built on Office Share-Point Server.

In this chapter, you learned about the following:

- ❑ The Report Center
- ❑ Report libraries
- ❑ KPI lists
- ❑ Building and using dashboards
- ❑ Building BI solutions outside of the Report Center
- ❑ Integrating with SQL Server Analysis Services

The next scenario you explore is using Excel Services to offload calculations from Excel client. Chapter 13 discusses how to set up the server and use it for this scenario.

Offloading Workbook Calculation to the Server

There are many scenarios in which you need to offload workbook calculation to the server. You may have workbooks that take a significant amount of time to calculate, and you can free up the client machines and specifically the end user's desktop by moving the calculation to the server. You may need to run multiple scenarios or parameters through a workbook and, although a single workbook calculation may not take long, iterating through thousands of parameters with that workbook may.

This chapter discusses these scenarios. It focuses on the setup and configuration considerations, as well as describing a few sample solution designs. Because there is no out-of-the-box functionality for offloading calculations, you need to write some custom code to create a solution that does this. You learn about the Excel Services API in the Chapter 14, so the actual code sample for one calculation scenario is in that chapter instead of here.

In this chapter, you learn about the following:

- ❑ The benefits of offloading workbook calculation to the server
- ❑ Setup and configuration considerations
- ❑ A few example solution designs
- ❑ Integrating with Windows Compute Cluster Server 2003

The Benefits

In general, Excel Services does not calculate a single workbook any faster than Excel client. In fact, if you take into account the network overhead, the need to send messages across boxes, and other factors, a single workbook usually calculates slower on the server than on the client. The value of moving a calculation to the server is not to make it faster, but rather to free up the end user's desktop machine so that he or she can continue working.

There are cases, however, in which moving the calculation to the server may actually improve performance. One such case is calculating workbooks that query a significant amount of external data. The server can benefit from being in the data center and, thus, both closer and with better connections to the data source than the end-user desktop machines.

There is an additional performance improvement if numerous users must calculate the same workbook, or calculate the same workbook with different input parameters.

In the first case, assume that each user in your organization needs to open and calculate a daily market analysis workbook. Each user who opens the workbook on the desktop incurs the cost of loading the workbook, potentially querying external data, and calculating the workbook. When the workbook calculation is moved to the server, the workbook is calculated once, and all the users can access the already calculated workbook. The calculated workbook can be saved out automatically for everyone to access, or loaded in cache so that the load time, query time, and calculate time are all saved.

A completely separate benefit to moving calculations to the server is the robustness that it provides. If you need to calculate a workbook or set of workbooks often and repeatedly, doing so on the client may require a relatively complex system for monitoring the processes and managing problematic states that Excel can go into while being automated. The client Excel application is designed as an end-user tool. There are various things that can get in the way of continuously calculating a workbook (such as pop-up dialog boxes). Excel Services is designed as a server, and, as such, is robust and has high availability. A common scenario that follows this description is doing parametric sweeps on models in workbooks.

Whether your goal is to free up the client, improve performance, or improve robustness, you should consider the setup and configuration scenarios presented in this chapter.

Setup and Configuration Considerations

There are a number of things to take into account when planning to use Excel Services to offload workbook calculations. First, if you are moving the calculation to the server because it takes a significant amount of time on the client, it is assumed that you turn automatic workbook calculation off. The workbook should be in Manual calculation mode, and your solution code on the server should programmatically trigger calculations. The rest of the considerations are outside of the workbook and specifically in Excel Services settings.

Excel Services Settings

The default settings for Excel Services are optimized for multiple users publishing and sharing workbooks. The server is optimized for business intelligence (BI) scenarios where many people are viewing the same workbook in a dashboard, and, thus, caching is highly leveraged. The default settings are also geared toward ensuring that the server is secure and tightly controlled out of the box. To this end, there are various limitations on workbook size, for example.

When you set up Excel Services specifically for solutions that offload workbook calculations to the server, you should revisit all the defaults settings and configure the server so that it is optimized for your scenario. You probably need to adjust the following settings (among others):

❑ *Workbook size* — The workbooks that you choose to be offloaded from the client to the server are most likely larger than the 10MB default. The maximum size is 2,000MB.

❑ *Maximum Request Duration* — You may want to adjust this to -1 so that sessions never timeout. In addition to the Excel Services settings, you need to increase the timeout settings within IIS (specifically, the settings for ASP.Net).

❑ *Volatile Function Cache Lifetime* — You may want to turn off all caching features (set this value to 0) so that each calculation is guaranteed to represent the latest values. Based on the assumption that workbook calculation takes a significant amount of time and there is no end-user wait time for the browser page refresh, the potential gain from caching volatile functions is often outweighed by keeping the values current according to the calculation of the workbook.

❑ *Session timeout* — Either increase the timeout or adjust this to -1 so that sessions never timeout.

❑ *Workbook Calculation Mode* — You can override the Calculation mode in the workbook and set this to manual. This is relevant if your solution requires setting multiple parameters or updating external data before calculating the workbook. If the workbook is saved with automatic calculation, you incur the calculation cost for each parameter set.

❑ *External Data Cache Lifetime* — For workbooks that include external data, you should consider changing this to 0.

❑ *Maximum Sessions Per User* — If your application is running all workbook calculation requests as the same user, consider raising the value on this setting.

❑ *Maximum Private Bytes* — If you have a dedicated server or servers for workbook calculation, you can increase the amount of memory they use by changing this setting to something higher than 50 percent of the physical memory (the default).

❑ *Caching* — You can adjust all workbook cache settings to disable caching altogether if your system will always be iterating through new workbooks being submitted. This frees up the memory for the active workbooks. You need to disable both the unused items cache (represented by the Caching of Unused Files setting) and the Maximum Size of Workbook Cache size setting.

To adjust these settings, you need to have administrative permissions to Excel Services. Chapter 7 discusses where and how to change these settings.

Deployment Topology Considerations

From a deployment perspective, to achieve the best performance and robustness, you should isolate the Excel Services boxes as an entirely separate farm. If you have an Office Server farm that you are using to support your solution, consider breaking out the Excel Calculation Services (ECS) boxes to dedicated hardware. In addition, consider locking down the access to this farm or to the Excel Services functionality to prevent usage of other features from affecting the server performance and reliability.

You can consider a dual-usage farm, in which, for example, the resources are used during the day for normal end-user scenarios and during the night for offloading calculations. In addition, you should use 64-bit machines for such scenarios, because the additional memory capacity can help you scale your applications.

Yet another element that you should take into account is the load-balancing scheme used by Excel Services. The default load-balancing scheme sends all requests for any specific workbook to the same ECS machine. If you have only one workbook that gets calculated repeatedly with a large number of parameters, or you have a very small number of workbooks, and you have more than one ECS machine, consider using the round-robin load-balancing scheme instead of the default.

Sample Solution Designs

There are many different scenarios and solutions that take advantage of offloading the workbook calculation to the server. Because there is no out-of-the-box functionality, these are, by definition, custom solutions that you need to develop. As such, you can fit them to your specific needs and use cases. To start you off, here are a couple of different solutions you can build. The solutions are described in broad terms and are meant to give you a starting point on which to develop the designs further.

The first solution is the most straightforward one. Workbook authors can submit workbooks to be calculated on the server. When the workbooks are calculated, the end users are notified and they can retrieve the updated workbook. There are a number of ways you can build this solution. Chapter 14 presents a very simple program that watches a specified file folder for any updated workbooks. Each time a new or updated workbook is placed in the folder, Excel Services is used to open the workbook, calculate it, and save an updated copy of the workbook to a second location. You can imagine extending this solution to include notification to the user when the updated workbook is made available, or perhaps send specific calculated result cells, ranges, or sheets from the workbook back.

A similar solution can be implemented using a custom workflow deployed to Office SharePoint Server. Workflows can already be triggered based on a document changing. All you need to develop is a custom workflow that opens the workbook, calculates it, and saves it back (either to the same or a different location). You can then leverage the Office SharePoint Server alerting or RSS functionality to notify the user when the workbook calculation is complete.

You can also add a scheduling component. This allows users to use Excel or a browser-based UI to submit a workbook to be calculated on a schedule, either as a one-time calculation or as a recurring event. For example, a workbook that includes complex modeling based on plant inventory could be scheduled to calculate every morning prior to the start of the workday. That way, plant managers can have the latest reports available to them without needing to first open the workbook on their desktops and then wait the many minutes or hours it takes to update and calculate the workbook.

Extending even further from simple workbook submission and scheduling, you could design a system that supports iterating through a workbook or set of workbooks with a set of input parameters. Such a solution could perform a parametric sweep against a model and collect the results. To do this, you can have one part of the solution generate the parameters based on user input, or require users to submit two files, one with the parameters and one with the model. The application then iterates calculating the workbook for each set of parameters. The results could be stored in the original workbooks, in workbooks or workbook snapshots created on the side, or extracted programmatically and placed in a database or some different output.

This section described each of the solutions at a high level. They are far from being complete, and serve only to stimulate your thinking about how you can leverage Excel Services to offload workbook calculations from the client to the server.

Integrating with Windows Compute Cluster Server 2003

Windows Compute Cluster Server 2003 is a Microsoft product that provides a high-performance computing platform based on Windows. With this product, you can set up a compute cluster that has Excel Services installed on it. It provides simplified deployment and management of new machines that you add to a cluster, which enables you to grow your cluster as your needs grow.

Another key component is a robust job scheduler that you can call programmatically. You can use the job scheduler to schedule workbook calculations on the cluster. The functionality that is most relevant to the scenarios described earlier is the error-recovery provided by the job scheduler. The error-recovery features take over when a certain job fails to execute. In such a case, the scheduler automatically reschedules the job. If the problem is with the compute node the job has been scheduled to, the scheduler is capable of working around such nodes and routing jobs to other available nodes. As nodes become available again, the job scheduler automatically adds them to the pool of available resources.

For applications such as the parametric sweep scenario described in the previous section, this functionality can be critical. If it is imperative that all iterations or all workbooks get calculated, leveraging the job scheduler provided with Windows Compute Cluster can solve this need without you having to develop your own solution to the problem.

As is true for all the scenarios described in this chapter, there is no out-of-the-box integration between Excel Services and Windows Compute Cluster. This is something you can explore outside the scope of this book.

Summary

Excel Services provides robust and scalable server-side workbook calculation. There are many cases in which offloading workbook calculation from client machines to the server makes sense. By doing this, you can free up the end user's desktop, provide a more robust environment for performing many workbook calculations, and, in certain cases, reduce the overall time it takes to calculate the workbooks.

Though Excel Services and Excel client do not provide out-of-the-box functionality for offloading calculations, you can build custom solutions that best suit your needs using the web service API provided by the server.

In this chapter, you learned about the following:

❑   When you should consider offloading workbook calculation to the server

❑   The benefits of offloading workbook calculation

❑   Setup and configuration considerations

❑   A few example solution designs

❑   Integrating with Windows Compute Cluster Server 2003

Chapter 14 discusses building custom solutions using the server and extending the server's calculation capabilities. It covers the web service API, as well as working with the Excel Web Access Web Part programmatically. Chapter 14 also includes a sample code solution for offloading workbook calculations to the server.

Building Custom Solutions

Excel Services is a strong product out-of-the-box, but you can always customize it to better suit the unique needs of your enterprise. Multiple programmability surface areas exist that you can leverage individually or together to extend the capabilities of Excel Services. This chapter introduces concepts geared toward extending the feature set through custom solutions.

In this chapter, you do the following:

- ❑ Become familiar with the Excel Services web service methods
- ❑ Learn how to create an application that makes Excel Services web service calls
- ❑ Learn how to author and deploy an Excel Services user-defined function (UDF)
- ❑ Become familiar with calling a UDF from an Excel workbook
- ❑ Learn about customizing xlviewer.aspx
- ❑ Discover approaches for interacting with the EWA through JavaScript and managed code

Excel Services Web Service

An important feature of Excel Services is its web service, also referred to as the API. This is a powerful programmability feature that enables solution developers to harness the power of Excel Services. One benefit of the web service is that developers are not tied to a specific technology when building solutions that interact with the API. The API exposes a wide range of methods that you can use to manage workbooks through Excel Services.

This chapter covers some of the terminology and good-to-know information about the API. With that information, you can then move toward creating a managed-code solution to make API calls. The chapter focuses on each of the public API methods by explaining their signatures, as well as by providing a code snippet on making calls with the methods. At the conclusion of the chapter, a comprehensive API solution is shown that ties together the API concepts.

First-Use Information

The Excel Services web service is fairly straightforward and easy to use. Understanding some of the Excel Services concepts can help you get more out of the API methods. This section draws attention to parameters and concepts that are standard across the majority of the API methods.

Session ID

Each time Excel Services opens a workbook, a new session is created. Each created session has an associated session ID that is unique. The session ID becomes a key for the Excel Services web service methods to perform operations on the caller's session, and maintain state for the life of the session. To perform any operation on the workbook using an API method, a valid session ID is required, which implies that the session is still active.

A session ends when the API `CloseWorkbook` method is called. A session can also time out after a period of inactivity, or be forced to time out prematurely under some Excel Calculation Server (ECS) error-handling conditions. Use the Excel Services administration settings to configure the session timeout associated with inactivity.

A session ID is a string that is similar to the following, which is a composite ID built with components such as the data culture and UI culture from the `OpenWorkbook` method call, time zone details, and an internal ECS session ID:

```
"64.21702262-ee93-48c6-9975-dcce27465ac940AMLTI2IPpxVF/+dMuBeZOwYeQ=
118.22.49JgQS2MbkuI3p3gVmbSfB90.5.en-US5.en-US73.+0480#0000-11-00-
01T02:00:00:0000#+0000#0000-03-00-02T02:00:00:0000#-0060"
```

Cultures

The *data culture* is equivalent to the configurable SharePoint site locale ID. The data culture specifies the language culture to be used when formatting numbers, currencies, and dates.

The *UI culture* is equivalent to the SharePoint site language ID. The UI culture specifies the language culture to be used for menus, drop-down lists, toolbars, and error messages. An Excel Services web service method uses the UI culture for error messages being returned to the method caller.

Both the data culture and the UI culture are set on each session created by the API `OpenWorkbook` method, and those culture settings are used for the life of the session. Excel Services supports the same set of languages that is supported by Microsoft .NET Framework version 2.0. The .NET Framework package includes the `System.Globalization` namespace, which contains the `CultureInfo` class that can provide the supported cultures. Neutral culture languages are not supported by Excel Services for data cultures. A *neutral culture* is one that is expressed in the form of `en` instead of `en-us`, for example. A neutral culture is handled by Excel Services as an unsupported data culture.

Excel Services defaults to a fallback culture for both the data culture and the UI culture when an unsupported or uninstalled culture is used by an API method call. If the fallback culture logic is invoked by Excel Services, the API method's `out Status` parameter provides the information about the culture fallback.

Status Class

Each of the Excel Services web service methods has an `out` parameter or a return value of type `Status`. The `status` object is used to return alerts with a next component state of Continue and for status messages. The default `Status` return value is `null` (not a zero-length array), which occurs when there are no alerts or status. The API returns an array of `status` structures when there are one or more alert or status messages. The items in the array are in the order they were received from the ECS. The status array is returned along with the normal return value of the method.

Following is an example of when a status is returned. In this example, an unsupported culture is used for the `OpenWorkbook` method's `uiCulture` parameter. The `status` structure includes three properties: `Message`, `Name`, and `Severity`.

```
try
{
    xlSessionId = xlEcsApi.OpenWorkbook(
        @"\\TheExcelServer\files\workbook.xlsb",
        @"aa-ZZ",
        @"en-US",
        out xlStatus);

    Console.WriteLine("Message: {0}", xlStatus[0].Message);
    Console.WriteLine("Name: {0}", xlStatus[0].Name);
    Console.WriteLine("Severity: {0}", xlStatus[0].Severity);
}
```

This code writes the following information to the console, which shows the properties of the `Status` that was returned for the `OpenWorkbook` method call. In this case, Excel Services is an English installation (operating system and MOSS).

```
Message: UI culture  (aa-zz) is not supported. Excel Services is using English
(U.S.) (en-US) instead.
Name: UnsupportedUICulture
Severity: Error
```

SOAP Fault Message

The ECS and WFE Excel Services components can return a second type of alert referred to as a Stop alert. This type of alert is returned when the called method must be stopped and is not allowed to finish. The `out` parameters of the method and the normal return value of the method are not output when a Stop alert is returned.

Unexpected exceptions can also be returned. These exceptions and the Stop alerts are returned to the caller as a SOAP Fault message. The following code is an example of a `try-catch` statement used to catch a SOAP Fault for an Excel Services web service call:

```
try
{
    //Excel Services Web Service method called from here
}
```

```
catch (System.Web.Services.Protocols.SoapException soapE)
{
    //code to handle the SOAP exception goes here
}
```

A1 Notation

Many of the Excel Services web service methods have a parameter that references one or more cells. The use of R1C1 notation to reference a cell is not supported. You can reference cells with A1 notation, object names, or a defined name.

The Excel A1 notation uses column letters and row numbers to refer to a cell. The syntax of the A1 notation can vary slightly to allow for references to cells, columns, or even rows. The following table lists some examples of supported cell references.

A1 Notation	Description
"A1"	Cell A1
"A1:B5"	Cells A1 through B5
"A:A"	Column A
"1:1"	Row 1
"A:C"	Columns A through C
"1:5"	Rows 1 through 5

Creating a Custom API Application

This section focuses on creating a managed code application that accesses the Excel Services web service. Creating the application has the following prerequisites:

- ❑ Microsoft Office SharePoint Server 2007 must be available.
- ❑ Excel Services must be set up and ready to load workbooks.
- ❑ An Excel workbook must be published to a trusted location where at least view permissions are set.
- ❑ Microsoft Visual C# and Microsoft Visual Studio 2005 must be available (to reproduce the steps noted here).

Creating the C# Console Application Project

Follow these steps to launch Visual Studio and create the C# console application:

1. Start Visual Studio.
2. Select File ➪ New ➪ Project to open the New Project dialog box.

3. In the Project Types frame, expand the Visual C# node and select Windows. In the Templates frame, select Console Application.

4. In the Name field, enter **xlWebService**.

5. Set the Location field to the location where you want to create the solution.

6. Select OK to create the application. The New Project dialog box closes and Visual Studio opens the `xlWebService` solution with `Program.cs` opened and visible. The namespace is `xlWebService`.

Adding the API Web Reference

Follow these steps to add the API Web reference.

1. Select Project ➪ Add Web Reference to open the Add Web Reference dialog box.

2. In the URL field, enter the URL to obtain the service description of the API. The URL should be in the form of `http://<wfe_server>/_vti_bin/ExcelService.asmx` or `http://<wfe_server>/<site>/_vti_bin/ExcelService.asmx`. This URL must support at least View permissions.

3. Click Go to retrieve the available web service. The service appears in the list as ExcelService.

4. In the Web Reference Name field, enter **ExcelWebService**.

5. Click the Add Reference button to add the ExcelService web service as a web reference to the solution.

Calling the API

Follow these steps to call the API:

1. In Program.cs, add a directive for the ExcelService web reference namespace. At the beginning of `Program.cs`, add the following `using` statement:

```
using xlWebService.ExcelWebService;
```

2. Add a second directive to `Program.cs` for handling SOAP faults:

```
using System.Web.Services.Protocols;
```

3. In the `Main(string[] args)` method, instantiate, and initialize the API with the following statement:

```
ExcelService xlEcsApi = new ExcelService();
```

4. Credentials must be explicitly set. Add the following statement to use default credentials:

```
xlEcsApi.Credentials = System.Net.CredentialCache.DefaultCredentials;
```

5. Create a status array and a string for the session ID:

```
Status[] xlStatus;
string xlSessionId = "";
```

6. Create a string and initialize it with the workbook to be opened by the API:

```
string xlWorkbookPath =
@"http://TheExcelServer/xlSite/Documents/workbook.xlsb";
```

7. Create and initialize additional strings to capture the UI culture and the data culture:

```
string uiCultureName = "en-US";
string dataCultureName = "en-US";
```

8. Add the API `OpenWorkbook` method call to have the ECS open the workbook and return a `sessionId`:

```
try
{
    xlSessionId = xlEcsApi.OpenWorkbook(
        xlWorkbookPath,
        uiCultureName,
        dataCultureName,
        out xlStatus);
```

9. Add the API `CloseWorkbook` method call to close the workbook and end the session:

```
xlStatus = xlEcsApi.CloseWorkbook(xlSessionId);
```

10. Complete the `try` block by adding the following `catch` block for SOAP exceptions:

```
}
catch (SoapException soapE)
{
    Console.WriteLine("Soap Fault: {0}", soapE.Message);
}
```

Following is the complete solution. This sample represents a starting point for trying the API. In the spirit of reducing the size of the sample, many good coding practices have been overlooked. Return values are not validated, error handlers are not present, and a number of values are hard-coded, to name a few of the shortcuts used here.

```
using System;
using System.Collections.Generic;
using System.Text;
using xlWebService.ExcelWebService;
using System.Web.Services.Protocols;

namespace xlWebService
{
    class Program
    {
        static void Main(string[] args)
        {
            ExcelService xlEcsApi = new ExcelService();
            xlEcsApi.Credentials = System.Net.CredentialCache.DefaultCredentials;

            Status[] xlStatus;
            string xlSessionId = "";
```

```
            string xlWorkbookPath = @"http://theexcelserver/testsite/shared
    documents/book1.xlsx";
            string uiCultureName = "en-US";
            string dataCultureName = "en-US";

            try
            {
                xlSessionId = xlEcsApi.OpenWorkbook(
                   xlWorkbookPath,
                   uiCultureName,
                   dataCultureName,
                   out xlStatus);
                xlStatus = xlEcsApi.CloseWorkbook(xlSessionId);
            }
            catch (SoapException soapE)
            {
                Console.WriteLine("Soap Fault {0}", soapE.Message);
            }
        }
    }
}
```

Local Linking

A second approach is to link the code directly to the web service assembly and call methods in-process instead of using SOAP. For this approach to work, the web service calling code must have Windows SharePoint Services (WSS) site context, which means the code runs within WSS.

The Excel web service assembly is located on MOSS servers at C:\Program Files\Common Files\ Microsoft Shared\Web Server Extensions\12\ISAPI\Microsoft.Office.Excel.Server.WebServices.dll. When you need to leverage local linking, simply add the project reference from the noted location. In Microsoft Visual Studio 2005, the assembly is available as a reference on the .NET tab of the Add Reference dialog box. If you want to use local linking, your project development environment must be on a MOSS server.

Visual Studio shows different signatures for Excel web service methods depending on whether the assembly was added as a web reference or as a reference (local linking). Any method with a void return and an out parameter has a different signature. When you use the web reference, the out parameter becomes the return. The API method explanations in this chapter present signatures as web references.

An example solution that uses local linking for accessing the API is shown in the "Managed Code Approach" section, later in this chapter.

Web Service API Methods

This section begins the coverage for each of the web service methods. For each method, a code sample is shown that focuses strictly on the method being discussed. The code isn't complete, but you can copy it into the previous API solution and execute it. The in, out, and return parameters are explained, as well as any intricacies for the methods.

GetApiVersion

The `GetApiVersion` method of the Excel Services web service returns the version information for the Excel Services web service. The declaration for the `GetApiVersion` method looks like this:

```
public string GetApiVersion(out Status[] status)
```

Parameter

The parameter for this method is `Status` (out). See the "Status Class" section, earlier in this chapter, for an explanation of the `out` parameter.

Return Value

A string is returned that is the version information for the Excel Services web service.

Calling GetApiVersion

The `return` value of the following `GetApiVersion` method call returns the string `"Excel web services (12.0)"`:

```
try
{
    string apiVersion;
    Status[] xlStatus;
    apiVersion = xlEcsApi.GetApiVersion(out xlStatus);
}
```

OpenWorkbook

The `OpenWorkbook` method of the Excel Services web service loads an Excel workbook in a new session by the ECS. The declaration for the `OpenWorkbook` method looks like this:

```
public string OpenWorkbook(string workbookPath, string uiCultureName, string
dataCultureName, out Status[] status)
```

Parameters

Following are the parameters for this method:

❑ `workbookPath` (in) — A string that includes the path and name of the workbook to be opened. The path must be in a UNC, HTTP, or SharePoint trusted file location. The workbook must be in an Excel 12 supported file format.

❑ `uiCultureName` (in) — A string that is used for the UI culture. See the "Cultures" section, earlier in this chapter, for an explanation of the (in) parameter. You can use the `String.Empty`, `null` or `""` instead of an actual culture string.

❑ `dataCultureName` (in) — A string that is used for the data culture. See the "Cultures" section, earlier in this chapter, for an explanation of the (in) parameter. You can use the `String.Empty`, `null` or `""` instead of an actual culture string.

❑ `Status` (out) — See the "Status Class" section, earlier in this chapter, for an explanation of this (out) parameter.

Return Value

A string is returned that is the `sessionId` created by the ECS for this `OpenWorkbook` call. The `sessionId` is a parameter for other Excel Services web service methods that may get called for this session.

Calling OpenWorkbook

The following `OpenWorkbook` method call is made to open a workbook from a SharePoint trusted file location using English data and UI cultures. The `xlSessionId` variable holds the session ID for the session created by the `OpenWorkbook` call.

```
ExcelService xlEcsApi = new ExcelService();
Status[] xlStatus;
string xlSessionId;

xlEcsApi.Url = "http://" + "TheExcelServer" + "/_vti_bin/ExcelService.asmx";
xlEcsApi.Credentials = System.Net.CredentialCache.DefaultCredentials;

try
{
    xlSessionId = xlEcsApi.OpenWorkbook(
        @"http://TheExcelServer/testsite/Shared Documents/workbook.xlsb",
        @"en-US",
        @"en-US",
        out xlStatus);
}
```

GetSessionInformation

The `GetSessionInformation` method of the Excel Services web service returns information about the ECS session. The declaration for the `GetSessionInformation` method looks like this:

```
public string GetSessionInformation(string sessionId, out string uiCultureNameUsed,
    out string dataCultureNameUsed, out Status[] status)
```

Parameters

Following are the parameters for this method:

- ❏ `sessionId` (in) — The `sessionId` string returned from a prior `OpenWorkbook` call. The session must still be active at the time of the `GetSessionInformation` call. Making a `GetSessionInformation` call using a `sessionId` that has timed out results in a SOAP exception.

- ❏ `uiCultureNameUsed` (out) — A string that represents the `uiCulture` that was set on this session when the session was created using the `OpenWorkbook` method. See the "Cultures" section, earlier in this chapter, for an explanation of this (out) parameter.

- ❏ `dataCultureNameUsed` (out) — A string that represents the `dataCulture` that was set on this session when the session was created using the `OpenWorkbook` method. See the "Cultures" section, earlier in this chapter, for an explanation of this (out) parameter.

- ❏ `Status` (out) — See the "Status Class," section, earlier in this chapter, for an explanation of this (out) parameter.

Return Value

A string is returned that contains the version information for ECS. The return value of the `GetSessionInformation` method call shown next returns the string `"Excel Calculation Services (12.0)"`.

Calling GetSessionInformation

The following example makes an `OpenWorkbook` call and then the `GetSessionInformation` method is called. The `uiCulture` and the `dataCulture` used for the `OpenWorkbook` call were en-US and de-DE, respectively.

```
try
{
    string xlSessionId, uiCultureUsed, dataCultureUsed, sessionInfo;
    Status[] xlStatus;

    xlSessionId = xlEcsApi.OpenWorkbook(
        @"http://theexcelserver/testsite/Shared Documents/workbook.xlsb",
        @"en-US",
        @"de-DE",
        out xlStatus);

    sessionInfo = xlEcsApi.GetSessionInformation(
    xlSessionId,
    out uiCultureUsed,
    out dataCultureUsed,
    out xlStatus);

    Console.WriteLine("Session Information: {0}", sessionInfo);
    Console.WriteLine("UI Culture Used: {0}", uiCultureUsed);
    Console.WriteLine("Data Culture Used: {0}", dataCultureUsed);
}
```

This code writes the following information to the console, which shows the `uiCulture` and the `dataCulture` properties that were set on the session:

```
Session Information: Excel Calculation Services (12.0)
UI Culture Used: en-US
Data Culture Used: de-DE
```

CloseWorkbook

The `CloseWorkbook` method of the Excel Services web service closes the session. Closing the session allows any cached data associated with the session to be released. Every `OpenWorkbook` call should have a corresponding `CloseWorkbook` call. The declaration for the `CloseWorkbook` method looks like this:

```
public Status[] CloseWorkbook(string sessionId)
```

Parameter

The parameter for this method is `sessionId` (in). This is the `sessionId` string that was returned from a prior `OpenWorkbook` call. The session must still be active at the time of the `CloseWorkbook` call. Making a `CloseWorkbook` call using a `sessionId` that has timed out results in a SOAP exception.

Return Value

A `status` object is returned by default with a value of `null`. See the "Status Class" section, earlier in this chapter, for an explanation of this return type.

Calling CloseWorkbook

The following code makes an `OpenWorkbook` call and assigns the returned `sessionId`. The `sessionId` is a parameter when `CloseWorkbook` is called.

```
try
{
    string xlSessionId;
    Status[] xlStatus;

    xlSessionId = xlEcsApi.OpenWorkbook(
        @"http://theexcelserver/testsite/Shared Documents/workbook.xlsb",
        @"en-US",
        @"de-DE",
        out xlStatus);

    xlStatus = xlEcsApi.CloseWorkbook(xlSessionId);
}
```

CancelRequest

The `CancelRequest` method of the Excel Services web service attempts to cancel any active request that is using the session. The `CancelRequest` method call is considered successful if there is no active request to cancel. The declaration for the `CancelRequest` method looks like this:

```
public Status[] CancelRequest(string sessionId)
```

Parameter

The parameter for this method is `sessionId` (in). This is the `sessionId` string that was returned from a prior `OpenWorkbook` call. The session must still be active at the time of the `CancelRequest` call. Making a `CancelRequest` call using a `sessionId` that has timed out results in a SOAP exception.

Return Value

A `status` object is returned by default with a value of `null`. See the "Status Class" section, earlier in this chapter, for an explanation of this return type.

Calling CancelRequest

You can make the following `CancelRequest` call when a `sessionId` is available after a successful `OpenWorkbook` call:

```
try
{
    string xlSessionId;
    Status[] xlStatus;

    xlSessionId = xlEcsApi.OpenWorkbook(
    @"http://theexcelserver/testsite/Shared Documents/workbook.xlsb",
        @"en-US",
        @"de-DE",
        out xlStatus);

    xlStatus = xlEcsApi.CancelRequest(xlSessionId);
}
```

Refresh

The `Refresh` method of the Excel Services web service requests updated query results for one or more external data sources used by the workbook associated with the session. The declaration for the `Refresh` method looks like this:

```
public Status[] Refresh(string sessionId, string connectionName)
```

Parameters

Following are the parameters for this method:

❑   `sessionId (in)` — The `sessionId` string that was returned from a prior `OpenWorkbook` call. The session must still be active at the time of the `Refresh` call. Making a `Refresh` call using a `sessionId` that has timed out results in a SOAP exception.

❑   `connectionName (in)` — Use this string to specify one connection that is to be refreshed, or to indicate that all connections in the workbook are to be refreshed. Specify the specific connection name to refresh a single connection. Use values of `String.Empty`, `null` or `""` to refresh all workbook connections. Specifying a nonexistent connection name results in a `Status` return that contains a message indicating that there was a problem refreshing the data.

Return Value

A `status` object is returned by default with a value of `null`. See the "Status Class" section, earlier in this chapter, for an explanation of this return type.

Calling Refresh

The following example makes two `Refresh` calls. The first call refreshes all external data sources in the workbook. The second call refreshes only the connection with a name of `"oneSource"`, if it exists in the workbook.

```
try
{
    string xlSessionId;
    Status[] xlStatus;

    xlSessionId = xlEcsApi.OpenWorkbook(
        @"http://theexcelserver/testsite/Shared Documents/workbook.xlsb",
        @"en-US",
        @"de-DE",
        out xlStatus);

    xlStatus = xlEcsApi.Refresh(xlSessionId, "");

    xlStatus = xlEcsApi.Refresh(xlSessionId, "oneSource");
}
```

CalculateA1

The `CalculateA1` method of the Excel Services web service calculates the entire workbook, a single sheet, a named range, a named object, or a range that is specified with A1 notation. The declaration for the `CalculateA1` method looks like this:

```
public Status[] CalculateA1(string sessionId, string sheetName, string rangeName)
```

Parameters

Following are the parameters for this method:

❑ `sessionId (in)` — The `sessionId` string that was returned from a prior `OpenWorkbook` call. The session must still be active at the time of the `CalculateA1` call. Making a `CalculateA1` call using a `sessionId` that has timed out results in a SOAP exception.

❑ `sheetName (in)` — Use this string to specify the name of the sheet containing the `rangeName` that is to be calculated.

❑ `rangeName (in)` — Use this string to specify the single cell or range to be calculated. You can specify the `rangeName` using a defined name that represents the range to be calculated, or an A1 notation. The name of an object (such as `"Table1"`) is also a valid value.

The behavior of `CalculateA1` is dependent on the values provided for both the `sheetName` and the `rangeName` parameters. Following are common uses for the `CalculateA1` method:

❑ *Calculate workbook* — The `sheetName` is either `String.Empty` or `""`, and the `rangeName` is either `String.Empty` or `""`.

❑ *Calculate sheet* — The `sheetName` is the name of a sheet, and the `rangeName` is either `String.Empty` or `""`.

❑ *Calculate a range* — The `sheetName` is the name of a sheet, and the `rangeName` is a defined name on the sheet used for `sheetName`. `rangeName` can reference a single cell or a contiguous range.

❑ *Calculate a range* — The `sheetName` is the name of a sheet, and the `rangeName` is the A1 notation that references a single cell (such as `"B2"`) or a contiguous range (such as `"C4:F10"`).

Return Value

A `status` object is returned by default with a value of `null`. See the "Status Class" section, earlier in this chapter, for an explanation of this return type.

Calling CalculateA1

The following example makes four `CalculateA1` calls. Comments are provided prior to each `CalculateA1` call to describe what is going to be calculated.

```
try
{
    string xlSessionId;
    Status[] xlStatus;
    xlSessionId = xlEcsApi.OpenWorkbook(
        @"http://theexcelserver/testsite/Shared Documents/workbook.xlsb",
        @"en-US",
        @"de-DE",
        out xlStatus);

    //calculate the entire workbook
    xlStatus = xlEcsApi.CalculateA1(xlSessionId, "", "");

    //calculate only Sheet3
    xlStatus = xlEcsApi.CalculateA1(xlSessionId, "Sheet3", string.Empty);

    //calculate the RangeOne named range on Sheet3
    xlStatus = xlEcsApi.CalculateA1(xlSessionId, "Sheet3", "RangeOne");

    //calculate range A1:B3 on Sheet1
    xlStatus = xlEcsApi.CalculateA1(xlSessionId, "Sheet1", "A1:B3");
}
```

Calculate

The `Calculate` method of the Excel Services web service calculates a single sheet or a range using range coordinates. The declaration for the `Calculate` method looks like this:

```
public Status[] Calculate(string sessionId, string sheetName, RangeCoordinates
rangeCoordinates)
```

Parameters

Following are the parameters for this method:

- ❑ `sessionId (in)` — The `sessionId` string that was returned from a prior `OpenWorkbook` call. The session must still be active at the time of the `Calculate` call. Making a `Calculate` call using a `sessionId` that has timed out results in a SOAP exception.

- ❑ `sheetName (in)` — Use this string to specify the name of the sheet containing the range coordinates that are to be calculated.

❑   rangeCoordinates (in) — Use this RangeCoordinates type to specify the range that is to be calculated. The range can be a single cell or a contiguous range. The rangeCoordinates type has the following four properties:

> ❑   Column — The zero-based integer index, where column A is 0.
>
> ❑   Row — The zero-based integer row index, where row 1 is 0.
>
> ❑   Height — An integer greater than 0, which represents the row height of the range.
>
> ❑   Width — An integer greater than 0, which represents the column width of the range.

The behavior of Calculate is dependant on the values provided for the rangeCoordinates. Following are common uses for the Calculate method:

❑   *Calculate sheet* — The sheetName is the name of a sheet, and the rangeCoordinates are initialized to 0.

❑   *Calculate cell A1* — The sheetName is the name of a sheet, and the rangeCoordinates are initialized as Column=0, Row=0, Height=1, and Width=1. This calculates cell A1.

❑   *Calculate cell B1* — The sheetName is the name of a sheet, and the rangeCoordinates are initialized as Column=1, Row=0, Height=1, and Width=1. This calculates cell B1.

❑   *Calculate cells A1:A2* — The sheetName is the name of a sheet, and the rangeCoordinates are initialized as Column=0, Row=0, Height=2, and Width=1. This calculates cells A1:A2.

❑   *Calculate cell A1:B1* — The sheetName is the name of a sheet, and the rangeCoordinates are initialized as Column=0, Row=0, Height=1, and Width=2. The result is that cells A1:B1 are calculated.

Return Value

A status object is returned by default with a value of null. See the "Status Class" section, earlier in this chapter, for an explanation of this return type.

Calling Calculate

The following example makes a Calculate call. The range is defined using the RangeCoordinates object, and then the Calculate method is called to calculate range A1:A2 on Sheet3.

```
try
{
    string xlSessionId;
    Status[] xlStatus;

    xlSessionId = xlEcsApi.OpenWorkbook(
        @"http://theexcelserver/testsite/Shared Documents/workbook.xlsb",
        @"en-US",
        @"de-DE",
        out xlStatus);

    RangeCoordinates xlRange = new RangeCoordinates();
    xlRange.Column = 0;
    xlRange.Row = 0;
```

```
    xlRange.Height = 2;
    xlRange.Width = 1;

    //calculate range A1:A2 on Sheet3
    xlStatus = xlEcsApi.Calculate(xlSessionId, "Sheet3", xlRange);
}
```

CalculateWorkbook

The `CalculateWorkbook` method of the Excel Services web service calculates the entire workbook using one of the two supported types of calculation. The declaration for the `CalculateWorkbook` method looks like this:

```
public Status[] CalculateWorkbook(string sessionId, CalculateType calculateType)
```

Parameters

Following are the parameters for this method:

❑   `sessionId (in)` — The `sessionId` string that was returned from a prior `OpenWorkbook` call. The session must still be active at the time of the `CalculateWorkbook` call. Making a `CalculateWorkbook` call using a `sessionId` that has timed out results in a SOAP exception.

❑   `CalculateType (in)` — Use this `CalculateType` type to specify the type of calculation to be performed. There are two supported enumerators for `CalculateType`:

    ❑   `CalculateFull` — All formulas are calculated, but the dependency tree is not rebuilt.

    ❑   `Recalculate` — Only dirty formulas are calculated.

Return Value

A `status` object is returned by default with a value of `null`. See the "Status Class" section, earlier in this chapter, for an explanation of this return type.

Calling CalculateWorkbook

The following example makes a `CalculateWorkbook` call using the `CalculateFull` enumerator:

```
try
{
    string xlSessionId;
    Status[] xlStatus;

    xlSessionId = xlEcsApi.OpenWorkbook(
        @"http://theexcelserver/testsite/Shared Documents/workbook.xlsb",
        @"en-US",
        @"de-DE",
        out xlStatus);

    xlStatus = xlEcsApi.CalculateWorkbook(
        xlSessionId,
        CalculateType.CalculateFull);
}
```

GetRangeA1

The GetRangeA1 method of the Excel Services web service returns the calculated values for a single cell, a named range, a named object, or a range that is specified with A1 notation. The declaration for the GetRangeA1 method looks like this:

```
public object[] GetRangeA1(string sessionId, string sheetName, string rangeName,
bool formatted, out Status[] status)
```

Parameters

Following are the parameters for this method:

- ❑ sessionId (in) — The sessionId string that was returned from a prior OpenWorkbook call. The session must still be active at the time of the GetRangeA1 call. Making a GetRangeA1 call using a sessionId that has timed out results in a SOAP exception.

- ❑ sheetName (in) — Use this string to specify the name of the sheet containing the rangeName. You can pass the sheetName as String.Empty or "" when you use a defined name or the name of an object for the rangeName.

- ❑ rangeName (in) — Use this string to specify the single cell or range to be retrieved. You can specify the rangeName using a defined name or an object name that represents the range to be retrieved. You can also use A1 notation.

- ❑ formatted (in) — Use this Boolean to specify whether formatted strings (true) or raw values (false) are to be returned.

- ❑ Status (out) — See the "Status Class" section, earlier in this chapter, for an explanation of this (out) parameter.

The behavior of GetRangeA1 is dependent on the values that you provide for the sheetName and the rangeName parameters. Following are common uses for the RangeA1 method:

- ❑ *Retrieve a single cell* — Specify a sheetName. Set the rangeName to a defined name that references a single cell or set the rangeName using A1 notation. For example, set the rangeName to "B1:B1" to retrieve the contents of cell B1.

- ❑ *Retrieve a range* — Specify a sheetName. Set the rangeName to a defined name that references a range or set the rangeName using A1 notation For example, set the rangeName to "B1:C10" to retrieve the contents of the cells in the B1:C10 contiguous range.

- ❑ *Retrieve a range associated with an object* — Specify a sheetName. Set the rangeName to the name of an object. For example, set the rangeName to "Table1" to retrieve the range of data contained within Table1. (The column header row for Table1 is not returned.)

Return Value

An array of values for the requested range is returned. The returned array has the same dimensions as the requested range. When the formatted parameter is true, string.empty is returned for empty cells. When the formatted parameter is false, null is returned for empty cells.

GetRangeA1 returns the values from cells in hidden rows and columns. If column A is hidden and the rangeName is "A1:B1", then two objects would be returned: one for cell A1 and one for cell B1.

Calling GetRangeA1

The following example makes three `GetRangeA1` calls. Comments are provided prior to each `GetRangeA1` call to describe what is going to be retrieved.

```
try
{
    string xlSessionId;
    Status[] xlStatus;
    object[] rangeResult;

    xlSessionId = xlEcsApi.OpenWorkbook(
        @"http://theexcelserver/testsite/Shared Documents/workbook.xlsb",
        @"en-US",
        @"de-DE",
        out xlStatus);

    //get the unformatted value for cell B1 on Sheet1
    rangeResult = xlEcsApi.GetRangeA1(
        xlSessionId,
        "Sheet1",
        "B1:B1",
        false,
        out xlStatus);

    //get the formatted value for the range associated with Table1 on Sheet1
    rangeResult = xlEcsApi.GetRangeA1(
        xlSessionId,
        "Sheet1",
        "Table1",
        true,
        out xlStatus);

    //get the unformatted value for the range H5:L15 on Sheet1
    rangeResult = xlEcsApi.GetRangeA1(
        xlSessionId,
        "Sheet1",
        "H5:L15",
        false,
        out xlStatus);
}
```

GetRange

The `GetRange` method of the Excel Services web service returns the calculated values for a single cell or a range that is specified using range coordinates. The declaration for the `GetRange` method looks like this:

```
public object[] GetRange(string sessionId, string sheetName, RangeCoordinates
rangeCoordinates, bool formatted, out Status[] status)
```

Parameters

Following are the parameters for this method:

- ❑ sessionId (in) — The sessionId string that was returned from a prior OpenWorkbook call. The session must still be active at the time of the GetRange call. Making a GetRange call using a sessionId that has timed out results in a SOAP exception.

- ❑ sheetName (in) — Use this string to specify the name of the sheet containing the rangeCoordinates.

- ❑ rangeCoordinates (in) — Use this RangeCoordinates type to specify the range that is to be retrieved. The range can be a single cell or a contiguous range. The rangeCoordinates type has four properties:

  - ❑ Column — The zero-based integer index, where column A is 0.

  - ❑ Row — The zero-based integer row index, where row 1 is 0.

  - ❑ Height — An integer greater than 0, which represents the row height of the range.

  - ❑ Width — An integer greater than 0, which represents the column width of the range.

- ❑ formatted (in) — Use this Boolean to specify whether formatted strings (true) or raw values (false) are to be returned.

- ❑ Status (out) — See the "Status Class" section, earlier in this chapter, for an explanation of this (out) parameter.

Following are common uses for the GetRange method:

- ❑ *Retrieve a single cell* — The sheetName is the name of a sheet, and the rangeCoordinates are initialized as Column=0, Row=0, Height=1, and Width=1. This retrieves the value of cell A1.

- ❑ *Retrieve a range* — sheetName is the name of a sheet and the rangeCoordinates are initialized as: Column=0, Row=0, Height=1, and Width=2. This retrieves the values in the range A1:B1.

Return Value

An array of values for the requested range is returned. The returned array has the same dimensions as the requested range. When the formatted parameter is true, string.empty is returned for empty cells. When the formatted parameter is false, null is returned for empty cells.

GetRange returns the values from cells in hidden rows and columns. If column A is hidden and the rangeName was "A1:B1", then two objects would be returned: one for cell A1 and one for cell B1.

Calling GetRange

The following example makes a GetRange call. The range is defined using the RangeCoordinates object, and then the GetRange method is called to retrieve the value in range E5:J9 on Sheet2. This represents a range that is 5 rows by 6 columns.

```
try
{
    string xlSessionId;
```

```
       Status[] xlStatus;
       object[] rangeResult;

       xlSessionId = xlEcsApi.OpenWorkbook(
           @"http://theexcelserver/testsite/Shared Documents/workbook.xlsb",
           @"en-US",
           @"de-DE",
           out xlStatus);

       RangeCoordinates xlRange = new RangeCoordinates();
       xlRange.Column = 4;
       xlRange.Row = 4;
       xlRange.Height = 5;
       xlRange.Width = 6;

       rangeResult = xlEcsApi.GetRange(
           xlSessionId,
           "Sheet2",
           xlRange,
           true,
           out xlStatus);
   }
```

GetCellA1

The `GetCellA1` method of the Excel Services web service returns the calculated values for a single cell that you specify with A1 notation, or a single cell that you reference by a defined name or object name. The declaration for the `GetCellA1` method looks like this:

```
public object GetCellA1(string sessionId, string sheetName, string rangeName, bool
formatted, out Status[] status)
```

Parameters

Following are the parameters for this method:

❑   `sessionId (in)` — The `sessionId` string that was returned from a prior `OpenWorkbook` call. The session must still be active at the time of the `GetCellA1` call. Making a `GetCellA1` call using a `sessionId` that has timed out results in a SOAP exception.

❑   `sheetName (in)` — Use this string to specify the name of the sheet containing the `rangeName`. You can pass the `sheetName` as `String.Empty` or `""` when you use a defined name or the name of an object for the `rangeName`.

❑   `rangeName (in)` — Use this string to specify a single cell to be retrieved. Specify the `rangeName` using a defined name or an object name that represents the cell to be retrieved. You can also use A1 notation.

❑   `formatted (in)` — Use this Boolean to specify whether formatted strings (`true`) or raw values (`false`) are to be returned.

❑   `Status (out)` — See the "Status Class" section, earlier in this chapter, for an explanation of this (out) parameter.

Return Value

An object is returned that is the value of the requested cell. Empty cells are represented as `null`. If the returned range is not a 1x1 range, a SOAP exception occurs.

Calling GetCellA1

The following example makes two `GetCellA1` calls. Comments are provided prior to each `GetCellA1` call to describe what is going to be retrieved.

```
try
{
    string xlSessionId;
    Status[] xlStatus;
    object cellResult;

    xlSessionId = xlEcsApi.OpenWorkbook(
        @"http://theexcelserver/testsite/Shared Documents/workbook.xlsb",
        @"en-US",
        @"de-DE",
        out xlStatus);

    //get the formatted value for cell A1 on Sheet1
    cellResult = xlEcsApi.GetCellA1(
        xlSessionId,
        "Sheet1",
        "A1",
        true,
        out xlStatus);

    //get the unformatted value for the cell with the OneCell defined name
    cellResult = xlEcsApi.GetCellA1(
        xlSessionId,
        "",
        "OneCell",
        false,
        out xlStatus);
}
```

GetCell

The `GetCell` method of the Excel Services web service returns the calculated values for a single cell that you specify using range coordinates. The declaration for the `GetCell` method looks like this:

```
public object GetCell(string sessionId, string sheetName, int row, int column, bool
formatted, out Status[] status)
```

Parameters

Following are the parameters for this method:

❑   `sessionId (in)` — The `sessionId` string that was returned from a prior `OpenWorkbook` call. The session must still be active at the time of the `GetCell` call. Making a `GetCell` call using a `sessionId` that has timed out results in a SOAP exception.

❑ sheetName (in) — Use this string to specify the name of the sheet containing the cell that is the focus of the GetCell call.

❑ row (in) — Use this integer to specify the zero-based row containing the target cell that is to be retrieved.

❑ column (in) — Use this integer to specify the zero-based column containing the target cell that is to be retrieved.

❑ formatted (in) — Use this Boolean to specify whether a formatted string (true) or a raw value (false) is to be returned.

❑ Status (out) — See the "Status Class" section, earlier in this chapter, for an explanation of this (out) parameter.

Return Value

An object is returned that is the value of the requested cell. An empty cell returns an object containing a zero-length string. GetCell returns the value from a cell in a hidden row or hidden column.

Calling GetCell

The following example makes a GetCell call. The GetCell call is made against Sheet1 to return the formatted value from cell E7.

```
try
{
    string xlSessionId;
    Status[] xlStatus;
    object cellResult;

    xlSessionId = xlEcsApi.OpenWorkbook(
        @"http://theexcelserver/testsite/Shared Documents/workbook.xlsb",
        @"en-US",
        @"de-DE",
        out xlStatus);

    cellResult = xlEcsApi.GetCell(
        xlSessionId,
        "Sheet1",
        6,
        4,
        true,
        out xlStatus);
}
```

SetRangeA1

The SetRangeA1 method of the Excel Services web service sets values into a range that is specified using the A1 notation, a named range, or a named object. The declaration for the SetRangeA1 method looks like this:

```
public Status[] SetRangeA1(string sessionId, string sheetName, string rangeName,
object[] rangeValues)
```

Parameters

Following are the parameters for this method:

❏ sessionId (in) — The sessionId string that was returned from a prior OpenWorkbook call. The session must still be active at the time of the SetRangeA1 call. Making a SetRangeA1 call using a sessionId that has timed out results in a SOAP exception.

❏ sheetName (in) — Use this string to specify the name of the sheet containing the rangeName. You can pass the sheetName as String.Empty or " " when you use a defined name or the name of an object for the rangeName.

❏ rangeName (in) — Use this string to specify the range where the values are to be set. Specify the rangeName using a defined name or an object name that represents the range where the values are to be set. You can also use A1 notation.

❏ rangeValues (in) — This is the array of values that are to be set in the specified rangeName. Empty cells are represented in the array as null.

A SOAP exception occurs when the dimensions of the rangeValues object do not match the dimensions of the rangeName.

Return Value

A status object is returned by default with a value of null. See the "Status Class" section, earlier in this chapter, for an explanation of this return type.

Calling SetRangeA1

The following example makes two SetRangeA1 calls. Comments are provided prior to each SetRangeA1 call to describe what is going to be set.

```
try
{
    string xlSessionId;
    Status[] xlStatus;

    xlSessionId = xlEcsApi.OpenWorkbook(
        @"http://theexcelserver/testsite/Shared Documents/workbook.xlsb",
        @"en-US",
        @"de-DE",
        out xlStatus);

    //define and create the data for the rangeValues
    int height = 2, width = 3;
    object[] rangeValues = new object[height];
    object[] firstRow = new object[width];
    object[] secondRow = new object[width];

    for (int x = 0; x < width; x++)
    {
        firstRow[x] = x + x;
        secondRow[x] = x + x + 1;
    }
```

```
    rangeValues[0] = firstRow;
    rangeValues[1] = secondRow;

    //set values for the cells in the K5:M6 range on Sheet1
    xlStatus = xlEcsApi.SetRangeA1(
        xlSessionId,
        "Sheet1",
        "K5:M6",
        rangeValues);

    //set values for the cells in Table2
    xlStatus = xlEcsApi.SetRangeA1(
        xlSessionId,
        string.Empty,
        "Table2",
        rangeValues);
}
```

SetRange

The `SetRange` method of the Excel Services web service sets values into a range that you specify using range coordinates. The declaration for the `SetRange` method looks like this:

```
public Status[] SetRange(string sessionId, string sheetName, RangeCoordinates
rangeCoordinates, object[] rangeValues)
```

Parameters

Following are the parameters for this method:

- ❑ sessionId (in) — The `sessionId` string that was returned from a prior `OpenWorkbook` call. The session must still be active at the time of the `SetRange` call. Making a `SetRange` call using a `sessionId` that has timed out results in a SOAP exception.

- ❑ sheetName (in) — Use this string to specify the name of the sheet containing the `rangeCoordinates`.

- ❑ rangeCoordinates (in) — Use the `RangeCoordinates` type to specify the range that is to be set. The range can be a single cell or a contiguous range. The `RangeCoordinates` type has four properties:
    - ❑ Column — The zero-based integer index, where column A is 0.
    - ❑ Row — The zero-based integer row index, where row 1 is 0.
    - ❑ Height — An integer greater than 0, which represents the row height of the range.
    - ❑ Width — An integer greater than 0, which represents the column width of the range.

- ❑ rangeValues (in) — This is an array of array of objects that is the array of values to be set in the specified `rangeCoordinates`. Empty cells are represented in the array as `null`.

A SOAP exception occurs when the dimensions of the `rangeValues` object do not match the dimensions of the `rangeCoordinates`.

Following are common uses for the GetRange method:

❑ *Set a single cell* — The sheetName is the name of a sheet, and the rangeCoordinates are initialized as Column=0, Row=0, Height=1, and Width=1. This sets the value of cell A1 with rangeValues.

❑ *Set a range* — The sheetName is the name of a sheet, and the rangeCoordinates are initialized as Column=0, Row=0, Height=1, and Width=2. This sets the values in the range A1:B1 with rangeValues.

Return Value

A status object is returned by default with a value of null. See the "Status Class" section, earlier in this chapter, for an explanation of this return type.

Calling SetRange

The following example makes a SetRange call using a range that is 2 rows by 6 columns. The range to be set is E7:J8.

```
try
{
    string xlSessionId;
    Status[] xlStatus;

    xlSessionId = xlEcsApi.OpenWorkbook(
        @"http://theexcelserver/testsite/Shared Documents/workbook.xlsb",
        @"en-US",
        @"de-DE",
        out xlStatus);

    //define and create the data for the rangeValues
    int height = 2, width = 6;
    object[] rangeValues = new object[height];
    object[] firstRow = new object[width];
    object[] secondRow = new object[width];

    for (int x = 0; x < width; x++)
    {
        firstRow[x] = x + x;
        secondRow[x] = x + x + 1;
    }

    rangeValues[0] = firstRow;
    rangeValues[1] = secondRow;

    //define range for E7:J8
    RangeCoordinates xlRange = new RangeCoordinates();
    xlRange.Column = 4;
    xlRange.Row = 6;
    xlRange.Height = height;
    xlRange.Width = width;

    //set values for E7:J8 on Sheet1
```

```
        xlStatus = xlEcsApi.SetRange(
            xlSessionId,
            "Sheet1",
            xlRange,
            rangeValues);
    }
```

SetCellA1

The SetCellA1 method of the Excel Services web service sets a value into a single cell that you specify using the A1 notation, a named range, or a named object. The declaration for the SetCellA1 method looks like this:

```
public Status[] SetCellA1(string sessionId, string sheetName, string rangeName,
object cellValue)
```

Parameters

Following are the parameters for this method:

❑   sessionId (in) — The sessionId string that was returned from a prior OpenWorkbook call. The session must still be active at the time of the SetCellA1 call. Making a SetCellA1 call using a sessionId that has timed out results in a SOAP exception.

❑   sheetName (in) — Use this string to specify the name of the sheet containing the rangeName. You can pass the sheetName as String.Empty or "" when you use a defined name or the name of an object for the rangeName.

❑   rangeName (in) — Use this string to specify the range where the value is to be set. Specify the rangeName using a defined name, or an object name that represents the cell where the value is to be set. You can also use A1 notation.

❑   cellValue (in) — This is an object that is the value to be set in the specified rangeName. An empty cell is represented in the object as null.

If the rangeName is not a 1x1 range, a SOAP exception occurs.

Return Value

A status object is returned by default with a value of null. See the "Status Class" section, earlier in this chapter, for an explanation of this return type.

Calling SetCellA1

The following example makes two SetCellA1 calls. Comments are provided prior to each SetCellA1 call to describe what is going to be set.

```
try
{
    string xlSessionId;
```

```
        Status[] xlStatus;
        object cellValue;

        xlSessionId = xlEcsApi.OpenWorkbook(
            @"http://theexcelserver/testsite/Shared Documents/workbook.xlsb",
            @"en-US",
            @"de-DE",
            out xlStatus);

        \\set a cell value in a 1x1 named object
        cellValue = "some text";
        xlStatus = xlEcsApi.SetCellA1(
            xlSessionId,
            string.Empty,
            "Table2",
            cellValue);

        \\set cell C2 on Sheet1 to a date
        cellValue = "5/30/2008";
        xlStatus = xlEcsApi.SetCellA1(
            xlSessionId,
            "Sheet1",
            "C2",
            cellValue);
}
```

SetCell

The `SetCell` method of the Excel Services web service sets a cell value into a range that you specify using range coordinates. The declaration for the `SetCell` method looks like this:

```
public Status[] SetCell(string sessionId, string sheetName, int row, int column,
object cellValue)
```

Parameters

Following are the parameters for this method:

- ❑ `sessionId (in)` — The `sessionId` string that was returned from a prior `OpenWorkbook` call. The session must still be active at the time of the `SetCell` call. Making a `SetCell` call using a `sessionId` that has timed out results in a SOAP exception.

- ❑ `sheetName (in)` — Use this string to specify the name of the sheet containing the cell that is the focus of the `SetCell` call.

- ❑ `row (in)` — Use this integer to specify the zero-based row containing the target cell that is to be set.

- ❑ `column (in)` — Use this integer to specify the zero-based column containing the target cell that is to be set.

- ❑ `cellValue (in)` — This is an object that is the value to be set in the specified `cell`. An empty cell is represented in the object as `null`.

Return Value

A `status` object is returned by default with a value of `null`. See the "Status Class" section, earlier in this chapter, for an explanation of this return type.

Calling SetCell

The following example makes a `SetCell` call. The `SetCell` call is made against `Sheet1` to set a date value into cell `K6`.

```
try
{
    string xlSessionId;
    Status[] xlStatus;
    object cellValue;

    xlSessionId = xlEcsApi.OpenWorkbook(
        @"http://theexcelserver/testsite/Shared Documents/workbook.xlsb",
        @"en-US",
        @"de-DE",
        out xlStatus);

    cellValue = "5/30/2008";
    xlStatus = xlEcsApi.SetCell(
        xlSessionId,
        "Sheet1",
        5,
        10,
        cellValue);
}
```

GetWorkbook

The `GetWorkbook` method of the Excel Services web service returns the workbook using one of the three supported modes. The declaration for the `GetWorkbook` method looks like this:

```
public byte[] GetWorkbook(string sessionId, WorkbookType workbookType, out Status[]
status)
```

Parameters

Following are the parameters for this method:

❑ sessionId (in) — The `sessionId` string that was returned from a prior `OpenWorkbook` call. The session must still be active at the time of the `GetWorkbook` call. Making a `GetWorkbook` call using a `sessionId` that has timed out results in a SOAP exception.

❑ workbookType (in) — Use this `WorkbookType` type to specify the mode to be used when retrieving the workbook. There are three supported enumerators for `WorkbookType`:

   ❑ FullSnapshot — Maps to the entire workbook that is being used, and returns the workbook in its current state, including the private state view if one exists.

❑   FullWorkbook — Maps to the entire workbook that was published to the server, taking into account the caller's permissions. This does not return the private state view of the workbook.

❑   PublishedItemsSnapshot — Maps to the items that were marked as viewable when the workbook was published, and returns those items in their current state, including the private state view if one exists.

❑   Status (out) — See the "Status Class" section, earlier in this chapter, for an explanation of this (out) parameter.

Return Value

A byte array is returned that represents the workbook content based on the specified WorkbookType. The file format loaded into the session is used.

Calling GetWorkbook

The following example makes a GetWorkbook call using the PublishedItemsSnapshot enumerator:

```
try
{
    string xlSessionId;
    Status[] xlStatus;
    byte[] bits;

    xlSessionId = xlEcsApi.OpenWorkbook(
        wkbk2,
        @"en-US",
        @"en-US",
        out xlStatus);

    bits = xlEcsApi.GetWorkbook(
        xlSessionId,
        WorkbookType.PublishedItemsSnapshot,
        out xlStatus);
}
```

API Sample

Chapter 13 described how you can leverage Excel Services to offload calculations from the client. This method is used primarily for workbooks that take a significant amount of time to calculate. Because there is no Excel Services out-of-the-box functionality for offloading such workbooks to the server, a custom solution is needed.

This section provides a sample application that enables the scenario described at the end of Chapter 13. It makes use of the Excel Services web service presented in this chapter.

The sample illustrates how you can use Excel Services to offload calculations from the client to the server. With this program, users of calculation-intensive workbooks can save those workbooks to the target folder, the workbooks are calculated on the server, and the updated workbooks are made available to the users in an output folder.

The sample creates a program that monitors the addition of workbooks in a target file location (provided by the second argument). Excel Services opens workbooks that get added to the target location, force a calculation of the workbook, and then save the calculated workbook to an output file location (provided by the first argument). As far as the usage of Excel Services API is concerned, this is a straightforward example. The program calls on the OpenWorkBook method, the CalculateWorkbook method, and the GetWorkbook method to complete the steps described previously.

Here is the sample code:

```
namespace ExcelServicesCalcDemo
{
    using System;
    using System.Collections.Generic;
    using System.IO;
    using System.Text;
    using System.Threading;
    using ExcelServices;

    class Program
    {
        // The destination directory holds the location
        // to which the calculated workbooks will be saved
        private static string DestinationDirectory;

        static void Main(string[] args)
        {
            DestinationDirectory = args[0];

            // Listen for any new *.xlsb files created in a given folder.
            // Call the OnFileCreated method for every such file
            FileSystemWatcher fileWatcher = new FileSystemWatcher(
                args[1],
                "*.xlsb");
            fileWatcher.Created += new FileSystemEventHandler(OnFileCreated);
            fileWatcher.EnableRaisingEvents = true;

            Console.ReadLine();
        }

        private static void OnFileCreated(object source, FileSystemEventArgs e)
        {
            // Create the Excel Service web service caller
            ExcelService service = new ExcelService();
            service.Credentials = System.Net.CredentialCache.DefaultCredentials;

            // Open the workbook, calculate it, get the workbook
            // into a byte array and close the session
            Status[] status;
            string sessionId = service.OpenWorkbook(
                e.FullPath,
                "en-US",
```

```
        "en-US",
        out status);
    service.CalculateWorkbook(sessionId, CalculateType.CalculateFull);
    byte[] savedWorkbook = service.GetWorkbook(
        sessionId,
        WorkbookType.FullWorkbook,
        out status);
    service.CloseWorkbook(sessionId);

    // Save the workbook to the destination folder
    string newFileName = Path.Combine(DestinationDirectory, e.Name);
    BinaryWriter writer = new BinaryWriter(File.Open(
        newFileName,
        FileMode.CreateNew));
    writer.Write(savedWorkbook);
    writer.Close();
        }
    }
}
```

This sample is very rudimentary. In a real-world application, additional functionality is needed to provide notifications or SharePoint alerts as steps in the process are completed. In addition, such a real-world application sends multiple requests in parallel to Excel Services. The formula for calculating the number of parallel requests is the number of ECS machines available in the farm multiplied by the number of processors on each ECS machine.

User-Defined Functions (UDFs)

Excel Services UDFs represent another tier in the Excel Services capability to support custom solutions. UDFs provide a means to call custom-managed code functions from within a workbook. Without UDFs, a workbook is restricted to using only the intrinsic Excel functions. With UDFs, custom functions can be called from the workbook as well.

UDFs are very instrumental to custom server solutions because Excel Services does not support loading workbooks that contain code behind (VBA). Nor does Excel Services support the Excel client add-ins used by workbooks to extend functionality. With the right UDF-managed wrapper solution, you could leverage existing custom client solutions on the server, but that topic isn't discussed here.

This section describes how to author managed UDFs and deploy them to the server to make them available to workbooks that are loaded from the trusted file locations. An example solution is provided to demonstrate the authoring and building of a UDF assembly. Additional material is provided to explain how the workbook interacts with UDF methods, and how to pass and return arguments to the workbook.

UdfMethodAttribute Class

Each public method in the public UDF class must have the [UdfMethod] attribute if the UDF is to be treated as a public UDF. The UdfMethodAttribute has two Boolean properties: IsVolatile and ReturnsPersonalInformation.

The `IsVolatile` property has a default value of `false`. When set to `true`, the UDF method is treated like an Excel volatile function. A volatile function always calculates when any part of a workbook needs to be calculated. UDF volatile methods are called when the Volatile Function Cache Lifetime setting has passed. This setting is defined on the trusted file location where the workbook was loaded.

The `ReturnsPersonalInformation` property also has a default value of `false`. When set to `false`, the thread's Windows identity is hidden, so all callers of the UDF method share the same results cache. When set to `true`, the UDF method returns results based on the identity, which ensures that callers of the method are not sharing cached values. If a UDF method is expected to return results based on the caller's identity, then the `ReturnsPersonalInformation` should be `true` so that each caller gets only their identity-specific results.

Argument Data Types

The supported UDF argument data types are in the .NET `System` namespace. Excel supports a smaller set of data types that can be applied to data in cells. The following table describes the behavior that you can expect from combinations of UDF argument types and Excel types. The first column represents the UDF argument data type. The remaining columns represent the Excel types that are passed into the UDF through the argument. The contents of the table indicate the error that is returned if the pair is unsupported, or what to expect if an error is not going to be returned.

	Excel Data Type			
UDF Argument Data Type Notation	**Double**	**String**	**Boolean**	**Empty**
Numeric	Tries to cast; `Byte` and `Sbyte` return #NUM	#VALUE	#VALUE	0
String	#VALUE	String	#VALUE	String.Empty
Boolean	#VALUE	#VALUE	Boolean	False
DateTime	Double*	#VALUE	#VALUE	#VALUE
Object	Boxed double	Reference to a string	Boxed Boolean	Null

Here is a further explanation of the data types in the table:

❑ Numeric — Refers to the following `System` namespace types: `Byte`, `Double`, `Int16`, `Int32`, `Sbyte`, `Single`, `UInt16`, and `UInt32`. The `Int64` and `UInt64` types are not supported.

❑ DateTime* — Internally, Excel treats dates as a double. The ECS converts a `DateTime` double from Excel into a .NET `DateTime`.

❏ Object — Defines the behavior for each cell in the range that is passed into the array.

❏ #VALUE — Can be returned for different reasons, including the following:

  ❏ The Excel type is an error, such as division by zero (#DIV/0!).

  ❏ The UDF argument is an unsupported type, such as Int64.

  ❏ The Excel and .NET type pair is not supported by ECS.

  ❏ The type conversion fails, which can occur for a DateTime type.

Ranges as Arguments

A UDF argument can be either a one-dimensional or two-dimensional array argument. Only object arrays are supported; strong typed arrays are not. #VALUE! is returned if the dimensions of the array argument are insufficient to hold the passed-in range. A single cell range can fit into a one-dimensional array, and a one-dimensional range can fit into a two-dimensional array.

A one-dimensional array can receive a range consisting of a single row. The following UDF method has a single object array argument (xlRow) and returns an integer that represents the number of columns (xlRow.Length) in the array argument. A row is passed in, and the number of columns in that row is returned.

```
[UdfMethod]
public int ReturnNumberOfColumns(object[] xlRow)
{
    return (xlRow.Length);
}
```

In Excel, you call the ReturnNumberOfColumns by entering the following code into a cell. Excel evaluates the method as #NAME?. The example noted here uses E5:H5 as the argument to pass in, and 4 is the return value to represent the column count in that range.

```
=ReturnNumberOfColumns(E5:H5)
```

A two-dimensional array can receive a range that spans one or more rows. The following UDF method has a single object array argument (xlRange) and returns an integer that represents the number of cells (xlRange) in the two-dimensional array argument. One or more rows are passed in, and the number of cells in that range is returned.

```
[UdfMethod]
public int ReturnNumberOfCells(object[,] xlRange)
{
    return (xlRange)
}
```

In Excel, you call the ReturnNumberOfCells method by entering the following code into a cell. Excel evaluates the method as #NAME?. The example noted here uses E5:H6 as the argument to pass in, and 8 is the return value to represent the cell count in that range.

```
=ReturnNumberOfCells(E5:H6)
```

Parameter Arrays as Arguments

You can also use a parameter array argument to get values into a UDF. This approach provides the flexibility of passing in a variable number of scalar arguments (such as an `int` type) or as an object-array type.

A one-dimensional parameter array can receive values or single cell references. The following `ReturnNumberOfCellsReceived` UDF method has a single `params` array argument (`xlCells`) and returns an integer that represents the number of cells passed in through the `params` array argument:

```
[UdfMethod]
public int ReturnNumberOfCellsReceived(params int[] xlCells)
{
    return (xlCells.Length);
}
```

In Excel, you call the `ReturnNumberOfCellsReceived` method by entering the following code into a cell. Excel evaluates the method as `#NAME?`. The example noted here provides one value (6) and two cell references (F2 and E5) as the arguments being passed in, and 3 is the return value that represents the number of items (or cells) passed in from Excel.

```
=ReturnNumberOfCellsReceived(6,F2,E5)
```

A second way to use parameter arrays as arguments is to create a two-dimensional array argument that can receive multiple ranges. The following `ReturnCountOfCellsReceived` UDF method has a two-dimensional object array argument (`xlArray`), and returns an integer that represents the number of cells in the items passed in from Excel.

```
[UdfMethod]
public int ReturnCountOfCellsReceived(params object[][,] xlArray)
{
    int elements = 0;
    for (int x = 0; x < xlArray.Length; x++)
    {
        elements += xlArray[x].Length;
    }
    return (elements)
}
```

In Excel, you call the `ReturnCountOfCellsReceived` method by entering the following code into a cell. Excel evaluates the method as `#NAME?`. The example noted here provides one value (6), a cell reference (F2), and a range (G2:H3) as the arguments being passed in, and 6 is the return value that represents the number of cells passed in from Excel.

```
=ReturnCountOfCellsReceived(6,F2,G2:H3)
```

Return Data Types

The supported UDF return data types are in the .NET `System` namespace. Excel supports a smaller set of data types that can be applied to data in cells. The following table describes supported return types, as well as the behavior that you can expect from combinations of UDF return types and Excel types. The first column represents the UDF return data type. The second column represents the Excel behavior.

UDF Return Type	Excel Behavior
Numeric	Cast to double
String	String
Boolean	Boolean
DateTime	Recognizes the Double as a DateTime
Object[] Type[]	Array (first value goes into the first cell, and so on)
Object[,] Type[,]	Array (first value goes into the first cell, and so on)
Object	Excel tries to map to one of the types noted above and handles it accordingly
Object(Null)	Empty/Null String

The Numeric data type refers to the following System namespace types: Byte, Double, Int16, Int32, Sbyte, Single, UInt16, and UInt32. The Int64 and UInt64 types are not supported.

Returning a Range

In addition to returning single-valued data types (also referred to as *scalar data types*), a UDF can return one- or two-dimensional arrays. Only object arrays are supported; strong typed arrays are not.

A one-dimensional array can hold a range consisting of a single row. The following UDF method has a single object array argument (xlRow) and returns an object array that represents the object that was passed in. A row is passed in and the same row is returned.

```
[UdfMethod]
public object[] Return1dObjectArray(object[] xlRow)
{
    return (xlRow);
}
```

In Excel, you call the Return1dObjectArray method by entering the following code into cell C7. To create the array formula, select cells C7:F7, press F2, and then press Ctrl+Shift+Enter. Excel automatically inserts the formula between {} (curly braces). The C7:F7 range represents the cells where the object[] returned from Return1dObjectArray is applied. Excel evaluates the method as #NAME?. The example noted here uses E5:H5 as the argument to pass in. After Return1dObjectArray returns, C7:F7 contains the same values as E5:H5.

```
=Return1dObjectArray(E5:H5)
```

A two-dimensional array can receive a range that spans one or more rows. The following UDF method has a single two-dimensional object array argument (xlRange) and returns a two-dimensional object array that represents the object that was passed in. One or more rows are passed in, and the same rows are returned.

```
[UdfMethod]
public object[,] Return2dObjectArray(object[,] xlRange)
{
    return (xlRange)
}
```

In Excel, you call the `Return2dObjectArray` method by entering the following code into cell C11. To create the array formula, select cells C11:E15, press F2, and then press Ctrl+Shift+Enter. Excel automatically inserts the formula between {} (curly braces). The C11:E15 range represents the cells where the `object[,]` returned from `Return2dObjectArray` is applied. Excel evaluates the method as #NAME?. The example noted here uses H8:J12 as the argument to pass in. After `Return2dObjectArray` returns, C11:E15 contains the same values as H8:J12.

```
=Return2dObjectArray(H8:J12)
```

Creating a UDF

This section focuses on creating an Excel Services UDF, deploying the managed UDF assembly to the ECS, and calling the UDF methods from an Excel workbook. Here are a few prerequisites that must be met before you get started:

❑ Microsoft Office SharePoint Server 2007 must be available.

❑ Excel Services must be set up and ready to load workbooks.

❑ There must be an Excel 12 client and an ECS trusted location where at least View permissions are set.

❑ A Microsoft .Net Framework 2.0 development environment must be set up (The procedures use Microsoft Visual Studio 2005.)

Creating the C# Class Library

Follow these steps to launch Visual Studio and create the C# class library:

1. Start Visual Studio.

2. Select File ⇨ New ⇨ Project to open the New Project dialog box.

3. In the Project Types frame, expand the Visual C# node and select Windows. In the Templates frame, select Class Library.

4. In the Name field, enter **xlUdf**.

5. Set the Location field to the location where you want to create the solution.

6. Click OK to create the library. The New Project dialog box closes, and Visual Studio opens the xlUdf solution with `Class1.cs` open and visible. The namespace is xlUdf.

Adding the UDF Run-Time Reference

The Excel Services run-time assembly is installed with each Complete or Stand-Alone (evaluation) type of MOSS installation. The run-time assembly may be available as a download some day, so you might want to search www.Microsoft.com for this. Obtain a copy of the assembly (Microsoft.Office.Excel.Server.Udf.dll) and place it in a location where your project can access it. Ensure that the assembly is compatible with the ECS that will ultimately host the UDF by using either a 32-bit or a 64-bit version of the assembly.

Follow these steps to add the UDF run-time reference:

1. Select Project ⇨ Add Reference to open the Add Reference dialog box.

2. Select the Browse tab in the Add Reference dialog box. Navigate to the directory that contains the Microsoft.Office.Excel.Server.Udf.dll run-time assembly, and select the file. Click OK. The Solution Explorer shows the run-time assembly as a reference for the xlUdf solution.

3. In Class1.cs, add a directive for the run-time assembly namespace. At the beginning of Class1.cs add the following using statement:

```
using Microsoft.Office.Excel.Server.Udf
```

Adding Attributes and a Method

Follow these steps to add attributes and a method:

1. In Class1.cs, add the [UdfClass] attribute to the class. Enter the following on the line immediately preceding public class Class1:

```
[UdfClass]
```

2. Define a UDF method within Class1. Add the following [UdfMethod] attribute to any public UDF method being created:

```
[UdfMethod]
public string EchoInput(string userInput)
{
    return "Input: " + userInput;
}
```

The complete solution for the UDF assembly is as follows:

```
using System;
using System.Collections.Generic;
using System.Text;
using Microsoft.Office.Excel.Server.Udf;

namespace xlUdf
{
    [UdfClass]
    public class Class1
    {
        [UdfMethod]
        public string EchoInput(string userInput)
```

```
        {
            return "Input: " + userInput;
        }
    }
}
```

Deploying the UDF Assembly

UDF assemblies are enabled at the Shared Services Provider (SSP) level. Any UDF method calls in a workbook to a UDF assembly that is not enabled will fail. Each ECS server in an SSP must be able to access all of the enabled UDF assemblies, so ensure that the assemblies are accessible to each ECS that needs access.

Follow these steps to make the UDF assembly accessible:

1. Build the xlUdf.dll assembly if you have not already done so.

2. Copy xlUdf.dll to a local folder on the ECS server. For example, place the assembly in D:\Udfs\xlUdf.dll on the ECS server.

Follow these steps to add xlUdf.dll to the list of trusted UDF assemblies for the SSP:

1. Open the MOSS Central Administration by selecting Start ⇨ All Programs ⇨ Microsoft Office Server ⇨ SharePoint 3.0 Central Administration. The Central Administration page loads in the browser.

2. Navigate to the trusted UDF assemblies administration page by clicking the SSP name (ShareServices1, for example). Locate the link for the UDF assemblies and click it.

3. Register and enable the UDF by clicking the Add User-Defined Function Assembly link. The page to add the UDF assembly is displayed.

4. Enter the assembly full path. For example, enter **D:\Udfs\xlUdf.dll**. You can use a network share or a local file path. A second option is to add the assembly to the Global Assembly Cache (GAC) and enter the Strong Name here instead of a file path.

5. If you entered a file path in the previous step, select File Path in the Assembly Location section of the page. If instead you added the UDF assembly to the GAC and entered a Strong Name in the previous step, select Global Assembly Cache.

6. Click the Assembly Enabled check box to enable the UDF.

7. Select OK to save the UDF Assembly settings and close the page. The xlUdf.dll assembly is now registered and enabled.

8. Reset IIS. (This is necessary to enable a workbook to make calls to the UDF.)

Follow these steps to enable UDFs at the trusted file location level:

1. Click the Trusted File Locations link. The Trusted File Locations page loads and a list of the defined trusted locations is displayed.

2. Click the trusted location where UDFs are to be supported. The Trusted Location edit page is displayed. Scroll to the bottom and select the User-Defined Functions Allowed option.

Calling the UDF

The syntax you use to make a UDF method call from a workbook is essentially the same as the syntax to call a built-in Excel function. Follow these steps to create the workbook, create a defined name to be used as a parameter, and make a UDF method call that takes the parameter input as an argument:

1. Create a new workbook by launching Excel 12 and selecting File ➪ New ➪ Blank Workbook ➪ Create.

2. Create a defined name by selecting Formulas ➪ Define Name. For the name, enter **String_Input** and set the Refers To field to **=Sheet1!A1**. Click OK to create the defined name.

3. Make the UDF method call by selecting cell A3 on Sheet1 and typing the following code.

```
=EchoInput(String_Input)
```

4. Press Enter. The UDF method call evaluates to #NAME? because Excel doesn't know about the UDF method.

5. Publish the UDF to a trusted file location by selecting File ➪ Publish ➪ Excel Services. Type the trusted file location path in the File Name field. Uncheck the Open In Excel Services box to deselect this option. Click Save.

6. Configure the defined name as a parameter and use the EWA to load the workbook by selecting File ➪ Publish ➪ Excel Services. Click the Excel Services Options link to open the Excel Services Options dialog box. Click the Parameters tab and then select Add. Click the check box next to the String_Input entry on the Add Parameters dialog box. Select OK on both the Add Parameters and the Excel Services Options dialog boxes. In the Save As dialog box, select the Open in Excel Services option and then click Save.

   A browser launches and displays the EWA with the workbook. There is a Parameters pane on the right side of the EWA, and cell A3 contains Input:.

7. Enter text in the String_Input parameter field and click Apply. The ECS applies the parameter value to cell A1, calculates cell A3 by passing the String_Input value to the EchoInput UDF method, and then returns the new value for cell A3. The EWA reloads and displays the new values in cells A1 and A3.

ECS XLL UDF

The Excel client supports UDFs in Excel add-ins (or XLLs). This type of UDF implementation is very common for Excel, and many customers have invested heavily in the XLL type of add-in. As mentioned earlier in this chapter, you can craft a solution that will wrap existing functionality and essentially create a UDF solution for the server. Because Excel Services supports only managed UDFs, the XLL requires a managed wrapper to make the calls to the XLL UDF.

Xlviewer Customizations

You can use the Excel Services Excel Web Access Web Part in one of two ways: embedded in a Share-Point page or by leveraging the built-in xlviewer.aspx solution. When the EWA is embedded, the configurable Web Part properties are exposed through SharePoint's Modify Shared Web Part interface. The xlviewer.aspx solution doesn't expose the Web Part properties through any user interface. The xlviewer.aspx page isn't coded to accept URL parameters for the properties either.

This section demonstrates the steps necessary to create a solution based on the functionality provided by the xlviewer.aspx method of using the EWA. The more popular EWA properties are explained and code examples are provided for setting the EWA properties.

There are a couple of scenarios in Excel Services where the xlviewer.aspx is used to render workbooks with the EWA. A SharePoint document library functionality called View in Web Browser uses xlviewer.aspx to render the workbook. Each EWA Web Part in a SharePoint page has a clickable title that loads the workbook using xlviewer.aspx. By default, xlviewer.aspx takes over the entire browser window and renders the workbook using the EWA. This provides better viewing of the workbook, with less scrolling, because the EWA isn't sharing screen space with other SharePoint components. You can also construct links in web pages or in e-mail messages that use xlviewer.aspx to load a workbook (for example, `http://TheExcelServer/_layouts/xlviewer.aspx?id=\\fileShare\trustedLocation\workbook.xlsb`).

Creating a customized version of xlviewer.aspx is a straightforward operation. In the following section, you create a copy of xlviewer.aspx and add code for setting EWA properties.

> *You could apply the changes described here directly to xlviewer.aspx, which would affect the behavior for all consumers of xlviewer.aspx. This may be your intention. However, for this example solution, you modify a copy of xlviewer.aspx.*

Setting New Defaults and URL Parameters

Follow these steps to create a customized version of xlviewer.aspx:

1. Locate the xlviewer.aspx file at C:\Program Files\Common Files\Microsoft Shared\web server extensions\12\TEMPLATE\LAYOUTS. Make a copy of xlviewer.aspx and keep it in the same directory. For this solution, name the copy **xlEwa.aspx**.

2. Open xlEwa.aspx in a text editor (such as Notepad) or, if you like extra bells and whistles, use a program like Visual Studio. Locate the following statement in the file and change the `AutoEventWireUp` attribute's value to `true`:

```
<%@ Page language="C#" Codebehind="XlViewer.aspx.cs" AutoEventWireup="true"
Inherits="Microsoft.Office.Excel.WebUI.XlViewer,Microsoft.Office.Excel.WebUI,
Version=12.0.0.0,Culture=neutral,PublicKeyToken=71e9bce111e9429c" %>
```

3. Insert the following code into xlEwa.aspx between the opening `<html>` tag and the opening `<head>` tag:

```
<script runat="server">

private void Page_Load(object sender, System.EventArgs e)
{
    try
    {
        if (Request.QueryString["RowsToDisplay"] != null)
        {
            m_excelWebRenderer.RowsToDisplay = Int32.Parse(
                Request.QueryString["RowsToDisplay"]);
        }
        else
        {
            m_excelWebRenderer.RowsToDisplay = 50;
        }

        if (Request.QueryString["ColumnsToDisplay"] != null)
        {
            m_excelWebRenderer.ColumnsToDisplay = Int32.Parse(
                Request.QueryString["ColumnsToDisplay"]);
        }
        else
        {
            m_excelWebRenderer.ColumnsToDisplay = 30;
        }
    }
    catch (Exception exc)
    {
        //error handler
    }
}
</script>
```

The xlEwa.aspx file is now a customized alternative to using xlviewer.aspx. This version of xlEwa.aspx renders the workbook and displays a grid size of 50 rows by 30 columns by default. In contrast, the xlviewer.aspx always renders a grid size of 75 rows by 20 columns.

In addition, the code you added to the xlEwa.aspx file enables you to input URL parameters and apply values to both the RowsToDisplay and the ColumnsToDisplay properties. You can now use xlEwa.aspx as shown in the following URL:

```
http://TheExcelServer/_layouts/xlEwa.aspx?id=\\fileShare\trustedLocation\work
book.xlsb&RowsToDisplay=77&ColumnsToDisplay=15
```

Configurable Properties

The EWA Web Part has approximately 43 configurable properties. About half of these are applicable for using the EWA in a nonembedded manner, as is the case with xlEwa.aspx.

The following table shows the properties that you can use for this solution. Instructions for obtaining the complete list of properties are provided after the table. Each of the configurable EWA Web Part properties exposed through xlEwa.aspx is also available through the EWA Web Part properties task pane that is displayed when an EWA is embedded in a SharePoint page.

Property Name	Type	User Interface Equivalent	Default Value
RowsToDisplay	int	Rows	75
ColumnsToDisplay	int	Columns	20
VisibleItem	string	Named Item	
ShowVisibleItemButton	bool	Named Item drop-down menu	true
WorkbookUri	string	Workbook	
AllowInExcelOperations	bool	Open In Excel; Open Snapshot In Excel	true
AllowPeriodicData-Refresh	bool	Refresh Selected Connection; Refresh All Connections	true
AllowRecalculation	bool	Calculate Workbook	true
AllowNavigation	bool	Workbook Navigation	true
AllowHyperlinks	bool	Hyperlinks	true
AllowInteractivity	bool	All workbook interactivity	true
AllowParameter-Modification	bool	Parameter modification	true
ShowWorkbookParameters	bool	Display Parameters task pane	true
AllowSorting	bool	Sorting	true
AllowFiltering	bool	Filtering	true
AllowPivotSpecific-Operations	bool	All PivotTable interactivity	true
AllowManualDataRefresh	bool	Periodically Refresh If Enabled In Workbook	true

Property Name	Type	User Interface Equivalent	Default Value
AutomaticPeriodic-DataRefresh	enum Automatic-PeriodicData-RefreshMode	Display Periodic Data Refresh prompt	Always
CloseWorkbookSessions	bool	Close Session Before Opening A New One	false
ToolbarStyle	enum Toolbar-Visibility-Style	Type of toolbar	Full

You can obtain a complete listing of the EWA Web Part properties by exporting the Web Part from a SharePoint page. Follow these steps to see all of the properties:

1. Navigate to a SharePoint page that contains an EWA Web Part, or add one to an existing page.
2. Open the EWA Web Part menu and click Export.
3. Save the .webpart file to disk and then open the file using Notepad. The available EWA Web Part properties are displayed in the file.

The AutomaticPeriodicDataRefresh and ToolbarStyle properties expect an enum value, as follows:

❑ AutomaticPeriodicDataRefresh — Has three supported values: Disabled, Optional, and Enabled. The user interface choices are Always, Optionally, and Never.

❑ ToolbarStyle — Has four supported values: FullToolbar, SummaryToolbar, NavigationOnlyToolbar, and None. The user interface choices are Full, Summary, Navigation Only, and None.

Add the following code to the previous xlEwa.aspx sample solution to try out the Automatic-PeriodicDataRefresh and the ToolbarStyle EWA properties. With these settings, if you use periodic data refresh, the data refresh happens automatically without prompting the user. Also, the EWA toolbar functionality is reduced to navigation operations only.

```
m_excelWebRenderer.AutomaticPeriodicDataRefresh =
AutomaticPeriodicDataRefreshMode.Enabled;
m_excelWebRenderer.ToolbarStyle = ToolbarVisibilityStyle.NavigationOnlyToolbar;
```

EWA and API Working Together

This section describes two approaches for using custom code to interact with an EWA session when the EWA Web Part is embedded as part of a SharePoint page. The first approach leverages the Content Editor Web Part, JavaScript, and Excel web services. The second approach is a bit more advanced, and makes use of a custom web application and managed code, the Page Viewer Web Part, and Excel web services. Each approach demonstrates how the Excel API can interact with an active EWA session.

JavaScript Approach

Of the two approaches, this one is easiest to implement, but it isn't nearly as powerful as the managed-code approach that is discussed later. Anyone who is well-versed in client-side browser scripting can probably take this approach and make it quite impressive. The usage described here stops well short of accomplishing anything extraordinary, but it provides a starting point and hopefully causes you to think about what could be possible.

To implement this approach, you create a web page that contains an EWA and a Content Editor Web Part. You then use the Content Editor Web Part to host the HTML and `<script>` that gets the session ID from the EWA instance. The `<script>` uses the session ID to make an Excel Services web service `GetSessionInformation` call. This approach also demonstrates the use of three EWA JavaScript functions.

Before you begin, the following prerequisites must be met:

- ❏ Microsoft Office SharePoint Server 2007 must be available.
- ❏ Excel Services must be set up and ready to load workbooks.
- ❏ An Excel workbook must be published to a trusted location where at least View permissions are set.
- ❏ You must have at least the Designer permission on a web page.

Creating a SharePoint Web Page

If you do not already have a web page where you can try out this approach, follow these steps to create one:

1. Use the browser to navigate to site where you want to create the web page.

2. Select Site Actions ➪ Create.

3. On the create.aspx page, click Web Part Page. When the New Web Part Page is displayed, provide a name for the page. For this exercise, name the page **testPage1.aspx**. Choose the Full Page template and click the Create button. The testPage1.aspx page loads in Design mode.

4. Click the Add A Web Part button and add two Web Parts: Context Editor Web Part and Excel Web Access Web Part. The testpage1.aspx page now contains both Web Parts and remains in Design mode.

5. Configure the EWA to load a default workbook by opening the Properties task pane. To do this, click the edit link on the EWA Web Part and click Modify Shared Web Part. In the Workbook input field, enter the full path to a workbook from a trusted location. Click OK to apply the change. The workbook loads in the EWA.

6. Before moving to the coding part of this approach, you need to provide the EWA Web Part ID. To obtain the ID, right-click the page above the Full Page label near the top of the page. Select View Source from the IE context menu, and then search the source for the ID of the EWA Web Part. The ID will be similar to WebPartWPQ4. Make a note of the ID, because you will need it later.

Configuring the Context Editor Web Part

Follow these steps to configure the Context Editor Web Part:

1. Webservice.htc must be in the same directory as the testPage1.aspx file, because it is used as part of the solution to make Excel Services web service calls. Obtain Webservice.htc from `http://msdn.microsoft.com`.

2. Click the edit link on the Context Editor Web Part and click Modify Shared Web Part. Click the Source Editor button to open a Text Entry window where you can enter HTML and `<script>`.

3. Enter the following code into the Source Editor. Search for `'WebPartWPQ4'` and replace the string with the EWA Web Part ID that you noted in a previous procedure. Search for `theexcelserver:38712` and replace the string with your server information.

```javascript
<SCRIPT LANGUAGE="JavaScript">
<!--

var iSessID;

function callSvc()
{
    service.useService(
        "http://theexcelserver:38712/_vti_bin/ExcelService.asmx?WSDL",
        "EcsWs");
}

function callGetSessionInfo()
{
    callSvc();
    var sessionId = document.getElementById('_sessionId_xl').value;
    iSessID = service.EcsWs.callService("GetSessionInformation", sessionId);
}

function onWSGetResult()
{
    // Error was returned
    if((event.result.error)&&(iSessID==event.result.id))
    {
        // Get the error details
        var errCode   = event.result.errorDetail.code;
        var errString = event.result.errorDetail.string;
        var errSoap   = event.result.errorDetail.raw;

        // Add code to handle specific error codes here
        if(iSessID==event.result.id)
        {
            document.getElementById('_sessionInfo_xl').value = "ERROR";
        }
    }

    // No error
    else if((!event.result.error)&&(iSessID==event.result.id))
```

```
      {
          // Put results in input control
          if(iSessID==event.result.id)
          {
              document.getElementById('_sessionInfo_xl').value =
                  event.result.raw.parentNode.firstChild.parentNode.text;
          }
      }
      else
      {
          // Not an event to be caught here
      }
  }
  // -->
  </SCRIPT>

  <div id="service" style="behavior:url(webservice.htc)"
  onresult="onWSGetResult();" />

  <input type="text" style="width:150px" id="_sessionId_xl" />
  <input type="button" style="width:100px" value="Get Session"
  onclick="document.getElementById('_sessionId_xl').value =
  (EwaGetSessionId('WebPartWPQ4'));" />
  <br />
  <input type="text" style="width:30px" id="_reload_xl" />
  <input type="button" value="Reload EWA"
  onclick="document.getElementById('_reload_xl').value =
  (EwaReloadWorkbook('WebPartWPQ4'));" />
  <br />
  <input type="text" style="width:150px" id="_cellFocus_xl" />
  <input type="button" style="width:100px" value="Selected Cell"
  onclick="document.getElementById('_cellFocus_xl').value =
  (getHighlightedCellA1Reference('WebPartWPQ4'));" />
  <br />
  <input type="text" style="width:160px" id="_sessionInfo_xl" />
  <input TYPE="button" VALUE="Session Info" NAME="GetSessionInfo"
  onclick="callGetSessionInfo()" />
```

4. Click Save to keep the code. Click OK in the Properties pane to apply the changes to the Web Part and close the pane. The web page reloads, no longer in Design mode.

Solution Functionality

The web page you created loads the workbook in the EWA and the Content Editor renders the custom code. Figure 14-1 shows what the page looks like when the custom code is executed.

Note the following:

❑ *Get Session button* — Clicking this button makes a call to the EWA EwaGetSessionId function, which returns the sessionId of the currently loaded workbook.

❑ *Reload EWA button* — Clicking this button makes a call to the EWA EwaReloadWorkbook function, which returns a TRUE or FALSE status to reflect whether or not the EWA reload call was successful. The function reloads the original workbook, so any private state that existed previously is lost.

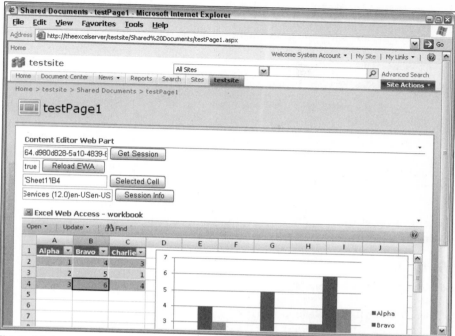

Figure 14-1

- *Selected Cell button* — Clicking this button makes a call to the EWA `getHighlighted-CellA1Reference` function, which returns the currently selected cell in the EWA grid. The string is returned in the format `'Sheet1'!C15`. When no cell is selected, `null` is returned.

- *Session Info button* — Clicking this button makes an Excel Services web service `GetSession-Information` method call using the `sessionId` of the currently loaded workbook.

Managed-Code Approach

To implement this approach, you create a .NET Web application using C#. Next, you create a web page that contains an EWA and a Page Viewer Web Part. The Page Viewer Web Part hosts the web application to get the session ID from the EWA instance. The application then uses this session ID to make Excel Services web service calls through local linking (not as a web reference).

Before you begin, the following prerequisites must be met:

- Microsoft Office SharePoint Server 2007 must be available.

- Excel Services must be set up and ready to load workbooks.

- An Excel workbook must be published to a trusted location where at least View permissions are set.

- You must have at least the Designer permission on a web page.

- Microsoft Visual C# and Microsoft Visual Studio 2005 must be available (to reproduce the steps described here).

Creating the C# Web Application Project

Follow these steps to launch Visual Studio on the MOSS server and create the C# Web Site application:

1. Start Visual Studio.

2. Select File ➪ New ➪ Web Site to open the New Web Site dialog box.

3. In the Templates frame, select ASP.NET Web Site. Set the Location to HTTP and the Language to Visual C#.

4. Enter the path for the web application in the form of http://<server>/_layouts/ <applicationName>. For example, http://TheExcelServer/_layouts/EwaCustApp creates the application in C:\Program Files\Common Files\Microsoft Shared\web server extensions\12\TEMPLATE\LAYOUTS.

5. Select OK to create the application. The New Web Site dialog box closes and Visual Studio opens the EwaCustApp solution with Default.aspx displayed. The Solution Explorer shows that Default.aspx.cs has been created as well.

Adding References

Follow these steps to add references:

1. Select Website ➪ Add Reference to open the Add Reference dialog box.

2. On the .NET tab of the Add Reference dialog box, select each of the following components and then click OK to add them as references to the application:

   ❑ Windows SharePoint Services component to add the Microsoft.SharePoint.dll

   ❑ Excel web services component to add the Microsoft.Office.Excel.Server.WebServices.dll

   ❑ System.Windows.Forms to add the System.Windows.Forms.dll

Adding the Default.aspx Code

Enter the following code between the <div> and </div> tags in Default.aspx:

```
<asp:Button ID="_getApiVersionButton_xl" runat="server"
OnClick="_getApiVersionButton_xl_Click" Text="GetAPIVersion" Width="130px" />
<asp:TextBox ID="_getApiVersionTextBox_xl" runat="server"
Width="160px"></asp:TextBox>
<br /><br />
<input type="button" style="width:140px" value="Get EWA Session ID"
onclick="getElementById('_sessionIdTextBox_xl').value =
(window.top.EwaGetSessionId('WebPartWPQ4'));" />
<asp:TextBox ID="_sessionIdTextBox_xl" runat="server" Width="305px"></asp:TextBox>
<br /><br />
<asp:ListBox ID="_workbookTypeListBox_xl" runat="server" Height="35px"
Width="148px">
<asp:ListItem Value="FullWorkBook"></asp:ListItem>
<asp:ListItem Value="FullSnapshot"></asp:ListItem>
<asp:ListItem Value="PubishedItemSnapshot"></asp:ListItem>
</asp:ListBox>
<br />
```

```
<asp:Label ID="_saveworkbookLabel_xl" runat="server" Text="Workbook Name:"
></asp:Label>
<asp:TextBox ID="_fileNameTextBox_xl" runat="server" Width="200px"></asp:TextBox>
<asp:Button ID="_getWorkbookButton_xl" runat="server"
OnClick="_getWorkbookButton_xl_Click" Text="GetWorkbook" Width="130px" />
<br /><br />
<input type="button" style="width:160px" value="Reload EWA Workbook"
onclick="window.top.EwaReloadWorkbook('WebPartWPQ4');" />
<br /><br />
<input type="button" style="width:160px" value="Get Selected EWA Cell"
onclick="getElementById('_cellWithFocusTextBox_xl').value =
(window.top.getHighlightedCellA1Reference('WebPartWPQ4'));" />
<asp:TextBox ID="_cellWithFocusTextBox_xl" runat="server"
Width="160px"></asp:TextBox>
```

Adding the Default.aspx.cs Code

Use the Solution Explorer in Visual Studio to open Default.aspx.cs. Enter the following code in Default.aspx.cs. You can replace the entire contents of Default.aspx.cs with the code provided here.

```csharp
using System;
using System.Data;
using System.Configuration;
using System.Web;
using System.Web.Security;
using System.Web.UI;
using System.Web.UI.WebControls;
using System.Web.UI.WebControls.WebParts;
using System.Web.UI.HtmlControls;
using Microsoft.Office.Excel.Server.WebServices;
using System.Windows.Forms;
using System.Web.Services.Protocols;
using System.IO;

public partial class _Default : System.Web.UI.Page
{
    ExcelService xlEcsApi = new ExcelService();
    Status[] xlStatus;

    protected void Page_Load(object sender, EventArgs e)
    {
    }

    protected void _getApiVersionButton_xl_Click(object sender, EventArgs e)
    {
        try
        {
            _getApiVersionTextBox_xl.Text = xlEcsApi.GetApiVersion(out xlStatus);
            if (xlStatus != null)
            {
                for (int i = 0; i < xlStatus.Length; i++)
                {
                    // Status handler
                }
```

```csharp
            }
        }
        catch (SoapException exc)
        {
            // Error handler
        }
        catch (Exception exc)
        {
            // Error handler
        }
    }

    protected void _getWorkbookButton_xl_Click(object sender, EventArgs e)
    {
        WorkbookType wbType = WorkbookType.FullWorkbook;
        switch (_workbookTypeListBox_xl.SelectedIndex)
        {
            case 0:
                wbType = WorkbookType.FullWorkbook;
                break;
            case 1:
                wbType = WorkbookType.FullSnapshot;
                break;
            case 2:
                wbType = WorkbookType.PublishedItemsSnapshot;
                break;
        }
        try
        {
            byte[] bits = xlEcsApi.GetWorkbook(
                _sessionIdTextBox_xl.Text,
                wbType,
                out xlStatus);
            if (xlStatus != null)
            {
                for (int i = 0; i < xlStatus.Length; i++)
                {
                    //status handler
                }
                if (0 < bits.Length)
                {
                    string saveToPath = @"e:\savedFiles\";
                    using (BinaryWriter binWriter = new BinaryWriter(File.Open(
                        saveToPath + _fileNameTextBox_xl.Text,
                        FileMode.CreateNew)))
                    {
                        binWriter.Write(bits);
                        binWriter.Flush();
                        binWriter.Close();
                    }
                }
            }
        }
        catch (SoapException exc)
```

```
        {
            // Error handler
        }
        catch (Exception exc)
        {
            // Error handler
        }
    }
}
```

When you have finished entering the code, save the application. Then build the application to confirm that there are no errors.

Creating the Web Page

If you do not already have a SharePoint Web Part Page where you can load the web application, follow these steps to create one:

1. Use the browser to navigate to the site where you want to create the web page.

2. Select Site Actions ⇨ Create.

3. On the create.aspx page, click Web Part Page. When the New Web Part Page is displayed, provide a name for the page. For this example, name the page **testPage2.aspx**. Choose the Full Page template and click the Create button. The testpage2.aspx page loads in Design mode.

4. Click the Add a Web Part button and add two Web Parts: Page Viewer Web Part and Excel Web Access Web Part. The testpage2.aspx page now contains both Web Parts and remains in Design mode.

5. Configure the EWA to load a default workbook by opening the Properties task pane. To do this, click the edit link on the EWA Web Part and click Modify Shared Web Part. In the Workbook input field, enter the full path to a workbook from a trusted location. Click OK to apply the change. The workbook loads in the EWA.

6. Obtain the EWA Web Part ID by right-clicking the page above the Full Page label near the top of the page. Select View Source from the IE context menu, and then search the source for the ID of the EWA Web Part. The ID will be similar to WebPartWPQ4.

7. Update the Default.aspx code to use the EWA Web Part ID for your web page. Search for 'WebPartWPQ4' and replace the string with the EWA Web Part ID.

Configuring the Page Viewer Web Part

Next, you configure the Page Viewer to load the Web application. Follow these steps:

1. Click the Edit link on the Page Viewer Web Part.

2. In the Link field, enter the URL of the application. This is the same value that you used when you created the web application in Visual Studio (for example, http://TheExcelServer/ _layouts/EwaCustApp/default.aspx).

3. Click OK in the Properties pane to apply the changes to the Web Part and close the pane. The web page reloads, no longer in Design mode.

Solution Functionality

The web page you created loads the workbook in the EWA and the Page Viewer renders the custom code. Figure 14-2 shows what the page looks like when the custom code is executed.

Note the following:

❑ *GetAPIVersion button* — Clicking this button makes an Excel Services web service `GetApiVersion` method call. The returned version information is displayed in the adjacent text box.

❑ *Get EWA Session ID button* — Clicking this button makes a call to the EWA `EwaGetSessionId` function, which returns the `sessionId` of the currently loaded workbook.

❑ *Get Workbook button* — Clicking this button makes an Excel Services web service `GetWorkbook` method call using the two adjacent controls as arguments. The drop-down control is used to select the `WorkbookType`, and the Workbook Name field is used to provide the name of the workbook to be saved. The sample code currently has a hard-coded target folder for these workbooks that you need to update to work in your environment.

❑ *Reload EWA Workbook button* — Clicking this button makes a call to the EWA `EwaReloadWorkbook` function, which returns a `TRUE` or `FALSE` status to reflect whether or not the EWA reload call was successful. The function reloads the original workbook, so any private state that previously existed is lost.

❑ *Get Selected EWA Cell button* — Clicking this button makes a call to the EWA `getHighlighted-CellA1Reference` function, which returns the currently selected cell in the EWA grid. The string is returned in the format `'Sheet1'!C15`. When no cell is selected, `null` is returned.

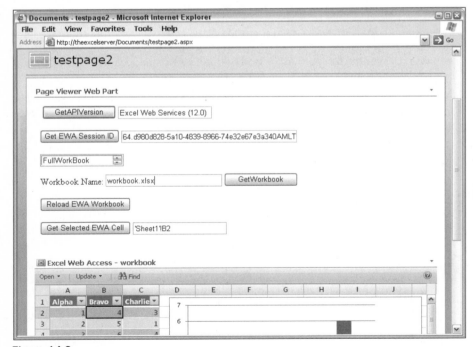

Figure 14-2

Summary

This chapter introduced some of the programmability options that you can use to extend the functionality of Excel Services. The chapter explained the API and all of its methods, and provided examples for writing a managed API solution. Server UDFs were identified as a means of calling custom functions from within workbooks, and you learned how to use the API to extend the EWA functionality within SharePoint pages. Examples were included for customizing the xlviewer.aspx file to allow EWA property values to be passed through the URL.

To summarize, you should now know how to do the following:

❑   Create a managed code application to use the Excel Services web service

❑   Author and deploy an Excel Services managed UDF assembly

❑   Customize xlviewer.aspx to set EWA properties

❑   Programmatically get the EWA session ID and author either JavaScript or managed-code to interact with the EWA and its session using the API

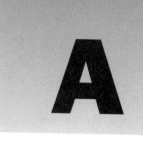

Troubleshooting

This appendix can help you troubleshoot the most common error messages after you have successfully installed Excel Services.

> **Access Denied**
>
> **You do not have permissions to open this file on Excel Services.**
>
> **Make sure that the file is in an Excel Services trusted location and that you have access to the file.**

The most common case for this error is that the workbook is not in a trusted location. For more details about trusted locations and permissions to access workbooks, see Chapter 8.

> **Unable to Load Workbook**
>
> **The workbook that you selected cannot be loaded because it contains the following features that are not supported by Excel Services:**
>
> **Comments, ActiveX controls, Shapes, Text Boxes, Pictures, WordArt, Clip Art, Embedded OLE objects, Ink Annotations, Forms Toolbar controls, Control Toolbox controls, Charts that are part of a group, Signature Lines, or Camera objects**
>
> **Contact the workbook author.**

Excel Services supports only a subset of the Excel features. Publishing a workbook with an unsupported feature results in this error message. See Chapter 4 for more information.

> **Data Refresh Failed**
>
> **Unable to retrieve external data for the following connections:**
>
> **My Connection**
>
> **The data sources may be unreachable, may not be responding, or may have denied you access.**
>
> **Verify that data refresh is enabled for the trusted file location and that the workbook data authentication is correctly set.**
>
> **How do I ensure a secure and valid refresh operation?**

If you are able to refresh data from the Excel client, the most common case for this error message is that the data access is not configured correctly on the server. Chapter 5 explains how to set up data access.

Index